T0366412

Money, Power, and the People

MONEY, POWER, and THE PEOPLE

The American Struggle to Make Banking Democratic

CHRISTOPHER W. SHAW

The University of Chicago Press

Chicago and London

The University of Chicago Press, Chicago 60637
The University of Chicago Press, Ltd., London
© 2019 by The University of Chicago
Published 2019
Printed in the United States of America

28 27 26 25 24 23 22 21 20 19   1 2 3 4 5

ISBN-13: 978-0-226-63633-7 (cloth)
ISBN-13: 978-0-226-63647-4 (e-book)
DOI: https://doi.org/10.7208/chicago/9780226636474.001.0001

Library of Congress Cataloging-in-Publication Data

Names: Shaw, Christopher W., author.
Title: Money, power, and the people: the American struggle to make banking
     democratic / Christopher W. Shaw.
Description: Chicago: The University of Chicago Press, 2019. | Includes
     bibliographical references and index.
Identifiers: LCCN 2018059623 | ISBN 9780226636337 (cloth: alk. paper) |
     ISBN 9780226636474 (e-book)
Subjects: LCSH: Banks and banking—Social aspects—United States. | Banks
     and banking—United States—Citizen participation. | Banks and banking—
     Government policy—United States—History—20th century. | Banks and
     banking—United States—History—20th century.
Classification: LCC HG2481 .S49 2019 | DDC 332.10973—dc23
LC record available at https://lccn.loc.gov/2018059623

♾ This paper meets the requirements of ANSI/NISO Z39.48-1992
(Permanence of Paper).

CONTENTS

Introduction

Some will rob you with a six-gun,
And some with a fountain pen.[1]

On April 14, 1913, a horse-drawn hearse solemnly transported the body of J. Pierpont Morgan from the splendor of the private library adjacent to his mansion, through the streets of Manhattan, to the Romanesque edifice popularly referred to as "Morgan's church." As the bell of St. George's Episcopal Church tolled overhead, one thousand spectators stood alongside the railing of Stuyvesant Square and watched the funeral cortege's approach. Inside the church, the pews were full, and the chancel was lavishly decorated with floral displays. These included a wreath of roses from the king of Italy and a spray of palm leaves decorated with golden tasseled silk streamers from the emperor of Germany. Among the prominent attendees were bearers of surnames that evoked the passing heroic age of American business: Harriman, Rockefeller, Vanderbilt. No less than three prelates of the Episcopal Church—to which Morgan had been a great benefactor over the years—were on hand to assist with the service. The bishops of New York, Massachusetts, and Connecticut all trailed dutifully behind the Jacqueminot rose-blanketed coffin.[2]

Morgan's death provoked a different reaction at a modest brick Episcopal church in the City of Brotherly Love that served a largely working-class congregation. The Reverend George Chalmers Richmond took to the pulpit of his parish church in Philadelphia's Northern Liberties section to reprove "men on Wall Street [who] have made a god out of Morgan for years." "Now let them read the gospel of Jesus," he admonished, "and see how far short of God did Mr. Morgan really appear to be." The Reverend Richmond's sermon followed from his censure of the very endeavor that had made Morgan's fame and fortune possible—namely, finance. "Mr. Morgan was a great financier," he instructed his parishioners, "but not a great man." "The country will get on much better without him." The men and women who heard these words would have left church that day with a sense of affirmation rather than revelation. "In all the tributes paid to his memory just now," Richmond observed, "we cannot find a single note of admiration from the American workingman." Thus, from within the Christian denomination that the preeminent figure of American finance had invested much of himself in—and a not-inconsequential amount of his fortune—arose a declaration of dissent, a condemnation of all that Morgan represented.[3]

The Reverend Richmond was not a voice crying in the wilderness. His challenge to the private financial system was merely one of many in the early twentieth century. In Boston, the ever-colorful James Michael Curley aggressively engaged in a decades-long struggle with his city's leading bankers. During his first term as mayor, from 1914 to 1918, he excoriated them as "insolent, arrogant sharpies, swindling the city of all they can get away with." Much to the displeasure of the big banks, Curley not only was elected mayor again in 1922, but he also immediately embarked on an ambitious public works program. And when the bankers refused to allow the city to borrow against future taxes, Curley declared war. He apprised one banker of "a water main with floodgates right under your building." "You'd better get that money up by three o'clock this afternoon," he advised, "or those gates will be opened, pouring thousands of gallons of water right into your vaults." The banker duly complied, but subsequently decided to again withhold funds from the city. This time Curley informed him that he would send a mass of municipal employees and contractors to the bank with payroll checks in hand and instructions to move their money to other institutions. "You don't want a run on your bank, do you?" he cautioned. Once again the banker complied.[4]

Curley was elected to four terms as mayor of Boston, four terms as a U.S. congressman, and one term as governor of Massachusetts. He possessed an intimate knowledge of the people he represented: remarkably, every year Curley tirelessly met, shook hands with, and individually spoke to 50,000 voters. He knew his constituents, and he knew what they thought about the power that bankers wielded. Opposed by this same banker for a third time, Curley did not pull any punches. "I have a nice picture of you," he informed his foe, "and I have a good picture of that beautiful estate you have." Unless money that the mayor needed to meet the city's payroll was forthcoming, he explained, he would make these pictures publicly available. "When a man gets hungry," Curley counseled, "he's likely to do something desperate. I'd keep away from that house if I were you." The banker retreated yet again.[5]

The dominant figure in Boston politics for half a century opposed the power that a handful of bankers exercised over the city through their control of money and credit. He considered leading bankers to be effete charlatans whose haughty manner, presumptuous attitude, and underhandedness warranted defiance. Curley proudly recalled keeping New England's foremost banker waiting for two hours while he was enjoying the aboveboard legerdemain of noted magician Harry Blackstone. "I can learn something from Mr. Blackstone, but I assure you that I never learn anything from bankers," he declared. Curley was confident that voters shared his viewpoint—and the bankers themselves evidently understood that there was no use in publicly confronting Curley, because he would prevail.[6]

Discontent with the banking system found sensational expression far to the west of the cheek-by-jowl wood-frame triple-deckers of Boston. In the depths of the Great Depression, Charles Arthur Floyd's ability to outmatch Oklahoma's bankers made him a folk hero—an American Robin Hood. "Pretty Boy" Floyd distinguished himself from such contemporaries as "Baby Face Nelson," "Machine Gun Kelly," and Bonnie Parker and Clyde Barrow by solely targeting banks. "I have robbed none but moneyed men," Floyd avowed. Stories circulated of "Pretty Boy" supplying schoolhouses with firewood, and of how families that shared their meals with him would discover large-denomination bills tucked away underneath his plate. During heists Floyd reputedly would place himself in even greater jeopardy by taking the time to destroy unrecorded mortgages. As one contemporary journalist observed: "He took money from those who had it—the banks—and divided the proceeds with the poor." Traversing the countryside behind the wheel of a Ford boasting a V-8 engine, submachine gun in tow, and sometimes sporting a bulletproof vest, Floyd proved so effective that bank insurance rates in the Sooner State rose to be the highest in the nation.

The governor offered a $7,000 reward for Floyd but found no takers. "The penniless tenant farmers kept their mouths shut," explained the same journalist. "They had no scruples about taking contraband wrested from bankers." One Oklahoman recalled that "the farmers liked Pretty Boy." "Pretty Boy would pay off a mortgage for a farmer if he was about to lose his home." Floyd finally met his end in an Ohio cornfield amid a hail of bullets as he fled from pursuing Federal Bureau of Investigation agents. His funeral was held back home in Sallisaw, Oklahoma, on October 28, 1934. No business tycoons were present, and foreign monarchs sent no floral arrangements. But there were twenty thousand men, women, and children in attendance, and teenage boys and girls wept openly. "Pretty Boy" Floyd's popularity did not diminish after his death. Children were named in his honor, and the legend of the "Sagebrush Robin Hood" continued to grow.[7]

This outspoken priest, big-city boss, and rural outlaw likely never crossed paths, yet they held a common outlook about the power of bankers and the private banking system. The men and women who took communion from Richmond, voted for Curley, and abetted

Floyd shared their viewpoint when it came to bankers. The popular grievance against finance found public expression through what I call "banking politics"—a political force that arose from the activism of ordinary people who joined together to oppose the power of finance. Numerous Americans believed that the banking elite exercised inordinate power and reaped unjust deserts. Working people formed institutions that nourished the web of words, ideas, and ideals that fueled banking politics. Workers and farmers found that banking politics provided insights that aligned with their beliefs, values, and experiences. This worldview made it clear that bankers benefited from an unjust financial system that oppressed working people. Indeed, bankers were seen as predatory parasites who exploited productive economic activity, caused recurrent depressions, and undermined social equality. The solutions, said adherents of banking politics, ranged from specific banking and monetary reforms to total financial reformation. Banking politics enabled a vibrant strain of American political culture to protest a social order in which the cash nexus directs human relations.[8]

A complex nineteenth-century tradition of dissent undergirded banking politics. Ethical principles rooted in mutual aid and Christian egalitarianism inspired popular criticisms of finance.[9] Diverse strands of intertwined political thought shaped various proposed reforms. Producerism, anti-monopolism, and Greenbackism animated public discussions of the financial system, as did the ideas of Populist political insurgents and such influential Gilded Age social critics as Henry George Sr., Jacob S. Coxey Sr., and Edward Bellamy.[10] Banking politics expressed an everyday intellectual tradition that eclectically drew from this political inheritance while also calling upon the burgeoning socialist and direct democracy movements of the Progressive Era.[11]

Banking politics was adversarial. Americans who took interest in banking and monetary questions recognized that finance is the engine of capitalism. Capitalism's most crucial figures are the gatekeepers who control the financial system: the moneylenders. Those controlling money and credit exercise power over those who do not. This arrangement appeared upside down to many working people, who observed that bankers produced nothing tangible. They concluded that bankers possessed spoils extracted through expropriation—that is, plunder. The blatant displays of inequality that such ill-gotten gains made possible were seen as an affront to the honest toil of working people and to the nation's democratic creed.[12]

The palpable economic and political power of bankers crystallized perceptions among working people that the private banking system was exploitative and undemocratic. Grassroots agitation aimed to nullify the power of the banking fraternity. Proponents of banking politics believed that true democracy required a financial system that served workers, farmers, and their families. Working people's faith in the principle of egalitarianism and insistence on the worth of manual labor gave rise to popular demands for a transparent banking system that prioritized security, affordable credit, and stability.

When people opposed banks, this did not mean they opposed all aspects of the capitalist order. Although banking politics adherents dissented from the rule of money and credit, their focus on financial affairs steered economic criticisms away from those capitalists who were not bankers. Nevertheless, banking politics challenged capitalism's cultural values. Its adherents objected to the subordination of social activity to the pursuit of profit and asserted the intrinsic value of human beings in the face of the immense power wielded by those who controlled money and credit. One Pennsylvanian avowed: "Money is a medium of exchange and not a power to control over human lives."[13]

Banking politics spread through both the printed and the spoken word. Americans pursued financial questions in the pages of newspapers, pamphlets, books, magazines, and journals that circulated communally in barbershops, libraries, pool halls, and streetcars, and were perused privately in crowded tenements and isolated farmhouses after the day's work was done. Whether broadcasting directly into listeners' homes over the radio, or lecturing from atop soapboxes planted on sidewalks and in public parks, speakers attracted audiences by expounding upon monetary and banking issues. "I am always talking about the money question," one Missourian related. "I talk about it at home, I talk it on the street corner, I talk it from the rostrum." Banking politics was a social endeavor. Americans channeled their discontent with finance through membership organizations that served as schoolhouses of banking politics. Worker and farmer organizations that were independent of the two major political parties and of other interest groups as well reinforced and transmitted this populistic political force. Workers at union meetings and farmers in Grange halls discussed banking policy, and national conventions of citizen organizations debated financial issues before resolving upon specific plans for reform.[14]

Practitioners of banking politics believed that government could remake finance into a democratically responsive force for good. During the Gilded Age, Greenbackers, Populists, and other reformers had fruitlessly sought banking and monetary reform. But then the Bankers' Panic of 1907 thrust financial legislation onto the national agenda. Up through the Great Depression, banking politics adherents nationwide rode an increasingly powerful wave of popular interest. This activism, joined with the support of other Americans who embraced more limited change, forced political elites to implement reforms they would otherwise not have considered, such as government guarantee of bank deposits and governmental provision of agricultural credit. The Federal Deposit Insurance Corporation and the Farm Credit System stand as institutional legacies of banking politics today. The fact that publicly appointed officials still govern the Federal Reserve System and determine national monetary policy further reveals how this widespread and committed early twentieth-century popular engagement with financial questions continues to shape the American economy.[15]

John Maynard Keynes once claimed that "questions about the economic framework of society . . . involve intellectual and scientific elements which must be above the heads of the vast majority of more or less illiterate voters." But banking politics demonstrates that in a democracy, working people can engage with recondite questions. No inability of ordinary citizens to apprehend the financial system hamstrung banking politics. Even as many aspects of modern life became increasingly complex around the turn of the twentieth century—

necessitating the establishment of bureaucracies, which increasingly relied on the specialized knowledge of experts—working people scrutinized finance all the more closely. While the undue power of bankers threatened democratic ideals, the articulate participation of ordinary citizens in these relatively complicated policy debates reveals democracy's promise.[16]

Banking politics was rooted in the middle stratum of farmers and workers, people who worried, justifiably, about social and economic security but had sufficient means to preclude the powerlessness that produces apathy. These farmers and workers possessed the self-confidence to demand fair remuneration for their own labor while objecting to bankers profiting from the toil of others. They took pride in the products of their skill and labor and looked askance at the paper profits of finance. Banking politics spoke to farmers whose income was at the mercy of distant authorities in faraway commodity markets, railroad workers whose labors were subject to the caprice of large corporate bureaucracies, and skilled tradesmen who were perpetually vulnerable to erratic economic conditions. Their experiences had made them averse to abusive power structures and conscious of the chasm between themselves and bankers.

Although working people nationwide believed the banking and monetary system was exploitative, the contours of popular concern with financial issues varied geographically. A range of financial reforms generally were advocated more vigorously in the West, upper Midwest, and Great Plains, and more sporadically in the South and Northeast. A large number of southerners had minimal contact with banks and currency, while the financial system was most functional in the Northeast. Agricultural credit reform was understandably a leading concern in rural areas. Bimetallism had a broad following in the silver mining states of the West. Greenbacker ideas still retained notable appeal in areas where Greenbackism and Populism had won adherents during the late nineteenth century. Government guarantee of bank deposits made distinct headway on the populistic Great Plains. This concept also found a significant following among small businessmen and professionals. Proposals for post office savings banks demonstrated cross-class appeal as well by attracting the charitable impulse of upper-middle-class reformers.

While public involvement with financial issues during the eighteenth and nineteenth centuries is not a secret, the persistence of this vital dimension of American political culture has been neglected.[17] Understanding how the thoughts and activities of ordinary people contributed to twentieth-century banking and monetary policy requires examining sources far beyond financial and policymaking circles.[18] My effort to recover the political lives of farmers and workers led me to seek out their voices in newspapers, organizational records, periodicals, manuscript collections, oral histories, and other materials scattered across the nation. And while I reveal how the grassroots influenced finance, I also consider the ideas and actions of bankers, politicians, and government officials. Enabling all of these actors to speak again for themselves resurrects the intellectual dialogue and political confrontation that produced the modern American financial system.

Appreciating the popular response to the power of the private banking system is essential for understanding the American encounter with capitalism. The vibrancy of banking politics well into the twentieth century provides needed perspective on claims that this nation and its people are fundamentally capitalist. Karl Marx alleged that the "capitalist economy and the corresponding enslavement of the working class have developed *more rapidly* and more *shamelessly* [in America] than in any other country," while Joseph A. Schumpeter contended that "the businessmen's attitudes" were "impressed . . . upon the soul of the nation." Max Weber cited Benjamin Franklin as embodying the "spirit of capitalism," which "was present" in America "before the capitalistic order." And Werner Sombart identified even those Americans who patently were not capitalists themselves to be disciples of capitalism. "Emotionally the American worker has a share in capitalism: I believe that he loves it." Thorstein Veblen assented to such characterizations, sardonically alleging, "Nowhere does the pecuniary personage stand higher or more secure as the standard container of civic virtues than in democratic America." But acquiescence to these assertions has serious contemporary implications, because it sanctions those political interests that insist a so-called "free market" economic order is destiny.[19]

Postwar intellectuals writing in the shadow of fascism, the Holocaust, and totalitarian communist regimes connected popular political action with menacing reactionary cultural tendencies. To them, populistic political movements tended to veer ominously toward irrational mass behavior, frequently pervaded by intolerance arising from provincial prejudices. This characterization is not consistent with twentieth-century American banking politics. Finance's adversaries did include such notable anti-Semites as Charles E. Coughlin and Thomas E. Watson, whose biases became particularly acute late in their political careers. Their anti-Semitism places them in rather awkward solidarity with leading financial figures who opposed them on financial questions such as A. P. Giannini, J. Laurence Laughlin, and J. Pierpont Morgan, who were anti-Semites as well. But Coughlin and Watson were exceptions among practitioners of banking politics.[20]

Banking politics largely faded from the American scene by the mid-twentieth century. This did not occur because of the devotedly capitalistic nature of America and Americans, nor because the financial system grew impenetrably intricate and unintelligibly complex; it resulted from a transformation of the nation's political economy. Progressive Era and New Deal reforms tempered aspects of capitalism that gave rise to banking politics in the first place (such as economic instability and inequality), reined in the power of business and finance by strengthening countervailing forces (both in civil society and government), and addressed specific outstanding banking issues (notably agricultural credit, home lending, and security of bank deposits). These developments led Americans to grow increasingly complacent about banking and monetary issues. Moreover, the New Deal's establishment of a pluralist policymaking structure discouraged oppositional politics and deterred farmer and worker organizations from confronting financial questions.

Political power in America has been variously identified as relatively dispersed, the preserve of a "power elite," and the domain of state actors. While a range of groups participated in financial debates

during the twentieth century, their influence varied. Government officials played important roles, but they did not drive financial policymaking. The outcome of this struggle can be interpreted as affirmation that a plutocracy rules America. The historical development of
American capitalism allotted elite private financial interests a privileged position that circumscribed policy debates among state officials. This circumstance helped private banking interests exert undue
influence over financial policy, because entrenched power structures
and the ideologies that justify them present formidable obstacles to
reform. Stressing elite dominance and the significance of path de-
pendency to the existing institutional framework, however, risks ne-
glecting the influence of civic activism on the broader political agenda
and specific policy debates. Numerous Americans far from the halls
of power forcefully decried imposing private financial interests during the first half of the twentieth century. Banking politics structured
their grievances in a way that empowered them to seek social change.
Public demands for financial reform reveal that popular mobilization
can effectively challenge the power of elites, especially when channeled through independent citizen organizations during moments of
crisis.[21]

The 1930s were a watershed moment when American politics became more inclusive. During the Progressive Era, policymakers had
hoped that expertise would serve an objective, unitary public interest by transcending competing interests. New Deal policymakers
pursued a different strategy: they incorporated workers and farmers
into the political process to an unprecedented extent, and then sought
to mediate between various interest groups. But the New Deal also
limited the parameters of national political debate by pressing groups
to aspire to partnership. Such attempts to forge consensus impaired
banking politics because of its inherent opposition to the power of
private financial interests. The New Deal allotted different interest
groups primary responsibility for discrete policy issues—their proper
sphere of influence. Questions explicitly related to labor became the
domain of unions, farmer organizations dealt with specifically agricultural concerns, and the financial system fell under the purview of

bankers. This arrangement impeded broader reform of the national economy, because each group focused on only one aspect of the larger economic system. And this settlement granted bankers sweeping powers since the financial system is integral to the entire economy. Dividing up questions of political economy in this manner, and diminishing space for oppositional political approaches, curbed the power of banking politics.[22]

Banking politics atrophied even further in the postwar era without the institutional support that organized labor and agriculture had long provided. But the legacy of banking politics was still felt during these years, because grassroots agitation had produced a financial system that emphasized the welfare of workers and farmers. Under this financial regime, millions of working people experienced economic stability and security for the first time. Generations of Americans had suffered through periodic economic depressions that the banking system either caused or magnified: "Panics" had defined 1819, 1837, 1857, 1873, 1893, 1907, and 1921, but sharp downturns were notably absent following the New Deal. This novel state of affairs reduced popular interest in financial questions. Consequently, by the 1970s, the nation's bankers were exerting private power in the pursuit of profit without regard to the public welfare. This development prepared the way for the economic instability that followed the savings and loan meltdown of the 1980s and the 2008 financial crisis, as well as the rise of ever larger, more powerful private financial institutions. In this light, the achievements of banking politics over the first half of the twentieth century appear all the more remarkable. Ardent, sincere popular engagement with financial questions gave birth to a vigorous banking politics that testifies to the dignity and intelligence of working people and their ability to be empowered citizens in a true democracy.[23]

1

The Bankers' Panic of 1907

"A Sthrange Business"

On March 17, 1908, Robert M. La Follette Sr. (R-WI) took to the Senate floor with the weighty charge that "it is difficult to find any sufficient reason outside of manipulation for the extraordinary panic of October, 1907." La Follette believed the economy was a political arena. "There was no commercial reasons for a panic," he contended, but "there were speculative, legislative, and political reasons why a panic might serve special interests. There were business scores to settle. There was legislation to be blocked and a currency measure suited to the system to be secured." La Follette's engagement with financial affairs reflected the American public's preoccupation with this subject. "I feel the deepest interest in the currency question," affirmed one self-described "quiet citizen."[1]

A diverse collection of Americans, especially farmers and workers, shared La Follette's critical outlook on finance and his conviction that economic events were intertwined with politics. The recently formed American Society of Equity was a growing midwestern farmer organization. "It was the banking trust that brought on the panic," these farmers insisted. "They wanted a panic to discredit Teddy [Roosevelt] and to loot the Treasury." "The Wall Street Panic," stated one railroad brotherhood, was "willfully started" by "kings of finance" opposed to "the power of organized labor" and the Roosevelt administration's efforts to combat "plutocratic domination of our economic and political system." The union saw this event as yet another episode in the ongoing struggle between "the people" and "the money barons."[2]

The banking fraternity emphatically denied that the Panic of 1907 was not simply an outgrowth of business conditions. The prominent Chicago banker James B. Forgan asserted that "the financial disturbance grew from causes plain to see and utterly different from those put forward by the Senator." Forgan was in high dudgeon. "I have never heard so much utterly sensational and untrue verbiage quoted as coming from the lips of any one man." Even the president, however, had concluded that powerful business magnates were culpable. "That the Harriman and Rockefeller interests," Roosevelt stated privately, "and those allied with them have been willing to see a panic and desirous of precipitating it, with purpose of discrediting my administration, I am quite prepared to believe."[3]

The Panic of 1907 marked the inception of an intense decades-long debate over the form and function of the American financial system. Banking interests were arrayed against farmers and workers who drew on a rich nineteenth-century legacy of heterodox financial thought. The ideas of Greenbackers, Populists, and silverites remained influential well into the twentieth century. Many workers, farmers, and their families believed that bankers possessed an undemocratic degree of political and economic influence, and they dissented from the orthodoxy that the pursuit of profit should determine how financial institutions functioned. Numerous Americans sought banking reforms that prioritized public accountability, macroeconomic stability, affordable credit, and secure savings. The ensuing impassioned political battle would establish the essentials of the banking institutions we have today.[4]

The War of the Copper Kings

The Panic of 1907 laid bare the great power held by a mere handful of financial figures. Their mercenary business rivalries inflicted an economic depression on the American people. The panic's immediate origins lie in a failed attempt to corner the shares of the United Copper Company. This mining enterprise was controlled by F. Augustus Heinze, who had brashly engaged in years of bitter struggle with the Amalgamated Copper Mining Company. Amalgamated Copper cast such a long shadow over Montana's politics and economy that the state's residents referred to it as simply "The Company." The giant copper trust was a venture of the confederation of aggressive speculators known as the Standard Oil Gang. H. H. Rogers, a notably ruthless robber baron whose business methods earned him the epithet "Hell Hound," was a leading member. "We are not in business for our health," Rogers bluntly acknowledged, "but are out for the dollars."[5]

Heinze's eventful years in Butte commenced in 1889, when the young mining engineer first arrived from New York. He set to work studying maps of the "Richest Hill on Earth" and familiarizing himself with the area's geology. In 1892 Heinze headed back east to discuss a proposed smelter project with his wealthy family. He also traveled to Europe to procure credit for his fledgling business venture. Heinze employed this initial funding, his knowledge of geology, and the legal system to become one of Montana's Copper Kings. His use of the "apex law" was a constant thorn in the side of Amalgamated Copper. This law allowed mine operators to claim possession of minerals located beneath the property of others, because it held that ore belonged to the owner of the land where a vein either outcropped or came closest to the surface. At one point, Heinze retained thirty-seven attorneys to conduct his mining litigation. Underground, the conflict between the two interests took the form of open combat, as miners employed by Amalgamated and Heinze did battle with dynamite, steam, water, smoke, electricity, and rocks. "I'll drive Heinze out of Montana," Rogers vowed, "if it takes ten millions to do it." In 1906 Amalgamated finally bought out Heinze's Butte operations for $10.5

million, thereby dismissing 110 lawsuits involving $70 million worth of property.[6]

Heinze promptly turned to finance, establishing control over the Mercantile National Bank of New York, while retaining remnants of the United Copper Company. In October 1907, his brothers Arthur P. Heinze and Otto C. Heinze Jr. conducted an audit of United Copper's stock and discovered there were more shares being traded in the market than actually existed. They sought to turn this situation to their financial advantage by cornering the company's stock, believing that brokers had loaned shares to speculators who thought United Copper's price would fall. The speculators planned to sell these shares with the expectation of later repurchasing them at lower prices, returning them to the brokers, and pocketing the spread. But if the brokers lacked sufficient shares to meet a call to deliver their holdings, there would be a bidding war for the stock. For the plan to work, however, the Heinze brothers needed to purchase additional shares. F. Augustus Heinze initially refused to aid this scheme. He was apprehensive about a recent unexplained drop in deposits at the Mercantile National, where $4 million had been withdrawn over the previous four months. But after repeated entreaties, he relented and arranged for provision of a loan from his bank. United Copper stock hit $60 per share on October 14, before tumbling to $10 two days later, destroying the attempt to corner the market; evidently there was no shortage of shares. "Some who remember financial history," reported the *New York World*, "saw the fine hands of H. H. Rogers and his Standard Oil associates raised in revenge."[7]

A story soon circulated that a friend of Heinze had indiscreetly told two of her friends about the corner. The *Chicago Daily Tribune* reported that this piece of gossip became known to a private detective agency whose managers recognized "such information would be of great value to the Amalgamated Copper interests . . . led by H. H. Rogers." These "foes of Heinze" made the most of this financial intelligence. "When the time was ripe for intervention by the Amalgamated people," related the *Washington Post*, "men known by them to be allied with Heinze in his pooling interest were sounded, and finally one was found who would dump his holdings." Whether the Standard Oil Gang had foiled the corner in such a manner or not, it was a bust.[8]

Following this financial misadventure, nervous depositors began withdrawing their funds from the Mercantile National, which forced Heinze to appeal for help from the city's other bankers—specifically the New York Clearing House Association, where his old adversaries exercised influence. A former president of the organization, James Stillman, president of National City Bank, was a key member of the Standard Oil Gang. Stillman's bank had played a pivotal role in establishing Amalgamated Copper. A longtime associate of Stillman's, Hanover National Bank president James T. Woodward, was currently chairman of the clearinghouse. Stillman served on the boards of both the giant copper trust and Woodward's bank. And Stillman worked closely with Woodward during the ensuing financial crisis. Otto C. Heinze Jr. recalled that "the clearinghouse refused to give assistance unless the control of the bank were turned over to them and F. A. immediately resigned its presidency." Heinze's career as a banker was over. He accepted banishment from financial circles in return for the clearinghouse's aid.[9]

Panic!

The financial drama of October 1907 remained far from over. Depositors at the Knickerbocker Trust Company had grown wary because its president, Charles T. Barney, was associated with Heinze and his confederate Charles W. Morse. The National Bank of Commerce initially extended loans to support the trust company. But on October 21, the bank announced it no longer would act as the Knickerbocker's clearinghouse agent, and Barney resigned his position. A sizable line formed outside the trust company's building on Fifth Avenue before its doors opened the following morning. Over the next few hours, the line continued to grow and the city's banks dispatched numerous messengers to the Knickerbocker's branches with stacks of checks drawn on the trust company. The Knickerbocker paid out over $8 million that morning before suspending all payments at 12:30 p.m. "My

God! Give me my money!" cried out one woman left standing at a teller window with passbook in hand.[10]

Bank runs soon spread. A city magistrate instructed one depositor charged with disorderly conduct that his money was safe in the bank. "Maybe you think that, Judge, but I don't," he retorted. Another institution associated with Barney—the Trust Company of America—was awash with frightened depositors. Governor of New York Charles Evans Hughes Sr. (R) received numerous telegrams urging him to take the radical step of declaring a bank holiday in the state. The panic placed money at such a premium that Hetty Green—the "Witch of Wall Street"—claimed she "easily" could have demanded interest payments of 40 percent on the loans she extended to wealthy men and major corporations caught short during the crisis.[11]

On October 23, Secretary of the Treasury George B. Cortelyou left Washington, DC, aboard a train bound for New York to meet with the most powerful financial figure in the nation: J. Pierpont Morgan. Early the following morning, Cortelyou announced that the federal government would deposit $25 million in New York banks. Management of this no-interest loan was left in the hands of Morgan. Later that afternoon, John D. Rockefeller Sr. made $10 million of his vast wealth available to the cause. The following days found Morgan ensconced in the opulence of his private library coordinating efforts to stem the panic. The *New York World* commented that Morgan was "in practical control of all the banks and all the trust companies. . . . [H]is word was law and his rule was absolute." A managed infusion of currency allowed beleaguered institutions to keep their doors open. Financial conditions improved toward the end of October, as demonstrated by the Trust Company of America becoming a net recipient of deposits. "No one," Stillman commended Cortelyou, "can appreciate more . . . than I do what this country owes to the present Secretary of the Treasury."[12]

By this point, however, the whole nation was suffering from a shortage of currency due to correspondent banks' inability to draw upon their New York reserves. Under correspondent banking, smaller banks maintained balances with larger banks and received services analogous to a clearinghouse and access to money markets. But correspondent banking also channeled funds toward New York City. "New York is a delinquent debtor," the *Oakland Tribune* alleged. Banks in two-thirds of all cities with populations over 25,000 suspended cash payments to some extent. "The lack of currency is felt everywhere," upstate New York's *Cortland Democrat* attested. In cities across the nation, clearinghouses circulated scrip as a substitute for currency. A Seattleite protested this ersatz currency by writing "don't let this happen again" directly on a $10 clearinghouse certificate. One Chicago depositor found the chaotic financial situation so alarming that he imagined imminent upheaval: "Unless the banks shall resume currency payments . . . so as to restore some feeling of confidence . . . there are apt to be . . . scenes of riot and bloodshed in this city."[13]

Desperate measures were taken in several western states. On October 24, a bank holiday was declared in Nevada. Oklahoma instituted a six-day holiday a few days later. The governor of Washington State proclaimed a five-day holiday. Before October was over, the governors of California and Oregon had introduced holidays that would last for close to two months. Conditions in California remained so perturbed that as November drew to a close, Frank B. Anderson, manager of the Bank of California, expressed concern that if the state's holiday was lifted, "some people might start a run on the banks." By December 17, the financial situation was sufficiently settled that the San Francisco Clearing House Association telegraphed the governor its opinion that continuing the bank holiday was "no longer required." The holiday was lifted a few days before Christmas.[14]

Many contemporaries concluded that the irresponsible actions of New York financiers had victimized the nation as a whole. *Michigan Farmer* maintained, "There would have been no financial stringency so far as Michigan is concerned had not the eastern banks first refused cash payment." "We of the Pacific Coast must be independent of New York and Wall Street operators," stated the *California Cultivator*. "Were this the case we would scarcely realize the present money stringency." New Orleans's *Daily Picayune* concluded that if locals' money were not "in the insatiable maws of New York speculators, we would have had no panic here, and as soon as we can get it back our panic will disappear." Many people thought the recent financial crisis had been created deliberately. "It seems to us," stated Kentucky's *Weekly Market Growers Journal*, "that it is all manipulated by a few of our 'Captains of Industry' and 'Frenzied Financiers' to loan on exorbitant rates of interest and purchase stocks at far below their value." The hope of Henry George Jr. that "some of these panic makers will disappear from their haunts in Wall street, and go to breaking stone," expressed broader sentiment.[15]

The Banking System

The Bankers' Panic had unsettled a complex network of around 20,000 banking institutions. The Northeast was better served than other regions, while the South's dearth of banks was conspicuous. Southern farmers habitually depended on expensive financing from crossroads retailers for essential supplies and equipment. Banking institutions also were scattered thinly across the sparsely populated West. At the apex of this multifarious financial system stood the private investment banks. These unincorporated partnerships assisted only the largest clients, arranging financing for domestic and foreign corporations and governments. Investment banks clustered in New York City, but notable firms operated in Boston and Philadelphia as well.[16]

The commercial banking system revolved around the over 6,500 national banks that were federally chartered under the auspices of the National Banking Acts enacted during the Civil War. National banks were the only private financial institutions that could issue banknotes. They focused on larger customers, including businesses and other banks. The linchpins of the national bank system were its largest banks, which were the centers of the correspondent banking networks. In 1905 National City Bank was the largest of these, with deposits of $201 million. More than half of the thirty-three national banks with deposits of more than $20 million were in New York.[17]

The most numerous banking institutions were almost 10,000 banks that individual states chartered. The diverse rules that regulated these institutions were less stringent than those governing national banks.

State-chartered banks occupied a particularly important position in rural areas because they were not limited by the strict real estate lending restrictions that encumbered national banks. These banks were the single largest source of farm mortgage loans. Local bankers loaned their institution's funds and also negotiated mortgage loans on behalf of other investors, including life insurance companies, mortgage bankers, and private investors. In addition to national and state banks, there also were a few thousand very small, unchartered private banks. In the Northeast, commercial banks faced increasing competition from trust companies. These institutions originally managed money for affluent clients, but were now pursuing additional profits by performing general banking functions. Trust companies operated under a variety of state regulations that often permitted them competitive advantages, such as the ability to attract depositors with higher returns obtained through speculative investments.[18]

Although banks and trust companies increasingly competed for savings deposits, savings banks were the financial institution designed to serve working people. Mutual savings banks were found almost exclusively in the Northeast. Operated on a nonprofit basis by trustees with philanthropic motivations, in 1909 they served almost half of the nation's 14.9 million savers. For-profit savings banks owned by stockholders provided additional opportunities for thrift, particularly in California and Iowa. More than 1.6 million aspiring homeowners turned to building and loan associations, cooperatives that used member funds to finance mortgages. They were most prevalent in the Northeast and Midwest, and approached savings banks in importance as sources of home mortgage financing.[19]

"Embittered by Competition"

A number of observers contended that conflict within New York's banking fraternity was responsible for the financial crisis. Alfred Owen Crozier was an attorney and critic of the private banking system who engaged in a wide range of pursuits, from manufacturing to writing novels. "It must not be forgotten," he counseled, "that there was among Wall street's national banks bitter hatred and envy toward the trust companies because they were not subject to the same legal restraints, and particularly because their high interest rate paid for deposits was attracting money the banks otherwise would have obtained." Trust company resources in New York State increased by 71 percent from 1901 to 1907, while the resources of national banks only grew 21 percent. New York trust companies' competitive advantages included having to maintain a reserve of only 5 percent of their deposit liabilities, as compared to the 25 percent required of the city's national banks. The financial journal *Trust Companies* felt compelled to defend the institutions against members of the New York Clearing House Association "who appear to be embittered by competition" and had made "derogatory statements against trust companies."[20]

It appears that Morgan was not initially inclined to prevent the independent trust companies from failing during the 1907 crisis. Noted muckraker Upton Sinclair later recounted that a knowledgeable friend informed him that Morgan was "determined to break . . . the independent trust companies." Two highly placed corporate lawyers told Sinclair the same story. Morgan later acknowledged that the crisis had provided "an opportunity for cleaning out the banking business." The crisis did disproportionately affect trust companies. Clearinghouse associations contributed to this discrepancy, because they served as a source of protection that trust companies lacked. The banks that comprised New York's clearinghouse demurred from interceding on behalf of their competitors. Joseph French Johnson, dean of the New York University School of Commerce, observed: "If the Clearing House banks of New York had supported the Knickerbocker Trust . . . there would probably have been no panic." The result was that trust companies experienced a significant contraction in their loans and deposits during the crisis while neither national banks nor state banks did. In fact, New York's larger banks gained new accounts.[21]

Sinclair concluded that Morgan "deliberately brought it [the panic] on to tighten his hold upon the credit of the country," but had been forced to intervene when the situation spiraled out of control. Some believed that leading business figures had wanted a depression because of their displeasure with recent political developments. In August, Rockefeller had warned: "The effect of the runaway policy of the present administration toward business combinations of all kinds can have only one result. It means disaster to the country, financial depression and financial chaos." And in the midst of the crisis, E. H. Harriman apparently was pleased to imagine: "The people are beginning to realize the unfairness of many of the attacks on corporations in the last few years."[22]

Morgan's actions fueled the public impression that financial manipulation was occurring. He plainly had turned the crisis to his advantage. For example, the House of Morgan's United States Steel Corporation had absorbed the Tennessee Coal, Iron and Railroad Company, one of the few remaining independent steel producers. One member of the syndicate that held a majority of the Tennessee Company's shares was financier Grant B. Schley, whose brokerage house faced bankruptcy when the crisis led the firm's creditors to call in their loans. Morgan seized on Schley's predicament to purchase the syndicate's Tennessee Company stock holdings.[23]

U.S. Steel used $34.6 million of its own bonds to purchase the Tennessee Company, though one industry expert estimated it was worth $90 to $100 million. "The Steel Corporation has secured a bargain which cannot be duplicated in a hundred years," observed a member of the deposed syndicate. "Messrs. Morgan and Harriman and Rockefeller and their allies," commented Raleigh, North Carolina's *News and Observer*, "find the money with which to pick up new bargains. . . . Let no one suppose that there is a dearth of money in New York."[24]

"Selfishness and Love of Money"

Widespread distrust of bankers stoked the public anger that followed the Panic of 1907. In the popular imagination, bankers were driven by greed and lust for power. Practitioners of banking politics spoke to the common belief that bankers' calculating mind-set yielded heartless behavior. John Peter Altgeld, former governor of Illinois (D), described the banker as "a cold, shrewd, fierce money-getter." "A banker, to be successful," he believed, "must be cold and severe, repressing all generous and humane emotions." "Greed enters every pore of his being." The popular understanding of what constituted productive labor further shaped how Americans viewed bankers. Those who performed physical work accorded their toil moral worth and cultural esteem. A Catholic priest affirmed the sentiment of railroad workers attending a 1908 union convention when he observed that "the dignity of manual labor was taught by Christ our Lord Himself who labored at the trade of a carpenter." This view of labor encouraged a celebration of productive economic activity that inspired criticism of the financial system.[25]

The popular belief that finance was predicated on the seizure and manipulation of wealth created by the labor of others was expressed succinctly in an article Henry W. Evans published in the *United Mine Workers Journal* following the Bankers' Panic. "The burden of all interest is on the workingman," he declared. Evans was an ordinary citizen who lived a remarkable life in which banking politics occupied a central role. Evans joined the ranks of labor at the age of eight, when he went to work in the coal mines of his native Wales. In 1864 Evans emigrated to Pennsylvania's anthracite coalfields, where he rapidly became a highly regarded member of his community. Evans eventually served as a leader of the local miners' union before leaving the mines and establishing a small produce farm.[26]

Evans was thoroughly embedded within his community. He was an active member of the Welsh Congregational Church, served on the school board, and helped organize such important community events as the local Eisteddfod (a Welsh cultural festival). But he was best known for his political activities, especially his engagement with banking and monetary issues. The *Wilkes-Barre Times* referred to Evans as "the well known champion of free silver." He had been active in the Greenbacker parties, Prohibition Party, and People's Party, and was a student of socialism. For decades, Evans regularly lectured on the "money question" in both English and Welsh, and wrote numerous articles on the subject for various periodicals. His commitment to this issue stemmed from a faith that financial reform offered a means for working people to exercise greater control over their lives. When Evans acted as the miners' spokesman during the inquest into the Avondale mine disaster, which claimed 110 lives, he protested the relative powerlessness of workers who "knew that to work in such mines was always dangerous, but they must work in them or starve." Evans believed that financial reform would help empower working people.[27]

Evans's producerist convictions led him to insist that "money does not produce anything, anywhere by itself." He saw exploitation in banking arrangements that placed the "masses of people" in debt, so that they were "all in servitude to the few rich people." Evans stressed that this state of affairs contradicted Christian ethics, since "the plain teaching of the Bible is that we should always lend to the poor, needy sufferer without any interest." He accordingly urged reforms designed to do away with the burdens of debt. Evans proposed establishing "government postal savings banks of loan and deposit where the treasury could loan all the money needed to all the people that needed money, at three per cent." Evans believed that a reformed financial system would give rise to a more stable economy that no longer operated in the interest of indulging the greed of the wealthy. He explained that "panics are caused by placing confidence in the schemes of men to get wealth without working for it, and promises to pay more interest or increase than the average producer makes. Selfishness and love of money are the roots of the systems of finance that makes a necessity of panics."[28]

Evans found an audience because his beliefs reflected the political and economic attitudes of many workers and farmers. Author Finley Peter Dunne's internalization of Irish American working-class life made his character Mr. Dooley a prominent contemporary representation of the common man's thoughts and opinions. Dispensing popular wisdom from behind his Chicago bar, Mr. Dooley inevitably turned to bankers. "I've put them down all me life as cold, stony-hearted men that wud as soon part wit their lives as with their money." The Irish-American sage explained that bankers' overriding greed fostered not only callousness, but also self-indulgent recklessness when they sensed an opportunity to turn yet another gratuitous profit. "They'll lend ye money on anything," he observed. "If ye broke into a bank in Ohio to-morrah ye'd prob'ly find th' vaults full iv Louisiana lotthry tickets, bets on th' races, an' rayports iv crystal gazin'."

Banking, in Mr. Dooley's words, was "a sthrange business." It enabled the banker to use the laborer's wages to grow rich and to obtain power. Discussing banks with two "rayspictable wurrukin'-men," Mr. Dooley explained to them what their deposits allowed bankers to do. "With ye'er money I [banker] build a house an' rent it to you. I start a railrood with it, an' ye wurruk on th' railrood. . . . Ye'er money makes me a prom'nent citizen. Th' newspapers interview me on what shud be done with th' toilin' masses, manin' ye an' Donohue." And the influence of bankers, Mr. Dooley revealed, extended beyond their personal wealth and prominence. They exerted great political power. "I consthruct th' foreign policy iv th' govermint; I tll ye how ye shu vote. Ye've got to vote th' way I say or I won't give ye back ye'er money." The banker, therefore, transmuted the money that workers had earned by their hard toil into power for himself. His riches were morally compromised, gleaned nefariously by means of a corrupt system.[29]

"Wonderful Morgan!"

In the wake of the panic, differing perspectives on the nation's leading financial figures—especially J. Pierpont Morgan—reveal the deep fissure between bankers and their supporters on one side and much of the general public on the other. Members of the Boston Stock Exchange approved a resolution "express[ing] their great and deep admiration for the timely, disinterested, courageous and wise action of Mr J. Pierpont Morgan and his associates." "No one can estimate," the *Wall Street Journal* declared, "the enormous value of the services which Mr. Morgan has performed for the country during the past three weeks." The *Morning Oregonian* editorialized that "Mr. Morgan crushed the stampede by the sheer force of his personality." According to the *Washington Post*: "When the occasion came for Messrs. Stillman, Rockefeller, and Morgan to show their colors they were equal to the emergency. . . . With superb poise and equanimity they met the crisis."[30]

Such expressions of admiration were dismissed and even condemned in other quarters. Rather than investing financial leaders with the admirable qualities of statesmen, critics believed that avarice motivated bankers. The Bricklayers and Masons International Union of America charged that "J. Pierpont Morgan, the so-called 'saviour,' and the men associated with him, recently made over twelve million dollars in the saving process." The *La Crosse Tribune* claimed that "there wasn't any real reason for the mighty 'hurrah boys' talk about Morgan and Rockefeller rescuing Wall street, when something like ten per cent of the rescued belonged to themselves and they couldn't rescue that 10 per cent without rescuing it all." "Columns of adulation and parasitic flattery have been written about this colossal figure [Morgan]," the *Berkeley Independent* derisively noted. "He is the greatest man in the country. . . . Wonderful Morgan! . . . Morgan, god-like in the power of his gold!"[31]

Thomas E. Watson was an exceptionally trenchant critic of banking interests. He had attained national stature as the vice-presidential nominee of the People's Party in 1896. Watson ran as the Populist candidate for president in 1904 and 1908, authored a number of books, and published a journal. Watson took offense at the glorification of financiers that had followed the crisis, denouncing "ignorant editors [who] have extravagantly eulogized Morgan and Rockefeller for the patriotic generosity with which they rushed to the relief of Wall Street. . . . Editors who write slush-gush tributes to these two insatiable money-grubbers render themselves ridiculous."[32]

There was, however, general agreement about the necessity of financial reform. In his annual message, Roosevelt instructed Congress: "We need a greater elasticity in our currency." Every fall, the monetary system underwent a period of stress when farmers sold their crops for cash, thereby straining the supply of currency. Following the panic, bankers began to agitate for more currency, a stance that incongruously evoked their adversaries from past decades—the Greenbackers and Populists. "It is really funny," observed the Iowa periodical *Wallaces' Farmer*, "to see how the source of demand for more currency has changed in the last twenty-five years." Finding themselves short of currency during the crisis, some bankers had abruptly adopted heterodox monetary practices associated with the Populists. For example, the Southern Farmers' Alliance's sub-treasury plan had proposed that farmers store their crops in federal warehouses as collateral for low-interest loans of paper currency. In Oregon, the Portland Clearing House Association issued over $1.1 million of scrip backed by warehoused commodities, including wheat and canned fish. Observers who had been "howled down" by "solemn oracles of high financial wisdom" in the past relished the Portland banks' renunciation of orthodox dogma. "Warehouse receipts," crowed Salem's *Capital Journal*, "repudiated Farmers Alliance riffraff, ragtag and bobtail wildcat currency are now the delight of our Napoleons of finance." "What was contemptuously denominated fiat money a few years ago has again bravely come to the rescue in the big bankers scare."[33]

The Monetary System

In the Gilded Age, the question of what constituted acceptable currency was inescapable. Enactment of the Gold Standard Act of 1900 had made the gold dollar official. Under this monetary standard, the dollar was convertible to gold, which protected its value and made the money supply dependent on the gold stock. While gold coins circulated as currency, the bulk of the money the national government issued came in other forms, including silver and minor coin, silver and gold certificates, and United States Notes. Silver and gold certificates were paper money representing silver and gold coin on deposit at the U.S. Treasury. The United States Note—commonly referred to as the greenback—was created by the Legal Tender Act of 1862, which had authorized the printing of currency that was not convertible to specie, and therefore derived value from its status as legal tender.[34]

There also were private institutions that enjoyed the privilege of currency issue: national banks could circulate their own banknotes by securing them with 2 percent government bonds they deposited with the U.S. Treasury as collateral. These banknotes were an obligation of the issuing national bank rather than legal tender. They were taxed at a rate of 0.5 percent per year. Many bankers wanted to replace the existing government-bond-backed paper currency with banknotes secured by the assets in a bank's portfolio—an asset currency. They claimed an asset currency system would avert financial crises because the amount of paper money in circulation could fluctuate as business needs required.[35]

Practitioners of banking politics criticized the banknote system for turning a public function over to private business. They habitually made the point that article 1, section 8 of the U.S. Constitution vested Congress with the authority "to coin money, regulate the value thereof." "Render to Caesar the things which are Caesar's," Watson demanded, "restore to the Government the sovereign power of issuing paper currency." Advocates of government currency claimed that the banknote system fostered economic instability by presenting bankers with a mechanism for engaging in reckless speculation. "Too much bank-made currency . . . is afloat," Watson declared over a year before the Panic of 1907, "the line of credits has been lengthened until it is about to snap; wild-cat speculation is rampant; and thousands of banks are dabbling in business which isn't legitimate banking." Many Americans further criticized the monopoly privilege of banknote issue for awarding national banks an undeserved "double profit." American Federation of Labor president Samuel Gompers protested that this arrangement "has the people coming and going, paying interest upon these bonds lodged with the Government, and the bank (as if there had been no money transaction at all, and as if it had kept its, say, $1,000,000) receiving the interest and then issuing its . . . money . . . and receiving all the advantages that come from the use of this million dollars." Adherents of banking politics wanted an adequate money supply that financial interests could not manipulate for their own pecuniary self-interest.[36]

On New Year's Day 1908, Watson claimed that "the money changers" had "brought on the panic—willfully, designedly—for the sinister purpose of compelling the government to yield to their demand for asset currency." "If they don't mind," he warned, "they will get a fight on their hands, such as the bankers have not known since the days of Andrew Jackson." The developing asset currency debate recalled the previous decade's Battle of the Standards, when gold standard apologists had pilloried silverites, who sought to increase the money supply by backing currency with both silver and gold. Silverites insisted that bimetallism would relieve financial pressure on debtors and provide a more stable monetary standard than gold alone. William Jennings Bryan had led the silver forces during this political contest. He was an anti-monopolist and steadfast proponent of direct democracy who demonstrated keen interest in financial issues. In the aftermath of the Panic of 1907, Bryan served as the most prominent spokesman of a strong current of public opinion that insisted that control over the national currency and the money supply was properly a function of government. "I am opposed to any increase in the banks' control over the currency of the nation," he affirmed.[37]

Opponents of the private banking system's power endorsed financial reforms that the Greenbackers and Populists previously had advocated. Greenbackers wanted the monetary system to be based on legal tender paper currency issued by the national government. They contended that money was a medium of exchange, which derived value from its legal status. They believed that making money more widely available at lower interest rates would help stabilize the economy and democratize the financial system. Populists had hoped to centralize control over money and credit under the democratically responsive national government. They had promoted the basic tenets of Greenbackism, in addition to bimetallism, federal farm loans, post office savings banks, and bank deposit guaranty. Practitioners of banking politics upheld this insurgent political tradition. The platform of the Michigan Federation of Labor, for example, endorsed: "Abolition of national banks, and substitution for their notes [by] legal tender treasury notes. Issue of all money directly by the government, and establishment of postal deposit savings banks." Immediately following the panic, workers and farmers who wanted to establish a more democratic, stable financial system pushed for heterodox forms of currency, a postal savings system, and deposit guaranty.[38]

Heterodox Currency

Down south, R. F. Duckworth, president of the Georgia Farmers Union, seized on the issuance of clearinghouse scrip to promote an adaptation of the Populist sub-treasury plan. "The Farmers' Union," he wrote Secretary Cortelyou, "has warehouses throughout the south. The majority of these warehouses are bonded, and I want to ask, for . . . the permission of your department to issue certificates backed by our cotton receipts backed by bonded warehouses." When Congress reconvened in December, Senator Benjamin R. Tillman (D-SC) introduced a resolution to investigate this proposal. He also spoke in favor of issuing greenbacks, as did Watson, who personally lobbied both Roosevelt and Cortelyou. "The Government," Watson urged, "has full authority to issue more than one hundred million dollars in greenbacks." A number of southern Democratic congressmen were in full accord with Watson's plan. Representative Charles H. Weisse (D-WI) introduced legislation authorizing the U.S. Treasury to issue $1 billion of greenbacks.[39]

In the Midwest, the venerable financial reformer Jacob S. Coxey Sr. had reappeared in the headlines. At the age of sixteen, Coxey had gone to work in the same Pennsylvania iron mill that employed his father as a stationary steam engine operator. He subsequently relocated to Ohio and purchased a farm and an unprofitable sandstone quarry. Coxey reorganized the quarry to produce high-quality silica sand for use in the iron, steel, glass, and ceramics industries. Business success allowed Coxey to pursue his interest in financial reform. He gained fame as an advocate of the federal government printing greenbacks to purchase non-interest-bearing bonds from state and local governments. This currency would then be used to fund employment generating infrastructure projects. In 1894 he had led a contingent of unemployed workers—the Commonweal of Christ, commonly referred to as Coxey's Army—on a march to Washington, DC, garnering national publicity. The 400-mile trek culminated in Coxey's arrest, when he attempted to deliver a speech outlining the marchers' grievances from the steps of the U.S. Capitol. Over a decade had passed since he had led the "petition in boots," but Coxey was again steadfastly publicizing his non-interest-bearing bond plan, which he had enlarged to allow states to gain control over utilities—including railroads.[40]

The Chicago Federation of Labor sanctioned Coxey's financial ideas when it resolved in favor of issuing greenbacks to create employment on public works projects. "We are not asking anything new in this," stressed the resolution's author Margaret A. Haley. "During war times the United States issued notes secured by government bonds." This Chicago Teachers Federation leader had been introduced to Greenbackism and the ideas of Henry George Sr. at a young age. She recalled that the experience of reading a Greenbacker pamphlet "with tense interest" when she was eleven or twelve years old had left "a tremendous effect on my point of view." Haley believed there was a crucial "association between a governmental currency system and the daily lives of the people." In the countryside, the American Society of Equity advanced a variation of the financial reforms that Coxey and the Populists had popularized. This farmer organization wanted to grant state governments the ability to issue "credit currency" by depositing state bonds with the U.S. Treasury as security. These funds could then be used for such purposes as infrastructure projects, developing mines and factories, and providing loans that would enable farmers to sell their crops "evenly throughout the year" so that "it will not be possible for speculators to force farmers to dump their crops at any time they see fit."[41]

Out west, the cry for free silver found new vigor. The *Nevada State Journal* asserted that "more silver coin" was "the one way permanently to settle the [money] question." Mining interests represented by the Commercial Club of Salt Lake City entreated Congress to remonetize the white metal. And one of the city's journals maintained that had silver been accepted as "basic money" in the 1890s, "there would have been no need of an elastic currency now." Silverites were heard from east of the Rocky Mountains as well. A resident of Albion,

New York, insisted: "We must yet . . . restore free silver to its constitutional rights and allow it to enjoy the same privilege with gold." A
Cleveland carpenter who had emigrated from Ireland as a young man
asked: "Would we have had to issue clearing house certificates [scrip]
to relieve a money famine if the abundant products of our silver mines
could be coined into money as gold is and made a legal tender for all
debts?" Thomas Murphy charged that the gold standard had fostered
both economic inequality and instability. "Under it this county has
produced a crop of millionaires and multimillionaires unprecedented
in the annals of any nation, while the poor man has had his spells of
feverish prosperity and panic chills."[42]

Postal Savings

The Bankers' Panic immediately ushered post office savings banks
into the political spotlight. "The heretofore strenuous objections of
the banks and their influence in opposition to postal savings banks
should certainly now," insisted one Texan, "after the experience before
us, have no influence with anyone having the welfare of the people at
heart." For decades, workers and farmers had sought postal savings
banks, which would be guaranteed by the national government. During the panic, the St. Louis Central Trades and Labor Union unanimously voted in favor of postal savings banks "where the working
people could deposit their few hard-earned dollars without fear of
losing them." The Socialist Party of St. Louis hastened to proclaim
that "for years socialists have been advocating postal savings banks."
Postal savings also was advanced as a defense against future economic
depressions. Henry George Jr. specifically advocated postal savings as
a means to prevent periods of currency scarcity.[43]

Postmaster General George von L. Meyer seized the moment to
campaign for a tempered version of postal savings. He even boldly
urged the idea before the economically orthodox members of the
Union League Club of Philadelphia. In early November, he stated
that "the psychological moment" for establishing postal savings had
arrived. Meyer claimed that allowing the postal system to operate a

savings bank would help stabilize the economy. He emphasized the potential benefits of postal savings during financial crises—with their concomitant hoarding and bank runs—because "what people want is absolute security." He contended that "the easiest way to get this immense mass of currency back into regular channels is through a postal savings bank."[44]

Meyer was no financial insurgent; he held conventional economic views. Raised in Beacon Hill and a graduate of Harvard College, Meyer was a public-spirited Boston Brahmin. In 1900 Morgan deemed Meyer sufficiently reliable to recommend he be appointed ambassador to Italy, and three years later Morgan hosted a dinner party in his honor. The postmaster general advocated a decidedly limited postal savings program and consistently acted to assuage the fears the idea aroused in bankers by reassuring them that "the Post Office Department is not going into the banking business." His proposed system would be strictly limited to savings accounts, offer a non-competitive 2 percent interest rate, and have a low deposit ceiling of $500. Roosevelt reportedly supported this conservative plan.[45]

Meyer's efforts helped raise the issue's profile. "The movement for postal savings banks is gaining strength," noted *Bankers' Magazine*, which disdained this "foolish movement." During the weeks immediately following the panic, Meyer even managed to obtain approval for his proposal from some prominent bankers and businessmen who were persuaded that the plan did not threaten their interests. Indeed, the postmaster general suggested banks would benefit from postal savings. He claimed that "the very people who had learned to deposit in postal depositories . . . would realize . . . they could double their income in the regular savings institutions."[46]

But the impetus behind postal savings came from workers and farmers who were not concerned with protecting the private banking system. Meyer's campaign inspired a new sense of resolve among the idea's proponents. The Boot and Shoe Workers Union declared that "every trade Unionist and reformer in the United States should unite in support of Postal Savings Banks." By Thanksgiving, the workers and farmers advocating a postal savings system included a mass meeting of the railroad brotherhoods in Indianapolis, the Spokane local of the International Typographical Union of North America, the Chicago Federation of Labor, a contingent of Nevada farmers, and the Hendrum, Minnesota, local of the American Society of Equity. "The time is now ripe for successful agitation for United States Postal Savings bank," urged the Central Labor Council of Bellingham, Washington. "[A] system that insures safety to the ordinary citizen . . . preventing money panics, which . . . line the pockets of the grafters with ill-gotten gains, and burden most heavily the wageworkers."[47]

National organizations such as the Farmers' National Congress and the National Grange soon declared their support for the idea. The American Federation of Labor instructed its legislative committee to draft a postal savings bill and see that it was introduced in Congress. The labor federation also added support for postal savings to its list of political demands. General Master Workman of the Knights of Labor John W. Hayes emphasized: "We have for more than thirty years been urging the passage of a law providing for a postal savings bank." The union now insisted that postal savings funds should be used to help finance federal government programs.[48]

Supporters of postal savings also included important purveyors of Progressive ideas. *Collier's* pointed out the conspicuous lack of an American postal savings system given their near ubiquity internationally, noting, "Almost all the civilized nations of the world successfully maintain postal savings banks." Agricultural periodicals overwhelmingly favored the idea. *Ohio Farmer* wrote, "If the money that is now hoarded . . . was in the hands of the government, in postal banks, there would be none of the financial stringency that is now paralyzing business." *Breeder's Gazette* concurred that the introduction of postal savings would mean "an end of lack of confidence and bank runs by depositors." And postal savings was not the only proposal for a government bank. The Federated Trades of Portland, Oregon, pursued establishing a state-owned and -operated bank through popular initiative.[49]

Bank Deposit Guaranty

Coincident with the postal savings discussion, William Jennings Bryan advocated using government programs to protect depositors in the private banking system. He wanted the federal government to guarantee national bank deposits and state governments to guarantee state-chartered banks. Bryan's newspaper the *Commoner* noted that Meyer's postal savings proposal limited deposits to $500. "These banks will do a great deal of good, but they will not entirely relieve the situation. Our state and national banks should be made so good that no one will be afraid to deposit with them." Bryan was not alone: farmers and workers were registering their support for bank deposit guaranty. The New York State Grange, Pennsylvania State Grange, and United Mine Workers of America all resolved in favor of guaranty.[50]

Members of Congress responded to the public demand for guaranteed deposits by introducing over thirty guaranty bills. A broad range of legislators—from veteran Republican senator Knute Nelson (MN) to freshman Democrat senator Robert L. Owen Jr. (OK)—submitted various proposals for protecting depositors. Proponents of guaranty stressed that securing bank deposits provided a means for preventing future economic depressions. Owen argued that "stability of the commerce of the United States . . . is dependent upon freedom from panic, and freedom of panic depends on the insurance of bank depositors." The Progressive magazine *Review of Reviews* similarly concluded that under federal guaranty, "the national banks at least would be practically immune from the outbreak of depositors' panics." It further noted that state banks could be protected along the same lines. The venerable *Farm Journal* reported: "There is a very general demand for the government insurance of national bank deposits, and no good argument has been offered against the proposition."[51]

Voices of banking heterodoxy saw no need to choose between deposit guaranty and postal savings. The Boot and Shoe Workers Union foresaw both of these reforms advancing economic stability. "Give us government responsibility to the depositors in government chartered banks, and give us Postal Savings Banks, and there will never be another money famine or industrial panic." The Hendrum, Minnesota, local of the American Society of Equity not only wanted postal savings, it also resolved in support of "federal guarantee of national bank deposits and state guarantee of state bank deposits." These farmers additionally declared their opposition to asset currency, advocating establishment of a federal bank to issue currency instead.[52]

The Panic of 1907 prompted vehement denunciations of the power that financial interests exercised. The *Sacramento Evening Bee* editorialized: "It is high time the clutch of the national bankers should be taken from the throat of the Government on the one hand, and of the people on the other." "The time is not far off when The People, looking backward," predicted the newspaper, "will wonder how in the name of common sense they ever permitted Wall Street and the National Banks to run this country to their own profit, as they once woke up to wonder how in the name of Christianity and Humanity they ever tolerated slavery." Farmers and workers began to campaign vigorously for postal savings and deposit guaranty, and to resist forcefully further privatization of the money supply and concentration of private financial power. Financial legislation was imminent and banking politics was in the air. A decades-long struggle over financial reform had begun.[53]

2

The Emergency Currency Act

"Part of Plutocracy's Plan"

In the wake of the Panic of 1907, socialist organizer Frank P. O'Hare orated on top of a wagon parked in front of an Arkansas bank. His audience, bristling with anger over recent events, listened intently to what he had to say about the "money question." That winter, Andrew Carnegie also delivered a speech on financial issues. His audience at Manhattan's Hotel Astor was the well-heeled membership of the Economic Club of New York. Other speakers present included former Secretary of the Treasury Lyman J. Gage and the prominent corporate lawyer Victor Morawetz. But an outsider to the financial and business worlds also offered his views: William Jennings Bryan. The club's members recognized that practitioners of banking politics would be heard in the ensuing financial debate and wanted to gain a better sense of where they stood.[1]

Landmark financial legislation loomed, and working people were injecting heterodox ideas into the banking reform debate. Bankers would need to defend their prerogatives. Big-city and small-town bankers nationwide started closing ranks. In response to the recent financial crisis, Congress enacted the Emergency Currency Act of 1908 as a stopgap solution. Deferring comprehensive financial reform provided bankers with the opportunity to regroup and unite around a legislative program. This measure also attempted to erect barriers against popular participation in banking policy discussions by creating the banker-friendly National Monetary Commission to study financial questions and issue recommendations. Yet practitioners of banking politics had demonstrated their ability to contest the banking fraternity—a power they would put to use.

Politicians

Bankers were wary of President Theodore Roosevelt. From the onset of the Bankers' Panic, they had blamed Roosevelt for it. J. Pierpont Morgan himself later claimed that in addition to "certain economic conditions," the "immediate cause" of this emergency was "certain attempts at legislation." Financial interests found the president's aggressive "trust-busting" posture threatening. A few months before the panic, Roosevelt had avowed that there would be "no change in the policy we have steadily pursued, no let up . . . for I regard this contest as one to determine who shall rule the Government—the people through their Governmental agents, or a few ruthless and determined men whose wealth makes them particularly formidable." Following the crisis, New York City bankers attending their annual banquet at the Waldorf-Astoria Hotel cheered and applauded when Morgan's name was mentioned, but greeted a toast offered to Roosevelt with silence.[2]

While Roosevelt's position on banking policy generally was not clear—he found finance "very puzzling"—bankers worried that his combative stance toward business interests pointed in a worrisome direction, especially in a volatile political environment. Following the panic, Roosevelt fanned their apprehensions. In late November, Morgan and George F. Baker Sr., president of First National Bank, met with the president at the White House, to address the administration's "dissatisfaction and resentment." It was an adversarial encounter, where the financial tycoons "heard facts plainly presented in the President's most vigorous English." Roosevelt even raised the possibility of establishing a federal bank to issue currency. Later, when Morgan learned Roosevelt was on safari in Africa, he confided to a friend, "I hope the first lion he meets does his duty."[3]

At the same time, the president was treating the banking fraternity's adversaries with respect. "I wish I could see you in person to talk over several matters," he wrote Thomas E. Watson. "I shall not 'surrender' to the bankers." Roosevelt invited Watson to the White House. To the further consternation of financial interests, Bryan and Roosevelt had a genial encounter at the White House, with the president showing "appreciation" for the opposition party leader's proposal to guarantee bank deposits. When representatives of the Farmers Union met with Roosevelt "on financial matters," they reported that he was "in sympathy" with their "aims" and thought favorably of Bryan's plan.[4]

Roosevelt had in fact reached certain conclusions immediately after the panic. He predicted that "big financial men . . . [would] seize the occasion to try to escape from all government control." "My judgment," he privately disclosed, "is more firmly than ever that they must be brought under control." Roosevelt declared publicly that "the panic showed the necessity for a general house cleaning in financial circles, and the sooner the house cleaning is started the sooner it is over with."[5]

On Capitol Hill, Senate Majority Leader Nelson W. Aldrich (R-RI) and Speaker of the House Joseph G. "Uncle Joe" Cannon (R-IL) provided economically orthodox leadership. Both men were bulwarks of the existing order who consistently sought to forestall the tide of reform. Cannon wielded iron-fisted control over the lower chamber and was suspicious of any non-routine legislation. Aldrich was a former bank president who championed big business. He had obtained great wealth from an investment in trolley lines that beneficiaries of his political efforts financed. Aldrich reportedly favored a central bank under the control of bankers, but conceded that such an institution would not be established in the immediate future.[6]

Bankers found Charles N. Fowler (R-NJ), the chairman of the House Committee on Banking and Currency, less dependable. Fowler had been pushing his own financial reform legislation for years and considered himself a leading authority on banking issues. He was a Skull and Bonesman at Yale College, former president of a mortgage bank, and financially orthodox. But he demonstrated a proclivity for independent action. Cannon found Fowler's overweening confidence in his own opinions, and consequent intransigence, troublesome. The Speaker appointed Representative Theodore E. Burton (R-OH) to the Committee on Banking and Currency so he could better keep abreast of Fowler's activities.[7]

Bankers

Public pressure for financial reform following the 1907 crisis was intense. Still, bankers sought to ward off programs that challenged their economic and social position. Although the financial fraternity had yet to reach agreement about its own reform agenda, bankers were united in adamant support for a private banking system firmly under their control. As the leading Chicago banker George M. Reynolds pronounced: "Capital must be managed by those who supply it." Opposition to such proposed government programs as postal savings and deposit guaranty further unified bankers. However, bankers did not view themselves as promoting their own interests, but instead felt they were the proper authorities on business and economic affairs, convinced that their lending decisions facilitated the all-important natural law of supply and demand. Similarly, bankers thought their judicious direction of credit to worthy borrowers generated local development and fostered a predictable business environment—indeed, that the remarkably rapid economic growth of the United States testified to the skill and wisdom of the banking fraternity. Adamant that the private banking system had been integral to national progress, they believed that future prosperity depended on conforming to financial orthodoxy.[8]

Prior to the panic, a group of influential bankers had become interested in reforms they believed would better adapt the financial system to an economy that increasingly was structured through large corporations, but they had lacked sufficient impetus to pursue re-form in a concerted manner. Their primary objective was to create a central bank. Now, they saw an opportunity. Some of this group also promoted branch banking. Other bankers concentrated on reforming the monetary system by proposing various plans for introducing asset currency and issuing additional currency during periods of financial crisis. Each proposed reform possessed a locus of strength within the banking fraternity: the chief proponents of a central bank were New York bankers, while urban bankers in the Midwest were the driving force behind asset currency.[9]

Those bankers who opposed a central bank, branch banking, and an asset currency system—such as many small-town bankers—favored former Secretary of the Treasury Leslie M. Shaw's proposal to issue emergency currency; Shaw used the term "supplemental cur-rency" to emphasize the conservative nature of his plan, under which national banks could issue additional banknotes with the important provision that they be taxed at a rate (5 percent) that hastened their retirement. Efforts to implement an asset currency system generated greater controversy. The asset currency legislation that Representa-tive Fowler had formulated in 1902 also promoted branch banking. Administrative practice precluded national banks from establishing branches. And although the various branching regulations govern-ing state-chartered banks varied, even those states that permitted the practice erected limitations. Fowler's attempt to foster branching aroused hostility to his legislation among officers of unit banks (single-office banks). At that year's American Bankers Association conven-tion, Andrew J. Frame, president of the Waukesha National Bank, attacked Fowler's bill. Frame's belief that asset currency would en-courage inflation further hardened his opposition. Although Fowler's legislative effort was not successful, many bankers continued to favor asset currency.[10]

Serious discussion of a central bank followed on the heels of the 1907 crisis. Bankers were mindful of the potential advantages of pool-ing reserves in an institution that members could turn to during pre-carious periods. The idea of a central bank had arisen in 1901, when

A. B. Stickney, president of the Chicago Great Western Railway Company, advocated it. The prospects for such a bank received a boost in 1906, when the New York State Chamber of Commerce and the American Bankers Association both investigated the concept. But a central bank remained a contentious proposal. Small-town bankers in particular distrusted proposals to centralize financial resources. They held long-standing misgivings about their dependence on financial institutions in major cities.[11]

Central bank proponents used the recent crisis to promote the idea, organizing a series of lectures at Columbia University that winter by luminaries of the banking world. "I am convinced," New York financier Paul M. Warburg declared, "we shall never . . . reach a completely satisfactory condition until we have worked our way to a central bank." Frank A. Vanderlip Sr., vice president of National City Bank, suggested that an "ideal solution would combine the Scotch system of branch banks with the German system of a central bank." Support for a central bank began to grow. The midwestern banking journal *Commercial West* reported that bankers in Chicago were settling on a central bank "as the final solution of our financial question." George E. Roberts, president of the Commercial National Bank of Chicago, already had outlined plans for one. An important government official also endorsed a central bank: the comptroller of the currency. "If we had such a bank in operation in 1907," William B. Ridgely claimed, "no such bank panic as we have had would have been possible."[12]

While the officers of large banks in big cities generally viewed a central bank more favorably than their counterparts in small towns, the typical small-town banker was becoming more amenable to the concept. Frame saw merit in the idea. He testified that "if by an evolutionary process, so as not to produce any shock . . . every national bank in the United States should be deprived of the privilege of issuing currency, and it was all done by one central institution . . . I believe it would be a good thing for the country." But Frame was adamant that no "branch banking feature" be included in such an arrangement.[13]

Whatever disagreement over the proposition existed within bank-

ing circles, it was public opposition to financial monopoly that presented the fundamental obstacle to a central bank. Charles G. Dawes,
a former comptroller of the currency who was president of the Central Trust Company of Illinois, warned: "Let the people of this country
. . . believe that there is a chance for the passage of a bill establishing
a central bank . . . and see what the opposition will be." Immediately
following the 1907 crisis, the *Commoner* alerted its readers to the possibility that financiers might attempt to create a central bank as "part
of plutocracy's plan to increase its hold upon the government." "The
dead hand of Andrew Jackson holds our banking development by the
throat," observed Senator Chauncey M. Depew (R-NY), "and a central bank . . . is a political impossibility."[14]

Coxey on the March

Popular unrest that winter threatened to upend the financial reform
debate. The Panic of 1907 had created a volatile situation among unemployed workers, as prospective recruits for Coxey's armies grew
restive. At the dawn of 1908, industry was running at a much diminished capacity. Numerous sectors were operating at only 28 percent
of the volume they had one year earlier. In Philadelphia, 18,000 of the
28,000 textile workers in Kensington were out of work. By March, the
city's social workers were handling almost five times more cases than
they had one year previously. The steel industry contracted dramati-
cally: at the end of 1907, only 154 blast furnaces were in operation,
as compared to the 329 that had been producing just a few months
earlier. An estimated five million workers could not find jobs.[15]

Financial and business interests maintained that economic depressions not only were inevitable but therapeutic. "This sort of thing
comes in cycles. It is periodic," explained George E. Roberts. "We are
going through a period of liquidation, and going through it with relative ease." The National Association of Manufacturers expressed hope
that "curtailment of production" would "tend to check the unparal-
leled rise in wages." That winter, Morgan observed that workers "have
got no jobs now" and ruthlessly insisted that they would "have to sub-

mit or they will starve." "They are to learn that they cannot control industry," Morgan continued. "We want wages that will make honest and profitable business possible." An incensed Samuel Gompers alleged that this "thought has been in the minds of many employers of labor for a considerable time." Morgan's fellow Wall Street financier Henry Clews advanced the same position less belligerently. "A lowering of wages has become absolutely necessary," he intoned. "Workmen should not forget that half a loaf is better than no bread." The multimillionaire scolded any worker who resisted wage cuts for pursuing a "narrow, selfish policy of living for himself alone."[16]

Workers regarded the depression less dispassionately. A social worker in Homestead, Pennsylvania, attested to the "idleness and deprivation" in the steel town that winter and characterized conditions as "pathetic" and "desperate." The extinguishing of furnaces in Granite City, Illinois, led to such hardship that the neighborhood of Hungary Hollow became known as "Hungry Hollow." Residents of Steelton, Pennsylvania, tried to subsist on bread and water that winter, and hunted for driftwood on the banks of the Susquehanna River to heat their homes. The "fierce" melee that occurred when free loaves of bread were distributed just south of Buffalo near the Lackawanna Steel Company revealed the extent of these workers' grim circumstances. The hundreds who turned up in the hope of receiving something to eat "fought among themselves like starving wolves." More than three-fourths of the community was out of work. Many were trying to survive the winter with no means to secure food or fuel. Desperation stalked the city of Buffalo as well. A contemporary reported that it was impossible to "walk along any thoroughfare off of Main Street at any hour of the day without being stopped by some unfortunate and asked to contribute a little toward procuring a meal to save him from actual starvation." Years later, one Buffalonian recalled that as a twelve-year-old boy, "my home was destroyed and I sold papers, ate garbage and slept just anywhere." Times were dire downstate too: John H. Long ran the bread line at the Bowery Mission in Manhattan, and he estimated that at the close of 1907 there were "100,000 or more" unemployed, homeless men in the city. "The distress is greater than ever before," the Salvation Army reported.[17]

Workers in a number of cities protested their plight. In January, several hundred jobless men marched to Cincinnati's city hall and demanded public works jobs. A few days later, 800 men marched on city hall in St. Louis, where their representatives met with the mayor. In Boston, former Coxey's Army lieutenant Morrison I. Swift led a peaceful demonstration of hundreds of unemployed men. In New Britain, Connecticut, 600 unemployed men marched to the mayor's house and appealed for work. Fully 2,500 out-of-work men and boys had marched in Detroit by the end of the month. Representatives of twenty-seven labor unions organized a similar parade of 1,400 unemployed men through the streets of Seattle.[18]

In early February, James Eads How, founder of the International Brotherhood Welfare Association, organized a national convention of the unemployed. Jacob S. Coxey Sr. was among the speakers who addressed the hundreds who gathered in St. Louis to consider marching on Washington. The convention forwarded a resolution to the president and every member of Congress that cited the $25 million no-interest loan the federal government granted New York banks during the recent financial crisis as precedent for "relief of the unemployed in this time of their distress." This resolution called for $150 million of greenbacks for developing transportation infrastructure, and legislation that would enact Coxey's plan to let state and local governments deposit non-interest-bearing bonds with the U.S. Treasury in return for greenbacks to fund public works projects. A few weeks later, more than 1,200 jobless men gathered in Baltimore to demand public works employment. They, too, resolved in favor of the national government funding infrastructure in this way.[19]

At the end of February, the president welcomed Coxey to the White House. The *New York Times* reported that although he remained noncommittal, Roosevelt "listened with interest and great pleasure to Coxey's ideas." A bill to enact his monetary program was introduced in Congress. Coxey announced that he planned to promote financial reform throughout the nation. "My campaign," he explained, "will be one of education. I propose to point out to the people the defects in the present money system. Start a fire back on their representatives in congress, so to speak."[20]

Emergency Currency Legislation

Due to the wide range of views on financial questions in the House, political commentators thought successful reform legislation would have to originate in the Senate. The chairman of the Senate Committee on Finance was Aldrich, who formulated a bill with the assistance of New York's three principal bankers—Morgan, James Stillman, and Baker. Aldrich's legislation proposed allowing national banks to issue emergency currency secured by municipal, state, and railroad bonds. Wall Street found the prospect of backing currency with railroad bonds appealing because it would increase demand for these securities. Aldrich's proposal alarmed Bryan. He began to rally congressional and public opposition to private corporations assuming greater control over the money supply and the national currency.[21]

Aldrich's bill provoked criticism inside financial circles as well. Bankers objected that the legislation required them to increase their reserves. Samuel A. Harris, president of Minneapolis's National Bank of Commerce, claimed this stipulation "would mean a shrinkage of the available cash means of this country in a very large amount." Any such contraction would contradict the purpose of emergency currency legislation. Moreover, many bankers argued that bonds—government or otherwise—lacked the requisite flexibility to secure currency. "Bond-secured currency," a New York banker explained, "is largely dependent for its elasticity on the price of bonds rather than the demands of trade." The bill's opponents further contended that such a currency would privilege the very large banks that held these bonds. A District of Columbia banker protested that "if the Aldrich bill becomes a law, we are expected to buy bonds which we do not want." "Our funds," explained one small-town banker, "are too busy in developing this territory to be invested in bonds of this character."

Critics of Aldrich's bill preferred an asset currency based on commercial paper (short-term, unsecured IOUs that firms sold to finance their operations). Alexander Gilbert, president of the New York Clearing House Association, thought that "even in New York it is only the very large banks that . . . might possibly be in favor of the Aldrich bill."[22]

Resistance to Aldrich's bill inside financial and business circles further increased as a result of amendments that Senator Robert M. La Follette Sr. forced. "Fighting Bob" was Aldrich's opposite, an anti-monopolist with a deep concern that business was corrupting politics. He led a political movement in Wisconsin that turned the state into a "laboratory of democracy," pioneering such reforms as the income tax, direct primary elections, public utility and railroad regulation, child labor laws, and workmen's compensation. He railed against financial mergers that were creating "masses of capital." La Follette believed a network of corporations had developed that allowed a handful of men to wield enormous power. He was concerned, therefore, about "banking institutions having community of interest with the powers that control the industrial and transportation life of the country." He thus sought means to check such power.[23]

La Follette successfully removed railroad bonds from the Aldrich bill's list of acceptable securities by arguing that the value of the railroads' physical property needed to be determined before their bonds were deemed acceptable. (The data collected would have provided new insight on railroad rates.) He also managed to insert an amendment that prohibited national banks from investing in the securities of any firm in which its directors were interested parties. La Follette later noted that his alterations provoked "consternation" among financial interests.[24]

Senator Knute Nelson introduced an additional amendment that bankers did not view favorably. The Norway-born Nelson came to America as a child and was raised on his stepfather's Wisconsin farm. In 1861 he enlisted in the Union army. Nelson was wounded and taken prisoner two years later. Following the Civil War, he homesteaded and practiced law before embarking on a successful political career. Nelson thought national banks ought to be of greater utility to the public and the federal government that chartered them. This outlook led him to conclude that national banks should pay interest on their government deposits. During debate on Aldrich's bill, Nelson attempted to establish an interest rate of 2 percent on federal deposits. When this proposal failed, he presented an amendment setting the rate at 1.5 percent. Aldrich insisted that it be reduced to 1 percent. Nelson responded by proposing to leave the precise rate to the discretion of the secretary of the treasury, though no less than 1 percent. This effort met with success and would become part of the Emergency Currency Act. As amended, the Senate passed Aldrich's legislation in late March.[25]

Despite objections to Aldrich's bill, there was no rush to embrace the banking legislation originating in the House, where Fowler once again had drafted a controversial measure. Fowler still wanted to institute asset currency. He boasted that his plan would ensure "a currency always responding to the varying demands of trade." Fowler's legislation also sought to make national banks more competitive by extending privileges to them that their rivals the trust companies enjoyed, such as acting as administrators, executers, and guardians. Although he omitted any provision for branch banking this time, Fowler included yet another idea that was considered beyond the pale: a government fund to guarantee bank deposits.[26]

Fowler's advocacy of a tenet of Bryanism shocked the banking fraternity. David R. Forgan, president of the National City Bank of Chicago, was "utterly amazed to find Mr. Fowler supporting [deposit guaranty]." Charles Elliot Warren, president of the New York State Bankers Association, articulated financial orthodoxy when he contended: "A guaranty of deposits would put a premium on doubtful, if not dishonest, banking methods." *Commercial West* admitted: "If it could be done with sound results we would still oppose it on the ground of its socialistic tendency." A. Barton Hepburn, president of Chase National Bank, maintained that bankers "would prefer no legislation at all than to run the risk of a guarantee of deposits." Fowler's bill was reported by his committee but advanced no further.[27]

Bryanism

While the financial reform debate was unfolding in Washington, DC, William Jennings Bryan was featuring deposit guaranty prominently in his 1908 presidential campaign. In addition to protecting depositors, Bryan argued that guaranty would avert financial crises, because when the public lacked confidence in banks, "money . . . is likely to be withdrawn just at the time when money is most needed." His plan to guarantee deposits found an enthusiastic reception on the hustings. In March, after "mingl[ing] with all sorts of people" in his travels around the nation, political reporter Walter E. Wellman concluded that guaranty "[had] met with instant response in all parts of the land." "Pass an act, as W. J. Bryan says," one Philadelphian urged, "let the State stand good for all deposits in local banks and the United States stand good for all national banks, and you will soon see the country in a prosperous condition." The Prohibition Party's decision to endorse guaranty at its 1908 convention further indicates the idea's broad appeal.[28]

Shortly after Bryan took up the cause of protecting depositors, the state of Oklahoma followed his lead. Bryan was so highly regarded in Oklahoma that the recently ratified state constitution expressed his political ideals. The Sooner State included a mandatory deposit guaranty program in the banking law it enacted immediately following the financial crisis in December 1907. The creation of this government program to guarantee state-chartered banks was a bold move that attracted national attention. "This is a radical experiment," stated *Outlook*, a leading newsmagazine, "but we are glad to see it tried in Oklahoma."[29]

Bryan foresaw guaranty providing new opportunities for curbing banker autonomy. "I welcome the prospect of guaranteed banks," he remarked, "because I think it will enable us to get some regulation that we need." Bankers fiercely defended their autonomy. One banker exemplified this attitude when a federal bank examiner pressed his concerns about an overdraft. This query provoked the banker to threaten: "We will throw in our national bank charter and start business tomorrow as a state bank." Another banker—having received letters from the Office of the Comptroller of the Currency outlining his bank's legal violations—sneeringly remarked to the deputy comptroller: "Here comes the man who writes those letters to the banks telling them how they should conduct their business." Any regulation was too much for partners of the House of Morgan, who elected to risk their personal wealth rather than incorporate and be subject to government oversight.[30]

The question of asset currency was another point of contention between Bryan and financial interests. He maintained the federal government should exercise authority over the national currency. "Do not," the *Commoner* exhorted its readers, "in this moment of financier-made panic . . . yield to the temptation to surrender more of the money issuing functions of the government." Bryan recommended providing for additional monetary flexibility through special issues of greenbacks when financial stringencies emerged. He insisted that currency should "be controlled by officials responsible to the people, and not by financiers, who would be tempted to act for their own interest rather than the interest of the public." Bryan's position had significant public support. The National Farmers Union wanted "all money . . . issued by and under the direct control of the Government." In Kansas, a former Populist leader instructed one of the state's congressmen, "when you get back there [Washington, DC,] we don't want any asset currency."[31]

Similarly, agitation for postal savings concerned the banking fraternity. The *Seattle Daily Times* reported that over the winter bankers "flooded" Congress with "hysterical letters" opposing postal savings. But springtime saw the president pushing hard for Congress to implement Postmaster General George von L. Meyer's plan, while public declarations of support for postal savings continued to accumulate: the recent conventions of the National Farmers Union, Bricklayers and Masons International Union of America, and Nashville Trades and Labor Council had endorsed the idea. The Central Labor Union of Evansville, Indiana, favored postal savings because it would foster economic stability. Granges across the country—from West Chazy,

New York, to Winlock, Washington—were petitioning Congress on behalf of the program.[32]

As the congressional session neared its close, Senator Thomas H. Carter (R-MT) introduced legislation that corresponded with Meyer's proposal. Carter was a loyal party man who promoted economic policies he believed would aid his adopted state. He thought the greatest beneficiary of this program would be "the sparsely settled sections of the West where facilities for the saving of small sums by the struggling poor are extremely limited." Carter also was convinced that postal savings would reduce hoarding, thereby ensuring more currency remained in circulation during periods of stress. "It is possible," he suggested, "that the amount of money concealed in the stoves of the country would prevent a panic."[33]

The banking fraternity was coping not only with the energetic reform agitation of workers and farmers, but also internal divisions and an unpredictable political climate. In this context, the idea of forming a commission to study banking reform rapidly took hold in financial and business circles. *Bankers' Magazine* hoped that a commission would help convert the general public to orthodox financial views, "shaping public opinion in favor of sound principles with respect to bank notes and currency and banking in general." Bankers' political opponents dismissed calls for a commission as a delaying tactic. "I believe we ought to legislate right away," Bryan argued. La Follette agreed that action should be taken while the issue retained a heightened hold on the public's attention. "The best time to work out the solution of any problem of national concern is when it engages public interest sufficiently to secure thorough and intelligent discussion."[34]

Emergency Currency Act

The House Banking and Currency Committee tabled Aldrich's unpopular legislation. But Roosevelt had concluded that because 1908 was an election year, it was imperative to pass financial legislation. Since the Republican Party controlled both the legislative and executive branches, it could enact any proposal that members could reach agreement about. With Cannon's backing, Representative Edward B. Vreeland (R), a banker from New York State, prepared a substitute measure. Cannon opposed letting busybody reformers meddle with existing economic arrangements that manifestly worked so well. "America is a hell of a success," he insisted.[35]

Although Vreeland approved of a central bank, he avoided associating his legislation with any controversial issue. Vreeland crafted a modification of Aldrich's bill that allowed groups of national banks to issue emergency currency backed by commercial paper, and established a commission to study financial reform. Vreeland's measure provided a mechanism for dealing with financial crises, while creating space for more consequential legislation in the future. Fowler resented that Cannon had marginalized him, and he led a House contingent against the Vreeland bill. Cannon was convinced that Congress had to pass a law "so that we can say to the people of the country we have made a panic due to currency stringency such as occurred last fall impossible in the future." The Speaker took the matter firmly in hand, successfully maneuvered the bill through the House, and hammered out its final form with Aldrich.[36]

During the House debate, John G. McHenry (D-PA) had articulated popular opposition to the measure by arguing that financial interests would use this new currency-issuing privilege to destabilize the economy when it suited their purposes. McHenry feared the ability to issue emergency currency provided "the Wall street rigger ... with an automatic device" so that "when the panic comes they have the money at hand to take advantage of the falling values." Worse, "Wall street never waits for a panic," he alleged. "It both anticipates and precipitates a panic." McHenry was actively involved in the Pennsylvania State Grange and oversaw its establishment of a number of small farmer-controlled banks. He had been raised on his father's farm in mountainous northeastern Pennsylvania. Whiskey was one of its products. He achieved business success by transforming this sideline into one of the state's larger distilleries. McHenry honored productive labor, not financial chicanery. He avowed that "the men and women who carry the dinner pail; and all toilers, whether by hand or brain, who by their production are contributing to our Nation's good, constitute the most useful members of society."[37]

The measure met with determined resistance in the Senate: La Follette led a filibuster, in part by reading aloud from Alfred Owen Crozier's novel *The Magnet*, which fittingly enough featured a senator's struggle against powerful financial interests. La Follette set a record by speaking continuously for over eighteen hours. The filibuster collapsed, however, when Senator Thomas P. Gore (D-OK), being blind, failed to notice that Senator William J. Stone (D-MO) was not in the chamber to relieve him. Nevertheless, "Senators La Follette and Gore," avowed the Knights of Labor, "deserve the thanks of the American people for the stand which they have taken against this bill."[38]

Congress approved the Emergency Currency Act on May 30. It established the National Monetary Commission to study banking and monetary policy, and permitted groups of national banks to issue emergency currency secured by almost any assets they held. A. Barton Hepburn stated that bankers "may well 'point with pride' to this achievement won in behalf of asset currency." The Emergency Currency Act not only postponed comprehensive financial legislation, it also sought to make banking reform a question of technical expertise, rather than of opposing economic agendas. The National Monetary Commission consisted of nine members of the House and nine members of the Senate. Aldrich served as chairman, and Vreeland was appointed vice chairman. Two of the banking fraternity's most reliable allies determined the rest of the commission's composition: Aldrich and Cannon. "We all felt uncertain as to what kind of men would have been selected by the President," Aldrich explained, "and we did not intend to take any chances."[39]

Following the Panic of 1907, bankers began to coalesce around a reform program that would bind them together: within financial circles, policy discussions increasingly focused on the question of a central bank. At the close of 1907, the *Washington Post* had surveyed bankers in the surrounding region and found them over two to one in favor of emergency currency and two to one against a central bank.

But even skeptical bankers were growing more amenable to a central bank. Although *Bankers' Magazine* did "not favor the establishment of a central bank," it did favor "a full and fair discussion of the merits of such a proposition." The banking fraternity would not be at liberty to simply concentrate on resolving its own internal divisions, however. Recent events had demonstrated that bankers would have to reckon with the public.[40]

3

Financial Heterodoxy Gains Ground

"I'll Trust Uncle Sam"

During the 1907 financial crisis, numerous Americans demonstrated their deep distrust of the private banking system and abiding confidence in government. The Bankers' Panic prompted one Iowa farmer to head to the local bank, withdraw all of his money, and take it across the street to the post office. He converted his savings into postal money orders made payable to himself. "I'll trust Uncle Sam," the farmer explained, "and nobody else." In addition to paying the fees for this transaction, he chose to forgo interest payments. But this Iowan was not in the least concerned. "I can go home now and breathe easy," he confided. He was not alone. In the year preceding March 1, 1908, Americans purchased at least 128,146 postal money orders made payable to themselves.[1]

Financial interests had sought to designate banking and monetary reform the province of the National Monetary Commission. But working people refused to be excluded. They demanded significant government involvement in finance, waging campaigns for postal savings, bank deposit guaranty, and agricultural credit reform. Bank-

57

ers were forced ever more on the defensive, as a number of state guaranty programs and a postal savings system were established.

As the political struggle over financial reform unfolded, the National Monetary Commission ponderously assembled the blueprint for a banker-controlled central bank. This agenda was deeply at odds with contemporary concerns. Farmers and ranchers, for example, believed that reform should stress easier access to agricultural credit. And Americans increasingly deplored that a "money trust" gave a handful of men vast influence over the nation's economy and politics. In response, Congress initiated a heavily publicized investigation of financial monopoly. The developing popular consciousness of concentrated financial power called into question the ability of bankers to control reform, and ultimately to maintain their grip on the nation's financial system.

Campaign Pledges

Americans habitually felt trepidation over the security of their bank deposits. As the Sailors' Union of the Pacific explained in a resolution that the California State Federation of Labor endorsed: "Through numerous bank failures very large numbers of small depositors have suffered great hardship, and a very large number of our people have lost faith in private banking institutions." Hall of Fame shortstop Honus Wagner—who came from the coal mines and steel mills of Carnegie, Pennsylvania—astutely divided his savings among the town's banks. "If one bank busts, there'll be some left," Wagner reasoned. Settlement house pioneer Jane Addams reported that bank failures in her Chicago neighborhood could produce tragic results. "When you consider that the meager savings of these people amount to so much to them, even life itself at times, it is not surprising that some of the victims of wrecked banks have become maniacs, while others have committed suicide."[2]

In 1908 President Theodore Roosevelt's Country Life Commission conducted a study of rural life that solicited the views of farmers nationwide. This investigation determined that "distrust of banks in country districts is very strong," and that small farmers and farm workers in particular had "little confidence in banks." The commission additionally found a "great strength of sentiment in favor of postal savings" that was "nearly unanimous." Popular enthusiasm for this innovation did not result simply from the private banking system's deficiencies. It was rooted in widespread faith in the nation's postal system, an expanding government service that Americans had time and again summoned to provide various public benefits. In the wake of the Bankers' Panic, a man in Pittsburgh hastily purchased $1,000 worth of postal money orders but left them as he rushed to leave. When the postal clerk called out after him, the man responded that he would retrieve them later. His trust was such that he left $1,000 for safekeeping without even requesting a receipt. Confidence in the Post Office Department encouraged Americans to pursue the possibility of grafting a banking system onto the arm of government that served its citizens day in and day out.[3]

During the 1908 general election, the Republican Party had to confront the popular appeal of William Jennings Bryan's deposit guaranty proposal. Campaigning before farmers and workers at the state fairgrounds in Fargo, North Dakota, Bryan asked his listeners to raise their hands if they supported guaranty. The crowd favored the idea almost unanimously. Public support for this Democratic policy proposal concerned Roosevelt. He was not averse to protecting depositors but dismissed Bryan's plan as "foolish and meaningless" because "a Government guaranty could not be given unless the Government possest [sic] absolute and complete control over the [banking] business and practically went into the business itself." As an alternative to guaranty, Roosevelt wanted the Republican Party to include a postal savings plank in its platform. Roosevelt's advocacy met with resistance from bankers who vigorously lobbied against the idea at the Republican National Convention. John L. Hamilton, president of the American Bankers Association, entreated the party not to endorse postal savings, and to instead leave the question to the National Monetary Commission.[4]

There also was conflict over the issue among party leaders. Bankers had a friend in Speaker Joseph G. Cannon, who opposed postal savings. But Roosevelt insisted that backing this groundbreaking service would encourage workers to vote Republican. His championing carried the day, and the party adopted the plank. The Democrats did not cede this popular issue to their opponents, however, endorsing postal savings at their convention as well. And a keynote speaker at the Democratic National Convention mockingly proposed that the Republican platform should be changed to read: "We did not establish postal savings banks."[5]

Both major parties had responded to the popular demand for postal savings. The American Federation of Labor had urged the party conventions to "pledge" their support for postal savings legislation. The Boot and Shoe Workers Union went so far as to propose that "a vote against postal savings banks is as much a vote against labor as a vote against the anti-injunction bill." Employers' use of injunctions was of prime importance to unions, because these orders prohibited such fundamental activities as organizing and striking. Linking postal savings with the injunction reflects the high significance workers accorded this proposed financial institution. Organized agriculture was no less supportive. In 1908 the Farmers' National Congress, National Farmers Union, and National Grange all resolved in favor of postal savings legislation. The names of Congress members who opposed postal savings were read regularly at meetings of Grangers. And the organization "call[ed] upon all members . . . to write their senators and representatives in Congress, urging them to vote for this bill."[6]

Public agitation for guaranty and postal savings were prime concerns at the American Bankers Association's 1908 convention. Arkansas banker Clifton R. Breckinridge stated: "I consider . . . those who are engaged in banking, is [sic] confronted by a very serious situation." The organization's president, J. D. Powers, complained that "the interests of bankers has been menaced for years by ill-advised, unfair and unjust legislation." The convention proclaimed that bankers were "unalterably opposed to any arbitrary plan looking to the mutual guaranty of deposits." The bankers called guaranty "misleading," "unsound," "subversive," and "revolutionary." Due to the influence of the staunch Republican banker A. Barton Hepburn, the convention was less thoroughly damning of postal savings, branding the idea merely "unwise and hurtful." Broader business interests sympathized with the bankers' position. At that year's National Association of Manufacturers convention, the relevant committee report cautioned that postal savings raised the issue of "paternalism," and included a statement from a "prominent business man" who called it "a dangerous, untried and dreaded idea."[7]

Small-town bankers objected to postal savings most bitterly. According to one incensed Washington State banker, postal savings was "Bryanistic, socialistic and paternal, and therefore un-American and hence undesirable." But prominent big-city financial figures like Henry Clews and George E. Roberts were outspoken opponents as well. The American Bankers Association's Federal Legislative Committee claimed that 98 percent of bankers opposed postal savings. Shortly after the election, Lucius Teter, head of the organization's anti–postal savings campaign, instructed bankers to communicate their opposition to members of Congress and to lobby local newspaper editors to editorialize against the idea. The campaign met with success. The momentum for postal savings in Congress ground to a standstill: the program failed to advance in 1908 or 1909.[8]

State Guaranty Programs

While postal savings legislation struggled to make headway nationally, states enacted laws guaranteeing the banks they chartered. Elected officials were responding to the popular outcry for deposit guaranty. "Guarantee bank deposits," enjoined one resident of Yakima County, Washington, "which would steady financial conditions and give people confidence." Guaranty's appeal extended beyond workers and farmers to professionals and small businessmen. "I have been specially interested in the law guaranteeing bank deposits," attested a civil engineer in York, Pennsylvania. The manager of a family-operated lumber company in Minnesota argued that if "bank depositors felt reasonably sure of the safety of their money . . . we would not have had such a panic as we had [in 1907]." Bryan spoke for this public demand to stabilize the banking system when he advocated guaranty laws in Nebraska, Kansas, and Texas.[9]

Bankers were guaranty's primary opponents, although the officers of some small state-chartered banks favored the idea because they hoped to better compete with national banks. In Oklahoma, guaranty initially had been welcomed at many state banks hoping to gain new deposits, while bankers at federally chartered institutions opposed the program. Less than one year after guaranty's inauguration, Oklahoma's national banks were said to "present an attitude of practically unanimous hostility to the law." And a state bank officer revealed that ambivalence now characterized "the position of state bankers" toward guaranty. He related that they "all view the law with more or less apprehension and treat it as an experiment," even though "it might be of temporary advantage to state banks in smaller towns."[10]

Public enthusiasm for guaranteed deposits overcame banker opposition in Nebraska, Kansas, and Texas. The *Lincoln News* observed that support of guaranty was "a very popular sentiment in Nebraska." A banker in Pawnee City "confess[ed] that the sentiment is for it in this vicinity undoubtedly." The incumbent Republican governor's knowledge of public opinion led him to press his party to endorse the idea at its 1908 state convention. Members of the necessary committee refused even to second this proposal, however, because they were either bankers or attorneys for banks. Meanwhile, Nebraska's Democratic Party endorsed guaranty, and the state's Populists and Prohibition Party also backed the idea. The *Omaha Daily Bee* called guaranty "the one real big issue of the campaign upon which the democratic candidates staked their all." A contemporary academic observed that Democratic support for guaranty was "undoubtedly of great force" in the party's electoral success that fall. Among the offices Democrats collected was the governorship.[11]

The electoral outcome was different in Kansas, where Republican leaders alive to guaranty's popular appeal prevailed. "The people want this law," observed the outgoing Republican governor. The state party incorporated the idea in its 1908 platform. The concept did find support among some Kansas bankers who were anxious about competition from guaranteed banks in neighboring Oklahoma and concluded their state should enact a similar program. But William H. Peck, president of the Kansas Bankers Association, condemned guaranty as representative of "the doctrine of the Socialist" that would "have the state own everything and the individual nothing." Following Grand Old Party victories in 1908, the bankers finally admitted defeat, but not before Jerome W. Berryman, former president of the Kansas Bankers Association, nearly came to blows over the issue with the new Republican governor. The enraged banker considered guaranty to be "a worse fallacy than the free silver craze." Berryman predicted that the program's "ultimate toppling would crush all industry, paralyze all business, and destroy confidence[,] leaving the state and country more prostrate than war or pestilence."[12]

Bankers in heavily Democratic Texas also resisted guaranty. One district convention of the Texas Bankers Association unanimously resolved against the idea. Another declared itself "unalterably opposed to the passage of any law guaranteeing deposits." Approximately 150 Texas bankers gathered in the state capital to lobby against proposed guaranty legislation. Leading politicians favored a guaranty law, however, and the state Democratic Party had pledged itself on the issue. Farmers were urging enactment of the program. And Commissioner of Insurance and Banking Thomas B. Love was an ardent Bryan supporter. He had moved from Missouri to work for Bryan's 1900 presidential campaign in Texas. Love insisted that "the overwhelming majority of the people of the State earnestly desire the redemption . . . of the platform pledge of the Democratic party by the enactment of a safe and sound law providing for the guaranty of State bank deposits." When progress toward a guaranty law stalled, the governor called a special session. "A law providing for the guaranty of deposits in State banks was demanded and the people mean it."[13]

By the summer of 1909, Nebraska, Kansas, and Texas had adopted guaranty programs. Shortly after the Nebraska measure passed, a group of bankers filed a lawsuit arguing it was unconstitutional. An earlier challenge to Oklahoma's law already was on the docket at the

U.S. Supreme Court. In South Dakota, bankers managed to make the state's guaranty law inoperative without seeking legal recourse. While guaranty was popular with South Dakotans, and both the state's Democratic and Republican parties accordingly endorsed the idea, the Speaker of the House was a bank president who took an active part in framing an ineffectual measure. The program that was enacted in 1909 made bank participation voluntary. The law also required that 100 banks (there were 485 in the state) join the program in order for it to take effect. The state's bankers successfully boycotted the program, so it failed to become operative. The president of the South Dakota Bankers Association expressed satisfaction that the law was "worse than useless."[14]

All of the states that had enacted guaranty programs were located west of the Mississippi River, but the concept held national appeal. The Department of the Treasury was receiving a growing number of letters on the subject. Guaranty legislation was under consideration in Colorado, Illinois, Indiana, Iowa, Maryland, Minnesota, Missouri, Montana, New York, North Dakota, South Carolina, Tennessee, and Washington State. Bankers were irate. One acknowledged before a convention of fellow bankers that he considered guaranty to be "such a heresy I could not touch upon it without dealing in criticism too caustic to have place in these proceedings." And such hostile feelings only grew as supporters of guaranty not only persisted, but also sometimes carried the day. According to Arthur Reynolds, chairman of the American Bankers Association's Federal Legislative Committee: "Bankers under their breath and to each other are expressing a fear that the scheme for guaranteeing bank deposits and postal savings banks will prevail."[15]

"Demands for Legislation"

After presiding over thirty public hearings in rural communities around the nation during the fall of 1908, Country Life Commission member "Uncle" Henry Wallace reported that "the people seem to be united" in demanding postal savings. A Michigan farmer wanted postal savings "so the holders of small sums can deposit them and keep them in circulation; then when I am ready to dispose of my crops the buyer will not say 'Money is scarce.'" Existing facilities to meet the savings needs of working people were limited. Approximately one-half of Americans lived in places where there were no savings banks. The ubiquity of post offices throughout the nation offered a potential network of thousands of secure savings depositories. "Massachusetts has probably as good a system of savings banks as any place in this world," pointed out Representative Joseph F. O'Connell (D-MA), "yet bank failures are not uncommon with us." O'Connell represented Quincy and the adjacent Boston neighborhood of Dorchester. He reported that "the people of my district desire a law establishing postal savings banks." In rural western Massachusetts, desire for both security and convenience prompted a mass meeting in Montague township to unanimously vote in favor of postal savings. Township residents explained: "It takes a full half day for one of our people to reach a savings bank."[16]

Key congressional leaders blocked postal savings legislation throughout 1909. Senator Nelson W. Aldrich insisted that action on postal savings should be postponed until after broader banking reforms had been enacted. Speaker Cannon appointed Representative John W. Weeks (R), a Massachusetts banker, to chair the Committee on Post Office and Post Roads in order to obstruct postal savings legislation. Cannon had little use for financial reform proposals. "Coming up from 90,000,000 of people are all kinds of demands for legislation," he said. "If a man has lost all other power to affect public opinion and cannot call attention otherwise to himself, he comes around with a currency scheme." Notwithstanding having such powerful allies, the American Bankers Association felt compelled to use "all honorable means to defeat the proposed [postal savings] legislation."[17]

Emerging victorious from the 1908 election, President William Howard Taft persevered in support of the Republican pledge to establish postal savings. In December 1909, Taft took the opportunity that the president's annual message to Congress afforded to reaffirm his desire for legislation on the subject. Weeks hastily appointed a subcommittee to handle the issue. He named an opponent of the measure, J. J. Gardner (R-NJ), as chairman, and stacked its membership with bankers.[18]

Adversaries of postal savings alleged the program would have disastrous consequences. The American Bankers Association's Committee on Postal Savings Banks claimed that were the system to be established, "the South, Southwest, Middle and Northwest and West would be overrun with bandits." Bankers frequently expressed their unyielding opposition in ideological terms. Nebraska banker Edmund R. Gurney indicted supporters of postal savings for seeking to "have the Government cast loose from its moorings of protection for the individual and plunge into the frightful slough of socialism." Another banker similarly classified his opponents on the issue as "those who hope for an early millennium on earth through the establishment of socialism."[19]

There were postal savings supporters, however, whose motivations were far removed from either socialist thought or utopian visions. "I am not a paternalist," Taft affirmed, "and I am not a socialist." He foresaw this program aiding bankers. Taft hoped to employ postal savings funds to purchase the 2 percent bonds that national banks used to secure their banknotes. This use of these funds would prepare the way for altering the monetary system without the banks suffering losses. *Bankers' Magazine* had staked out the position that there was "absolutely no justification" for postal savings, but Taft's solution prompted second thoughts. The journal reasoned that "any sensible plan which involved getting them [the bonds] out of the way is not to be lightly considered." By New Year's Day 1910, Aldrich had informed Taft that he no longer would oppose postal savings legislation.[20]

Benevolent Institution

Important proponents of postal savings imagined an institution constrained from competing with the private banking system. These reformers portrayed postal savings as a means for serving groups that did not use banks. They foresaw the institution facilitating uplift among its patrons. Postmaster General George von L. Meyer insisted that "the principal object of the postal savings banks would be to encourage habits of economy." He argued that expanding opportunities for working people to save would inculcate thrift, which in turn would foster respectability. Leading Progressive reformer Florence Kelley arrived at a corresponding conclusion. She had been a resident of Hull House, whose founder Jane Addams long advocated for postal savings on behalf of immigrants. Kelley lamented that "drinking, gambling, petty speculation in wildcat stocks . . . and patronizing vendors of patent medicines . . . are fostered by . . . [the] needless lack of accessible safe places for small savings." She put forward postal savings as a "stimulus to thrift on the part of small depositors." "The post-office is open early and late," Meyer added, "and the day-laborer returning home on Saturday night with his week's pay finds the regular banks closed, but the saloon open." The postmaster general hoped that postal savings would encourage these workers to exercise the restraint and self-discipline so central to the ethic of respectability that upper-middle-class reformers esteemed.[21]

Progressive reformers who lobbied for postal savings particularly emphasized the beneficent influence the institution would exert over immigrants. Lajos Steiner of the New York State Department of Agriculture believed that "postal savings banks will facilitate the Americanization of immigrants." Foreign-born workers often avoided banks because of their limited business hours and intimidating character. Immigrants frequently availed themselves of banking services offered by fellow countrymen who operated with minimal or no legal oversight, often lacked financial training, and sometimes acted dishonestly. Steiner denounced these immigrant bankers for facilitating insularity, and thereby "obstructing immigrants from absorbing Americanization." He added that frequently these "banks cause to their depositors total losses of their savings." Steiner believed that postal savings would ensure that immigrants no longer served as "easy prey" for immigrant bankers.[22]

Reformers further argued that postal savings would decrease the remittances of foreign-born workers to their homelands. Greeks sent home an average of $5 million annually; Swedes remitted up to $10 million to the old country each year. From 1906 to 1909, $312 million worth of postal money orders were made payable to people in foreign countries. Steiner pointed out that remitted money was "a total loss to American prosperity." Meyer insisted that postal savings would "encourage the foreign settler to deposit his earnings in this country." He further argued that postal savings would serve as a moderating social force, since "after he [the immigrant] had accumulated a few hundred dollars he would . . . possibly seek to purchase a home, and the moment he acquired real property here he would become a more conservative citizen." The belief that postal savings would promote political stability helped win support for the measure: "When a rabid disturber becomes a partner in an enterprise," submitted the *Morning Oregonian*, "his conservatism grows apace." The *Oregonian* hoped that postal savings would facilitate the transformation of potentially radical elements of society into defenders of the status quo, so they would cease "to hearken to apostles, like Bryan, of credit and currency buncombe."[23]

Public Bank

There was a fundamental divergence between the reformers who conceived of postal savings as a charitable program, and those who sought to challenge the existing banking system by counteracting financial concentration and providing working people with affordable loans. Farmers and workers frequently stressed the necessity of keeping postal savings funds in the localities where they had been deposited so this money would circulate there, rather than being funneled to large banks in the nation's financial centers. The Wisconsin State Grange, California Federation of Labor, and Michigan State Grange all lobbied to this effect.[24]

Many workers and farmers hoped to establish an actual postal bank. Chicago Federation of Labor founder James O'Connor believed that not lending postal savings funds would "work a positive injury to workingmen." He wanted "to have the government loan the savings on real estate at a low rate of interest and help the workers to own their own homes." Newspaper publisher William Randolph Hearst's numerous campaigns for political office primarily attracted a following among workers. The 1908 platform of Hearst's Independence Party recognized his constituency's perspective on postal savings by declaring: "Government postal savings banks should be established where the people's deposits will be secure, the money to be loaned to the people."[25]

Farmer organizations expressed particular interest in government lending. The American Society of Equity resolved that postal savings deposits should be "loaned to the people." An official journal of the National Farmers Union stated that the "best thing" would be "national postal savings depositories, with privileges of depositing any amount and also the privilege of borrowing from Uncle Sam's savings bank depositories on good security any amount at a small rate of interest for a long time or short." Farm tenancy rates increased over 45 percent nationally from 1880 to 1910. The Washington State Farmers Union wanted postal savings funds loaned to farmers at 3 percent, claiming that "cheaper money" would facilitate farm ownership and thereby help "solve the tenant problem."[26]

Workers and farmers also hoped to see postal savings serve as a counterweight to the private banking system. The New Hampshire State Grange saw the institution serving "as a regulator for the financial world." And the United Mine Workers of America resolved in favor of postal banks "paying a low rate of interest on deposits and loaning the money out on actual property values to the extent of one-half the value of the property . . . at a rate of interest not to exceed five per cent." For the union, the point of a low interest rate on deposits was not to make postal savings non-competitive with banks, but to ensure that the institution would be able to extend low-interest loans. Competition from postal savings presumably would compel private lenders to offer more affordable loans as well.[27]

Postal Savings Bank Act

The banking fraternity had managed to thwart postal savings legislation in 1909, but supporters of the idea redoubled their advocacy in 1910. In January, the national convention of the farmer organization the Ancient Order of Gleaners resolved in favor of postal savings. Meanwhile, the National Farmers Union and Postal Savings Bank League launched a joint lobbying effort. Senator Thomas H. Carter introduced yet another bill to establish a postal savings system later that month. This measure was modest, allowing individual account holders to deposit up to $500 at 2 percent interest. Money deposited at the post office would be re-deposited in local banks. The use of postal savings funds was a contentious issue. A contingent of senators pressed the popular demand that money deposited at a particular post office remain in that locality. But Taft threatened to veto legislation that did not grant the federal government access to these funds. He claimed the government had "a duty" to safeguard banks from financial loss on their 2 percent bonds. Taft further insisted that postal savings funds should be employed to protect the government's solvency during financial crises.[28]

The idea of using postal savings funds to purchase bonds provoked popular concern that this reform was being subverted. The Western Federation of Miners had envisioned postal savings as a haven where small depositors would be "reasonably secure from the 'frenzied financier.'" Any suggestion that Wall Street might handle these funds undercut this expectation. "The postal savings bank wanted by the people will not be established," the union concluded. "If a postal savings bank is established it will merely be an agency of the government to collect the savings of the masses of the people, to be turned over to such moneyed princes as Morgan or Rockefeller." The Senate arrived at a compromise that allowed the president to withdraw postal savings funds from local banks and invest them in federal bonds if an "exigency" necessitated such action. Senator William E. Borah (R-ID) then sought to prevent postal savings funds from being mobilized on behalf of 2 percent bondholders with a successful amendment prohibiting their investment in bonds bearing less than 2.25 percent. The revised measure passed the Senate in March.[29]

Meanwhile, a legislative opening had appeared in the House, where Cannon's reign had come to an abrupt end after disaffected Republicans had joined together with Democrats. But under the chairmanship of John W. Weeks, the Committee on Post Office and Post Roads continued to obstruct postal savings legislation. In April, Bryan visited Capitol Hill and encouraged House Democrats to push for legislative action. Working people continued to press postal savings as well. In early May, the National Farmers Union and American Society of Equity held a joint convention of thousands of farmers. The assembly adopted a declaration demanding postal savings, which was forwarded to the president and every member of Congress. Taft had acknowledged the political significance of this convention by speaking to it. Other prominent speakers included Missouri's governor, three U.S. senators, the secretary of agriculture, Samuel Gompers, Bryan, and Jacob S. Coxey Sr., who reminded farmers that "the citizens of this country paid a dear price for their present banking system."[30]

Armed with public support, Taft began to exert pressure on Weeks. The president spent one evening arguing with the "bitterly opposed" congressman until midnight. Legislation finally was reported to the House in June. The House acquiesced to Taft's demand for full authority to invest postal savings funds in securities, permitting up to 30 percent of deposits to be invested in government bonds, and granting the president discretion to invest an additional 65 percent in federal bonds when "the interests of the United States so require." The legislation passed the House following limited debate and was returned to the Senate. "It is most unfortunate," Senator Albert B. Cummins (R-IA) protested, "that we are called upon in these very closing hours of a long session to consider a new and a novel postal savings bill." He unsuccessfully tried to insert an amendment—similar to the one Borah had previously attached—requiring that postal savings funds be invested in government bonds paying at least 2.25 percent. There were rumors that a contingent of midwestern Republicans would mount a filibuster. Taft wanted the House version of the bill passed. On June 21, he announced his intention to wait all summer if necessary and put out a call for absent senators to be present for a vote on the measure. Taft's threat to keep Congress in session was aided by the oppressive 96-degree heat in Washington that day. On June 22, the Senate concurred in the bill as amended by the House.[31]

The Postal Savings Bank Act established a government savings bank that would operate only in designated post offices and pay patrons a non-competitive 2 percent interest rate on no more than $500. Lucius Teter boasted that the American Bankers Association "had a great deal to do in bringing about such favorable conditions as exist in the present law." Despite the limited nature of this reform, Lewis E. Pierson, president of the American Bankers Association, pronounced: "It can only be hoped that Congress will heed the unanimous warnings of our members as to the ultimate consequences of a Postal Savings Bank system and at an early date repeal the present law." On the other side, the Boot and Shoe Workers Union declared: "The chief value of this legislation is in the establishment of the principle of Postal Savings Banks and the opportuni[ti]es for amendment . . . which will come later."[32]

Agricultural Credit

The new law had notably failed to address farmers' and ranchers' concerns about securing affordable credit. Middling and small farmers depended on loans to finance their operations. One representative of a farmer organization in Oklahoma revealed how vulnerable farmers were: "He does not meet the banker on equal terms; ordinarily he is distressed in mind and body. He meets the banker, who is the very opposite of that, and he must have that money. Necessarily there is a cooperation among the banks as to their charges." Farmers believed that prevailing lending practices discriminated against them. Orthodox banking theory endorsed restricting bank lending to short-term commercial transactions to ensure liquidity. Because bankers sought to keep their assets as liquid as possible, they favored rapidly maturing business loans and harbored misgivings about offering loans for terms of six months and longer that farmers required. Senator Knute Nelson did not presume to transform orthodox lending theory, but he repeatedly attempted to expand farmers' opportunities to obtain financing. He campaigned to permit national banks to accept farmland as security for loans—an effort the *New York Times* characterized as "little hobby-horse journeys into dangerous country."[33]

Farm loans generally were most expensive in the Rocky Mountain states and parts of the South, and most affordable in New England, but no region lacked farmers who had difficulty obtaining credit. In 1912 a Department of Agriculture survey found that just under half of farm owners holding good security were able to procure sufficient credit. The periodical *Rural New-Yorker* reported: "Farmers write us that they are unable to get credit on any terms, and still more write that they can borrow only on terms that are ruinous." Farm mortgages presented special difficulties. In most western states, the average cost of such loans approached—or even exceeded—10 percent. Long-term credit was nearly as expensive for large numbers of farmers in the Midwest and South. Moreover, mortgage loans commonly were issued for only three to five years with no assurance of renewal. The risk that they would not be renewed was particularly acute during economic downturns or when money was tight. "The man of small means has no chance, under present conditions," deplored a farmer in Washington County, Iowa. "With small capital, high interest rates, and uncertain crop returns, he has little encouragement."[34]

In 1908 a National Farmers Union convention called for the national government to make low-interest loans to farmers. These farmers demanded that "citizens with land collateral shall all at times have the privilege of borrowing at not to exceed 5 per cent per annum." The following year, the Country Life Commission criticized the "lack of any adequate system of agricultural credit." The wide publicity the commission's findings received established agricultural credit as an issue that warranted the careful consideration of policymakers, who could no longer dismiss farm debt as merely a preoccupation of rural agitators.[35]

Against the background of the financial reform debate, bankers sought to curry favor with farmers by supporting various efforts that promoted agricultural improvement. Illinois banker Benjamin F. Harris acknowledged: "We want the people of Illinois to know that the Illinois Bankers' Association is with them." Bankers entered the "rural credit" discussion as the issue emerged onto the national political agenda in the 1910s. The banking fraternity's foremost spokesman on the question was Myron T. Herrick. This Ohio banker and Republican politician long had opposed proposals for public banking. He energetically publicized methods that private institutions employed for lending to farmers in Europe. Press coverage and editorial support in farm periodicals further bolstered efforts to promote nongovernmental solutions to agricultural credit reform.[36]

Taft's formal acknowledgment of agricultural credit deficiencies in 1912 affirmed that the issue demanded attention. Farmers recognized that this moment held new prospects for reform. The National Grange's 1912 convention expressed interest in loaning the Postal Savings System's funds to farmers. Senator Miles Poindexter (R-WA) assured Carey B. Kegley, master of the Washington State Grange, that he favored this idea. Public agitation for federal programs for affordable farm loans would intensify over the following years. "If President Taft is really in earnest about cheap money for the farmer," remarked a resident of Port Bolivar, Texas, "he ought to work for a change in the postal banking law." Popular demands for government to directly extend credit to farmers now accompanied calls to expand postal savings and establish guaranty programs in the national debate over banking reform.[37]

The National Monetary Commission

When Aldrich and his National Monetary Commission had commenced their study of financial questions in the summer of 1908, he was referred to as the "General Manager of the United States" and the term "money trust" received limited use. The commission submitted its report over three years later. Times had changed by 1912. The Postal Savings System was commencing, and agricultural credit reform had emerged as a national issue. Aldrich no longer held public office. The concept of a Wall Street financial monopoly had gained broad acceptance. The efforts of Aldrich and his commission to advance the interests of bankers had collided with effective, unwavering resistance from workers and farmers.[38]

In 1908 the *New York Times* reported that Aldrich wanted to make banking reform "the crowning work of his career, leaving it as a monument to his work in the Senate." He had eagerly convened the commission barely a month after Congress adjourned. He also promptly solicited the assistance of J. Pierpont Morgan and spent many hours discussing financial reform with him over the next few years. In August, Aldrich, Edward B. Vreeland, and other congressional members of the commission set sail to investigate banking in Europe. They were accompanied by the commission's secretary Arthur B. Shelton, and three advisers: Harvard University Professor of Economics A. Piatt Andrew Jr., Chicago banker George M. Reynolds, and New York banker Henry P. Davison Sr., whom Morgan had recommended to Aldrich. As the aging financial colossus withdrew from public life, Davison was assuming the role of his representative.[39]

Upon returning from Europe that fall, Aldrich announced that the commission would need at least two years to complete its report. The commission was amassing a mountain of material bearing an imprimatur of expert authority that would make its conclusions intimidatingly unapproachable. The commission sponsored the publication of twenty-three volumes on a range of financial subjects, aiming to overwhelm by sheer weight of information and burden of erudition any competing thoughts on the subject. (Aldrich had speculated that "out of the 90,000,000 of people in the United States, I suppose at least three-quarters of the heads of families think they are entitled to submit a plan, and have it considered.") Thomas E. Watson, however, directed ridicule straight at the heart of this project: he portrayed the commission's European research as an extended vacation, while simultaneously celebrating the labor of the working people the commission sought to silence.

> While the average man loafed through the summer, lightly tilling the soil, sporting with a hod of brick, merrily saluting the anvil with a 200-pound hammer . . . or similar amusements, *these* patriots were tracing the currency question all over Europe—pursuing it to the very summit of the snow-clad Alps, delving for it in the Catacombs of Rome, laboriously upturning the stones of Venice, that no financial system escape scrutiny. Yea, verily, they sought along the castled Rhine, the blue Danube and in the pure depths of romantic Lake Lucerne.

According to Watson: "The present Monetary Commission . . . is busy 'fixing' up a Central Bank scheme, under the direction of 'some of the ablest financiers of Wall Street.' The public is cordially invited not to meddle."[40]

One year after the commission embarked for Europe, reports indicated its interest in establishing a central bank. This energized practitioners of banking politics. The National Farmers Union contacted members of Congress to insist that they "defeat . . . the proposed central bank." This reaction reflected the increasing attention that the public was paying to financial concentration. In 1910 the business periodical *Moody's Magazine* noted that "steady and increasing concentration . . . is becoming more and more a matter of discussion in all walks of life." This was in part due to a merger movement under way among the nation's banking institutions—one popularly identified with the "triumvirate" of Morgan, James Stillman, and George F. Baker Sr., whom the newsmagazine *World's Work* reported were jointly "organizing more closely . . . the banking power." The Knights of Labor contended that Morgan's "recent activity in assuming control of big banks, trust companies, and insurance companies is all part of one general plan that was decided on by Morgan and his advisers following the panic of 1907. Closer control of banks."[41]

A deluge of articles in popular magazines both reflected and encouraged growing public interest in financial concentration. "Seven men in Wall Street," *McClure's Magazine* readers learned, "now control a great share of the fundamental industries and resources of the United States." The summer of 1910 provided further evidence of financial consolidation: two Chicago banks—the Continental National Bank and Commercial National Bank—combined to form the second largest bank in the country. And financial affiliation extended beyond mergers: Frank A. Vanderlip Sr. later acknowledged that J. P. Morgan & Company, National City Bank, and First National Bank had "an agreement that on any issue of securities originated by any of the three, the originating house was to have 50 per cent, and each of the other two was to have 25 per cent." According to Vanderlip, this arrangement was struck so as not to upset "the existing balance in the money power in Wall Street."[42]

The Aldrich Plan

The National Monetary Commission faced a difficult task. Davison suggested a clandestine retreat to formulate a plan at Morgan's hideaway in the exclusive Jekyll Island Club on the Georgia coast. Aldrich readily accepted and let Davison select the participants. In November 1910, a collection of powerful financiers surreptitiously gathered at the seaside resort for the professed purpose of hunting ducks. Present were Davison, Aldrich, Vanderlip, Andrew, Paul M. Warburg, and Shelton. Warburg's son later remarked that his father "had never had a gun and didn't know which end you shoot from." They spent more than a week in seclusion resolving the details of a plan. "We were working so hard," Vanderlip fondly remembered, "that we ate enormously." With evident relish, he recalled dining upon "deer, turkey and quail . . . pans of oysters . . . country hams," and the pièce de résistance: "wild turkey with oyster stuffing." After returning from Jekyll Island, participation in further deliberations was expanded slightly by involving a contingent of financial leaders from Chicago: James B. Forgan, J. Laurence Laughlin, and Reynolds.[43]

The result of these meetings was revealed publicly in January 1911. The Aldrich plan sought to establish a banker-controlled central bank and asset currency, packaged with a few cosmetic touches devised to win public favor. This banker's bank would be named the "National Reserve Association of the United States." California Bankers Association president William H. High noted that employing the term "Reserve Association" was "a concession to those who object to the centralization idea attached to the central bank." The central bank's fifteen branches would regulate the issue of asset currency and discount for member banks. (Discounting allows banks to borrow money from the central bank.) Those national banks that chose to join the system could purchase the institution's stock in proportion to their size. Bankers would elect, both directly and indirectly, thirty-nine of the central bank's forty-five directors.[44]

The Aldrich plan's proponents now sought the American Bankers Association's endorsement. Meetings between National Monetary Commission members and the organization's leadership that spring produced a revised version of the plan that its executive council approved unanimously. Extensive discussion of central banking within the banking fraternity following the 1907 financial crisis had swung support toward the idea. A 1909 poll revealed that three out of five bankers were in favor. They perceived benefits in an institution that would lend additional reserves and adjust the volume of currency. By September 1911, the American Bankers Association's journal was free to state that the Aldrich plan had "the approval of the banking fraternity." Chicago banker Charles G. Dawes observed that "gradually students of the question, originally far apart in their views, have become more united until now they are practically a unit for a National Reserve Association."[45]

Some small-town bankers who continued to harbor doubts about centralizing financial power expressed concern that the Aldrich plan threatened their independence. Frederick E. Lyford, president of the First National Bank of Waverly, New York, worried that the plan embodied "a new system . . . which will bring into existence a form of branch banking." Small-town unit bank spokesman Andrew J. Frame wanted a central bank to supply "a safety valve" and "act as servant of our splendid, independent banking system, and not as its master." The members of the Wisconsin Bankers Association were apprehensive that financial reform might promote branching. At the organization's 1911 convention, Frame observed, "I do not think there is one man in my hearing who is in favor of branch banking." Yet with his encouragement, the convention passed a resolution supporting the Aldrich plan while also declaring that branch banks should "not be permitted." Bankers in twenty-eight other states endorsed the Aldrich plan as well, and Continental and Commercial National Bank reported that its correspondent banks "generally" supported the idea.[46]

Winning public approval would be the Aldrich plan's crucial test, however. Many Americans were convinced this proposed reform served bankers, not the nation as a whole. "No financial scheme," the National Grange declared, "which could be launched would be more detrimental to the best interests of this country than such a centralizing of banking as shall put the reins of control into the hands of a few Wall Street magnates." Grangers stressed that currency issue was a public function. "The Grange will stand squarely on its carefully taken position in this matter and will use every means in its power to defeat the Central Bank scheme." The National Farmers Union's Committee on Legislation recommended enactment of a law that would specifically prohibit a central bank. Voices in both political parties disapproved of the plan. "We do not need it," stated the *Commoner*, "and we can not afford to build up such a gigantic money trust." Senator Robert M. La Follette Sr. alleged the plan was "backed by powerful financial and business interests to secure stronger control upon the capital and credit of our country."[47]

Bankers buttressed the pro–Aldrich plan campaign by establishing a surrogate organization to speak on their behalf. In January 1911, Warburg convinced the National Board of Trade to support an organization to "carry on an active campaign of education and propaganda for monetary reform, on the principles . . . outlined in Senator Aldrich's plan." In March, Warburg secured the New York State Chamber of Commerce's support for the proposed organization. The following month, the Chicago Association of Commerce formed the National Citizens' League for Promotion of a Sound Banking System, which was largely funded by clearinghouse associations.[48]

Professor J. Laurence Laughlin of the University of Chicago led the National Citizens' League. The leading academic goldbug during the monetary debate of the 1890s, Laughlin was a prolific and dogmatic author of materials upholding the gold standard for non-academic audiences. Although the League claimed to support a set of general principles rather than any particular plan, the ideas it espoused corresponded with the Aldrich plan. The organization distributed over one million pieces of literature during its initial year and was particularly diligent about supplying newspapers with materials. Moreover, Laughlin received personal advice from Aldrich on lobbying Congress. Laughlin also undertook an extensive speaking tour through congressional districts in the South and Midwest. Banking interests were highly appreciative of the organization's "splendid work."[49]

Representative Charles A. Lindbergh Sr. (R-MN) had a very different perspective on the National Citizens' League: he indicted the organization. Father of the famed aviator, Lindbergh had been brought to America as an infant by his Swedish parents. Lindbergh's father protested that back in the old country, "not half of the people are represented, only the rich, and pretty rich, too." Lindbergh's earliest years were spent in a log cabin on the Minnesota frontier. As a young man, he practiced law and operated a small farm before entering politics. Lindbergh was a man of strong convictions and great political courage. "The subtle and underground influence of Wall Street in furthering and advocating that [Aldrich] plan," he charged, "is illustrated in the formation of the National Citizens' League."[50]

Lindbergh emphasized that this organization was anything but a grassroots movement. "I believe in citizens' leagues," he affirmed, "but I would like to see them started voluntarily by the people themselves." Lindbergh charged that interested parties were promoting their political agenda by pouring large sums of money into the organization. "The dollar charged for [an individual] membership does not pay one-tenth part of the cost of the sums that are being expended," he pointed out. A Granger in Washington State was similarly critical, protesting that the National Citizens' League had "flooded" his town with literature declaring that members of Congress who "stood for our interest and voted against the Aldrich bill were traitors," and insinuating that "we should banish them if we did not want our industries interfered with."[51]

Business developments during the summer of 1911 undercut the pro–Aldrich plan campaign. Stillman envisaged his National City Bank assuming the role of a de facto central bank. The bank thus declared a special dividend to fund the creation of the state-chartered National City Company, which would take control of stock the bank's owners held in a large number of other banks and trust companies. And the National City Company would be free to engage in investment banking activities that federal regulations prohibited National City Bank from pursuing. This development inspired Lindbergh to seek an investigation of whether financial interests were combining "in restraint of trade." Lindbergh had emerged as the leading congressional spokesman of Americans who were opposed to financial concentration.[52]

The National City Company affair fueled the controversy swirling around the question of financial monopoly. "It is a waste of breath," observed the *New York Times*, "to urge upon the people of the country the acceptance of the Aldrich plan . . . so long as one National bank, through a holding company, may control twenty, fifty, or one hundred other National banks." In November, the National City Company announced that it had disposed of all its stock holdings in banks. This decision was made just days before Solicitor General Frederick W. Lehmann issued an unfavorable opinion on National City Company. Following a meeting with Vanderlip and Davison, Taft saw to it that Lehmann's opinion was not made public. Nevertheless, the formation of the National City Company further tainted financial interests in the public mind.[53]

The National Monetary Commission finally submitted its official report on January 8, 1912. The commission wanted to create a central bank with fifteen regional branches. The proposed National Reserve

Association would be controlled by bankers and empowered to issue asset currency. "Instead of overshadowing banks," the commission stated, "it is their representative." Farmers and workers vehemently denounced this idea. The Farmers Union local of Grayson County, Texas, believed "that such an institution would make the people of the United States victims of an Oligarchy of wealth and greed." "The big financial concerns . . . have the people pretty well chained up now," observed the Oregon State Federation of Labor, "but the infamous Aldrich currency bill would 'hog-tie' them and deliver them to the trusts." Opposition was voiced by all kinds of working people. A "hobo convention" in Cincinnati that drew together hundreds of highly mobile workers from all corners of the nation condemned the idea. The comparatively rooted participants in the burgeoning movement to organize farmer-controlled grain elevators throughout the Midwest were similarly against the plan. The Grain Dealers Association of South Dakota was "unalterably opposed" to the idea and resolved to "work for such men for congress as are opposed to the said measure, and only those."[54]

The Money Trust

A month before Aldrich's commission submitted its report, Lindbergh had renewed his push to investigate financial monopoly. The *Journal of Commerce* duly assailed him for introducing a "ridiculous resolution." The Knights of Labor observed that proposals for such an investigation had prompted "some allusions and even slight references to the threats of a terrible panic, if there was any Congressional meddling." There was substantial support in Congress for an investigation in spite of such intimations, however: Lindbergh's resolution was notably the single piece of legislation that a Republican sponsored that made headway in the Democratic-controlled House during that session.[55]

Commercial West attempted to discredit Lindbergh and his push for scrutiny of the financial world. "In banking circles Mr. Lindbergh and his 'money trust' hunting expedition is a joke." The journal scoffed that the congressman conceived of bankers as "a sort of 'money changer,' like those of Palestine 2,000 years ago,—who were driven from the temple." Yet the congressman attracted support precisely because he was attacking financial interests. For example, John J. Gallagher, a vice president of the Brotherhood of Railway Carmen of America, stated that "usury or interest are one and the same thing, that form of thievery that keeps the farmer and the worker in the grip of the banker . . . the money lending parasite that Christ . . . drove out of the temple."[56]

Banking interests were so opposed to an investigation that inaction remained a distinct possibility. The *Commoner* instructed its readers to "immediately write or wire" their representatives in support of House Democrats conducting a financial monopoly investigation. At the close of January 1912, Representative Robert Lee Henry (D-TX) introduced a resolution to investigate financial monopoly and its political influence, including the question of campaign contributions. Henry was a committed anti-monopolist, who as assistant attorney general of Texas in 1893 had drafted an indictment of such Standard Oil executives as John D. Rockefeller Sr., William Rockefeller, and H. H. Rogers for anti-trust violations. Henry now aligned himself with the mounting public demand to confront centralized financial power. "It is hoped," the United Mine Workers of America attested, "that the contemplated investigation of the Money Trust will materialize."[57]

Henry insisted that a special committee conduct the investigation, not the House Committee on Banking and Currency, which, Bryan contended, "contains some Democrats whose sympathies are with the 'money trust.'" At the urging of Majority Leader Oscar W. Underwood (D-AL), the House Democratic caucus approved a substitute measure that left the initiative to standing committees—not a special committee—to conduct "such investigation as may be necessary." Henry and his allies refused to concede defeat, however, and managed to strengthen the Democratic caucus measure by directing the banking committee "to make a full investigation."[58]

Henry then took to the floor of the House and avowed that "more than 75 per cent of our financial resources . . . [are] now dominated and controlled by not more than four small groups of financiers." Vreeland refuted Henry's analysis. Vreeland claimed that the credit system provided a model of equal opportunity and mass participation, involving "at least 15,000 or 20,000 money trusts." "Every city, every town, every village that has a bank has a money trust, and when a village is too small to have a bank some good old Deacon Jones, who has laid up his money . . . is the money trust." Jefferson Monroe Levy (D-NY) expressed the apprehension among financial interests. "We must cease entirely this utterly useless method of agitating, investigating, and experimenting," the wealthy congressman admonished.[59]

Such arguments were out of step with the tide of contemporary public opinion. The House voted overwhelmingly in favor of investigating financial monopoly. "If there be no Money Trust," Representative George W. Norris (R-NE) pointed out, "then no one can be hurt by an honest investigation, no matter how thorough it may be." The banking committee was split into two subcommittees: one would handle the financial monopoly investigation, and the other would consider banking reform legislation. Representative Arsène P. Pujo (D-LA) chaired the investigative subcommittee, while reform was assigned to Representative Carter Glass (D-VA). In April, the prominent New York corporate lawyer Samuel Untermyer was selected to serve as the Pujo subcommittee's counsel. A few months previously, Untermyer had delivered a speech that acknowledged the existence of centralized financial power, "a close and well defined 'community of interests,' and understanding among the men who dominate the financial destinies of our country."[60]

As a condition of accepting the position, Untermyer demanded broader powers than the enabling legislation had granted. Pujo responded by introducing a resolution that resembled Henry's original one, minus the special committee. By this time, the House recognized the public demand for a thorough investigation of financial concentration, and only fifteen members voted against Pujo's resolution. The banking fraternity was indignant. The journal *Trust Companies* avowed that there had never been "a more disgraceful abuse of the power vested in Congress" than that "perpetrated" by the resolutions approving this investigation.[61]

During May and June, the initial hearings of the Pujo subcommittee probed the scope and nature of concentrated financial power, revealing that leading bankers had an unwavering opposition to public accountability. In one telling exchange, Untermyer pressed A. Barton Hepburn about introducing some degree of public oversight to the New York Clearing House Association. "You think," he asked, "it ought to remain like a private club . . . above and beyond the courts of law?" "I do not think," Hepburn responded, "that you can provide any review of the men in charge here that would be an improvement." Untermyer's questioning demonstrated that the same bankers who vehemently rejected external oversight were liable to exercise their power arbitrarily. The hearings revealed that shortly after the 1907 financial crisis, the clearinghouse had forced a solvent bank to close. "It was a mistake," Hepburn admitted. Such revelations further undermined the banking fraternity's public standing. Bankers found the irreverent exchanges that characterized these forums both impertinent and unsettling. "What an outrage that our best men should be summoned . . . before a committee of cheap politicians and business ignoramuses to be cross-questioned by an unprincipled and pettifogging Jew," one banker commiserated with George F. Baker Sr.[62]

It was an election year, and the Pujo subcommittee wrapped up initial hearings in mid-June, shortly before the political parties held their conventions. Newspapers across the country were featuring front-page headlines about the "money trust" and Untermyer's interrogation of leading bankers. The Wisconsin Society of Equity stated that the first question to ask a candidate was: "How he stands on the Aldrich Currency Scheme?" The 1912 Republican Party platform neglected to endorse the Aldrich plan and pronounced: "Our banking and currency system must be safeguarded from any possibility of domination." With Bryan's encouragement, the Democrats were more explicit about the issue: "We oppose the so-called Aldrich bill or the establishment of a central bank." The party pledged "protection from control of dominion by what is known as the money trust."

Likewise, the Progressive Party opposed the Aldrich plan by name and proclaimed that control over currency "should be protected from domination or manipulation by Wall Street."[63]

The nation's political establishment had affirmed the public's rejection of the Aldrich plan and demonstrated that the concept of financial monopoly had become part of mainstream discourse. One aging advocate of a cooperative economy questioned the significance of this development. "The Money Power has this people—has this nation—by the throat," lamented Albert Kimsey Owen. The promoter of the ambitious—and failed—nineteenth-century utopian Topolobampo colony believed the power of finance "has changed the people of this country . . . into mad, crazy, soulless, 'business' creatures that struggle, lie, cheat, fight, steal." Owen thought American culture had been so thoroughly corrupted that "there can not be a Bill passed . . . that interferes with the Money Power." The banking fraternity, however, saw reform on the horizon. *Pacific Banker* urged bankers to wage a public relations campaign that would "speak to the people and explain to them that the bank's interest and the people's interest are identical."[64]

Given the public suspicion of finance, and the general tenor of the reform sentiment engulfing the nation, the future outline of the banking system appeared hazier than ever. Numerous Americans thought the power of finance was detrimental to the nation. Buffalo banker Elliott C. McDougal acknowledged there was "a general distrust of all measures proposed by bankers." One supporter of the National Citizens' League expressed deep-seated concern over contemporary political trends. "We are living in times of great political unsettlement," observed Cornell University president Jacob Gould Schurman. "Not only has Socialism received a tremendous impetus but Radicalism of a more or less revolutionary character is rampant in many states." But whether those who had so diligently harried concentrations of financial power would actually capture the initiative for banking reform remained an open question.[65]

4

Central Banking and Agricultural Credit

"Vigorous and Persistent Efforts"

In 1908 *Bankers' Magazine* had speculated about the "interesting possibilities" that a central bank raised. "If the Populists got control of the Government, should we expect to see Tom Watson made president of the bank? . . . Would he and his fellow directors make loans on the basis of the collateral offered by the applicant, or on the basis of his views respecting the initiative and referendum? Or on the length and luxuriance of his whiskers?" The journal's scorn betrayed deep-seated anxieties. But shortly before Christmas Eve 1913, the signing of the Federal Reserve Act relieved apprehensions within the banking fraternity over the central bank debate.[1]

While the Federal Reserve Act constituted a victory for bankers in important respects, it was not altogether a triumph for banking interests. Workers and farmers had influenced the shape of the Federal Reserve System in crucial ways. Popular opposition to financial monopoly produced a decentralized central bank rooted in a principle that practitioners of banking politics strongly advocated and bankers vociferously resisted: public authority. The governors of the system were presidential appointees who needed to be confirmed by the Senate. Furthermore, the campaign that banking politics advocates had waged during the central bank debate compelled agricultural credit reform. The resulting Federal Farm Loan System repudiated the creed of laissez-faire by pioneering government lending programs for ordinary citizens.[2]

"The 'Peoples' Banks"

As Woodrow Wilson prepared to assume the presidency in March 1913, practitioners of banking politics were primed to challenge the existing financial system. The Pujo subcommittee's investigation of financial monopoly had verified that a small circle of bankers and businessmen exercised vast economic power. A mere 180 men held 746 directorships in 134 corporations capitalized at over $25 billion. Senator Robert M. La Follette Sr. noted that in 1908 *Review of Reviews* had characterized his warnings about financial monopoly as "sensational and much to be regretted." However, the "money trust" investigation inspired the magazine to affirm that "to-day figures and cold statistics show that more power is lodged with a dozen men than La Follette, four years ahead of his time, dared ascribe."[3]

Public agitation to remake the banking system emphasized the power of bankers to both manipulate credit in their own interest and to withhold credit from others. Socialist thought advocated government banking as the means for combating such monopoly. Karl F. M. Sandberg—a noted physician, prominent member of Chicago's Norwegian community, vigorous advocate of banking reform, and committed socialist—wrote, "Government ownership of our credit system is the only cure for the evils resulting from the manipulation of credit for private profit." But agitation for government banking was hardly restricted to socialists. It also included avowed opponents of socialism. An alarmed Thomas E. Watson, for example, referred to socialism as "dynamite that is being planted at the very bases of our institutions." Yet Watson favored a government bank as a mechanism for making low-interest loans more widely available.[4]

Practitioners of banking politics routinely foresaw the Post Office Department as the nucleus of a new banking system. The Postal Savings System had expanded rapidly since its debut in 1911. On the system's inaugural day in Kansas City, eager patrons had formed a line in the post office lobby before the doors opened at nine o'clock. By the time postal clerks closed the windows at nine o'clock that night, 155 people deposited a total of $5,009. The *Brooklyn Daily Eagle* reported that the borough's postal savings depositors were "Americans, Hebrews, Italians, Germans; men, women, and children . . . people of many nationalities, divers[e] occupations and all ages." After one year, 5,185 post offices had been designated postal savings depositories, and patrons were depositing $1 million per week.[5]

Farmers and workers regularly advocated lending postal savings funds. "Let all our banks be located in the post-offices and be run by the government," urged Charles O. Drayton, president of the Farmers Equity Union. At its 1912 national convention, the American Federation of Labor resolved "that the money accumulated in the Postal Savings Banks be loaned to individuals in the community where deposited, preferably to laboring people striving to obtain a house." The Brotherhood of Painters, Decorators and Paperhangers of America wanted to do away with the deposit limit, introduce checking accounts, and use postal savings deposits to fund public works projects.[6]

Reformers holding a range of perspectives agreed that the institution's purpose should extend beyond assisting thrift. "There is no more excuse for a private banking system than there is for a private postoffice system," Sandberg insisted. "The government has provided savings depositories in our postoffices; it should provide full banking facilities for our use." Charles O. Boring, a Chicago proponent of the Social Gospel who was active in the cooperative and prohibition movements, foresaw the Postal Savings System making loans and becoming "the 'Peoples' Banks." Arizona state senator Albinus A. Worsley (D)—a former Populist, promoter of Henry George's single tax, proponent of direct democracy, and labor union advocate—proposed eliminating the postal savings deposit limit, increasing the interest rate paid depositors to 3 percent, and using the funds to extend 4 percent loans on real estate.[7]

The Authority of Expertise

The banking fraternity's ability to resist popular demands for sweeping financial reform was not simply a product of its economic and political power. The rise of Progressivism had promoted the application of professional expertise to political questions as a means for arriving at non-ideological policies that served the public interest. Theodore Roosevelt, for example, described "experts" as "men who should not represent any special interest or industry . . . [who are] single-minded in finding out, and telling, the truth." Progressives hoped that using expertise to guide policymaking would preclude conflict between different interest groups and social classes.[8]

In practice, this celebration of expertise justified granting bankers disproportionate influence over banking policy. Key policymakers privileged the opinions of bankers during the formulation of financial reform legislation. "There is no class in the community," President Taft had stated, "whose experience better qualifies them to make suggestions as to the sufficiency of a currency and banking system than the bankers." Progressive reformers did not fail to recognize that bankers constituted a special interest group, but as the political commentator Walter Lippmann stated: "Reform of the credit system does not consist in abolishing the financial expert. It consists in making him a public servant." President Wilson accordingly attempted to resolve the conflict between involving bankers in the Federal Reserve System as experts, and restraining them as representatives of a special interest, by creating a board to oversee the central bank that would be accountable to democratically elected officials.[9]

Government officials' repeated neglect—and sometimes outright dismissal—of non-bankers' views on banking policy reinforced the bankers' influence. The banking fraternity's unyielding self-assurance further inflated its influence. Bankers simply assumed it was their pre-rogative to guide the course of reform. "Is the opinion of 15,000,000 voters . . . to have more weight than 25,000 practical bankers?" *Commercial West* protested. "Has democracy gone mad in this country[?]" Such alarm proved premature. The cloak of expertise helped to main-tain the existing power structure. Influential political figures not only accorded bankers a privileged role in the reform process, they also in-hibited broader public involvement.[10]

Carter Glass

The election of 1912 had sealed the Aldrich plan's fate. Democrats now had an overwhelming advantage in the House, a solid majority in the Senate, and their first president since Grover Cleveland. Representa-tive Carter Glass had spent the preceding summer preparing a Demo-cratic Party alternative to the Aldrich plan. The son of a newspaper owner who had served as an officer in the Confederate army, Glass became a newspaper editor and owner himself. Elected to the Sen-ate of Virginia in 1899, he played a pivotal part at the state's 1901–1902 constitutional convention that disenfranchised black and poor white voters, thereby halving Virginia's electorate. Glass was a reactionary who rejected Bryanite banking and monetary views. He had retained J. Laurence Laughlin protégé H. Parker Willis for guidance on the in-tricacies of finance, and by October 1912 the two men had prepared a legislative draft.[11]

Glass intended to keep faith with the party platform's rejection of a central bank, but he supported asset currency and thought it was "imperative" to shield bankers from losing money on their 2 percent bonds during any transition from the existing government-bond-secured currency. The plan that Glass and Willis designed sought to establish a decentralized central banking institution composed of an undefined number of largely autonomous "local reserve banks." De-posit guaranty, pushed by Glass's fellow Democrats on the House Committee on Banking and Currency, also found a place in this ini-tial effort.[12]

Almost immediately following the 1912 election, Glass wrote to the president-elect requesting a meeting "concerning the matter of revising our currency system." When Glass and Willis met with Wilson for two hours on the day after Christmas, they discovered that the president-elect was amenable to their plan. Wilson had maintained his distance from the Democratic Party's Bryanite wing. His life had been spent in academic circles, enveloped by self-assured orthodox opinion on economic issues. But well before the Pujo subcommittee's investigation, Wilson had stated that "a money monopoly exists. It must be destroyed." He thought decentralizing the control of credit would provide opportunities for small businesses contending with large corporations. He hoped Glass's proposed system of regional "reserve banks" would decrease Wall Street's control over credit. At the meeting, the president-elect pressed his own idea as well: a supervisory board that would allow the national government to exercise greater influence over the central bank. Glass was doubtful about this idea. However, he relished the prominent political position that serving the incoming administration afforded and acquiesced.[13]

The hearings that the Glass subcommittee held were largely pro forma. The bill's essentials already had been determined. Still, since the ostensible purpose of holding congressional hearings was to solicit information, the subcommittee was obliged to invite a range of witnesses. But any spirit of intellectual open-mindedness was lacking. Glass had dismissively resolved that he was "not going . . . to be bothered by the scores of schemes presented by as many cranks on the subject."[14]

One witness who revealed himself to be remote from the views that Glass wanted to hear was William T. Creasy, master of the Pennsylvania State Grange. This hands-on advocate of modern farming techniques had formerly served as an effective Democratic state representative. As director of a small-town bank that Grangers had organized, Creasy possessed practical banking experience. He testified in favor of permitting national banks to accept farmland as security for loans. Glass, remarkably, expressed interest in this idea. Popular agitation had led the Democratic Party to endorse improving access to agricultural credit in its 1912 platform. And far-reaching agricultural credit reform proposals were under consideration in Congress. Representative Ellsworth R. Bathrick (D-OH) recently had introduced a bill to establish a government bureau for making farm mortgage loans. But Creasy also opposed a central bank, criticized the privilege of currency issue that national banks enjoyed, and objected to asset currency issued without government supervision. After the Grange leader was antagonistically quizzed about his knowledge of foreign monetary systems, the total amount of money circulating in the United States, and the definition of such terms as "asset currency" and "deposit," Glass disdainfully told Creasy: "You are not sufficiently well posted on banking details to cope with these gentlemen here."[15]

In contrast, Glass's attitude toward prominent bankers was solicitous. Glass inaugurated the hearings by asking a group of leading bankers: "Assuming that you think the Aldrich bill . . . is the best thing to be had, what is the next best thing to get?" The public's rejection of the Aldrich plan had convinced some influential bankers to accept that concessions would have to be made. Bankers consequently exhibited some willingness to accept the greater decentralization and government involvement in the measure Glass was drafting. But bankers were apprehensive about a rumor that guaranty might be included in the legislation. Glass assured the *Washington Post* that any bill in the House "would be framed along general lines in conformity with the well-known views of banking experts."[16]

Banking Politics in High Places

Robert L. Owen Jr. took charge of banking reform in the Senate, as chairman of the newly created Committee on Banking and Currency that he campaigned to establish. Prior to entering the Senate from Oklahoma, Owen gained prominence and wealth as an attorney and businessman in Indian Territory. Over the years, his inclination toward financial heterodoxy had led him to support free silver and postal savings. From the outset, Owen understood that the president approved of the legislation Glass and Willis had prepared. But the senator still pursued a reform he had long advocated: deposit guaranty. Although bankers had been relieved to hear Glass pronounce that this "bitterly controverted point . . . should not be permitted to endanger legislation," they were predictably perturbed when Owen declared his intention to establish a fund to aid depositors of insolvent banks. The senator had introduced further uncertainty to the legislative process.[17]

In May, Glass completed a legislative draft titled the "Federal Reserve Act." It possessed the essentials of the Aldrich plan, but proposed a more decentralized structure and a nine-member supervisory board. Six members of this body would be government appointees, and bankers would select the remaining three. The reserve banks would issue an asset currency backed by gold and commercial paper. The government would have no connection to this currency, which would be an obligation of the issuing reserve banks. Well before Secretary of State William Jennings Bryan was afforded an opportunity to read the Glass bill, what he heard about it caused him grave concern. In the first place, he did not approve of granting bankers representation on the institution's supervisory body. Owen concurred; the senator later wrote that he "insisted that the control of the system was a governing function to be exercised alone by the Government." Bryan also strongly opposed the proposed asset currency. He told Wilson "that the issue of money is a function of government and should not be surrendered to banks." Owen and Secretary of the Treasury William G. McAdoo raised objections to the bill's currency feature as well.[18]

Wilson had to decide how to address Bryan's opposition to the Glass bill. Bryan informed the president that he would resign from the administration if the objectionable features were not removed. The president was inclined to compromise with Bryan; from the very outset, he had feared Bryan's opposition. Bryan also made a convincing argument that the features he objected to contradicted Democratic Party platform planks. For guidance, the president turned to Progressive reformer Louis D. Brandeis, who had advised him on economic issues during the presidential campaign. "The function of the bankers," Brandeis recommended, "should be limited strictly to that of an advisory council." Brandeis also agreed with Bryan, McAdoo, and Owen that the national currency was properly the province of government. "The power to issue currency should be vested exclusively in Government officials, even when the currency is issued against commercial paper." To the displeasure of Glass, Brandeis's opinion settled these matters in Bryan's favor. The "Great Commoner" was relieved. Wilson's personal secretary recalled that it had been "evident" that Bryan was attempting "to find a way" that would "enable him to give the President his whole-hearted support."[19]

Thus modified, the Glass bill became an administration measure. The proposed Federal Reserve System would consist of no fewer than twelve Federal Reserve Banks controlled by independent nine-member boards. Bankers would elect six of these board members, and the supervisory Federal Reserve Board would select the remaining three. That seven-member board included the secretary of the treasury, secretary of agriculture, comptroller of the currency, and four additional presidential appointees. Federal Reserve Banks would discount commercial paper for member banks and issue "Federal Reserve Treasury notes"—secured by gold and commercial paper—declaring on the obverse their status as "obligations of the United States." National banks were permitted to make nine-month loans on farmland. The bill also allowed large national banks to establish foreign branches. This last feature was of particular importance to Frank A. Vanderlip Sr., who had international ambitions for National City Bank. "It seems to me," he concluded, "that considering the obstacles they have had in their way they have produced, on the whole, a very satisfactory measure."[20]

A Protean Summer

The bill was introduced in both the House and Senate on June 26, to both praise and criticism. Wilson's supervisory board helped win support from Progressive voices. "Presidential control of appointments to the Federal Reserve Board insures direct Government supervision over the operations of the National Banking System . . . and makes that supervision responsible to the popular will," *Outlook* magazine affirmed. Bankers naturally opposed this feature. New York banker Benjamin Strong Jr. protested that the "bill reflects a profound distrust of . . . the officers and directors of the National banks." Banker control was the paramount issue for bankers. "All other points of controversy . . . will yield to suggested modification and adjustment," *Trust Companies* stated. "But the insuperable barriers to successful currency reform . . . are the provisions which render the Federal Reserve Board susceptible to political influence."[21]

The president exhorted Congress to act swiftly. Contrary to his wishes, the bill's critics sought a more deliberative approach. Glass had difficulties with his committee right from the outset. Representative Charles A. Lindbergh Sr. presented a motion to open committee hearings to the public. He also promoted an amendment that established a governmental system for providing low-interest farm mortgage loans. Glass successfully evaded public hearings and further unwanted proposals from the opposition party by having the Democratic members undertake initial deliberations behind closed doors.[22]

Glass subsequently faced problems with members of his own party. Representative Otis T. Wingo (D-AR) presented an amendment banning interlocking directorates among member banks. And Representative J. Willard Ragsdale (D-SC) introduced an amendment he had prepared with Robert Lee Henry that altered the essentials of the Glass bill. It proposed that a "bona-fide representative of agriculture" and a "bona-fide representative of industrial labor" serve on the Federal Reserve Board. The amendment further sought to make credit more available in rural areas by authorizing Federal Reserve Banks to discount agricultural paper of longer maturities. Henry and Ragsdale also proposed issuing $700 million worth of three distinct classes of paper money. "Commercial currency" would be distributed through the Federal Reserve System to the tune of $300 million. Another $200 million of "agricultural currency" designed to support farm prices would be issued to farmers bearing warehouse receipts recording the value of stored commodities. A farmer who could borrow money on his crops, Henry explained, "will sell when he wants to sell, and will not be forced by poverty to give up his products at a sacrifice." The remaining $200 million of "industrial currency" would be available to states for employment-generating infrastructure projects.[23]

There were reports that a majority of the Democrats in the House supported the Henry-Ragsdale amendment. The Knights of Labor called this plan "the first strong move for even a small break from the grasp of the National bank combine." Democratic members of the Texas Farmers Union urged adoption of the amendment. "We cannot believe our party will commit such a wrong against the common people," the farmers protested. "If the party votes down the Henry amendments now and passes the Glass-Owen bill it will have spurned the prayer of sixty millions of people who toiled and filled the lap of luxury with additional millions." At this point, the president aggressively intervened in opposition to amending the bill. He brought pressure to bear on Henry, summoning him to the White House. Wilson charged Henry with challenging his leadership and informed the congressman that he was ready "to meet him and fight it out." Following this confrontation, both the Henry-Ragsdale and Wingo amendments were voted down. The Democratic committee members then approved the Glass bill and sent it to the party caucus. Glass later called the congressmen who had attempted to alter his bill "economic guerillas."[24]

The issues the insurgent congressmen had raised provided rallying points for practitioners of banking politics outside of Congress who sought to shape the legislation. The Hearst newspaper chain was soon supporting restrictions on interlocking directorates and calling for Federal Reserve Banks to assist farm lending. That summer, Grange leader Carey B. Kegley—a tireless reformer who had been active in the People's Party, Socialist Party, and most recently Theodore Roosevelt's Progressive Party—called for loaning postal savings funds to farmers, much as other champions of banking politics had been doing.[25]

While the ideas of banking politics advocates inspired the congressional insurgents, business interests supported the bankers' efforts.

George M. Reynolds had suggested that an "Advisory Board" of bankers should guide the Federal Reserve Board. The U.S. Chamber of Commerce in turn advocated a "definite . . . method of voicing . . . the judgment of the banking and business interests." The organization proposed a "Federal Reserve Council" that would advise the Federal Reserve Board and attend its meetings. The Glass bill accordingly was amended to add an advisory council composed of one banker from each Federal Reserve Bank. Bankers soon were pushing to expand the council's powers so that it would initiate policies, while the Federal Reserve Board would be reduced to a regulatory body with veto power over the council's proposals.[26]

Advancing the bill did not get any easier once it went to the Democratic caucus. During the deliberations, a contingent of congressmen jeopardized the legislation when they submitted a proposal to issue currency backed by warehouse receipts. Rural constituents inundated Congress in support of the idea. "Again and again during the discussion of the currency bill," the president observed, "it has been urged that special provision should be made . . . [for] the farmers of the country." Wilson committed to future agricultural credit legislation in an attempt to remove this issue from the central bank debate. "Special machinery and a distinct system of banking," he contended, "must be provided for if rural credits are to be successfully and adequately supplied." Congressional opponents of the Glass bill had demonstrated their political strength. "At this time," reported the *Washington Post*, "it may be frankly stated that a mere handful of courageous men are putting the proponents of the Glass bill to the utmost of their power and political prestige in order to prevail, with the issue in grave peril."[27]

Amid this volatile situation, the American Bankers Association's Currency Commission assembled in Chicago to address the pending legislation. Representatives of state bankers' associations and city clearinghouses were invited to participate in the conference as well. Karl F. M. Sandberg observed an "absence of the usual self-confidence and self-assurance on the part of the bankers." Many of the bankers present were frustrated that the bill did not more closely approximate their ideal measure. James B. Forgan had gone so far as to prepare a resolution urging Congress, the U.S. Chamber of Commerce, and the American Bankers Association to name three members each to a committee that would draft entirely new legislation.[28]

One major point of bankers' disapproval was the dissipating of the proposed institution's pool of reserves among multiple units. "Why should not the law create one central bank?" asked A. Barton Hepburn. Yet the bankers' wish for a unitary central bank—like their desire to avoid government supervision—had died with the Aldrich plan. Indeed, the Democratic Party had specifically ruled out this idea in its platform. "[Hepburn] might as well insist upon a revival of the old United States Bank," scoffed the *New York World*, "and bringing Nicholas Biddle back from the dead to manage it." Bankers found the political situation in Washington foreboding. They were well aware that Glass and the administration had been fending off heterodox reforms all summer long. Reynolds noted that the bill's congressional opponents included "men who are so extremely radical they would put us out of business if they could." The bankers elected to adopt a conciliatory tone, acknowledging: "The pending measure has many excellent features."[29]

Meanwhile, the Democratic caucus continued to debate the Glass bill. The insurgents refused to capitulate to the administration. Representative George A. Neeley (D-KS) presented an amendment prohibiting interlocking directorates like the one Wingo had introduced in committee. Glass responded by collaborating with Majority Leader Oscar W. Underwood to have the issue of interlocking directorates assigned to the Committee on the Judiciary in the following session. Then Glass played his trump card: a letter from Secretary Bryan that declared his support of the administration's position. Bryan assured his supporters that "whatever mistakes may be made in details can be corrected easily and soon." A subsequent push to eliminate the proposed bankers' advisory council was unsuccessful. The insurgents plainly lacked the backing of a crucial figure, and the Democratic caucus approved the bill, thus binding party members to support its passage in the House.[30]

Shortly after receiving the caucus's blessing, the Glass bill was the topic of "considerable discussion" among delegates attending the National Farmers Union's annual convention who felt "that the farmer is discriminated against as the bill is now drawn." Former National Farmers' Alliance leader Henry L. Loucks also appraised the legislation disdainfully. "I see no provision as to regulating the rate of interest for the use of money." Still, the House insurgents' efforts did force the inclusion of reforms designed to address farmers' short-term financing needs. The caucus had approved a provision that increased the maximum time period for national banks to issue farm mortgage loans from nine months to one year. And an amendment the insurgents sponsored affirmed the eligibility of agricultural paper for discount at Federal Reserve Banks.[31]

The bill was reported to the House on September 9. Practitioners of banking politics continued to criticize it. A mass meeting of Newport, Oklahoma, residents demanded that Congress "pass this bill with the amendments as offered by Mr. Henry." Representative Lindbergh believed the bill shielded the existing banking system rather than reforming it. "It is perpetuating a system the very purpose of which is to enable the money loaners, rent collectors, dividend beneficiaries, and speculators generally to take advantage of the actual producers so as to control production and fix prices." As a solution, he proposed establishing a "fiscal department" in the U.S. Treasury that would issue currency and provide low-interest loans to state governments, farmers, workers, and "legitimate industry, work, and enterprise of whatsoever character . . . promote the general welfare." But with a large Democratic majority bound to support the Glass bill by their caucus, there was little question about its fate. The House passed the measure on September 18.[32]

"Stand Back of the Bill"

In October, the American Bankers Association held its annual convention. Many bankers had not fully reconciled themselves to government supervision of the proposed central bank, and the convention gave them an opportunity to vent their displeasure. Conciliatory voices were lonely ones. When Arkansas banker Thomas C. McRae, a former Democratic congressman, spoke up in defense of the administration, other delegates repeatedly interrupted him. Despite the rancor at their convention, bankers increasingly conceded that government would play a central role in the Federal Reserve System. Robert H. Treman, president of the New York State Bankers Association, had informed Glass that he was "in sympathy with the Bill in general." An intransigent attitude toward government supervision had become politically untenable. *World's Work* now dismissed bankers who opposed the Glass bill as "habitual irreconcilables." Russell Lowry, vice president of San Francisco's American National Bank, spoke for many bankers when he demurred that the measure had "objectionable features," but nevertheless urged "the bankers of the country . . . to try to stand back of the bill." The National Citizens' League found the Glass bill sufficiently satisfactory to close up shop.[33]

Although opposition to the administration's legislation among bankers was subsiding, the measure was encountering serious resistance in the Senate Committee on Banking and Currency, where three defiant Democrats had forged an alliance with the body's five Republicans. "The Senate committee is unnecessarily delaying action on the bill," protested the president, who was growing livid. "The Democrat," he declared, "who will not support me is not a Democrat." The Senate hearings reopened issues the bill's framers considered resolved, and even presented a forum for the financial ideas of Jacob S. Coxey Sr. An apparently still-incensed Glass later objected that among those who testified before the Senate were "three of the most pestilential currency 'freaks' in the United States." While Coxey would have been unwelcome at any hearing Glass convened, Senator Knute Nelson assured the veteran campaigner, "You are the class of man that we want to hear from, rather than the bankers." An alarmed Vanderlip reported that Coxey "was gravely, respectfully listened to" by the committee members.[34]

Coxey pointed out that the national government operated the postal system as a democratic, nonprofit public service. "They engrave and print the postage stamps and furnish them at cost to the people," he observed. "John D. Rockefeller . . . if he needs 10,000 postage stamps . . . has no advantage over the man [laborer] who is tearing that brick building down over across the street when he needs only 1 postage stamp." Coxey wanted the "means of exchange" provided "at cost to the people" in the same manner. He proposed establishing a network of government banks that would make loans to citizens at 2 percent. Coxey also made his perennial appeal to allow state and local governments to deposit non-interest-bearing bonds with the federal government and receive funding for public works projects in return. "Your scheme is very interesting," stated Nelson, "and I wish you would prepare a skeleton bill and file it with the committee." Clearly, the Senate committee was open to banking reforms that were far afield from the Glass bill.[35]

By early November, the threat of administration retaliation had brought two of the three rebellious Democrats in line, leaving the committee evenly divided. The Democrats who supported the bill protested the resulting deadlock by boycotting committee proceedings. With the end of the congressional session fast approaching, the White House remained determined to enact legislation. In late November, Democrats took the drastic step of announcing their intention to keep the Senate in session every day for eight hours, take two hours for dinner, and then continue until eleven o'clock at night. If no bill had been passed by Christmas, there would be no recess, and Congress would break only for Christmas Day itself. Heterodox ideas were evident in the legislation that finally emerged from the committee. The Senate's counterpart to the Glass bill, for example, increased the time period for national banks to loan on farmland to five years, rather than the one-year maximum the House had permitted. Another notable alteration was a provision to create a deposit guaranty fund. New York's Wall Street–friendly *Sun* looked upon this prospect with extreme disfavor, disparaging guaranty as "one of the nostrums of Bryan finance . . . an old quack remedy for bad banking."[36]

On December 19, the Senate passed its version of the Federal Reserve bill. Six senators attended the hastily convened conference

committee, while Glass was one of only two House conferees. This arrangement amplified Glass's influence within the conference. "There
are things in this bill," he claimed, "which would bring calamity to this
country." Glass succeeded in removing the guaranty provision, which
prompted one financial journal to observe that bankers were "entitled
to felicitate." On December 22, the House passed the revised bill. The
Senate passed it the following day. The president signed the Federal
Reserve Act into law using four gold pens early that evening. "He is a
great man and a great President," declared financier Thomas Fortune
Ryan.[37]

All national banks were required to join the new Federal Reserve
System. The supervisory Federal Reserve Board included five individuals the president appointed with approval of the Senate, plus two
ex officio members—the secretary of the treasury and comptroller of
the currency. The nation would be divided into twelve districts, each
with its own Federal Reserve Bank to discount for member banks
and set the regional discount rate. The Federal Reserve Banks were
chartered as private corporations. Member banks held their stock
and received dividends. Nine-member boards would govern the Federal Reserve Banks. Member banks would elect six of the directors,
and the remaining three would be Federal Reserve Board appointees.
Federal Reserve Notes would be government obligations secured by
gold and commercial paper (and convertible to gold). National banks
were permitted to make loans on farmland for terms of no longer than
five years. Banks capitalized at over $1 million could establish for-
eign branches. The Federal Reserve Banks were empowered to purchase and sell government securities, which paved the way for the
open market operations that became an increasingly important tool
of monetary policy following World War I as their effects came to be
better understood.[38]

Arthur Reynolds, president of the American Bankers Association, lauded the Federal Reserve Act and singled out Glass for special
praise. "While the bill may not have been all that we expected, or that
he desires, yet we feel that he has been a very great benefit in assisting
the bankers and co-operating with them in bringing about the pas-

sage of the very best bill that was possible." But in a crucial respect, the Federal Reserve Act constituted a decisive victory for advocates of banking politics. The pressure of popular opinion had forced bankers to concede the principle of public authority that they contested so violently. J. Pierpont Morgan had anticipated a new economic order. "The time is coming," he remarked, "when all business will have to be done with glass pockets." He had perceived the import of the changes being wrought.[39]

"Establishing Government Banks"

Farmers and ranchers had extracted a notable victory by compelling the Wilson administration to commit to future action on long-term agricultural credit. This decision led the U.S. Chamber of Commerce to grow apprehensive about "a currency based upon farm loans." Secretary Bryan suggested the national government should lend directly to farmers at 4 percent. But the president opposed any governmental role in agricultural credit beyond establishing the program's basic structure. The legislation that won his approval proposed that the federal government charter privately owned "farm-land banks" to lend money obtained from selling bonds secured by farm mortgages. However, farmers supported reforms that attacked such fundamental precepts of the existing banking system as privately controlled banks and maximizing profit on loans. "We want the use of the Postal Savings Bank at a reasonable rate," an Idaho Granger insisted. The National Grange's program for farm mortgage lending sought to remove bankers from the agricultural credit system altogether.[40]

In 1914 the Grange and other farmer organizations threw their support behind Representative Bathrick's latest bill, which proposed that the Department of Agriculture issue government bonds to raise funds for farm mortgage loans at no more than 4.5 percent. The American Federation of Labor endorsed the Bathrick bill as well. The president responded to this insistent advocacy by removing agricultural credit from the Democratic legislative program for that congressional session. The banking fraternity's foremost spokesman on the issue,

Myron T. Herrick, promptly commended Wilson for his "wise position."[41]

Farmer organizations remained determined to achieve government lending. "Inasmuch as the United States Congress and cabinet are very much under fear of the money trust," stated North Carolina Farmers Union official J. Zeb Green, "it is going to take vigorous and persistent efforts to secure any adequate rural credit legislation." Green hoped that agricultural credit reform would aid tenant farmers. He foresaw implementation of "twenty or forty year loans under [the] amortization plan" helping to reduce tenancy. "What we want is a method to make the tenant a home-owner," agreed National Farmers Union president Charles S. Barrett. To achieve this end, he hoped to inaugurate "direct loans by the government to tenant farmers."[42]

Farmers maintained their campaign throughout 1915. On the evening of January 15, a "goodly number" of farmers and farm women gathered at the local Grange hall in Peshastin, Washington. The assembled Grangers charged that bankers were "restricting credit," which was a form of "coercion" designed to bring "the producers of America into submission to their service as slaves." They resolved "to wrest this power from the hands of the present banking system, by establishing government banks to care for the needs of the people." Similar discussions were taking place in rural communities across the nation. In July, the American Society of Equity, the National Farmers Union, and the National Grange jointly approved a plan to have the federal government extend thirty-year mortgages to farmers at 4.5 percent. At its annual convention that September, the National Farmers Union went still further, resolving that "the national government shall operate the banks for the benefit of the people, as it now runs the postoffices, turning the profits into the peoples' treasury, instead of into the coffers of private interests."[43]

The relentless popular pressure for government lending forced opponents of the idea to make concessions. When Congress convened in December 1915, a legislative compromise proposed establishing twelve privately owned Federal Land Banks under the supervision of a presidentially appointed five-member Federal Farm Loan Board.

These institutions would sell bonds backed by farm mortgages to raise funds for long-term loans to farmers. The Federal Land Banks would buy these mortgages from local borrower associations that farmers in their districts had organized. Eventually these associations would own the Federal Land Banks, because every time a Federal Land Bank bought a mortgage, the borrower association in turn purchased a corresponding amount of the institution's stock. The national government would help capitalize Federal Land Banks should they fail to secure adequate resources from private investors. This measure included no special assistance for tenant farmers.[44]

As the 1916 general election drew nearer, the president grew worried about facing voters without having established the long-term agricultural credit program he had promised. Wilson was particularly eager to compete for the midwestern and western farm vote. In January 1916, he abruptly decided to support the compromise legislation. The administration's blessing allowed the measure to pass easily in Congress, and the president signed the Federal Farm Loan Act in July. Farmers would benefit from lower interest rates and longer loan terms (up to forty years) than private lenders had offered. One decade later, Federal Land Banks held over $1 billion of long-term loans.[45]

This reform demonstrated how far the banking debate had progressed since the Panic of 1907. Bankers recognized that the Federal Farm Loan System was a landmark development. James K. Lynch, president of the American Bankers Association, warned that it was "certain" the act "contains great possibilities for evil." The organization predicted that "if the rural credits system . . . is developed and proves workable, the next step will be . . . the providing of government banks for all purposes."[46]

Contemporary developments stoked bankers' fears. The American Society of Equity and Cattle Raisers Association of Texas both had formulated plans that used the Postal Savings System to extend loans. And the Knights of Labor contended that government should "carry on the banking business directly." The American Federation of Labor noted that "the Federal Government has already established a rural credit system for the benefit of the farmer," and concluded that the government should "relieve the working people in the industrial centers of the unsanitary homes that are now unfit for habitation." The labor federation began pursuing legislation to establish a governmental home loan system, either by lending postal savings deposits to municipalities for home construction or by loaning directly to prospective homeowners "at a low rate of interest, to build their own homes."[47]

Practitioners of banking politics regarded further financial reform as imperative. "The Postal Bank is what we want," affirmed a Norwegian-American farmer in Iowa. In addition to ongoing public demands for easier credit, lack of confidence in banks persisted. Back in 1908, an observer reported that the Bryan campaign's advocacy of guaranty "made a profound impression on Vermont." Distrust of the state's banks remained salient in 1916, when elected officials in Barre withdrew the city's funds from a bank that refused to secure this deposit with a bond. The city sacrificed higher interest payments in favor of distributing its funds across multiple banks to mitigate the potential consequences of a failure. Banking reforms that promised greater deposit security, more affordable credit, increased macroeconomic stability, and enhanced democratic control of financial institutions possessed widespread support among working people. These workers and farmers believed they were the producers performing the labor that allowed the nation to prosper, and tenaciously insisted on their right to play a role in determining how the economy should function. They understood their opposition to be an exploitative financial system that was ruled by a grasping, parasitic, domineering special interest who manipulated the economy and the political process to serve their own selfish ends.[48]

Following the Panic of 1907, working people and their political allies had advanced an aggressive financial reform agenda. But this drive for reform collided with World War I. Although wartime mobilization helped women win the right to vote and organized labor to attain new prominence, the noted settlement house movement leader Helena Dudley lamented that "the socialists [are] broken up, and the social workers lining up with the bankers." Public discussion of many reform issues—including financial ones—grew muted. Nevertheless, contemporaries had witnessed the establishment of two national financial institutions that were explicitly intended to serve working people—the Postal Savings System and the Federal Farm Loan System. And banking politics had helped inscribe the principle of public authority on the Federal Reserve System. Farmers and workers would again agitate for a financial reformation once peace was declared.[49]

5

From Armistice to Depression

"Our Fight Is with the Bankers"

"The 'Money Question' has been lost sight of during the war," one Washington State farmer noted following the armistice. But the depression of 1920-21 soon placed banking heterodoxy back at the forefront of political discussion. Farmers and ranchers held financial interests responsible for the severity of this economic crisis. George F. Richardson was a Michigan farmer and Greenbacker prior to his 1892 election to the House of Representatives on a fusionist Populist-Democratic ticket. In 1921, amid surging popular criticism of finance, Richardson indicted the private banking system for undermining working people's efforts to attain a modicum of economic security. He believed the "complete monopoly of money control" that banks possessed made it difficult for Americans to "have the hope of a home, with family love to soften the heart and make sacred the privilege of citizenship in the United States." Richardson proposed a "government Home Loan department" to "give liberal loans on long time at low rates of interest."[1]

The Great Depression imparted financial issues with a political urgency that echoed that of the 1890s, when Richardson had advocated free silver. Unemployment rose from 2.9 percent in 1929 to 15.7 percent by 1931. It reached 22.9 percent in 1932. "We was all out of work," recalled one Philadelphia carpet weaver. "No work anywhere!" It was a frightening predicament. "Then, there was no such thing as unemployment or welfare," he explained. "You were on your own." "Surely a big country such as this one could do better in this hour of need," protested an unemployed Swedish immigrant. "But there is no help, one must be able to take care of himself or die." Comedian Groucho Marx captured just how disastrous the situation had become when he remarked that "the pigeons [had] started feeding the people in Central Park."[2]

As the Depression took hold, farmers were thrust into an increasingly adverse financial environment: they confronted a severe deflationary spiral, a shrinking money supply, and a frozen credit market. Moreover, politically, they faced obdurate banker opposition to policies intended to relieve agriculture's plight. The cumulative actions of financial interests from the post–World War I agricultural crisis forward engendered deep anger among many farmers. National Farmers Union president John A. Simpson called "big bankers . . . the biggest criminals in the country." "They should be completely ostracized . . . by every decent man and woman in this country," he declared. Workers were no less incensed that bankers were campaigning for wage cuts during such hard times. The American Flint Glass Workers Union, for example, objected when bankers instructed one plant's management "that unless the glass workers' wages were reduced no more money would be advanced." And when bankers initiated a movement to levy fees on depositors, they further fueled the growing public sense of outrage. The Montana State Federation of Labor decried the additional financial strain these charges imposed. "The small depositor is discriminated against and burdened by the banking institutions of the country by means of monthly charges for small accounts and special charges for checks." Bankers had managed to directly antagonize farmers, workers, and depositors.[3]

The Crime of 1920

The end of World War I ushered in economic crisis for America's farmers. Between July and December 1920, the average price of the nation's ten leading agricultural crops decreased 57 percent. Farmers found themselves squeezed between falling commodity prices and rising credit prices. As agricultural prices dropped, farmers' need for credit rose, but it was harder to borrow because in late 1919 the Federal Reserve System began implementing deflationary policies. The impact of the agricultural crisis on rural Americans was severe. Secretary of Agriculture Henry C. Wallace reported: "Many thousands of farmers have not been able to weather the storm, notwithstanding their most strenuous efforts." Agriculture had entered a downturn that would last until World War II.[4]

Many Americans concluded that the recently established Federal Reserve System bore significant blame for agriculture's predicament. The "sentiment" of a National Farmers Union meeting "was that readjustment was naturally to be expected after the war . . . but that the deflation policy of those in financial authority . . . is responsible for the tremendous decrease in prices." Political leaders in both major parties endorsed this interpretation. "The Reserve Board deflated the farmer," William Jennings Bryan stated. "It is largely responsible for the sudden drop . . . in farm prices." Senator Asle J. Gronna (R-ND) concurred. "It was the autocrats controlling the Federal reserve system who were largely responsible for the sudden deflation of prices in agricultural products."[5]

Farmers believed the Federal Reserve System had demonstrated its subservience to powerful financial interests. A meeting of farmers in Marshall County, Kansas, protested that deflationary policies had sacrificed the well-being of working people so that others could profit: "We believe that this contraction of currency and bank credits is in the interest and at the instigation of the fund-holding investment classes and to the detriment and ruin of the producing class." Elected officials responded to the popular outcry with proposals for reforming the central bank, such as making the secretary of agriculture a Federal

Reserve Board member. By the time of Thomas E. Watson's (D-GA) surprise 1920 election to the Senate, he was notorious for unbridled appeals to anti-Semitism, anti-Catholicism, Anglophobia, and white supremacy. But he continued to sympathize with struggling white southern farmers, and in 1921 introduced a resolution to replace the entire Federal Reserve Board with members "who shall not be bankers." In 1922 Congress took a more moderate step and added one member who represented agricultural interests.[6]

Other reform proposals focused on direct monetary fixes to falling commodity prices. Yale University Professor of Political Economy Irving Fisher's "compensated dollar" plan found a congressional following. Fisher believed the value of money could be stabilized by actively managing the gold content of the dollar. His plan failed to gain support from bankers, businessmen, or fellow economists. But the idea inspired Representative T. Alan Goldsborough (D-MD) to introduce legislation in 1922 that sought to maintain a stable price level by periodically adjusting the value of the dollar. "I never want to see agriculture and industrial enterprise struggling in the agony of a long period of falling prices," he explained. Goldsborough was an attorney from the eastern shore of Maryland who traced his interest in financial questions back to childhood. The experience of accompanying his country doctor grandfather on house calls to farms left the future congressman wondering why these hardworking people were continually in debt. When Goldsborough was eighteen years old, the vigorous 1896 debate over bimetallism inspired him to begin researching financial issues. Similar legislation to Goldsborough's would be introduced in following congressional sessions.[7]

The postwar depression fueled criticism of the private banking system. In December 1921, Senator Edwin F. Ladd (R-ND) convened a "national conference on credits and finance." Ladd recently had introduced legislation to establish a government bureau to provide farmers and homeowners with low-interest loans. He believed the existing banking system was "controlled by a small group of men for the benefit of the few and to the injury of the great masses of our people." A familiar face from the monetary debate of the 1890s made a timely appearance at this conference: William H. Harvey. A native West Virginian, "Coin" Harvey had been a schoolteacher and attorney before heading to Colorado, where he made successful mining and real estate investments. During the 1893 depression, he became a passionate spokesman for bimetallism. Harvey did much to popularize the free silver issue and win supporters to the silverite cause. Most notably, he was the author of the widely disseminated *Coin's Financial School*, which sold a remarkable 400,000 copies in its first year of publication. Harvey proposed amending Ladd's bill so the federal government would control banking.[8]

The ensuing legislative response to the agricultural crisis was significantly more restricted. A congressional commission investigating economic distress in the countryside recommended increasing the availability of agricultural credit for terms between six months and three years, because the Federal Reserve System did not discount agricultural paper with maturities greater than six months. Dueling proposals to address this deficiency emerged in Congress. One bill provided for the federal charter of privately funded loan corporations. The other bill proposed establishing twelve regional banks that would discount agricultural paper held by other financial institutions and would lend directly to agricultural cooperatives on the security of warehouse receipts. The U.S. Treasury would provide $5 million to capitalize each bank.[9]

Secretary of the Treasury Andrew W. Mellon protested that the latter measure "gets the Government further into the banking business." Corporate lawyer Russell C. Leffingwell seconded this objection. "I belong to a group that dreads unspeakably the thought of Government banks," he testified. Leffingwell shortly would be named a partner of J. P. Morgan & Company. However, the American Farm Bureau Federation, National Grange, and National Farmers Union all supported a new system of government banks. President Warren G. Harding, hoping that expanding credit opportunities for farmers would reduce rural hardship, strongly supported legislative action. Because neither side was willing to yield, the two bills were combined into one piece of legislation. In May 1923, Harding signed the Agricultural Credits Act into law. The twelve new government-owned and -operated Federal Intermediate Credit Banks would extend over $900 million of credit by the end of the decade. The private loan corporations proved ineffective: a mere three were ever organized, and only one of these was active for more than a couple of years before it, too, was liquidated in the mid-1930s.[10]

Labor Banks

Workers joined farmers in charging that financial interests manipulated the economy to serve their own selfish ends following the war. The unemployment rate is conservatively estimated to have almost tripled from 1919 to 1921. Those industrial workers who still had jobs saw their wages cut by 10 to 25 percent. American Federation of Labor (AFL) president Samuel Gompers alleged that leading financers were to blame for the suffering of "5,000,000 unemployed in the United States, men and women who are willing and anxious to work." Gompers attested that these unfortunate workers were the victims of "the contraction program, the object being to make people hungry." He claimed this "artificial period" had been "inaugurated by the profiteers who found in the Federal Reserve Board a willing instrument to aid their plans."[11]

This dissatisfaction with post–World War I financial policy led the AFL to avow that "labor will eventually wrest the power to control credit . . . from the control of private financiers." Gompers urged that "control of credit be . . . placed in the hands of a public trust." In 1921 organized labor in Illinois sought to achieve greater public control of credit, endorsing legislation that would establish a state bank there (as had happened recently in North Dakota). Union-owned banks became a particular focus of organized labor's push to reshape finance. Unions regularly denounced bankers for funding the open-shop drive that employers launched following the armistice. The AFL protested that "banking facilities are being used to destroy the trade union movement and to impoverish the workers through the savings deposited by the workers." Labor banks could ensure that labor's money would not be mobilized against its interests.[12]

Unions and union members controlled labor banks through ownership of their stock. Labor banks operated under the same charters as other banks and engaged in the full spectrum of banking activities. The Brotherhood of Locomotive Engineers was the union that waded into banking most aggressively. In 1920 the brotherhood opened its first bank in Cleveland. During its initial two years of operation, the bank's resources increased exponentially from $653,000 to $19.2 million. At the height of its activities, the union was connected to more than a dozen labor banks in major cities and small towns across the nation. Its success inspired other unions to establish banks. By 1928 a total of twenty-eight labor banks held resources of over $114 million.[13]

Labor banks introduced innovations that provided immediate benefits to workers. They offered extended hours of operation that better served people whose daily lives revolved around the workday. Labor banks also adopted the practice of declaring a dividend for depositors out of bank profits. Whereas many banks imposed a probationary period before new depositors began receiving interest payments, the Brotherhood of Locomotive Engineers' Cleveland bank paid interest on savings deposits from the initial day of deposit, which compelled other banks in the city to adopt this practice. The Amalgamated Clothing Workers Union's New York City bank was able to provide its depositors unsecured installment loans because it did not attempt to make a profit on this service.[14]

Labor banks implemented policies that advanced the cause of unionism as well. William H. Johnston, president of the International Association of Machinists, saw labor banks as a means for unions to establish a financial sector independent of the existing economic power structure. "I have believed for a long time that Labor should not permit its funds to be deposited in the hands of the enemy. . . . What do we find when you go on strike? You find . . . that the very funds you have accumulated . . . and deposited in the banks, are borrowed to fight you with." In Tucson, local unions established a labor bank in response to a campaign that local bankers conducted to make the "Old Pueblo" an open-shop town. An open-shop drive similarly led the Central Labor Union of Philadelphia to enter the labor banking movement. In Spokane, the cashier of the Brotherhood of Locomotive Engineers' bank declined to renew an employer's loan after he insisted on an open shop. Johnston believed that labor banks ultimately held the potential to change how the economy operated. "We are fighting for industrial democracy and we believe that the labor banks besides being of great aid to the workers will some day give them a share in the control of industry."[15]

The banking fraternity, predictably, did not embrace labor banks. The Cleveland Clearing House Association declined to extend membership to the Brotherhood of Locomotive Engineers' bank, which prompted its president to charge that "your primary reason rests on your determination to perpetuate a banking monopoly." He accused clearinghouse members of establishing "a mutual agreement . . . to regulate the rate of interest to be paid to depositors, and to fix the fees and interest charges to be levied on borrowers." In 1930 a run weakened the Brotherhood of Railway Clerks National Bank in Cincinnati. Queen City bankers "flatly told" the labor bank to "go to labor unions for help and not ask the bankers." Consequently, despite being declared solvent by federal bank examiners, the institution was forced to close.[16]

Insurgent Politics

Banking politics invigorated the insurgent political spirit that animated a large swath of the nation in the 1920s. An agrarian protest movement had won control of North Dakota's state government during World War I. The Nonpartisan League was elected on a platform that included "rural credit at cost." Once in power, the organization established the state-owned and -operated Bank of North Dakota. The Nonpartisan League inspired political unrest in a number of midwestern and western states where organizations of farmers and workers made common cause, including on public banking. The Farmer-Labor

Reconstruction League of Oklahoma won the governorship with a program that featured a state bank. The emerging Progressive Party of Idaho sought government control of money and credit. And the political insurgency testing Republican Party hegemony in South Dakota urged the establishment of a state bank. In 1923 Farmer-Labor organizations in Montana, North Dakota, South Dakota, and Washington State endorsed government control of money and credit "for service instead of profit." Reorienting the motivation of finance also inspired Arizona state senator Fred T. Colter's (D) proposal to establish a state bank. Such an institution's "existence," he explained, "calls attention to the Divine law and moral precept that it is a SIN to either pay or receive interest on money."[17]

In early 1924, a national convention of farmer organization leaders, union presidents, leading socialists, and other prominent reformers pledged to back politicians who supported reform of the Federal Reserve System that would "provide for direct public control of the nation's money and credit." Members of the Farm-Labor Union—primarily Arkansans, Oklahomans, and Texans—resolved in favor of public ownership of the Federal Reserve System. Grangers in Ada County, Idaho, previously had come to a similar conclusion. "We have no confidence in the banking system of the country," these farmers declared. "It is preposterous to have a law . . . that enables a small group to absolutely and privately own and control our finance and credit to their own personal interest, use and benefit. . . . [W]e again ask Congress," they urged, "to at once repeal the iniquitous Federal Reserve System, returning to Congress its constitutional power to coin money and regulate the value thereof."[18]

While the Federal Reserve System provided a new focus for banking reformers, they continued to advocate expanding the Postal Savings System. Following the armistice, the postmaster general recommended "a slight increase in the rate of interest paid to depositors." In 1921 Representative Halvor Steenerson (R-MN) introduced legislation to raise the postal savings interest rate to 3 percent. Both the National Grange and the American Federation of Labor endorsed this idea, which was modest in comparison to Representative M. Clyde

Kelly's (R-PA) legislation. He wanted the Postal Savings System to pay 4 percent interest and lend its funds at low rates to prospective home-owners.[19]

Bryan and Senator Robert M. La Follette Sr., who had carried the banking politics standard for years, now both embraced the postwar push for financial reform. Bryan claimed the Federal Reserve System he helped create was "instituted to benefit the people [but] had been captured by Wall Street." La Follette perceived a variation of the events he had excoriated following the Panic of 1907. "The masters of American finance and business devoted the year 1920 to 'deflating' the farmers, using as their agency the Federal reserve system." La Follette stated that once this objective had been accomplished, the American worker became the target. "The year 1921 has been devoted by these same masters of business and credit to the . . . task of 'deflating' labor and destroying their unions, which alone stand between them and serfdom." La Follette's 1924 Progressive Party presidential platform anticipated "reconstruction of the Federal Reserve and Federal Farm Loan Systems, so as to eliminate control by usurers, speculators and international financiers, and to make the credit of the nation available upon fair terms to all."[20]

Branch Banking

One of the more prominent financial policy debates during the 1920s addressed branch banking. Between 1920 and 1929, the total number of bank branches in the United States rose from 1,281 to 3,349. Unit bankers resisted this trend. In Missouri, for example, they formed an organization specifically devoted to opposing this "pernicious practice." Branching also worried anti-monopolists. "Fighting Bob's" son Philip F. La Follette assailed "chain banking" for constituting "a part of the monopoly system which is a declaration of war against every independent man and woman in America." Small businessmen fearing diminished credit opportunities, and uneasy about the rapid expansion of chain stores, objected to branching as well. In 1924 alarmed

Illinois residents voted to prohibit branching in the state. By that point, seventeen states had statutes authorizing branching by state-chartered banks, and five accepted branching by administrative practice. Branching critics claimed that large banks operating multiple offices drained wealth from local communities. In 1925 the National Grange affirmed that it was "absolutely opposed to branch banks" outside of large cities.[21]

The Banking Act of 1927 was a significant milestone in this debate. It granted branching greater latitude while seeking to restrain the practice. Representative Louis T. McFadden (R-PA), the president of a small-town national bank, introduced the measure in an attempt to stem a tide of national banks that were abandoning their federal charters in favor of state ones. The act allowed state banks that joined the Federal Reserve System to retain the branches they already had opened. But it also included branching restrictions: member banks could not establish branches outside of the municipality where their main office was located. While national banks could now open branches in their home office city in states that granted state banks branching privileges, they were prohibited from opening branches in towns with less than 25,000 people, and limitations were placed on the number of branches they could operate in more populous cities. In addition to branching, the act addressed the growing number of commercial banks that had entered investment banking during the 1920s by explicitly empowering national banks to buy and sell securities.[22]

Many branching opponents had deemed McFadden's bill insufficiently restrictive. Representative Morton Denison Hull (R-IL) drafted an amendment that sought to prevent branching from spreading into the twenty-six states that did not permit the practice. His position initially met with great support in Congress. Representative Otis T. Wingo reported that the House leadership was convinced the legislation would not pass without this amendment. But branching proponent Senator Carter Glass's opposition altered this calculus. He considered the amendment "an atrocious proposition," and an Ohio banker concluded after meeting with Glass that the only hope "to secure legislation which will place national banks . . . on a parity with state banks" was to "urge a reconsideration of the McFadden bill, with the view of eliminating the Hull amendments."[23]

Many bankers grew apprehensive that controversy over Hull's amendment was impeding legislative action. A Baltimore banker worried that absent "legislation that will allow the National Banks to properly compete with the State Institutions, the National System is doomed." The 1926 annual meeting of the American Bankers Association's National Bank Division resolved in favor of enacting the bill without Hull's amendment. This controversial provision subsequently was removed from the legislation, which facilitated its enactment. Just days after the measure was made law, the nation's most aggressive branch banking system—A. P. Giannini's Bank of Italy (later renamed the Bank of America)—became a national bank.[24]

Mellon vs. Patman

Popular demands for financial reform gained extraordinary intensity when the Roaring Twenties came to a screeching halt following the Great Crash of 1929. The scorn heaped upon Secretary of the Treasury Andrew W. Mellon reveals the extent to which the Great Depression cast orthodox economic opinion and leading financial figures into disrepute. One of the nation's richest men and most prominent bankers, Mellon presided over the Department of the Treasury for more than a decade beginning in 1921. He advocated cutting public spending and lowering taxes on corporate profits, inherited wealth, and personal incomes. His efforts resulted in substantial income tax reductions for wealthy individuals, decreased inheritance tax payments, and generous tax refunds for corporations. "Plutocracy has never been so brazenly championed by any other public man," Bryan protested.[25]

Mellon had led the unsuccessful effort to block enactment of legislation in 1924 awarding World War I veterans a bonus to be paid in 1945. In 1930 he maintained that early payment of this benefit to aid veterans struggling through the Depression would have "seriously detrimental" effects. Mellon thought the proper response to the

Great Depression was to "liquidate labor, liquidate stocks, liquidate the farmers, liquidate real estate . . . purge the rottenness out of the system." His belief that depressions constituted therapeutic processes of liquidation reflected a common perspective among bankers. In 1931 Mellon thwarted a plan that would have prevented a major bank failure (of one of his competitors) in his hometown of Pittsburgh. This suspension precipitated at least fifteen additional bank closures in western Pennsylvania.[26]

By the early 1930s, Mellon served as a focal point for popular disaffection and was subject to extensive public condemnation. A resident of Hutchinson, Kansas, referred to "old, moneyhog, hypocrite, brute, liar, soldier-hating Mellon." One Ohioan revealed that "there are even women in Wooster who would like to see Mellon and his kind blown to hell where they belong and they said it in just such words." Anger at Mellon was notably apparent in Pittsburgh. A young mother with a family of five and an unemployed husband stated: "Next to Satan I don't believe any one is more despised than our honorable Sec. Mr. A. W. Mellon." "He is the most hated man in Pittsburgh," affirmed one man, who reported that when Mellon's face appeared on the screen of a local movie theater, "the boys in the gallery, yelled ROBBER, ROBBER." "Most of us in his home town would be pleased to see him behind the bars where he belongs," one woman stated. She observed that "Pittsburgh vibrates Hatred of him to such an extent that visitors actually feel it."[27]

This widespread grievance found a political outlet in January 1932, when Representative Wright Patman (D-TX) presented articles of impeachment against Mellon for engaging in numerous business ventures while serving as secretary of the treasury. Patman was an anti-monopolist who believed: "We need an anti–Wall Street campaign in this nation that will disclose the corruption of those who have ruined the people of the county in order to promote their private greed." Born in a log cabin to east Texas tenant farmers with very little formal schooling, Patman passionately pursued education. His voracious reading included the *Congressional Record* and a magazine that Thomas E. Watson edited. Following high school graduation as valedictorian and service in the U.S. Army during World War I, Patman was elected to the state legislature in 1920. In 1929 he entered Congress and quickly made a name for himself by urging that fiscal policy be used to fight the Depression. He specifically championed immediate cash payment of the bonus owed World War I veterans. Patman argued that paying the bonus would combat the Depression by increasing the amount of money circulating in the economy. The money supply collapsed between 1929 and 1933, falling 33 percent. "As you reduce the per capita circulation of money," Patman testified, "you necessarily reduce purchasing power, and as you reduce purchasing power, the wheels of industry commence to slow up, and as they slow up, business is hurt and a depression comes on."[28]

Not all Americans rallied in support of Patman's challenge to the nation's financial establishment. One New York banker chastised Patman: "You are to be most heartily condemned for even suggesting the removal of the greatest Secretary of the Treasury, whoever held the office." But Patman's bold protest elicited a flood of praise. "Mellon has been a disgrace to the office and the U.S.A. long enough," stated the wife of the Episcopal bishop of Nevada. "You are brave to start this move to Impeach and as for me and my household we are with you." A few weeks later, the secretary of the treasury resigned his post and accepted the position of ambassador to the Court of St. James's in London. The American Legion post in Mineola, Texas, wryly commented that "England is too close get him sent to China."[29]

Farmers

Conditions in rural America during the early 1930s were dire. Between 1929 and 1932, the net income of farmers fell 70 percent. At one grain elevator in South Dakota, corn was actually listed at −3¢ per bushel. Farm foreclosures rose 162 percent from 1928 to 1932, while tax sales increased 136 percent. The inability of farmers to access credit compounded their plight. Bankers had grown apprehensive about maintaining liquidity and were reluctant to extend loans. "I am in need of help and I need it badly," confessed one desperate Farmers Union member in Colstrip, Montana. "If I could get a loan for enough to carry me through I would gladly mortgage my farm." One Virginia farmer's experience illustrates the kind of predicament many farmers faced. He made numerous fruitless trips to a bank in the hope of obtaining a loan that would allow him to pay off the $60 debt he owed a fertilizer dealer. Finally, the farmer secured a loan. However, the banker had decided the farmer's collateral only justified a $25 loan. So the farmer sold his hogs to obtain the additional $35, which jeopardized his ability to repay the bank loan and continue farming.[30]

The disinclination of bankers to make credit available provoked protests from prospective borrowers. One Texan objected that although banks commanded large cash reserves, they still refused to "lend a dollar to anybody." President Herbert C. Hoover stressed a different side of this issue when he launched an ineffective campaign against hoarding. Hoover chastised depositors for removing their savings from banks in response to numerous bank failures. Anti-hoarding efforts principally targeted small depositors, although much of this cached currency consisted of partial withdrawals by affluent people establishing emergency reserves. Hoover claimed the public was acting on "unnecessary fears and apprehension." "This building up of a large amount of hoarded currency by people . . . makes for serious deflation," Hoover intoned. Many Americans rejected the premise of this appeal. "If you want to know who's hoarding money," quipped an Arizona farm periodical, "try to borrow some from a banker."[31]

Rapid deflation confronted farmers with falling prices for their product, on the one hand, and inflexible debt payments that had been contracted before the downturn, on the other. With deflation forcing debtors to pay their creditors more than the amount they had borrowed, inflation—or what its proponents instructively referred to as "reflation"—found its way to the top of the farm agenda. As Edward B. Dorsett, master of the Pennsylvania State Grange, explained at the close of 1931: "A dollar today will buy 45 per cent more goods than it would in 1926. In other words, a dollar today, in terms of goods, is worth $1.45. If Congress should pass a law requiring every debtor to pay $1.45 for each dollar he borrowed, we would have a revolution in this country. Yet that is exactly what has been done by two years of deflation." This state of affairs gave rise to various inflationary plans. Farmers took great interest in printing greenbacks, government purchase and monetization of silver, and reduction of the gold content of the dollar. The Michigan State Grange resolved in favor of issuing greenbacks to expand the monetary base, while meetings of Iowa farmers discussed printing greenbacks and remonetizing silver. The Oregon State Grange also supported issuing greenbacks, "instead of having that credit dispensed to us in a circuitous round that makes us dependent upon big business financial banking institutions." And the National Farmers Union wanted Congress to control the money supply and the national government to issue greenbacks to fund public works projects.[32]

The 1930s heard echoes of the Battle of the Standards. Silver advocacy maintained a political presence during the previous decade, but the Great Depression introduced a renewed sense of urgency to this cause. Although the "Great Commoner" had passed on, his son stepped forward to champion bimetallism. "In 1896 the statement frequently was made that the silver question was dead," William Jennings Bryan Jr. observed. "Today we are painfully aware that the silver question was not dead, but sleeping." One contemporary reported that in Rocky Mountain states, "The word 'silver' fairly gleams from the daily press; you hear bimetallism in the street cars." The silver issue was attracting attention beyond its traditional base as well. When Senator William E. Borah raised the question of silver in Iowa, he was "amazed at the interest manifested in that part of the country."[33]

The white metal received influential political support from the western senators who collectively constituted the silver bloc. One of this group's members was Burton K. Wheeler (D-MT), whose interest in politics dated back to 1896, when he sided with the silverites. He had made his mark on Montana politics by challenging the all-powerful Anaconda Copper Mining Company (successor to Amalgamated Copper). In 1922 an alliance of the state's workers and farmers elected him to the Senate. Wheeler attained national prominence when he initiated an investigation that led to the attorney general's resignation, and then served as La Follette's running mate on the 1924 Progressive Party ticket. In 1932 Wheeler introduced a bill to reestablish bimetallism that appealed to both silverites and farmers. He claimed that remonetizing silver at the time-honored ratio of sixteen ounces to one ounce of gold "will enable the debtor to liquidate in honest dollars the value of those borrowed instead of in dollars of greater value."[34]

Silver advocacy in Washington, DC, extended beyond western legislators: in 1932 Representative Andrew L. Somers (D-NY), chairman of the Committee on Coinage, Weights, and Measures, promoted remonetization of silver, while Representative D. D. Glover (D-AR) introduced legislation to issue $1 billion of silver certificates and $1 billion of silver coin. Elements of all the major farmer organizations promoted silver. John A. Simpson, president of the National Farmers Union, was a vociferous critic of finance. He had taught school and practiced law before settling on farming. A supporter of the Populist movement in the 1890s, following World War I he emerged as a tireless organizer and dynamic leader of the Oklahoma Farmers Union. In 1932 he called for enactment of the Wheeler bill. The state Granges of Colorado, Oregon, and Washington all favored remonetization of silver. And the Utah State Farm Bureau wanted "a recognition of silver in our financial structure."[35]

Criticism of the gold dollar was concomitant with the appeal that silver held for farmers. A politically diverse group of agricultural representatives articulated varying challenges to the gold standard. *Wallaces' Farmer* insisted: "It is time to begin expanding credit in the United States even tho [*sic*] it involves temporarily going off the gold standard." "The gold standard," Simpson decisively concluded, "has proved inadequate not only for this nation, but for the whole world as well." Cornell University Professor of Agricultural Economics George F. Warren Jr. stated that "ultimately we have got to come to an all-commodity dollar of some form, rather than a one-commodity [gold] dollar." Warren believed that "the thing to correct is not the organization of society but the tool [money] that is not working properly." He warned that in the absence of monetary reform, "there is

danger of forcing some kind of a socialistic state." Warren had compiled statistics showing that if rising economic production was not
matched with a corresponding increase in the supply of gold, the
price level fell. Conversely, if the gold supply expanded more rapidly
than production, prices rose. Warren proposed to raise commodity
prices, therefore, by increasing the gold supply through reducing the
amount of gold in the dollar. His critique found an eager audience. In
1932 over 14,000 people attended the fifty-four speeches he delivered,
and thousands more listened to his two national radio addresses. "I
am in perfect accord with Doctor Warren," testified the president of
the New York State Farm Bureau Federation. Governor of New York
Franklin D. Roosevelt numbered among those who took note of Warren's ideas.[36]

Farmers' discontent with the financial status quo found legislative
expression in 1932. That January, the leaders of the American Farm
Bureau Federation, National Farmers Union, and National Grange
jointly adopted a "unified program" that urged "immediate action"
to expand credit and "stabilize the purchasing power of money." This
program sought the eventual "readjustment of the entire banking and
fiscal policies and structures of the United States." As an immediate
mechanism for achieving financial reform, farmer representatives
settled on legislation that Representative Goldsborough introduced.
The Goldsborough bill sought to inflate the purchasing power of the
dollar and then stabilize it at the average level of commodity prices
during the period from 1921 through 1929. The Federal Reserve System would then expand and contract credit as needed to maintain
price stability. The American Federation of Labor supported this
effort. A legislative representative of the organization testified to Congress that "we are in favor of the principles involved here."[37]

Bankers strongly opposed the Goldsborough bill as impractical
and inflationary. When the House overwhelmingly passed the measure anyway, *Trust Companies* called it "proof of the degree of asininity
to which the present House of Representatives can attain." *Wallaces'
Farmer* contrastingly celebrated a victory in which "big bankers were
against our bill, but organized labor and agriculture were too much

for them." However, the journal noted that there was a "stumbling-block" in the Senate: Carter Glass, the bankers' powerful ally who had proclaimed his "utmost aversion" to the bill. The three major farmer organizations wrote the Senate Banking and Currency Committee to "urge an early favorable report on this measure." But Glass proceeded to devise a substitute that blocked the legislation. In this manner, the financial reform that agricultural interests had rallied around met its end.[38]

Bankers' opposition to the Goldsborough bill encouraged the idea that they were orchestrating the farmer's plight. The president of the American Farm Bureau Federation, Edward A. O'Neal, testified that "five great banking institutions completely control the flow of currency." "Our big bankers of America have been extremely selfish," he stated. "They want to control the flow of money in the channels of trade. They are surely doing it now with disaster to American agriculture." Simpson concluded: "There can never be a permanent and secure prosperity until we have destroyed the money power of the country." While bankers and farmers had long held conflicting perspectives on financial issues, the gulf between the two groups rarely had been so glaring.[39]

Workers

The animosity between bankers and organized labor during the 1920s is indicated by the outright refusal of certain Los Angeles and San Francisco banks to accept communications with a union label printed on them. Relations between these two groups only worsened in the early 1930s. Unions forcefully condemned bankers for seeking wage reductions. "The theory that a high rate of wages is necessary in order to stimulate rapid consumption . . . calls for critical debunking," the *American Bankers Association Journal* urged in the fall of 1930. The president of the organization's National Bank Division added, "Our standard of living is too high." A few months later, one of the nation's most prominent bankers sanctioned these assertions. Albert H. Wiggin, president of Chase National Bank, stated: "It is not true that high wages make prosperity." He recommended that labor "accept a moderate reduction in wages." American Federation of Labor president William Green swiftly condemned Wiggin.[40]

The banking fraternity, however, continued to call for lower wages. Rome C. Stephenson, president of the American Bankers Association, declared: "If any banker as an individual student of conditions reaches a conclusion that wage cuts are inevitable, he is fully within the rights and proprieties of his position to say so." Bankers claimed that wage reductions resulted from natural economic developments. Chase National Bank economist Benjamin M. Anderson Jr. explained that "reduction of wages is necessary as a part of the general readjustment." "Wage rates cannot be held *inflexible* when everything else is changing, without gravely retarding the process of recovery." Organized labor rejected both bankers' disavowals of agency and their justifications for cutting wages. "There is no longer any doubt about the brutal and greedy policy of certain banks and bankers in relation to wages," attested the labor press. "This group, headed by the huge Chase National, in New York, is hell bent on destroying wage standards."[41]

Organized labor concluded that bankers sought to force a lower living standard upon workers by making business loans dependent on wage cuts. Alfred J. Ahern, secretary of the Baltimore Building Trades Council, charged that the city's bankers had made loans to contractors contingent on this basis. Similarly, United Mine Workers of America official Patrick T. Fagan claimed that in numerous instances bankers had instructed firms "to make these fellows [employees] take a reduction, or your credit is cut off." Green stated that as the Depression worsened, bankers were pushing for lower wages more aggressively. "Millions of men are out of work," observed the *United Mine Workers Journal*, "and evidently these bankers believe now is a good time to take advantage of this situation to cut wages." Union officials were not alone in reaching this conclusion. Senator James J. Couzens (R-MI) agreed that bankers "were waiting for the psychological moment to put it [wage reductions] over."[42]

A number of union leaders thought the banking fraternity wanted to institute dominion over working people. John P. Frey, secretary of the AFL's Metal Trades Department, denounced bankers for "dominating industrial policy and attempting to dictate the terms of employment and conditions of labor." Joseph O'Malley, an American Flint Glass Workers Union official, reported that "a big man in the banking and financial world" had told him that "the working class of people have been too damn extravagant. They have been living too high . . . and they have to be taught a lesson in thrift. Their wages . . . have got to be reduced." "I consider," O'Malley related, "[he] was simply expressing the attitude of all the big international bankers of our country."[43]

The banking fraternity's push to reduce wages was most visible in the public sector. A substantial proportion of property taxes in Cook County, Illinois, dating back to 1928 remained uncollected, because previous real estate valuations had been conducted on the basis of political connections and a court order had ruled that no taxes could be collected until a reappraisal was completed. By 1930 the county had borrowed $300 million to pay for current expenses. A leading Chicago banker reported that due to the county's deteriorating fiscal condition, banks would refuse to purchase any additional tax anticipation warrants (securities backed by future tax revenues). Moreover, Oscar F. Nelson, a city alderman and labor union official, alleged: "No banker outside of Chicago will buy the tax warrants without the Bankers Association's sanction." He held this "bankers' agreement" responsible for Chicago's unpaid public schoolteachers and unfunded mothers' pensions. When school closed for the summer in 1932, the district's teachers had been paid in currency for only five of their previous fourteen months of service. Much of their salaries had been issued in tax anticipation scrip that banks and many stores did not accept. Upon exhausting their savings, hundreds of teachers resorted to running up debts with loan sharks who charged over 40 percent interest. John Fitzpatrick, president of the Chicago Federation of Labor, charged that "LaSalle Street bankers are holding a club over the heads of public officials . . . [threatening that] unless they enforce lower standards of wages they cannot get any money."[44]

When New York City ran into fiscal difficulties during the Depression, Mayor James J. Walker (D) initially assumed an aggressive posture toward the bankers. He protested that "the banks have raised the interest charges on short-term loans to prohibitive rates and are imposing almost impossible conditions." Walker contacted Congress to urge that President Hoover's proposed Reconstruction Finance Corporation, which was to lend money to troubled banks, provide loans to cities. Walker declared that for the national government "to extend a helping hand to the bankers while hundreds of thousands of its people face starvation for lack of means for relief is deplorable." He was eyewitness to a city where "our institutions are filled to capacity with broken bodies and broken hopes." "The question," he insisted, "is whether New York shall be compelled to turn its government over to bankers in exchange for the right to feed its starving citizens."[45]

A group of the city's largest financial institutions responded by reiterating that the municipality "must undertake measures of strict economy." When federal assistance was not forthcoming, the city met the bankers' demands. Once public officials committed to retrenchment in January 1932, the banks granted the city an eleven-day $12.5 million loan to meet immediate short-term obligations. Shortly thereafter, upon coming to "complete satisfaction" with the city's spending cuts, a $350 million high-interest loan package was extended. The bankers had achieved a signal victory. "The banks of New York have done an epoch-making thing," proclaimed the American Bankers Association. "They have compelled the application of some degree of economy to the administration of the affairs of New York City."[46]

The city's fiscal situation deteriorated further over the remainder of 1932. By December, New York City was facing bankruptcy. Charles E. Mitchell, chairman of National City Bank, had commanded city officials: "Cut your budget or go elsewhere for your money." The city accordingly rewrote its budget to satisfy the bankers and announced salary reductions of 6 to 34 percent. The La Follette family's magazine the *Progressive* stated that "New York bankers figuratively held a pistol to its [the city's] head." The union journal *Labor* called the whole affair a "brutal and brazen piece of financial domineering."[47]

The city's teachers were appalled. Abraham Lefkowitz had taught in the school system since 1903. He earned his doctorate from New

York University and was a founder of the American Federation of Teachers. The Hungary-born history teacher's advocacy of his political ideals was unflinching. "Our fight is with the bankers of this country," Lefkowitz roared. "They are determined to destroy educational standards. . . . They have every city by the throat. Talk about Democracy! It is a shame. You have a government by money and for money." The American Federation of Teachers claimed that bankers were undermining basic principles of democratic governance. "The power to tax is one of the greatest powers possessed by governments. If the banks insist upon not only the right to determine the amount of taxes the city may raise but also how the taxes are used, they usurp the most vital functions of government." Lefkowitz was outraged that banking interests were dictating public policy because "their allegiance is to the god of profit and not to the community." "I shall not cease fighting," he pledged, "until the credit power of the bankers is completely destroyed by nationalization." The joint salary committee of seventy-three New York City teacher organizations called for the establishment of a municipal bank "in which patriotic citizens may deposit the money they would like to withdraw from the banks of these dictators."[48]

Organized labor had concluded that bankers were imposing control over employment conditions and government policies. The International Brotherhood of Electrical Workers contended: "The strategy of the banking group . . . consists of continued attacks upon wage scales, all along the line, and in warring against the social welfare measures of the national, state and city governments." Unions further alleged that the bankers' self-serving economic agenda was delaying the nation's recovery by suppressing consumption. "Up, wages, readjust UPWARD!" urged the Boot and Shoe Workers Union. "Stop the bank propaganda. Get big purchasing power into the hands of workers." Organized labor argued that wage reductions had set a vicious economic cycle in motion where diminished purchasing power led to decreased consumption, which brought about additional cuts in production that further magnified the Depression. Both workers and farmers had constructed analyses of the Depression that demanded financial reform. "The money powers . . . have too much to say both in industry and government," objected the journal the Central Labor Council of Stanislaus County, California, jointly published with the local Farmers Union. "This depression is their depression. . . . [A]nd if we permit them to continue running the works they are liable to make things a whole lot worse than they are."[49]

Depositors

Even as bankers remained hidebound in their adherence to financial orthodoxy, they were promoting a notable innovation: deposit account fees. As banks extended fewer loans, they began to search out new profit sources. Depositors provided a promising candidate. A Georgia bank cashier captured the spirit when he urged his colleagues to "eliminate those forms of service which do not permit our banks to make adequate profit." A St. Louis banker hopefully predicted that "customer resistance . . . will be virtually eliminated from the start if banks go into the plan in group formation." One Minnesota banker claimed banks that failed to impose a "service charge upon small accounts" were "negligent or worse."[50]

From the banking fraternity's perspective, the Depression presented a unique opportunity. According to *Southern Banker*, it was "the best time that has ever come, or will ever come again, to add new sources of income by the adoption of proper service fees and exchange charges and by cutting out every free function that represents value to the public while meaning expense to the bank." The economic crisis presented bankers with an ideal pretext. The president of a Chicago bank went so far as to claim, "Free service given to the public by banks has been, to some extent, the cause of the trouble in banks that have had to close."[51]

Not surprisingly, the public did not warm to this innovation. When banks in Kearney, Nebraska, started charging farmers 10¢ to cash their checks from the local Farmers Union creamery, its manager James C. Norgaard concluded that "the bankers are trying to relieve the farmers as much as they possibly can." A resident of Madison, Wisconsin, called checking account fees "a scheme that helps the rich and penalizes the small depositor." The introduction of such fees in Hartford, Connecticut, prompted a resident to warn that "if the movement to 'socialize' the banks get increasing momentum, it is quite certain that the activity charge will be one of the causes."[52]

One stockman penalized with a mercenary 50¢ fee for letting his account balance drop below $50 seized an opportunity to protest the charge. When he entered the bank with $150 worth of checks, the teller began to make out a deposit slip. "Never mind," the rancher interjected. "As my account is such a nuisance, I can take care of that much money myself." Organizational commitments to resist the new fees joined such individual acts of protest. "We will not accept this outrageous charge on small accounts without a fight," avowed Charles C. Hulet, master of the Oregon State Grange. "Perhaps we can find an answer to this problem in a Postal bank." Although their grievances with the private banking system differed, farmers, workers, and depositors all had reasons to seek reform.[53]

6

The 1930s Banking Crisis

"You Have Taken My Money"

B ank failures became so commonplace during the early 1930s that the possibility of imminent closure haunted the national imagination. Dramatic bank runs in cities and towns across the nation manifested this tense situation. It was a period when a line forming outside of a movie theater could prompt an anxious passerby to ask: "What's that—a bread-line or a bank?" In the fall of 1929, there had been 229 banks operating in Chicago. By July 1932, only around sixty remained open. Despairing depositors lingered outside the locked doors of banks in the Back of the Yards neighborhood, hoping that somehow they might reopen. Masses at Catholic churches in the city that summer exhorted parishioners to remain calm amid the wave of bank failures. "From now on I am depositing what funds I have in the postal savings bank," a *Chicago Defender* reader reported. "Look at the banks in Chicago, and then praise Jesse James for being a gentleman."[1]

Americans nationwide could appreciate the distress that Chicago's depositors felt. Approximately 4,500 banks failed from January 1930 through June 1932. "Working men and women, in the shops and factories, over washtub and scrubbing brush, suddenly saw wiped out the savings which they had coined out of their sweat and blood and tears," Representative J. Will Taylor (R-TN) observed. "And following in the dismal and desolate wake of the wreckage has trailed a grim and ghastly procession of human distress, suicides, and unutterable anguish." Although the Hoover administration attempted to prop up the private banking system, the financial situation did not improve. A new generation of Americans hopefully embraced heterodox financial ideas that veteran practitioners of banking politics had advocated for decades. Banking politics had long pervaded the American experience, but the harsh everyday reality of the Great Depression transformed what was a rumble of discontent during the 1920s into a roar.[2]

Failing Banks

The numerous bank failures of the 1920s had been geographically concentrated in areas bearing the brunt of the agricultural depression. From 1921 to 1929, 70 percent of all suspensions occurred in twelve midwestern and southern agricultural states. These small-town banks often held limited assets, and not infrequently were under incompetent management. The center of financial weakness shifted from rural to urban areas in late 1930, when large banks in cities began failing. The banking fraternity portrayed the 1930s banking crisis as a product of mass hysteria. But long lines of distraught small depositors clutching their passbooks were more a symptom of this crisis than the cause. Large depositors—including financial institutions and businesses—with access to inside information about weak and mismanaged banks removed their funds first. Bankers also alleged they were victims of a sinister communist plot to destroy the financial system. The western journal *Coast Banker* stated that "'Reds' and others who want to see the country going to hell in a hanging basket" were conducting "whispering campaigns" to undermine depositor confidence. "Slander," *Commercial West* exclaimed, "has become the slinking, whispering weapon of Communism in its campaign to assassinate American finance."[3]

Claims of communist sabotage notwithstanding, in fact, in addition to heavy withdrawals, bank suspensions resulted from such factors as falling asset values, loan defaults, illiquidity, and mismanagement. White-collar crime played a prominent part in the 1930s banking crisis. In January 1932, Henry J. Bruère, president of the Bowery Savings Bank, acknowledged: "We have seen millions of dollars of savings lost through inexpert and fraudulent management of banks." Sensational cases of banker criminality were abundant. A banker in Binghamton, New York, skipped town after having embezzled $2.5 million to play the stock market. The manhunt lasted for one year before he faced criminal charges alongside three fellow bank employees and directors. In Missouri, a banker pointed his revolver at a bank examiner and pulled the trigger. He was a poor shot. The unharmed examiner soon discovered that the bank's assets were largely spurious. The signatures of people who did not owe the bank a cent had been forged in order to make it appear otherwise. The bank's president, vice president, and cashier all were sentenced to prison.[4]

The Depression's first major wave of bank failures demonstrated the far-reaching consequences of mismanagement and misfeasance. The collapse of Caldwell and Company set in motion the flood of bank suspensions that struck the South in late 1930. Poorly managed banks in the region that were already in precarious positions proved unable to withstand the ensuing period of stress. The origins of Caldwell and Company's weakness dated to the 1920s. Financier Rogers C. Caldwell had transformed his small Nashville, Tennessee, bond operation into a financial empire that controlled the largest chain of banks in the South. This rapid expansion, however, had been at the expense of securing an adequate financial foundation. In November 1930, the firm's Bank of Tennessee was placed in the hands of the state superintendent of banks. This action called into question the safety of all the institutions associated with Caldwell and Company. Over the next couple of weeks, approximately 120 banks in seven states closed. Criminal prosecutions of bankers soon followed, for such offenses as breach of trust, filing fraudulent reports, and conspiring to defraud.[5]

Bank runs subsequently struck the urban North. On December 10, reports of problems at the Bank of United States triggered a run at one of the bank's sixty-two New York City branches that attracted 15,000 people. A chaotic scene unfolded as rain fell and long lines of depositors quickly developed at branches in the Bronx, Brooklyn, and Manhattan. Depositors claimed that at the branch where the initial run had begun, mounted police officers aggressively used their horses to control the crowd and some people were beaten. Those who remained in spite of such conditions likely did not regret their fortitude, because the Bank of United States failed to open the following morning. State officials had attempted to effect a merger or some other solution that would aid the bank's 400,000 depositors, but the city's bankers declined to help.[6]

New York was on edge, and public officials pleaded for calm. Depositors were understandably incensed: management at the Bank of United States had recklessly employed deposits in risky real estate ventures and unsecured loans to directors. The bank also had extended loans to its investment banking affiliate that were used to fund purchases of the bank's own stock, inflating its price. Six months after the bank's suspension, its president and executive vice president received prison sentences. A large crowd outside the courtroom applauded and cheered the convictions, and then "booed and hissed" the disgraced bankers as they were led away to Sing Sing.[7]

The following year proved to be an even worse one for America's bank depositors. There were a total of 2,293 bank failures in 1931, as compared to 1,350 in 1930. Toledo was particularly hard hit: its average deposit losses per person were a full one-fifth higher than any other large city during the crisis. On June 17, one of Toledo's largest financial institutions—the Security-Home Trust Company—did not open. Ensuing bank runs prompted three major banks to place sixty-day holds on withdrawals. Two months passed, and these banks failed to open. The following day saw another bank failure and the suspension of eleven building and loan associations. One Toledo Mudhens outfielder prudently had divided $10,000 among five of the city's banks. Fortunately for him, one of the banks did not fail, so his was not a total loss.[8]

"The Toledo banking situation was fundamentally sound," Cleveland banker Leonard P. Ayres claimed. "There has been no betrayal of faith by the banking officials in Toledo, no dishonesty in the banking operations, no dissipation of assets." This was false. The failed banks were severely compromised by bad assets risked in speculative ventures. Moreover, all indications pointed to considerable dishonesty on the part of management. Subsequent prosecutions were mishandled, however, and consequently ineffectual—likely due to the power and influence of the bankers. Numerous Depression-era bankers who committed white-collar crimes escaped the full consequences of their actions.[9]

Business and political leaders in many communities implemented radical measures on behalf of local banks. In Urbana, Illinois, all nonessential commercial activity was halted following bank runs in January 1932, as the mayor declared a five-day business moratorium. Canvassers went house to house securing depositors' signatures on pledges not to withdraw money from their bank accounts. Other Illinois towns soon followed Urbana's lead. Aurora adopted this approach following heavy bank withdrawals. Mendota's mayor suspended business for one week. "Restored confidence among citizens in their banks and other businesses," he explained, "is the purpose of the order." That summer witnessed additional towns in the Land of Lincoln emulating this practice. Normal business resumed following a bank failure in Chicago Heights only after depositors in the town's one remaining bank committed to limiting their withdrawals. The same was true in the city of North Chicago.[10]

The era's bank suspensions produced a new collective consciousness among depositors. In Portland, Oregon, a handbill circulating after one closure protested that while "small depositors" faced "ruin, hunger, suffering, breadlines," "big bankers" enjoyed "greater wealth and power." It announced an upcoming meeting where a depositors' committee would be established. "DON'T ACCEPT BREADLINES! DEMAND 100 CENTS ON THE DOLLAR! ORGANIZE SMALL DEPOSITORS. ELECT DEPOSITORS COMMITTEES!" A survey of unemployed families in Chicago reported that they were "enraged by bank failures." Fully 12,000 Chicagoans attended an animated gathering ten days after the Sheridan Trust and Savings Bank closed. The assembled depositors appointed a committee to investigate the causes of failures. The young son of an organizer of a Chicago depositors' committee carried a sign that denounced banker greed: "I AM A BOY. YOU HAVE TAKEN MY MONEY. DOES MONEY MEAN AS MUCH TO YOU AS IT DOES TO ME IN YOUR BANK?"[11]

In Manhattan, former depositors of the Bank of United States protested in front of city hall. One such mass meeting attracted a thousand people who called for the arrest and prosecution of the bank's board of directors. The state Banking Department and the Federal Reserve System were criticized for exercising inadequate oversight. "Change bank laws to protect savings," protestors demanded. At another rally, depositors carried signs reading: "Bankers Don't Go Hungry, Workers Do" and "Pay the Small Depositors in Full." Israel Greenbaum, chairman of the depositors' committee, claimed that the bank's failure had led to five suicides and the eviction of fifty families. "This is the start of a mass movement of workers and depositors," he announced. "We want what has been ours."[12]

Reactions were not always so measured. An aggrieved depositor kidnapped and severely beat the former president of a failed downstate Illinois bank who had been sentenced to prison for embezzlement, but then released pending appeal. In Chicago, a police guard was posted over one closed bank and the home of its president due to bomb threats made by "irate depositors." In the interest of preventing any further bank failures, a resident of one of the city's suburbs went so far as to suggest that "a law should be passed by the United States and each state government stipulating that officers of any bank that fails should be executed." Comments a founder of the Southern Tenant Farmers Union made decades later reveal a still-smoldering sense of outrage. "China had the best system of all," he related. "When a bank went broke there, why they took the leaders in that bank and beheaded them, so they didn't have any banks fail."[13]

"Make Bank Deposits Safe"

"We have many laws making it a crime to rob a bank," observed a rancher who lived in Buffalo, South Dakota, "but we have no laws to protect the depositor from being robbed by the banker." Chronic bank failures had provoked a demand to remedy this situation. A local union of waitresses in Seattle protested the hardships that befell depositors of failed banks. Members who had entrusted their savings to these institutions—including those "in their old age and perhaps ill and unable to work longer"—had subsequently been unable to "draw the money that belongs to them, even in cases of death, some of our people have been unable to get enough money for burial of their loved ones." "I saved all I could," recounted a widow in Miami. "I wanted to protect myself in my [old] age." She had labored for twenty years— "long hours, small salary and hard work." And all her efforts were for naught. A bank failure had dealt "a terrible blow to me for today I am penniless after such hard struggle for my living." "Now my strength is gone and my health is poor—I have no one to depend on."[14]

Now semi-retired, Frank A. Vanderlip Sr. inferred that with the exception of "unemployment, there is probably no other subject in the economic phase so sharply in the minds of people as . . . securing safety for their bank deposits." The movement to establish bank deposit guaranty had suffered a setback in recent years, however. Numerous bank failures in the heavily agricultural states that had guaranty programs severely strained the resources of their reimbursement funds. None of the state programs remained in operation. But this precedent did not deter guaranty's supporters. Elmer B. Christie, an Episcopal priest in Washington State, pointed out that "federal authority has often been successful where the states have failed." In 1931 governor of Nebraska Charles W. Bryan (D)—William Jennings Bryan's brother—excoriated the state's bankers for having waged "a continuous effort . . . to amend or repeal [Nebraska's guaranty program]. . . . Every amendment weakened the law, or lowered the assessment rate on the banks, or weakened the state's control over the banks." He thought the banking crisis demanded that Nebraska revive its guaranty program. In the absence of guaranty, Governor Bryan proposed that the state establish and operate a system of government banks. Organized agriculture and labor furnished guaranty political support. In 1932 such diverse groups as the Chicago Federation of Labor, the Michigan State Grange, the Nebraska Stock Growers Association, and the United Mine Workers of America declared in favor of guaranty.[15]

Congress was mindful of this public demand. More than two dozen guaranty bills were introduced from 1930 through 1932. Representative Henry B. Steagall (D-AL) had great admiration for William Jennings Bryan and had supported guaranty legislation for years. His elevation to the chairmanship of the Committee on Banking and Currency in 1932 presented an opportunity to advance the idea. Steagall formulated a guaranty bill that promptly was reported to the House. It included a cap on deposit interest rates in order to discourage banks from offering higher yields made possible by reckless practices.[16]

Supporters of guaranty dating back to Bryan's 1908 campaign testified in favor of the idea before Steagall's committee. Robert L. Owen Jr. returned to Capitol Hill to register his support. In 1907 William H. D. "Alfalfa Bill" Murray (D) had spearheaded enactment of Oklahoma's pioneering guaranty program. A quarter century had not dulled his enthusiasm for the idea. Now governor of Oklahoma, Murray affirmed "that a sound guaranty law would cause all citizens to deposit their money in banks, and there would never be such a thing as hoarding." Steagall's hearings demonstrated that guaranty's opponents could not dismiss the idea as the hobbyhorse of men bearing such monikers as "Alfalfa": Professor Irving Fisher testified that guaranty was "of prime importance to help us out of this depression."[17]

Steagall's bill easily passed the House by voice vote at a time of deep-seated apprehension over the banking system. But guaranty now had to face the rigid opposition of Senator Carter Glass. The elderly Virginian's views were on full display at the Democratic National Convention in Chicago early that summer when he opposed the guaranty plank that Senator William G. McAdoo (D-CA) proposed. "The preponderant sentiment of the country," McAdoo enjoined, "is . . . to save from loss those who put their money in banks for safe keeping." Glass refused to countenance guaranty, which he claimed would cause "loss to the depositors . . . and the breakdown of the banking system." Glass won the day at the convention and in the Senate, where guaranty legislation failed to advance.[18]

Glass's banker allies appreciated his stubborn resistance. *Southern Banker* called guaranty legislation "the most deadly threat that has yet been aimed at sound banking practices in this country." And that year's American Bankers Association convention declared guaranty "unsound and in practice . . . unworkable," and resolved that it was "opposed to the passage of any law carrying a guarantee of bank deposits." The U.S. Chamber of Commerce opposed the idea as well.[19]

Supporters of guaranty were not deterred. A watchman at a packinghouse in Fresno County, California, declared his "hope to see the day when this system [guaranty] will be tried out by all national and state banks." His appeal was moderate in comparison to other reforms that were the topic of public conversation. "When the Federal Government takes over the banks and operates them as out and out Federal institutions—then and not until then—will we be immune from bank failures," stated a North Carolina railroad worker. "There is no cure other than Government operation of the banks."[20]

Hoover's Reforms

While many farmers, workers, and depositors supported reforms that alarmed bankers, the Hoover administration developed a legislative program the financial fraternity found more agreeable. As Hoover neared the end of his term, he concluded that the "major fault in the [economic] system as it stands is in the financial system." But his abiding faith in business autonomy had prevented him from pursuing fundamental change. Hoover thought that "increasing complexity" of the economy necessarily had resulted in government and business growing "more dependent upon each other." However, he was deeply concerned this development would "extinguish the enterprise and initiative which has been the glory of America." Hoover's most concrete response to the banking crisis involved remedial legislation designed to bolster the existing system. His administration pressed for enactment of the Banking Act of 1932, creation of the Reconstruction Finance Corporation, and establishment of the Federal Home Loan Bank system. The rapidity of these three measures' legislative progress directly corresponded to the positions bankers assumed toward them. The American Bankers Association declared its "unhesitating approval" of the first two proposals, and both promptly became law. The association opposed the latter one, however, and its passage proved more challenging.[21]

In late 1931, Hoover grew concerned about gold withdrawals by foreigners forcing the nation off the gold standard. By law, Federal Reserve Banks were required to cover not less than 40 percent of Federal Reserve Notes with gold reserves. The remaining 60 percent could be secured by commercial paper or gold. But there was such a dearth of eligible paper that large quantities of gold were tied up securing notes beyond the statutory 40 percent. In February 1932, the president explained this predicament to congressional leaders. Legislation addressing the situation was introduced simultaneously in the House and Senate two days later. Its passage through Congress was rapid. In a little over two weeks, the Banking Act of 1932 was law. Federal Reserve Banks could now back Federal Reserve Notes with government bonds and lend to member banks on a broader range of collateral. These adjustments buttressed the gold standard and permitted more expansionary monetary policy. The Hoover administration's support of the gold standard had signaled its continued commitment to financial orthodoxy.[22]

As 1931 came to a close, Hoover called for establishing "an emergency Reconstruction Corporation" to make government loans to struggling financial institutions and businesses. Congress responded with swift action and with the approval of financial interests. Melvin A. Traylor, president of the First National Bank of Chicago, testified: "It is in the interest of the whole banking structure that this . . . corporation . . . be enacted at the earliest possible moment." In January 1932, the Reconstruction Finance Corporation was created. It made $2 billion of federal resources available to banks, trust companies, insurance companies, and railroad corporations.[23]

The establishment of a government agency for the explicit purpose of funding large private corporations with public resources was unprecedented. Representative Fiorello H. La Guardia (R-NY) denounced the agency as "a millionaire's dole." A union steelworker in McKees Rocks, Pennsylvania, observed acerbically: "Here we find our government has passed the Reconstruction Finance Corporation Law to establish a fund to take care of . . . the banks or railroad owner, while thousands of our people lose their little homes and farms without so much as an effort made on their behalf." Senator Burton K. Wheeler gave legislative expression to such criticisms when he introduced a bill that mimicked the Reconstruction Finance Corporation Act in all respects, save one: its funds would be loaned directly to farmers. Wheeler contended that "the farmers of the country need refinancing more than the bankers need it. . . . [We] are not going to have prosperity in this country unless we begin at the bottom rather than at the top." Similarly, Representative Thomas R. Amlie (R-WI) insisted: "It would have been infinitely better if this money had been used to help the people at the bottom." Although the RFC assisted powerful economic interests rather than relieving the Depression's victims, it did raise radical possibilities. "Uncle Sam has been compelled to go to the rescue of the banks to the tune of billions," pointed out one resident of Winifred, Montana. "Why not make a good job of it by taking over the whole business?"[24]

The RFC was not the sole financial institution Hoover proposed in late 1931 to aid economic recovery. The home credit market had ground to a virtual halt. A survey of 117 communities found first mortgages were available only in two cities. Nearly 60 percent of existing homeowners had mortgage payments to make, and at a minimum one out of five—and possibly up to one-half—were unable to keep up their payments. Annual foreclosures of non-farm properties had risen from 116,000 in 1928 to 252,400 by 1932. "If things keep up like this . . . there's going to be trouble," one Chicagoan warned. "It doesn't feel good to get kicked out of your house." Foreclosure—and fear of this possibility—could have tragic consequences. In a Queens neighborhood where more than half the residents lost their homes between 1928 and 1933, the five members of one family were hospitalized, ostensibly with the flu. The mother died. Their condition actually resulted from starving themselves for three years in order to keep up the house payments.[25]

Hoover's response was to suggest "home loan discount banks" that would generate liquidity in the housing market. The Federal Reserve System did not discount for home mortgage lenders. By doing so, these proposed banks would increase the supply of credit in the housing market. The banking fraternity disapproved of this idea. National City Bank denied the need for such an institution. "The best way to revive residential construction is to reduce its cost," the bank declared. "Wage reductions in the building trades are spreading widely." The American Bankers Association wanted to see action on such legislation "deferred," claiming that building new homes "would not seem advisable to encourage at this time." And, revealingly, that it was "unwise public policy for the Federal Government to create additional banking corporations of a permanent character." Hiram S. Cody, president of the Mortgage Bankers Association of America, maintained legislative action was unwarranted, a claim that a homeowner in Chicago disputed. "I . . . would like to see some evidence of that statement," he demanded, "as would thousands of others who have tried to refinance their property." Charles W. Ervin of the Amalgamated Clothing Workers Union rebuked bankers for pursuing their own self-interest. "The reason for the opposition is self-evident—it cuts into the profits of the bankers and releases somewhat the stranglehold which they now have."[26]

While bankers lobbied against the measure, building and loan associations waged a spirited campaign on its behalf. These lenders had attained greater significance in the home mortgage field during the 1920s. William E. Best, president of the United States Building and Loan League, claimed the reform would "do much to hasten recovery and steady . . . residential real estate deflation." The support of the

National Association of Real Estate Boards further bolstered the campaign. And business interests that expected to benefit from a rebound in housing construction—such as lumber companies—lent their support as well. The idea of aiding homeowners struck a chord with an important group of voters. One Greensboro, North Carolina, homeowner stated: "I feel that the time has come when something must be done for the man that is trying to own his home."[27]

The Home Loan Bank bill finally was sent to the president for his signature as the congressional session came to a close in July. The Federal Home Loan Bank Act established a system of twelve regional government banks modeled on the Federal Reserve System to advance funding to member lending institutions. The new law included no effective provision for directly aiding distressed homeowners. Representative Wright Patman claimed this reform "was intended only to finance the financiers." A Dallas resident offered a solution. "Change The Federal Home Loan Bank's plan of doing Business and arrange so as to do business direct with the Home owner."[28]

Glass's Reform

Another proposed financial reform that garnered significant attention in 1932 was a project of Carter Glass. Bankers impeded Glass's legislative effort, despite his long-standing political advocacy on their behalf. Edmund Platt, vice president of Marine Midland Corporation, affirmed, "Senator Glass's name has always been associated with constructive legislation." Yet Platt and other bankers opposed the Glass bill nevertheless, because they opposed reforms that would permanently alter the banking system. "The banking laws should be changed just as little as possible," an Alabama banker insisted.[29]

Glass had assumed a proprietary attitude toward the Federal Reserve System. He considered the central bank his legacy and was apprehensive about its survival. In the late 1920s, the use of member bank funds in stock market speculation had attracted Glass's notice after Senator Robert M. La Follette Jr. (R-WI) and other congressional critics raised the issue. La Follette wanted "to restrict the further expansion of loans by member banks for speculative purposes." Glass concluded that unless speculation was reduced, Congress would enact wide-ranging reforms he considered "inimical." Even prior to the Great Crash of 1929, therefore, Glass inveighed against the "enormous funds of the banks" being "thrown into the maelstrom of stock speculation." He encouraged the Federal Reserve Board to take the initiative in curbing speculative activity. "This situation should be corrected administratively without forcing the dangerous expedient of statutory readjustment." Following the stock market's collapse, Glass assumed a more proactive position. In November 1929, he announced that it was necessary to enact "banking laws to prevent by penalization such disasters in stock gambling operations."[30]

In 1930 Glass made his initial effort to legislate financial reform. This bill failed to advance in a Republican-controlled Congress, and in January 1932 he made another attempt. His second effort immediately met with unabashed opposition from the banking fraternity. In the words of *Southern Banker*: "The Glass bill . . . is without friends." Allan M. Pope, president of the Investment Bankers Association of America, reported that in conversations with hundreds of investment bankers "without a single exception" they opposed the measure. Glass presented a modified version of the legislation in March that proposed to create a liquidating corporation for failed banks, permit statewide branch banking by national banks, separate banks from their investment banking affiliates following a three-year grace period, restrict member bank speculation with Federal Reserve System credit, remove the secretary of the treasury from the Federal Reserve Board, and formalize the existing coordination of Federal Reserve Banks' open market operations. Bankers remained steadfastly resistant to reform. "This is little better than the first Glass Bill," maintained the Guaranty Trust Company of New York.[31]

Glass then submitted yet another version of the bill that retained the salient features of his previous proposal. At this point, the American Bankers Association changed tack and extended a mock endorsement, in which it "approved" of the legislation but urged amendments that upheld the banking system's autonomy. The organization was amenable to a liquidating corporation, but did not want funding for it "forced from the banks"; it accepted that speculation with Federal Reserve credit should be addressed, but did not want any action of "an autocratic extent"; it approved of branching, but thought this practice "should be extended by the states"; and it was willing to submit to some controls on investment affiliates, granting that they "should report to and be supervised by the bank supervisory authorities."[32]

The banking fraternity's position on the Glass bill reveals just how out of touch bankers were with the contemporary political situation. In a time of crisis, their perennial ally Glass had assembled a mild reform package, but they remained stubbornly resistant nonetheless. Glass was frustrated. "If the bankers generally would have the good sense to get behind this conservative measure," he reflected, "we could legislate this winter and avert radical legislation at the session of the new Congress." The veteran legislator's political sense was astute. The nation's financial plight had precipitated a situation where even traditionally moderate voices sounded radical. "The injustices which the debtors of the United States are suffering from today," *Wallaces' Farmer* claimed, "are more serious than those which provoked the American Revolution."[33]

Demands to overhaul American finance were routine. John A. Simpson called on farmers "to unite in the battle to destroy the present banker-controlled money system." Grassroots activism was seeking to make bankers superfluous, such as the effort of teachers to establish a municipal bank in New York City. One thousand miles to the west, there was a campaign in Iowa to establish a state bank. Out on the Pacific coast, both the Oregon State Grange and Oregon State Federation of Labor favored a state bank. North of the Columbia River, the Washington State Federation of Labor resolved that due to bankers' "organized program of wage slashing"—and also their "gross mismanagement and often times criminal handling of the people's savings"— the organization would "launch a state-wide movement" to establish "a state-owned and operated banking system." A convention of the state's unemployed had gone a step further and advocated that banking be nationalized.[34]

Coxey and "Coin" Ride Again

Banking and monetary issues had become so salient that financial reformers who had attained prominence in the 1890s received renewed
public attention. Jacob S. Coxey Sr. had never stopped campaigning
and now found the wind squarely at his back. In 1930 he addressed
the American Federation of Labor's annual convention and traveled
through the Midwest speaking about his proposed financial reforms.
Representative Guy E. Campbell (R-PA) introduced Coxey's bill for
issuing government currency backed by non-interest-bearing bonds
to fund public works projects. And after numerous unsuccessful for-
ays into the electoral arena, Coxey assumed political office on New
Year's Day 1932, when he was sworn in as the mayor of Massillon,
Ohio. Coxey received a deluge of congratulatory letters, including
ones that requested information on his financial ideas.[35]

The dynamic septuagenarian was not satisfied with local political office: he announced his intention to seek the Republican Party's
presidential nomination. The Grand Old Party demurred, but Coxey
remained undeterred. By that summer, Coxey was headlining the
Farmer-Labor Party's ticket. The party's platform championed heterodox banking and monetary reforms, demanding free silver and greenbacks, as well as abolition of the Federal Reserve System and all existing banking laws. The party also wanted to allow the Postal Savings
System to offer checking accounts and loans at 2 percent interest.[36]

Coxey was not the only reformer of the 1890s making waves again.
When William H. "Coin" Harvey announced a convention at his Arkansas home, the *New York Times* reported that he received "great
piles of mail from his organizers throughout the country." In August
1931, 768 delegates from twenty-five states journeyed deep into the
Ozark Mountains to form the Liberty Party. They nominated Harvey
for the presidency and adopted a program that sought to enact his
financial ideas. "The Money Subject is the Paramount Issue," proclaimed the new party's platform. Its planks included free silver and
greenbacks, in addition to "repeal of all present financial laws," and

the establishment of a financial system "owned exclusively by the government; no other banks permitted."[37]

Not all presidential candidates who championed financial reforms
were established campaigners. A new voice emerged in Pittsburgh,
where Catholic priest James R. Cox had organized bread lines and
soup kitchens in response to the Depression. But the growing need
for relief soon overwhelmed his efforts. Following in the footsteps of
Coxey, Father Cox decided to lead a march of the jobless to Washington, DC. On January 5, 1932, thousands of unemployed workers set
out in a motley caravan for the nation's capital. One observer reported
there were participants who rode on "car bumpers, rear tires and fend-
ers the entire distance." Upon reaching their destination, a delegation
had the opportunity to meet with Hoover. Cox's Army was filled with
patriotic sentiment. Cox himself had served in France during World
War I as a hospital chaplain. Before the marchers departed town, they
sang "America," recited the Pledge of Allegiance, and placed a wreath
of flowers at the Tomb of the Unknown Soldier. Father Cox left the
capital a national figure. One week later, he floated the possibility of a
run for the presidency before a rally of 55,000 people in Pittsburgh.[38]

Further reflection led Cox to investigate the possibility of merging
his political efforts with the Liberty Party's campaign. Harvey oblig-
ingly dispatched a representative to Pittsburgh who met with Cox
for two days. The priest then approved the party's platform. A joint
convention of Cox and Harvey supporters was arranged that summer
in St. Louis. But the two factions could not agree on which candidate would be the presidential nominee. The newly created Jobless
Party subsequently nominated Cox for president on a platform that
included federal control of banks and direct no-interest government
loans to farmers. The party's existence proved short-lived. At the end
of August, Cox embarked on a campaign tour that started out well,
with thousands turning out in such Ohio cities as Akron and Youngstown. By the end of September, however, Cox had run out of money
and found himself stranded in Tucumcari, New Mexico. A few weeks
later, lack of funds forced the priest to announce that he no longer

was campaigning. Within days, Father Cox pulled out of the race altogether and threw his support behind Democratic Party nominee Franklin D. Roosevelt.[39]

The presidential campaigns of Coxey and Harvey also ended in disappointment. Restrictive ballot access laws impaired third-party efforts. In November, Harvey received votes in only ten states, while Coxey managed a mere four. But there were additional undermining factors. Coxey was seventy-eight years old, had a city in Ohio to run, and lacked the support of such key Farmer-Labor Party leaders as governor of Minnesota Floyd B. Olson and Representative Paul John Kvale (MN), who both made the pragmatic decision to support Roosevelt. In one notable campaign speech, the Democratic nominee had proposed "to correct, by drastic means if necessary, the faults in our economic system." Roosevelt appealed to anti-banker sentiment by identifying the "questionable methods" of "great bankers" as one of those faults.[40]

The fate of Harvey's campaign is more suggestive of the attraction that a third-party banking reform ticket presented to voters. Harvey was over eighty years old, and his electoral efforts consequently suffered from the handicaps of advanced age. As the *New York Times* reported: "Once Mr. Harvey was a sparkling orator . . . but now he has grown too feeble for much activity." Harvey had difficulty making his voice heard at campaign events. It fell upon the party's vice-presidential nominee, California's Andrae B. Nordskog, therefore, to, in the words of one supporter, "shoulder the campaign of the Liberty Party." Nordskog had delivered a stirring address at the party's convention that won him a place on the ticket.[41]

The son of Norwegian immigrants to Iowa, Nordskog was an accomplished musician who had managed the Hollywood Bowl. He was drawn to politics and entered into the contentious debates over Southern California water policy. In response to the Great Depression, Nordskog proposed a recovery program that hinged on heterodox financial ideas: ending the gold standard, remonetizing silver, printing $1 billion worth of greenbacks to fund infrastructure projects, repealing the National Banking Acts and Federal Reserve Act, enacting immediate payment of the veterans' bonus, and extending the Postal Savings System by removing the deposit limit, introducing checking accounts, and offering loans to the public at cost. Nordskog claimed that in Southern California he was "speaking to crowds that in many cases have crowded the halls to overflowing." But the Liberty Party's campaign was severely disrupted when an ugly public dispute erupted between its presidential and vice-presidential nominees over campaign expenses, public acclaim, and control of the party. "I blame both Nordskog and Harvey for their folly!" exclaimed a disappointed supporter.[42]

The split between Harvey and Nordskog did not bring the party's campaign to a complete halt. Harvey managed to make a tour through Washington State that fall, which included a banquet presided over by the mayor of Tacoma, and a speech (with the assistance of a sound system) before a large audience at the state fairgrounds. Moreover, the Liberty Party's campaign in the state did not depend exclusively on Harvey's personal efforts, because the party also had congressional candidates spreading its message in three districts. One of these candidates netted over 18 percent of the vote, and the lowest vote-getter of the three received over 8 percent. Harvey received only 53,199 votes nationwide, but, instructively, more than half of these ballots were cast in Washington State, where he polled almost 5 percent of the total vote.[43]

The platforms of other 1932 third-party campaigns further indicate the broad attraction of banking reform. The Prohibition Party adopted a plank reprimanding banks for "hoarding untold millions in their vaults, refusing to lend even on prime security," and calling for the national government to purchase state and municipal bonds with "legal-tender treasury notes" in order to expand the money supply and liquefy credit markets. And the Socialist Party sought "the complete governmental acquisition of the Federal reserve banks and the extension of the services of postal savings banks to cover all departments of the banking business."[44]

New Movements Arise

Discontent with the existing financial system was also facilitating the rise of new movements and leaders outside of the electoral arena. In the 1920s, World War I veterans had confronted banks that denied them loans when they attempted to exercise their option to borrow against the bonus they were scheduled to receive in 1945. Once the Depression struck, the banking fraternity strongly objected to paying the bonus early. American Bankers Association president Rome C. Stephenson testified: "I have the viewpoints on this proposition of many of my associates in banking and in the American Bankers Association. Universally they are unalterably opposed to it." In the spring and summer of 1932, hard-pressed veterans assembled in the nation's capital to demand immediate payment of the bonus. A pamphlet that the Bonus Army circulated in support of their cause was titled *Don't Let the Bankers Fool You*. Bonus Army leader Walter W. Waters reported that veterans frequently denounced "Wall Street and the bankers" at their tent encampment. A sign at the Anacostia Flats camp asked: "What did Morgan do for the country that we didn't do?" Waters observed that many veterans bore a deep-seated sense of outrage over "the little bank in their home town that had pressed down on them or had failed, from crookedness within." "Billions for the bankers but nothing for the hungry," one veteran remarked caustically.[45]

By the summer of 1932, farmers were engaging in direct, organized, militant action. Northwestern Iowa witnessed a Farmers' Holiday Association–organized blockade, inspired by grievances against bankers and intended to halt the movement of agricultural products to market. Farmers picketed roads and were prepared to enforce their will with pitchforks for tires, rocks for windshields, and clubs for drivers. There were banks in Iowa denying savings account withdrawals and limiting checking account withdrawals. Farmers believed that if bankers were effectively going on strike, they were entitled to declare "holidays" as well. The *New Republic* reported: "Even conservative farmers who take no part in the Farmers' Holiday movement seem pleased to see the bankers squirm when their own trick is turned against them." As summer turned to fall, the farm holiday idea spread to Nebraska, Minnesota, the Dakotas, and Illinois.[46]

The bankers' campaign to prevent depositor withdrawals inspired some farmers to call for the suspension of farm debts. A Farmers Union convention at Wolf Point, Montana, resolved that "any farmer has who has been foreclosed shall stay right on his land and take the full value of the crops without interference." It further resolved "to enforce this right by mass action." Grangers in Fairview, Idaho, advanced a debt moratorium and resolved "to take any other steps that may be determined necessary for the protection of the farmers against the mortgage holders and the creditors." A North Dakota banker decided not to foreclose on a widow's farm after a group of farmers told him: "If you foreclose on that woman, we'll hang you." In his successful 1932 campaign for the state's governorship, William L. Langer instructed farmers to "shoot the banker if he comes on your farm."[47]

Urban Americans also were attracted to social movements that opposed the private banking system. In Detroit, the eccentric Alfred W. Lawson accrued a following through his advocacy of financial reform. The son of English immigrants, as a young bootblack Lawson noted that "people who did the least work toward the production of wealth wore the best boots and those who did the hardest work . . . wore the worst boots." At the age of eighteen, he began a twenty-year career in professional baseball as a player, manager, and owner. Following Lawson's retirement from baseball in 1908, he abruptly transitioned to the fledgling field of aviation. In 1931 he shifted course again by founding the Direct Credits Society, which operated the School for Direct Credits, offering free night classes to those who were interested in financial reform. Lawson sought to eliminate interest payments and insisted that "private banking must be prohibited" because "all credits must be issued by the government direct." Thousands of midwesterners found his message compelling.[48]

A more prominent voice seeking banking reform had arisen from the Motor City as well. Raised in a devout Canadian family of Irish descent, Catholic priest Charles E. Coughlin had been ordained in 1916 at the age of twenty-four. In 1926 he was assigned a parish in the Detroit suburb of Royal Oak. Coughlin soon began broadcasting weekly religious programs over the radio. His mellifluous voice was custom-made for this emergent technology. When the Depression hit, Coughlin's initial response was to organize God's Poor Society to distribute food and clothing in the Detroit area. But he also started addressing political questions in his broadcasts. In 1930 the Columbia Broadcasting System began transmitting his sermons nationally. Father Coughlin developed a large following in working-class neighborhoods throughout the urban Northeast and Midwest by stressing financial issues. To his millions of listeners, he exhorted that there should be "government owned banks controlled by duly elected or appointed Government officials." By 1932 Coughlin was receiving so many letters from supporters that he employed more than a hundred mail clerks. The rapid emergence of diverse popular voices who excoriated bankers and urged the reformation of finance demonstrates the degree to which Americans hungered for change.[49]

As 1932 drew to a close, bankers occupied a precarious position. The American Bankers Association recognized that "the next Congress will be governed by the people back home to an extent not carried out in practice for a number of years, because recent issues have aroused back home a deeper interest in economic and political problems." The organization further warned that "unsound banking legislation is a constant threat." A Pacific Northwest financial journal acknowledged the popular sentiment that had made possible the Liberty Party's surprising electoral showing in Washington State, reporting that in Seattle a "tidal wave of votes swept into office some men who are hostile to banks and who openly campaigned for measures deemed inimical to banking interests." David Levine, past president of the Seattle Central Labor Council, illustrated this political climate when he proclaimed: "The Nation must own the Banks or the Banks will own the Nation."[50]

Despite the unfavorable political environment, bankers had been able to draw consolation from the knowledge that Hoover upheld financial orthodoxy. George M. Reynolds had faith that "President Hoover can be relied upon to exercise the veto power on most of the [heterodox economic] measures if, by any chance, they should be passed by Congress." In 1932 one New York bank accordingly instructed its employees "to vote for Hoover—or else." But the election of Franklin D. Roosevelt had set a firm expiration date on this source of solace. As the private banking system was collapsing, banking politics was finding new voice.[51]

7

The Emergency Banking Act

"MENE MENE TEKEL UPHARSIN"

As 1932 came to a close, millions of Americans faced a bitter, hungry winter. Unlikely sources betrayed how widespread disaffection with the existing financial system had become. "Are bankers intelligent?" asked an article in the thoroughly respectable *North American Review*. While at one time conventional opinion could have reflexively dismissed this as the impudent question of an economic radical, recent developments had shaken such assumptions. Alive to the widespread popular outrage, the fiery old Texas Populist James H. "Cyclone" Davis eagerly anticipated a battle he had looked forward to since the 1890s. He claimed that "thousands [of Americans] . . . now confess that my harangues on the money question were a vision of foresight." Davis accordingly hoped to see "a row over the Wall Street domination of this country."[1]

The financial system had wreaked havoc on the lives of ordinary citizens. The self-serving actions of numerous bankers and disastrous state of the nation's banks forged strong popular demand for sweeping change following the collapse of the private banking system in March 1933. Public anger toward bankers was pervasive and unmistakable. At this moment, President Franklin D. Roosevelt could have remade the nation's banking system entirely. "Practices of the unscrupulous money changers," he observed, "stand indicted in the court of public opinion, rejected by the hearts and minds of men." But rather then embarking on a new epoch in American financial history, Roosevelt elected to save the existing banks. The bankers thus survived this moment of crisis. A strong current of public opinion, however, demanded that the banking fraternity be deposed once and for all.[2]

"Damned by Many"

Events in the nation's least populous state during the fall of 1932 exemplify the banking fraternity's public disgrace. Nevada's foremost banker was George Wingfield Sr., who controlled a chain of banks that dominated economic affairs in the state. As a young man, Wingfield found wealth as a successful gambler and later as a casino owner. The "Boy Gambler" subsequently engaged in lucrative mining ventures in Goldfield that involved the ruthless repression of union miners before relocating to Reno in 1909. Wingfield possessed sizable real estate holdings, had interests in numerous mining concerns, operated the state's leading hotels, and was rumored to be the silent partner in bootlegging, gambling, and prostitution operations. His economic power accorded Wingfield great influence over Nevada politics, which he exercised as the state's kingmaker.[3]

Nevada's economic life and existing power structure were severely disrupted on November 1, 1932, when its governor declared a twelve-day bank holiday. The imminent insolvency of the Wingfield chain of banks had forced his hand. Nevada's economy rested upon mining and ranching, both of which the Depression had crippled. In an attempt to protect his existing investments and sustain the state's livestock industry, Wingfield had extended and increased loans against doubtful security. His political power meant that state banking officials had turned a blind eye to these practices.[4]

The Wingfield chain was so financially impaired that the bank holiday had to be extended until mid-December. Members of the state's establishment expressed their enduring support for the beleaguered banker. "George Wingfield is a man of rugged character," proclaimed the *Las Vegas Age*, "the one man in a thousand who could come through such a terrible ordeal without any man having the hardihood to charge that he took unfair advantage of any depositor." But as the extravagant nature of this praise betrays, esteem for Wingfield was far from universal. "Some people," the *Battle Mountain Scout* disclosed, "are taking advantage of the present banking moratorium . . . to belittle George Wingfield's banking ability." "He was damned by many," reported one contemporary. Another Nevadan later recalled that "there was animosity toward Mr. Wingfield. You could see it on every turn." Wingfield himself acknowledged that "attacks over the radio have been very bitter." The Wingfield banks never reopened.[5]

While Americans had long considered bankers to be coldhearted and greedy, they were now rapidly concluding that bankers also were inept at best and criminal at worst. "Do you see any of the bankers themselves ruined?" one man angrily demanded. "They're still riding in their big cars. . . . It takes about as much brains and honesty to run a bank now as it used to take to run a peanut stand." John H. Puelicher, former president of the American Bankers Association, acknowledged: "I find myself astonished by the general conversation about the incompetence of bankers." Indeed, bankers were losing any ability to command authority. The Washington State Grange pronounced it was "evident that the private ownership and control of the financial and banking system of the United States has failed." The Boot and Shoe Workers Union unflinchingly demanded: "What right have bankers in Wall Street got to expect respect for their opinions?" The labor press adamantly pressed the deficiencies of bankers: "Are they wiser than others? No! Are they more far-seeing for the public good? No! Are they more honest? No!"[6]

During this crisis, there was no shortage of suggestions for improvement. In November 1932, the *American Bankers Association Journal* imagined apprehensively, "At this moment, tucked away in pigeon-holes and desk drawers, or existing solely as hunches, are hundreds of plans for restoring prosperity tomorrow morning by the simple method of hampering the operation of banks." Such plans commonly sought to inaugurate a publicly controlled, service-oriented banking system. "Banks should be controlled and operated by states and national government," proposed a *Chicago Defender* reader in Detroit who held bankers responsible for "having brought poverty and misery to thrifty American citizens." A Texan submitted that Congress "should cancel the present banking charters and create national banks, not allowing any individual to own a dollar of bank stock." And a Norwegian-American farmer in Ada County, Idaho, suggested that "interest or usury for private profit should be forever prohibited under penalty of life imprisonment."[7]

As disapprobation of finance became ubiquitous, businessmen gained new prominence among the bankers' critics. One Brooklyn wholesaler believed that powerful financial interests wanted to see "small manufacturers and jobbers and middle-class department stores . . . go by the wayside leaving a clear road for those in control of money." Andrew S. Greenfield foresaw this development culminating in a nation of "two classes." "The upper with everything in control, and the lower, which will eventually be likened to the slaves in the days of Egypt." Some businessmen produced radical plans for restructuring banking. The millionaire progenitor of numerous ventures in Nevada and California drafted a blueprint for running the banking system as a public utility. An Ohio manufacturer who had moved to California and become the state's leading fig producer recommended that the government take over banking. One small Philadelphia manufacturer declared: "Sooner or later the Government must go into the banking business."[8]

The era's most widely recognized representative of American business numbered among the banking critics. Negative public attitudes toward finance help explain why Henry Ford was uncommonly popular for a business leader. "When it is organized as it must be," Ford submitted, "banks will be the servants of industry. . . . Business will control money instead of money controlling business." He once claimed that the "difference between me and a capitalist" was that "I earn my living honestly," unlike the "capitalist [who] loans out his money, collects the interest, and lets the other fellow do the work." Although Ford made reasoned public appeals for banks to eschew speculation in favor of providing business with credit and depositors with security, his animosity toward bankers was part of a complex personal hatred that included anti-Semitism. During the 1920s, he waged a poisonous campaign against Jews, and he later claimed nefarious Jewish financiers caused both world wars.[9]

Ford illustrates how anxieties about monopolistic financial power could be reconciled with conspiratorial ideas about Jews. This interpretation was most present among businessmen whose faith in the status quo led them to conclude economic problems must be the result of sabotage. In 1933 Representative Louis T. McFadden, who had served as treasurer and president of the Pennsylvania Bankers Association, delivered an ugly speech alleging a global Jewish financial conspiracy. McFadden had completed an abrupt transition from respectable Republican leader to political pariah months earlier, by presenting articles of impeachment against President Hoover in reaction to his moratorium on Europe's war debts. McFadden had grown increasingly paranoid in response to the Depression. In 1930 he had claimed a cabal of foreign and New York bankers were conspiring to seize power in the United States. McFadden's prejudiced outbursts were instrumental to his subsequent electoral defeat. Anti-Semitism occupied a marginal position in banking politics, akin to its unseemly place in American society more broadly.[10]

"Talking It Over"

In the face of widespread demand for reform, bankers spent the Great Depression disclaiming any pressing need for change. As 1931 dawned, Rome C. Stephenson, president of the American Bankers Association, declared the year would witness "the strongest banking situation we have ever enjoyed." As 1931 closed, Chicago banker Melvin A. Traylor maintained that "the disaster which has overtaken the banking business is not due to the system of banking we have; it is not due to the character and quality of the supervision, nor is it attributable to the management of the banks." The banking fraternity continued to stubbornly deny the need for reform during the winter of 1932–33. "Is sweeping and radical legislation of a permanent nature called for?" asked Francis H. Sisson, the new president of the American Bankers Association. "I think not."[11]

Practitioners of banking politics thought otherwise. The United Mine Workers of America noted recent news reports of substantial bank stock dividends: "Millions are hungry while banks pay 14 to 200 per cent dividends." The union warned that "those who are in authority and have the power to change the conditions had better get busy and change them while they still have a chance." "The day has arrived," the Reverend Charles E. Coughlin informed his listeners, "when our Federal Government must establish its own banks throughout the nation for the purpose of safeguarding depositors' money." Coughlin thus urged the establishment of "a nationally owned banking system as sound as our army and as honest as our post office."[12]

As Coughlin's comment reveals, the Postal Savings System continued to provide a starting point for heterodox banking reform. A few months after Black Tuesday, October 29, 1929, Representative John T. Buckbee (R-IL) introduced a bill to double the postal savings deposit limit to $5,000. While it made no progress, he reintroduced it during the following session of Congress. Such proposals were numerous. Representative Emanuel Celler (D-NY) wrote President Hoover in support of temporarily doubling the deposit limit in order to combat hoarding. Representative Martin L. Sweeney (D-OH) set the bar still higher, a permanent increase to $10,000. The Post Office Department testified in favor of this proposal, while the American Bankers Association predictably opposed any action along these lines. The National Federation of Post Office Clerks reported that bankers "carried on an active fight, deluging members of Congress with telegrams."[13]

Bankers also combated proposals to have the Postal Savings System offer checking accounts. In 1931 both the Public Ownership League and the Chicago Federation of Labor resolved that in order "to stabilize . . . the financial basis of the nation," it was necessary to authorize "the enlargement and extension of the Postal Savings Bank System, . . . [including] the necessary provisions for checking accounts." The Washington State Federation of Labor declared it would "insist" on checking accounts. Senator Clarence C. Dill (D-WA), who had idolized William Jennings Bryan in his youth, seized political leadership on the issue. Dill was first elected to the Senate in 1922 by a coalition of workers and farmers, and was a noted advocate of public power projects and government radio regulation. In 1932 he introduced legislation to raise the deposit ceiling to $5,000 and permit checking accounts. A number of labor organizations endorsed the measure, including the Central Labor Council of Buffalo, the Montana State Federation of Labor, the Niagara Falls Central Labor Union, and the Central Labor Council of Portland, Oregon. While many working people approved of Dill's legislation, public discussion of the proper role for postal savings extended beyond checking accounts. "Nationalize the banks," proposed a retired carpenter and farm laborer. "Then money used formerly to create debts could be used to eliminate them. A year from the establishment of post office banks, all internal debt could be retired."[14]

The Great Depression left jobless Americans with plenty of free time to consider banking reform programs. Over one-quarter of all union members were unemployed by 1933, including over 70 percent of those in the building trades. The International Molders and Foundry Workers Union of North America urged its members: "Use your public library—it is your friend." Public libraries played a central role in the daily lives of the unemployed. Libraries in cities across the nation reported that 40 to 100 percent more books were being circulated than before the Depression. One librarian later recalled that in the neighborhood branch in Buffalo where she worked, "you couldn't keep a book on the shelf." And these new patrons increasingly used public libraries to pursue financial questions. The New York Public Library reported that large numbers of its patrons were studying economic issues. Carl H. Milam, secretary of the American Library Association, remarked on "the unprecedented demand . . . for books and other material on economic planning, unemployment insurance, gold standard, business cycles and suggested methods of recovering prosperity." According to *Scientific American*: "The average person now knows more of the mysterious inner workings of economic laws; he is talking it over with the butcher, the baker, the candle-stick maker, and they all answer in kind."[15]

The Banking System Fails

By January 1933, over one million Americans were using barter and scrip to escape the need for currency and credit. Banking conditions had deteriorated to the point where state governments resorted to extraordinary measures. On January 20, Iowa authorized the state's superintendent of banking to directly take control of any state-chartered bank's operations. The next state to intervene in banking was Louisiana, which declared a surprise bank holiday on February 4, nominally to honor the anniversary of the severance of diplomatic relations with Germany in 1917. This holiday was deemed necessary to address a major New Orleans bank's shaky financial condition. The novel observance proved successful: Reconstruction Finance Corporation support quickly arrived.[16]

Banks in the Motor City presented more intransigent difficulties. Detroit's industrial economy was in shambles. National motor vehicle production in 1932 was only one-quarter of what it had been in 1929. The automobile industry's collapse had compounded the existing defects of the city's banks. The immediate origin of Detroit's financial debacle was the condition of the Union Guardian Trust Company. Its weakness dated back to irresponsible lending practices during the 1920s real estate bubble. In 1933 the Union Guardian held only $6.3 million in assets against $20.5 million in deposit liabilities. The Union Guardian was a member of the Guardian Detroit Union Group, which had been formed at the end of 1929 and either controlled outright, or held significant interest in, thirty-two Detroit financial institutions.[17]

The other banking group that dominated finance in the city, the even larger Detroit Bankers Company, had been formed in early 1930 to unite five of the region's largest banks. It subsequently absorbed additional financial institutions. Together, these two groups controlled fully 92.5 percent of the city's total bank resources and over 80 percent of its trust company resources. Dubiously, both groups had declared dividends well in excess of earnings, released false financial reports, and made questionable insider loans. In May 1932, the Guardian group's principal component—the Guardian National Bank of Commerce—was carrying $7.8 million in loans to its own directors. In November 1932, Acting Comptroller of the Currency F. Gloyd Awalt determined that "the banking situation in Michigan is decidedly menacing and unstable."[18]

The Union Guardian sought $65 million from the Reconstruction Finance Corporation to keep its doors open. The agency denied this loan since the Guardian group offered collateral valued at only $35 million. Anxious government officials turned to Henry Ford. James J. Couzens, Michigan's wealthy senior senator, had proposed a joint intervention by Ford and himself. The automaker, however, blamed reckless financiers for precipitating the nation's economic distress. Ford rejected efforts to salvage banks as counterproductive. Early on the morning of February 14, Michigan's governor declared an eight-day bank holiday. One week later, the holiday was declared officially over, but effectively remained in place because a strict limitation on withdrawals was imposed.[19]

Michigan soon had company. Large withdrawals in Baltimore prompted Maryland's governor to declare a three-day bank holiday. Member banks of the Indianapolis Clearing House Association limited depositor withdrawals. In Ohio, Dayton's city government proclaimed a three-day bank holiday. All of the banks in Akron and Youngstown imposed withdrawal limitations on depositors, and a number of banks in Canton and Lima operated under heavy restrictions. With one exception, members of the Cleveland Clearing House Association allowed depositors to withdraw only 5 percent of their account balances. The banking collapse struck the West on March 1, when California announced a three-day bank holiday. Six western states quickly followed the Golden State's lead. By March 3, bank holidays and restrictions on withdrawals had been implemented in thirty states plus the District of Columbia.[20]

Time vividly reported that the "banking disease had reached Manhattan, heart of the nation's banking system." Over the preceding years, as New Yorkers lost confidence in the city's banks, the Bowery Savings Bank had been the exceptional institution that saw its deposits increase. But depositors now besieged the famed savings bank, as "bootblacks, Jewish matrons, silk-stockinged stenographers and shawled immigrants carried off cash from the paying windows." The bank's president recalled: "We were busy securing funds from the Federal Reserve Bank until they had no more cash." Any remaining public confidence in the nation's private banking system had evaporated. Frank Brescani, the owner of a small poultry shop in Akron, Ohio, had such little regard for bankers that he would not entrust even a safe deposit box with his savings. "Suppose they'd think up some way to take even that," he explained.[21]

Hoarding was pervasive: heavy bank withdrawals produced a record high amount of money in circulation by February 15, and a $900 million increase over the course of the month. The Postal Savings System had become a haven for large numbers of Americans. "Go down to the Postal Savings in the post office," advised one observer, "and take a look at the money being deposited there and draw your own conclusions." The Detroit Federation of Labor pointed out that postal savings deposits were not loaned to postal officials. "Uncle Sam does not do business that way." One North Carolinian revealingly wanted "the post-office inspector [to] be a bank examiner also." Postal savings deposits surpassed the $1 billion mark that February, and they rose a further 10.6 percent in March. The total amount on deposit had increased by almost 500 percent over the previous three years. Americans trusted the government's savings bank.[22]

The Bank Holiday

Franklin D. Roosevelt was inaugurated on March 4, just as the banking meltdown struck the center of the nation's financial system.

Shortly after four o'clock that morning, the governor of New York State had declared a bank holiday. Illinois followed suit ten minutes later. Stock and commodity exchanges across the nation—including the New York Stock Exchange and Chicago Board of Trade—closed as well. "We were in a terrible situation," recalled Secretary of Labor Frances Perkins. "Banks were closing. The economic life of the country was almost at a standstill." Even as the financial system collapsed around them, however, autonomy remained paramount to influential bankers. "I believe in all seriousness that the emergency could not be greater," J. P. Morgan & Company partner Thomas W. Lamont Jr. wrote Roosevelt at the end of February. Yet he and other leading New York bankers recommended that no federal action be taken. Senator Carter Glass also advised the president-elect not to declare a bank holiday. But Roosevelt disregarded these financial authorities and declared a four-day national bank holiday commencing March 6.[23]

The bank holiday halted financial activity nationwide, as the Department of the Treasury permitted banks to perform only a severely limited set of functions, including making change and providing access to safe deposit boxes. In Grants Pass, Oregon, bearded prospectors from the surrounding hills were fortunate enough to possess a commodity they could exchange for currency at the town's banks: gold dust. Meanwhile, millions of Americans whose labors had not secured personal gold reserves attempted to navigate daily life without money. Three traveling salesmen, stranded in North Carolina with no access to funds, struck upon a creative solution to their predicament. They marched down to a bus station and had themselves shipped as freight COD.[24]

Despite the disruption Roosevelt's proclamation created, there was a sense of relief that action finally had been taken. "No money, no banks," the influential humorist-philosopher Will Rogers noted. Nevertheless, he observed that "America hasn't been as happy in three years." The bank holiday gave pause to some, however. It threatened to further burden people who could little afford any additional strain. In Boston, Mayor James Michael Curley (D) sought to shield the vulnerable during this crisis. He secured assurances from local electric and gas companies that no one would lose service. Curley also instructed the city's water department not to perform any shutoffs. The welfare department cared for families lacking credit or access to currency. It was an unfortunate time to be due for release at the state prison in Elmira, New York. Those inmates were delayed in tasting freedom because discharge payments—needed for their train fares—entailed the use of checks.[25]

Such worries did not press upon the president of the California Bankers Association. J. F. Sullivan Jr. was incensed over the recent conduct of the nation's depositors. He lambasted these "yellow shirkers who withdrew their savings . . . and thereby precipitated the present situation." Sullivan was indignant that prevailing opinion held bankers, and not depositors, responsible for the banking crisis. "The persons who . . . became frightened at nothing," he contended, "and withdrew their funds to hide it at home or to store it in deposit vaults were as unpatriotic as the slackers in the war." California state senator Chris N. Jespersen (R) was incredulous: "A statement of this kind coming from the source that it does, to say the least, is unbecoming. These people are more to blame than the depositors who withdrew their accounts."[26]

Emergency Banking Act

"The first test of the sincerity of the new administration will come on the money question," the Wisconsin Equity Union declared. "If the people are to have a new deal the control of money and credits must be taken from New York bankers and given back to Congress." This farmer organization surely was disappointed when the Roosevelt administration elected to rely on much of the same financial leadership that had presided over the banking disaster. "The money changers," Roosevelt had declared in his inaugural address, "have fled from their high seats in the temple of our civilization. We may now restore the temple to the ancient truths." Yet the president did not believe that sweeping banking reform was necessary. "I've had every assurance of co-operation from the bankers," he explained.[27]

Roosevelt entered office convinced of the need for swift action to end the banking crisis. His choice for secretary of the treasury was a suitably expedient one: corporate executive William H. Woodin, whom *Business Week* described as "Big Business, holding all the orthodox views about sound money, guarantee of bank deposits." Roosevelt initially offered the position to Carter Glass. "We might just as well have Andy Mellon as Senator Glass," protested Roy L. Rickerd, president of the Farmers' Holiday Association of Oklahoma. Glass, however, had declined the post after concluding that the president-elect could not be depended on to reliably back financial orthodoxy. Although circumspection characterized Roosevelt's handling of the banking crisis, he was prepared to challenge conventional beliefs and practices. "New conditions," he affirmed, "impose new requirements upon Government and those who conduct Government." Roosevelt had hinted that inflation was necessary. He used the bank holiday to break with the gold standard. A series of measures over the following months would formalize this monetary innovation.[28]

Roosevelt's closure of the banks bought some time. Officials of the incoming administration—such as Woodin and Raymond C. Moley—worked closely with prominent holdovers from the Hoover administration, including Awalt, Secretary of the Treasury Ogden L. Mills, and Undersecretary of the Treasury Arthur A. Ballantine. But they were far from alone. "The Treasury," recalled financier James P. Warburg, "was overrun with bankers." Officials settled on a plan to save the banks by providing sufficient currency to meet public demand and gradually reopening institutions as their financial position allowed. Both the president and congressional leadership summarily approved this approach.[29]

The administration's plan was hastily given legislative form, introduced on March 9, and rushed through Congress. "I am suspicious of this railroading of bills," protested Representative Ernest Lundeen (FL-MN). "No one has told us who drafted the bill." "The bill has been driven through the House with cyclonic speed." The whole process was completed in less than eight hours. That very night, Roosevelt signed the measure into law and issued a proclamation extending the bank holiday until further notice. Moley recalled that the Emergency Banking Act was "greeted with loud shouts of approval by all articulate conservatives." The *Journal of Commerce* approvingly called the law "a sound, conservative measure."[30]

The Emergency Banking Act permitted Federal Reserve Banks to issue paper money backed by government bonds and commercial paper—with no gold reserve requirement. It authorized so-called "conservators" to reorganize illiquid national banks with the aid of Reconstruction Finance Corporation loans. There were insolvent banks that remained closed. The Reverend Billy Graham's father was convinced the North Carolina bank holding his savings would re-open. But it never did. "He had to start over from scratch," Graham remembered. Within a month, however, 80 percent of Federal Reserve System member banks and 67 percent of state-chartered banks had fully reopened, and most of the others operated on a restricted basis. The Roosevelt administration had resurrected the private banking system.[31]

The moment had presented radical possibilities for banking reform. During the debate on emergency banking legislation, Senator Robert M. La Follette Jr. observed: "The Government can do almost anything with the banks of the country in this situation except to leave them to themselves. We at last have reached a situation in which no one will deny that the Government and the Government alone can restore the financial activity of the Nation." La Follette and Senator Edward P. Costigan (D-CO) presented the president with a plan for "a Federal banking system entirely within the control of the Federal government." Civic organizations also had called for government banking. John Dewey submitted a proposal on behalf of the leftist academics and intellectuals of the League for Independent Political Action designed to "make our banking system function as a social institution rather than as an instrument in the hands of private promoters." The League "look[ed] forward to the eventual nationalization of banks and credit." The Chicago Federation of Labor wired Roosevelt that due to the "financial morass" created by "the incompetent and dishonest bankers," the organization had resolved in favor of "a new deal which will lead to government ownership of all banks." The Public Ownership League of America agreed that "the Government . . . should assume the ownership and control of money, credit and banking."[32]

The small circle of men who formulated the administration's response to the banking emergency disregarded heterodox financial perspectives. Moley recalled that during the bank holiday he and Woodin "were determined to exclude from the group of major participants . . . all the reputedly radical and visionary individuals who were hovering in the background with novel, even revolutionary, ideas." The Nebraska Farmers Union observed that "a great many of us on the outside of the marble counters feel that we could tell the president a lot about banking." But when a decision needed to be made about the future of banking, the administration had consulted the bankers. The organization's journal concluded, "There is no getting away from the reality that he who owns controls."[33]

Investigate and Expose

The Emergency Banking Act had addressed the immediate crisis, but comprehensive banking legislation remained outstanding. And revelations about the banking fraternity were emerging that portended far-reaching reform. Senator George W. Norris had publicized the full extent of financial monopoly, while a congressional investigation was uncovering the details of leading bankers' reckless use of depositor funds and fraudulent promotion of securities. Labor leader John P. Frey spearheaded this movement to draw back the curtain on the banking fraternity. An iron molder by trade, Frey was a veteran union official and committed craft unionist who had begun working full-time at the age of twelve. Frey's rise to union leadership began when he was elected president of his local in Worcester, Massachusetts, after confronting a foreman who kicked a Swedish immigrant molder. He went on to become a personal friend and close adviser of Samuel Gompers, and he authored studies on a variety of labor issues. During the Depression, Frey decided to examine how finance achieved its influence. "I have, for many years, believed that Wall Street siphoned off about all the loose wealth which was created. . . . My present purpose has been to indicate the mechanism—interlocking directorates by which the job is done."[34]

Frey's research traced the numerous corporate directorships that bankers occupied. "When the president or the chairman of the board of directors of one of the large New York banks makes a public statement," he explained, "he also speaks directly through his board of directors to hundreds of corporations who depend upon him for credit." Frey concluded that "the political, industrial and commercial influence which the bankers exert, the part they take in shaping national and international relations, could not be adequately described by anything less than a series of books." Andrew Furuseth, president of the International Seamen's Union, was appalled at what Frey's research documented. Furuseth was a legend in his own time whose long struggle to ameliorate the often-brutal lives of sailors had won him the title "Abraham Lincoln of the Sea." This austere eminence proposed that Frey replace the terms "banker and director" for the subjects of his study with "racketeer."[35]

In late January 1933, Frey's research attracted attention when he testified before Congress that the directors of the eight largest New York banks held a total of 3,741 corporate directorships. Senator Hugo L. Black (D-AL) reported that the committee received "many favorable comments upon your testimony." "Stick with this banker racket and you will find the people with you," advised J. Whidden Graham of New York City, a lifelong apostle of the single tax. A Philadelphian proposed a bank boycott, urging Frey to "start a movement to have people never to bank their money." The acclaim prompted the Chicago Federation of Labor to boast: "Labor may feel proud that it is a man from its ranks who has done this magnificent piece of work."[36]

Frey's testimony piqued Senator Norris's interest. This highly respected legislator was the son of a struggling Ohio farm family who had taught school to pay for his legal education. First elected to the House in 1902, Norris emerged as a key congressional leader of the Progressive movement. His critical view of financial interests was

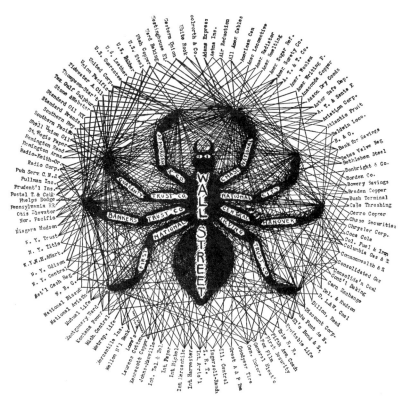

Fig. 1 The Spider of Wall Street. Courtesy of the International Association of Machinists and Aerospace Workers.

forthrightly stated on the eve of the American entry into World War I, when he charged bankers with favoring a conflict they would profit from at the cost of many lives. "We are going into war upon the command of gold. We are going to run the risk of sacrificing millions of our countrymen's lives in order that other countrymen may coin their lifeblood into money." The Great Depression posed another moment of national crisis, and Norris again confronted the culpability of bankers. He delivered an address to the Senate on the power that bankers wielded through interlocking directorates. Norris also represented financial monopoly visually with the aid of an eight-foot square chart that Frey had prepared. It featured a spider labeled "Wall Street" in the middle of its web with legs bearing the names of eight large banks.

The strands of the spider's web connected these banks to the names of 120 corporations arranged around the chart's perimeter. His fellow senators listened intently and inspected the chart carefully.[37]

Norris held that financial monopoly dominated economic life: "We are gradually reaching a time, if we have not already . . . when the business of the country is controlled by men who can be named on the fingers of one hand, because those men control the money of the Nation." Norris's searing condemnation of concentrated economic power urged reform. "How much longer will we stand for it before we realize that we are just hired men of corporations; that we are just slaves; that we have nothing to say about anything that shall be done unless we get the consent of some great big corporation which through its interlocking directorates controls practically every avenue of human activity?"[38]

Proceedings on the floor of the Senate had to compete with the dramatic events transpiring in its hearing rooms, where Wall Street was being exposed as unscrupulous and even criminal. Senator Peter Norbeck (R-SD) had retained Ferdinand J. Pecora as chief counsel of the Committee on Banking and Currency's investigation of the Great Crash. Both Norbeck and Pecora had supported Theodore Roosevelt's Progressive Party in 1912, and they also shared modest origins that contrasted sharply with many of the bankers called before the committee. Norbeck, an unpretentious but physically imposing presence, had been born on his Scandinavian immigrant parents' homestead in a dugout cellar carved from the prairies of Dakota Territory. Prior to entering politics, he found business success as an artesian well driller. In the Senate, his legislative efforts focused on aiding farmers. Pecora had emigrated to New York from Sicily with his parents. He left school at fifteen to help support his six younger siblings, but managed to work his way through City College of New York and New York Law School. He had gained familiarity with white-collar crime while serving as chief assistant district attorney of New York City.[39]

The hearings these two men convened served as a scathing public rebuke to Wall Street. Most notably, the committee exposed National

City Bank chairman Charles E. Mitchell to public opprobrium. This banker's family circumstances had afforded him advantages that were only magnified as he rose in the financial world. Mitchell was the descendant of a colonial New England family and a graduate of Amherst College. His father was a successful businessman who served as the mayor of Chelsea, Massachusetts. When young Charles had wanted a pony, the elder Mitchell purchased one for him. First and foremost a salesman, Mitchell led his bank's aggressive campaign to sell stocks and bonds to the public during the 1920s. In a move the noted advertising executive Bruce F. Barton deemed "revolutionary," Mitchell established sales offices and trained his employees to seek out investors. He believed that the ability to "come up smiling day after day" could "carry a man to the top and keep him there." Ever the outspoken optimist, as late as August 1929, Mitchell had likened the stock market to "a weather-vane pointing into a gale of prosperity." The financial world venerated "Sunshine Charley." One awestruck subordinate reverently lauded his boss's genius, comparing Mitchell's mind in action to "a great wheel in a Power House." Mitchell harbored no doubt about his own superiority: he traveled exclusively by special train and once fired an employee who had dared to discreetly inform him that the fly of his pants was unbuttoned.[40]

But this powerful banker's time was at an end. The committee's work shone a bright light on activities that outraged the nation, including the disquieting fact that National City Bank had shamelessly promoted its own stock, selling a total of almost two million shares for inflated values. Moreover, it had engaged in short selling of these shares over the course of this lucrative multiyear sales campaign. The revelations did not end with these illegalities, however. It was further divulged that National City Bank had established a $2.4 million fund for extending loans to its executives following the Great Crash — not more than 5 percent of which had been repaid. Over a three-year period, Mitchell himself had received almost $3.5 million in bonuses. This disclosure prompted Senator Smith Wildman Brookhart (R-IA) to suggest that it would "be a good idea . . . to consider regulating the salaries of these national-bank presidents." It was further revealed that Mitchell had sold his wife National City Bank stock to create a paper loss of $2.8 million and evade income tax payments.[41]

By the time the committee dismissed Mitchell, his personal and professional reputation had hit rock bottom. "The best way . . . to restore confidence in the banks," an indignant Senator Burton K. Wheeler proposed, "would be for them to remove these crooked presidents from the banks and treat them the same as Al Capone." The *New Republic* was led to conclude the banking system suffered less from individual greed than from a systemic defect: "The only answer is to dissociate banking operations entirely from the realm of private operation for profit." A month later, Mitchell was arrested at his five-story Fifth Avenue mansion for tax evasion.[42]

Mitchell's disgrace symbolized bankers' loss of authority. "Hitherto," *Catholic World* reported, "we have been but half convinced that highly respected bankers of the richest banks in the world were but magnified shell-game gamblers. But now we know it." It was not clear whether the private banking system could ever be redeemed. *Christian Century* affirmed that "nothing can be more immoral than to invite the public to give its confidence again to a type of financial leadership which has demonstrated that it is unworthy of confidence." Many Americans believed bankers stood convicted as the cause of the Great Depression. "All the best minds of the country have been for three years trying to find out who stopped the pump and why," noted John Possehl, general president of the International Union of Operating Engineers, "but we are at last discovering through investigation that the intricate system of high finance did the trick."[43]

"Many Attacks"

Anger toward finance was palpable. A restive public censured banker avarice with rising vehemence. In January 1932, Herman J. Hahn, a minister of the German Evangelical Synod of North America, had prepared a radio address that Buffalo's WGR censored due to its threateningly "radical" tone. One of his pronouncements was that although the nation's "wealth production has been increasing by leaps and bounds," prosperity failed to benefit the American people, because this bounty had been "*piped off* . . . into the capacious, Gargantuan pockets of . . . high priests of finance—leaving the people a mere trickle." The tightening grip of the Depression had only strengthened such sentiments, placing Hahn's perspective firmly within the realm of prevailing opinion. A few days before Roosevelt's inauguration, Senator Huey P. Long Jr. (D-LA) had confronted an associate of the House of Morgan at the Mayflower Hotel. "I don't like you and your goddamned banker friends!" he growled.[44]

Millions of Americans likely would have made the same declaration. Shortly after the bank holiday, mayor of Detroit Frank Murphy (D) fired a former banker from his position on a city commission. "I propose to have no bankers in my administration," he avowed. When former Iowa state senator Lars J. Skromme (R) addressed a meeting of farmers, he knew how to win over the audience at the outset: "with an assault on the international bankers." During a trial of two bankers in Philadelphia, the courtroom audience "cheered when an attack was made by a witness on bankers in general." The North Dakota Farmers' Holiday Association resolved that it had "declared war against the International Bankers and the lesser money barons of the country." Numerous Americans were convinced that the future welfare of the nation necessitated striking against the power of bankers. James Maloney, president of the Glass Bottle Blowers Association, thought that "just a few individuals through their control of credits are in possession of the wealth of this country and are able to direct and control the destinies of the American people." He insisted that "this yoke must be thrown off if we are to continue to remain a free people."[45]

The banking fraternity's power weighed heavily on the seasoned Farmers Union activist G. T. McElderry, who informed his senator that "farmers were producers of wealth while Bankers were parasites, that produce no wealth, but lived by the sweat of the other fellow's brow." This common belief fortified support for government banking. "I very strongly favor public ownership of banks and credit. The people whose industry and intelligence support the credit of these United States should be entitled to that credit direct," explained Minneapolis locomotive engineer Maurice W. Murphy. "We are under no obligation to private individuals who have had the complete control of banking and credit for private profit — and the impoverishment of the people."[46]

Dissatisfaction over the existing financial order could prompt a desire for direct confrontation with the bankers. A member of the Workers Unemployed Union of Oelwein, Iowa, predicted, "I hardly think that the big bankers will give up the racket of loaning the people their own money, without a fight. Direct action will be necessary before they will get off the people's Backs." A resolution was presented in the West Virginia state legislature to petition Congress for a law "providing for the beheading of the officers and directors of any National Bank that fails." One New Yorker felt so enraged about bankers forcing wage cuts that he was "willing to lead a gang like myself and blow up every one of their homes and to make sure that all their families are in it at the time." While many Americans disapproved of such a sentiment, they also felt sympathy for the motivation behind it. Accordingly, bankers looked to the future with apprehension.[47]

8

The Banking Act of 1933

"Roosevelt Saved the System"

"For many years in this land of ours we have had a government of the bankers, by the bankers, and for the bankers," Representative Charles V. Truax (D-OH) protested following the national bank holiday. This reign was now precarious. President Roosevelt's decision to end the era of the gold dollar signaled a new financial order was at hand. "All banking laws need revision," editorialized Philadelphia's *Public Ledger*. "Obviously, banking policies are due for a change," affirmed the *Stockton Daily Evening Record*. "Public sentiment has been so strong that it cannot be ignored or muzzled." A spirited national conversation explored guaranteeing bank deposits, expanding the Postal Savings System, and nationalizing banking.[1]

The Banking Act of 1933 forced bankers to adapt to a new regime whose contours practitioners of banking politics had molded over the course of many years. Those who had long struggled to blunt Wall Street's power achieved a striking victory: this reform curbed financial centralization and speculation by separating commercial banking and investment banking. Banks either could accept deposits and provide loans, or raise funds for clients in financial markets. They no longer could do both. The decades-long agitation of workers and farmers for bank deposit guaranty saw results as well. Establishment of the Federal Deposit Insurance Corporation brought peace of mind to millions of small savers and unprecedented stability to the financial system. Recurring banking crises came to an end. Although government exercised new authority over finance, the private banking system still existed. Thus, while the Banking Act of 1933 constituted a triumph for banking politics advocates, financial interests had been granted a reprieve.[2]

"The People Are Aroused"

In the spring of 1933, a chorus of voices called for replacing banker control of the financial system with public control. One self-deprecating resident of Coffee, California, made plain his perspective on the issue. "Now to a hill-billy, it seems the best thing to do would be to call in all the letters of marque that the banks have been raiding under, and the government take over the business and make all the profit for the people." Many Americans found hope in the prospect of government banks that served the commonweal. An Akron, Ohio, resident anticipated the day of public banks when "you . . . could proudly say 'I am depositing my money in my bank,' and when you borrow you would pay not more than 2 per cent. and when you paid your interest you would say 'I am paying my interest to my own government, through my own government, through my own bank and not to 'Andy' [Mellon] or 'J.P.' [Morgan].'" An Astoria, Oregon, resident believed that "were our Uncle Sammy to establish banks backed by the U.S. treasury," such institutions "would bring forth all the hidden wealth in the country." A railroad freight checker in Ithaca, New York, demanded swift action to inaugurate government control over banking. And he entreated the president not to shrink from extraordinary measures. "If there is no law that will allow you to take them [banks] over in the name of the government, then let Congress create one," he urged. "If the Supreme Court should declare such a law unconstitutional, then let Congress increase membership of that court until you have a safe majority of its members."[3]

Organized groups of workers and farmers advanced the grassroots demand for government banking. "Now is the time to make the strong and insistent demand for government ownership of banks," the Detroit Federation of Labor declared. "Now while the people are aroused." The Colorado State Federation of Labor, the Lake County Central Labor Union of Indiana, the National Farmers' Holiday Association, and the National Farmers Union all held similar sentiments. Soon, the idea was finding support on Capitol Hill. Representative Denver S. Church (D-CA) called nationalization "a proposal that appeals to me very much."[4]

The Socialist Party had advocated nationalizing the banks prior to the Great Crash, but the banking crisis brought its financial reform program new attention. The party's 1932 presidential nominee Norman Thomas had made a respectable showing in the general election, receiving 883,990 votes and winning over 3 percent of the vote in seven states. During the bank holiday, National City Bank complained to the police about stickers that had been affixed to their buildings, which read: "If the Socialist party were in power this bank would be open."[5]

Socialist banking ideas found a welcome at the White House. As banks were reopening, Thomas presented the president with a reform program that proposed making the Federal Reserve Banks government banks and establishing a new "publicly owned banking system" with the Postal Savings System serving as its "nucleus." Thomas also wanted to nationalize all banks that had received public assistance. "What the government has had to save, the government should keep." Other banks would be permitted to operate "for the time being," but would have to join the Federal Reserve System, divorce any investment banking affiliates, and guarantee deposits. The *Houston Post* predicted that the nation would be newly receptive to Thomas's proposals, because Americans were "only too well aware of the truth of his indictments."[6]

Representative William Lemke (R-ND) had drafted a similar proposal. The son of a prosperous German immigrant farmer, Lemke received his legal education at Yale University, and then returned to North Dakota, where he served as an official of the Nonpartisan League. Following the bank holiday, the zealous freshman congressman announced his belief that "75 percent of the people of this Nation are ready and willing to repeal the Federal Reserve Banking System if you give them a chance." The "Crime of 1920" remained fresh in Lemke's mind as he castigated the "Federal Reserve octopus" for having "increased the money in . . . circulation" during World War I "and then in 1920 and 1921 contracted it." This belief that "the international bankers and Wall Street" dominated the Federal Reserve System led Lemke to propose replacing it with the "Bank of the United States"—modeled on the Bank of North Dakota—in order to "give the Nation a banking system owned, controlled, and operated by the Government of the United States."[7]

Lemke claimed that "many of the members [of Congress] are whole-heartedly with me, but the party whip falls strong on their backs, and as yet, they are not quite willing to break." Beyond the nation's capital, however, his proposed bank met with open support. According to Minnesota's *Farmers Union Herald*, such a bank would be "an instrument of public service rather than one of private exploitation." Lemke planned to campaign on behalf of his proposal. "I intend to make a nation-wide fight for the Bank of the United States."[8]

While proposals for government banking were flourishing, bank deposit guaranty had reached the top of the political agenda. "No doubt exists," observed Senator Arthur H. Vandenberg (R-MI), "about the strength of the general demand for some practical and satisfactory system of guarantee." On Inauguration Day, the grand master of the Louisiana Masons sent a telegram to Roosevelt urging the "guaranteeing of bank deposits in full" in order to "restore confidence in banking institutions of nation." Over the next few days, the Kansas Live Stock Association's annual convention resolved in favor of "national legislation for guaranteeing bank deposits," and the American Farm Bureau Federation's board of directors wired Roosevelt to urge "governmental guarantee of the new deposits of all banks." Shortly thereafter, Edward A. O'Neal, the organization's president, insisted: "Banks must be made safe for the depositors. . . . Nothing short of government guarantee of deposits will do it."[9]

Some sufficiently alarmed businessmen endorsed guaranty. "Let's try something radical," New Jersey manufacturer Jay R. Monroe proposed. Similarly, a Southern California business leader claimed that guaranty provided the "only sound cure of this situation." The Texas Retail Dry Goods Association reported: "Merchants of Texas in the face of [the] bank situation seem to be at one in urging some measure [of] governmental guarantee of bank deposits." But leading representatives of business interests had not realigned their positions. The U.S. Chamber of Commerce would affirm that it remained "against government guaranty of deposits."[10]

Public support for guaranty was broad and adamant, however. American Federation of Labor president William Green observed: "It seems quite clear that public opinion will crystallize in favor of some form of guarantee." Senator George W. Norris sensed guaranty "'percolating' through many brains which have always bitterly opposed any system of guaranteeing deposits." A North Carolina attorney—who on "general principle" always had opposed guaranty—claimed, "It is imperative that some measure be enacted whereby deposits will be guaranteed." The largely Polish-American depositors' committee of a failed Philadelphia bank charged that "the defunct bank was mismanaged and looted, through improper and unsecured loans." They wanted "a Federal law with full guarantee of deposits." A former Chicago postal clerk who had moved to a citrus orchard in San Bernardino County, California, outlined two possible courses of action: "either an act to guarantee Bank Deposits 100% or the Federal Government must take over the entire banking system."[11]

In April, the American Bankers Association apprehensively noted the "numerous bills for various forms or degrees of Government guaranty of deposits." But the organization perceived another alarming prospect as well: "serious proposals to widen the services of the postal savings system." Once again, legislation in Congress proposed raising the postal savings deposit limit: one bill advocated $5,000, another

$7,000. Moreover, congressional support for Senator Clarence C. Dill's effort to introduce checking accounts was continuing to grow. Like many working people, an Irish-American railroad delivery clerk in Quincy, Massachusetts, insisted that the postal system affirmed the advantages of government banking. "When you mail a letter in the letter box you expect safe delivery of same. When you make a deposit in the bank why shouldn't you be protected with safe return of same?" "If the postoffice can be run by the government," he asked, "why not the banks?"[12]

Whether supporters of banking reform favored nationalization, guaranty, or an expanded Postal Savings System, all shared a commitment to curbing the power of the private banking system. And they all opposed the nation's bankers. One Californian surmised, "We should not listen to the bankers in this crisis. It is time now for the government and the people to free themselves from the bondage of the money lenders." The International Brotherhood of Electrical Workers wanted to separate banks from their investment affiliates and guarantee deposits, "preferably by making the Postal Savings banks not only repositories but . . . [adding] checking privileges." However, the union's journal noted that these popular reforms "would not end the pernicious practice now exercised by big bankers of controlling industrial and social policies through the control of credit." "Only full and unqualified public ownership of banks" would end this state of affairs and restore "real government by constituted authorities." An unnerved *Saturday Evening Post* responded by exhorting: "It seems at once futile and juvenile to turn in a sort of mental panic, as so many people are doing, to devices like the guaranty of bank deposits, Government ownership or monopoly of banks, and the nationalization of credit."[13]

"Fight the Glass Bill"

Senator Carter Glass certainly agreed with the sentiment the *Saturday Evening Post* expressed. And he had been trying to stave off radical reform with his own bill. By December 1932, the American Bankers

Association had relaxed its opposition but still asked for certain modifications. Specifically, the organization focused on preventing the separation of banks and their investment affiliates. Glass had secured an initial hearing for his legislation shortly after New Year's Day. However, Senator Huey P. Long Jr. then proceeded to block the measure. He adamantly opposed the Glass bill's promotion of branch banking. Long was known for his flamboyant, egotistical behavior as governor of Louisiana, but he did have a policy agenda, championing the interests of ordinary citizens against oil companies and the wealthy elite who had long dominated the state. His populistic policy positions and irreverent manner were tailor-made to antagonize the imperious egoist Glass, who exclaimed: "I'd vote to expel that scalawag without raising a finger to find out what the charges were against him."[14]

Long introduced an amendment prohibiting banks from operating branches outside of the municipality where they were headquartered. According to Long, "Practically every disaster from which the country is suffering is by reason of the concentration of authority and the concentration of wealth in the hands of a few." Policies that encouraged branching, therefore, conflicted with economic recovery. Long hoped to "decentralize . . . bank authority . . . [and] put the control back among the people." He led a filibuster of the Glass bill that lasted for nearly three weeks.[15]

A number of Long's colleagues supported his efforts. They were heartily approved of by Senator Elmer Thomas (D-OK), whose initial interest in financial questions had been piqued during William Jennings Bryan's 1896 presidential campaign. Thomas had been born and raised on an Indiana farm and was politically allied with the Oklahoma Farmers Union. He believed branching would ultimately result in "the centering of all the wealth of the Country in a few banks in New York, and . . . this would mean the complete domination, by these few banks, of not only the financial policies of our Country but also all other policies of our government." Ohio members of the Oil Field Workers Union shared Thomas's perspective and commended his opposition to the bill. "My sentiments," agreed the mayor of Chickasha, Oklahoma, "are to fight the Glass bill if it takes all winter." By the time the Senate had finally passed Glass's measure, the damage had been done. As the banking system descended further into crisis in February 1933, President Hoover had urged the House to pass the bill "to reestablish confidence," but President-elect Roosevelt had declined to support what he deemed an unsatisfactory reform. The bill failed to advance any further.[16]

Banking Legislation

Following the bank holiday, Glass tried again, introducing his bill two days after the Emergency Banking Act was passed. Meanwhile, Representative Henry B. Steagall was in charge of reform in the lower chamber, where deposit guaranty topped the agenda. While Glass had successfully opposed guaranteeing deposits for decades, he now faced both overwhelming public demand for guaranty and powerful congressional support for it—including from Steagall and a member of the relevant Senate subcommittee, William G. McAdoo. Glass acknowledged which way the political winds blew and muted his hostility to guaranty. But Secretary of the Treasury William H. Woodin opposed the idea, as did Roosevelt, echoing arguments that bankers had made for years. "We do not wish," he stated, "to make the United States Government liable for the mistakes and errors of individual banks, and put a premium on unsound banking in the future." During the bank holiday, he had instructed former Secretary of the Treasury Ogden L. Mills to reassure leading bankers on this score. But other members of the administration supported guaranty, including Vice President John N. Garner and Jesse H. Jones, chairman of the Reconstruction Finance Corporation.[17]

Proposed inflationary measures further challenged orthodox opinion. "When we speak of inflation, the reply is that it means trouble, disaster, and greater distress," Senator Burton K. Wheeler observed. "To my mind the answer to that is that unless we can arrest the fall of prices, the distress which is ahead is infinitely worse than anything we have experienced in the past." In April, therefore, he introduced an amendment to the Agricultural Adjustment bill that sought to re-

establish bimetallism. Public and congressional support for inflationary action had continued to climb as the economy's protracted slide
dragged on. In January, one Iowan had called "inflation . . . the most
imperative need of our country today." Two months later, Senator
Peter Norbeck declared his willingness to "vote for any radical change
in our currency . . . that will lead to inflation." Wheeler's amendment
failed but demonstrated significant support by collecting thirty-three
votes.[18]

Although Roosevelt instructed Wheeler that "Bryan killed the remonetization of silver in 1896," the president supported mildly inflationary policies. He decided to endorse an amendment Elmer Thomas
had offered to the Agricultural Adjustment bill that unified inflationists by permitting the president to issue greenbacks, monetize silver,
and alter the dollar's gold content. Roosevelt's backing of the measure rested on certain modifications, however. The Thomas amendment accordingly was rewritten to place initial responsibility for increasing the money supply on Federal Reserve System open market
operations. But if this method should prove ineffective, the president
was provided with other options: issuance of up to $3 billion of green-
backs, reduction of the gold value of the dollar by as much as 50 percent, and acceptance of foreign nations' debt payments in silver—to
be issued as silver certificates. At this point, Glass made his opposition
to inflationary action public knowledge, which threatened "a political
sensation," but proved to be in vain, as the amendment was adopted.[19]

The ever-present postal savings issue joined the political struggles
over guaranty and inflation. One New York banker expressed an
anxiety that was widely shared within the banking fraternity. "If the
alarming rate of increase in the Postal Savings System continues, it
will ultimately result in the destruction of our entire banking system."
In May, Senator Thomas T. Connally (D-TX) catered to banker demands by introducing a measure to prohibit the Postal Savings System
from paying interest on its deposits. The New York State Bankers Association lobbied Congress in support of this amendment. The United
Brotherhood of Carpenters local in Cedar Rapids, Iowa, rushed to defend the government's savings bank, passing a resolution "condemn-

ing the efforts of Iowa bankers to secure the elimination of interest on Postal Savings Bank accounts." The city's Central Trades Council and the District Council of Carpenters endorsed this position as well. The Connally amendment was not adopted.[20]

In the meantime, banking reform legislation had continued to advance. The divide between Steagall and Glass over guaranty remained evident in their respective bills. The House permitted state-chartered banks that were not members of the Federal Reserve System to participate in the program, whereas the Senate denied this privilege. Steagall insisted that "any plan established for the insurance of bank deposits should embrace deposits in State banks, regardless of membership in the Federal Reserve System." Members of the Senate were pushing Glass to accept a less restricted guaranty program as well. The proposed "Federal Bank Deposit Insurance Corporation" was not scheduled to commence operations until July 1, 1934. Senator Vandenberg insisted: "The most important single contribution that can be made to the economic recuperation of the country . . . [is] immediate Federal bank-deposit insurance." He therefore inserted an amendment that provided for a temporary one-year guaranty program to take effect on July 1, 1933. Vandenberg secured this provision with the aid of a timely parliamentary maneuver that Vice President Garner devised.[21]

The bill that passed the Senate at the end of May fixed the framework of the Banking Act of 1933. In addition to guaranteeing deposits, it sanctioned branching by national banks to the extent that state laws permitted. It also established the Federal Open Market Committee to formalize the coordination of open market operations between Federal Reserve Banks. The bill included important reforms that encouraged the commercial banking sector to stress prudence rather than risk. It restricted use of Federal Reserve member banks' credit for speculative purposes. Because banks attempted to attract deposits by paying high interest rates, which created an incentive to make imprudent investments and offer risky high-interest loans, the bill prohibited the payment of interest on checking accounts and granted the Federal Reserve Board the power to regulate savings deposit interest rates (which it would implement by issuing Regulation Q). Finally, the measure required financial institutions to choose between operating as commercial banks or investment banks.[22]

Roosevelt had campaigned on separating commercial and investment banking, and in the wake of the public backlash to the recent revelations about Charles E. Mitchell and the National City Bank, opposition to this reform evaporated. United Mine Workers of America economist W. Jett Lauck had emphasized the necessity of preventing speculation one year previously, when he concluded there was a "clear and irrefutable" need for government to tame investment banking. Lauck avowed that investment banks must be prohibited from accepting deposits and "brought under strict Federal supervision and control." In the popular mind, investment banking was bracketed with Wall Street intrigue. When Senator Hiram W. Johnson (R-CA) met with Roosevelt and Woodin at the White House during the bank holiday, he urged that "the whole Wall Street crew" be "thrown into the street" in order to "allay the present fear and restore the confidence of our people."[23]

Johnson had his finger on the pulse of national opinion. "Speculative activity in America is out of control," stated a Chinese-language San Francisco newspaper. "Financial sharks have seized funds through deceitful transactions. Ordinary people have been exploited." During the early 1930s, public discussion had dwelled repeatedly on the destructive power of Wall Street. In the fall of 1930, a Pottstown, Pennsylvania, resident had foreseen a cold, hungry winter. "I hope that Wall St will never have the power again to cause such a panic upon the people." By 1933 the labor press observed that "resentment against big bankers, especially Wall Street bankers, is expressed on every hand." The public was crying out for protection against the reckless— and even criminal—financial schemes that unfolded on Wall Street. "There has never yet been a panic in this country but started in Wall Street," charged a coal dealer in Columbus Grove, Ohio, who insisted, "We must put up a determined fight against them."[24]

During the bank holiday, National City Bank had acknowledged the course of contemporary events by announcing plans to separate from its investment affiliate. Chairman of Chase National Bank Winthrop W. Aldrich (son of Nelson W. Aldrich) was so alarmed at the popular outcry that, after consulting with the noted public relations specialist Ivy L. Lee, he had preemptively announced his bank also would divorce its investment affiliate. Moreover, he endorsed a complete separation of commercial and investment banking, commenting that "the spirit of speculation should be eradicated from the management of commercial banks." The labor press heralded this unforeseen development, proclaiming that Aldrich's action constituted "smashing confirmation of every charge made by John P. Frey." The Bricklayers, Masons and Plasterers International Union of America declared: "The great banking royalty is to be stripped of its purple." The Detroit Federation of Labor, however, inferred that bankers' "fear of government ownership of banks" had caused them to "change their attitude and their practices in the hope that they may escape the fury of the storm, and continue in business." "Farmers and workers should not be misled by this," the labor organization counseled.[25]

"Monopolistic Power"

The Banking Act of 1933's separation of investment banking and commercial banking produced a less centralized financial system. But the law also contributed to concentration in the commercial banking sector by encouraging branch banks, which advocates argued allowed banks to better withstand financial stress by commanding greater resources and holding more diverse assets. Glass said he was "thoroughly convinced" that branch banks were a "real necessity . . . in order to save the situation that now confronts the country."[26]

Bankers had remained divided over branching. Charles F. Zimmerman, president of the First National Bank of Huntingdon, Pennsylvania, threatened that if the American Bankers Association did not oppose branching, unit bankers would be forced to find a means "to be heard through some other avenue." Whereas Arthur Reynolds, chairman of Bank of America, claimed that if "branch banking [had] been generally permitted . . . hundreds of bank failures would have been avoided." Due to this friction, the American Bankers Association re-solved at its 1932 convention that "it should not attempt at this time to formulate a definite attitude aimed to commit all types of bankers on this many-sided question."[27]

Rural Americans were particularly apprehensive about the power of large banks, especially as banking concentration had been increas-ing. The total deposits held by the nation's one hundred largest banks surged by more than 46 percent from 1924 to 1930. By then, a mere 1 percent of the nation's banks held over 46 percent of total bank re-sources, with just twenty-four New York banks controlling 15 percent of all resources. In the aftermath of the bank holiday, the *Progressive* specifically urged against further banking concentration. "There is danger of setting up a new financial structure in which the big banks will emerge with dominant power over the banking business. . . . We do not believe that simply because a bank is a BIG bank that it is nec-essarily a SOUND bank." Recent events in Detroit and Nevada lent credence to this viewpoint.[28]

During the banking crisis, Senator Thomas J. Walsh (D-MT) had apprehensively imagined "how our financial structure would be shaken to its very foundation should disaster overtake . . . the chain of banks comprising the Bank of Italy system." (Bank of Italy recently had been renamed Bank of America.) The federal government prevented such a catastrophe from occurring: the Reconstruction Finance Corporation extended over $90 million in loans to Bank of America and the affili-ated Bankitaly Mortgage Company. And A. P. Giannini's bank was af-forded special treatment during the bank holiday, since with one mil-lion depositors it was considered what we now call "too big to fail." The large amount of government financial aid given to giant banks re-veals that as a whole they were no more sound than the nation's small unit banks. During the first five months of the RFC's existence, it lent $113 million to Chicago banks—almost 80 percent of which went to one institution. In total, the agency's lending to large banks was in proportion to their overall share of the banking system. Of the $950 million the RFC loaned to banks and trust companies in 1932, a mere twenty-six institutions received $330 million.[29]

Deposit Guaranty

While bankers were deeply divided over the question of branching, proposals for guaranty routinely elicited angry reactions from the banking fraternity. There were exceptions, such as Gustav J. Moen of the First National Bank of Canton, South Dakota, who previously had "never favored a guarantee of deposits." Competition from postal savings, however, compelled him to conclude that it was necessary "to perfect some national guarantee of bank deposits." But one North Carolina banker articulated the prevailing opposition to guaranty among bankers when he categorically declared: "I am entirely opposed to any guarantee of bank deposits on any basis whatsoever."[30]

The controversies surrounding guaranty and branching loomed over the June deliberations of the conference committee charged with reconciling the House and Senate bills. The House won an important concession: state-chartered banks were granted the opportunity to participate in the Temporary Federal Deposit Insurance Fund (precursor of the Federal Deposit Insurance Corporation) when it commenced operation on January 1, 1934. Deposits up to $2,500 would be fully covered. But House conferees capitulated on branching to secure this provision. National banks were free to establish branches to the extent permitted state banks under state law. "After a great deal of deliberation," Representative T. Alan Goldsborough recounted, "we were forced to the conclusion that we should yield, because we could not have gotten any sort of legislation if we had not yielded." "A majority of the Senate conferees did not want any bank-deposit insurance bill at all," he explained. A Federal Reserve System official recalled that Glass had been "very unhappy" about guaranty. Glass had resigned himself to the program's inevitability, however, concluding that "it will be better to deal with the problem in a cautious and conservative way than to have ourselves run over in a stampede." The branching feature, therefore, was a concession Glass extracted in return for acquiescing to guaranty.[31]

The administration's position on the banking bill had remained unsettled throughout the spring. Senator Josiah William Bailey (D-NC) reported: "We hear one day that the President is for it, and the next day that he is not." Even after the House and Senate had passed legislation incorporating guaranty, Roosevelt remained resistant to the idea. In reaction to this uncertain situation, the Allied Building Trades Council of Buffalo anxiously registered its demand for a city-owned and -operated savings bank "until such time" as deposits were guaranteed. The American Bankers Association instructed its members to contact the White House and urge a veto. "The American Bankers Association fights to the last ditch deposit guarantee provisions . . . as unsound, unscientific, unjust and dangerous," declared Francis H. Sisson, the organization's president. The popular demand for guaranty was overpowering, however. In a meeting that included Roosevelt, Glass, and Woodin, Comptroller of the Currency J. F. T. O'Connor stressed that the political reality was that "people were impatient and demanded security on deposits." Roosevelt followed the politically expedient course and signed the bill into law on June 16. *Commercial West* expressed relief that the legislative process had concluded. "As long as it was before Congress . . . with no one knowing just what might happen, bankers felt that it was a constant menace."[32]

"Big Things Are Happening"

The achievement of deposit guaranty was a seminal moment for practitioners of banking politics. A further tenet of Bryanism was ratified when the United States departed the gold standard. "Big things are happening," Representative Wright Patman observed. "We did in a half day yesterday what there was almost a war over thirty-five years ago — going off the gold standard." Roosevelt was determined that the gold standard must no longer constrain management of the monetary system. "We are now off the gold standard," he remarked privately after signing the bank holiday declaration. This directive stopped gold transactions. It was followed by an executive order a few days later that extended the suspension of gold payments. Over the following months, a series of policies confirmed this new financial order. In April, Roosevelt issued an executive order that prohibited gold hoarding by requiring the surrender of private holdings of gold coins, gold certificates, and gold bullion to the Federal Reserve System in exchange for dollars. The transfer of gold to foreign nations was prohibited shortly thereafter. In June, Congress finalized the break when it annulled gold clauses in legal contracts so debts would be paid in dollars, not gold. The legal tender dollar was now the monetary standard. Although gold reserves still backed paper money, American citizens could no longer redeem currency for gold.[33]

Inflationists provided Roosevelt with political support during the push to give government officials greater control over the monetary system. Gold's disciples had included Glass, who claimed that deviation from the gold standard "means dishonor . . . it is immoral." The octogenarian goldbug J. Laurence Laughlin publicly praised Glass's objection. "We should never allow a doubt to arise as to our maintenance of the gold standard," he remonstrated. But the deflationary spiral called for abrogation of the gold standard, and many bankers accepted the administration's course of action. J. P. Morgan & Company even encouraged Roosevelt to take this step. Departing the gold standard stimulated economic activity by creating inflationary expectations. The Department of the Treasury subsequently would pursue policies that greatly increased the money supply, which grew at an annual rate of almost 10 percent between 1933 and 1937.[34]

The legal tender dollar's debut evoked less opposition from the banking fraternity than the impending inauguration of guaranteed deposits, which would necessitate increased government oversight. Bankers remained intransigent about the Federal Deposit Insurance Corporation throughout 1933. "Of course," *North Pacific Banker* stated, "the American Bankers Association should do all in its power to have this law changed." George V. McLaughlin, president of the New York State Bankers Association, declared before the American Bankers Association's annual convention that guaranty "should be eliminated" from the Banking Act of 1933. The convention contacted the White House to recommend postponing the program's implementation.[35]

The bankers' recalcitrance proved futile. Guaranty's supporters were firmly in command of the political situation. The labor press issued a warning: "Since the bankers are getting so particular about what kind of banking they want to do with other people's money. . . . May we rise to remark, that there is one kind of bank in which an increasing number of people have a lot of confidence. We refer to the United States Postal Savings Banks." And the American Federation of Labor's annual convention put the bankers on notice: "We are in accord with the thought of further liberalizing the Postal Savings Bank."[36]

The popular judgment favoring guaranty was emphatic. After decades of agitation, public pressure had secured the enactment of a federal program to secure bank deposits. As Steagall observed: "The insurance of bank deposits is written today as a law of the land because the voice of the long suffering and long abused people arose to the point where it could not longer be ignored." The bankers' position on guaranty was utterly out of step with the political reality. Vandenberg identified the American Bankers Association's opposition to be a "mistake . . . an attitude which tends to close the door to any future suggestions that association may have." The Temporary Federal Deposit Insurance Fund became operative as planned on January 1, 1934.[37]

During the guaranty debate, some bankers sought a silver lining in the proposition. *Coast Banker* hopefully suggested that "Postal Savings may be eliminated . . . [if] insurance of bank deposits goes through." In September, Comptroller O'Connor said as much when he told the American Bankers Association's annual convention that once guaranty took effect, "Congress would be justified in repealing the Postal Savings Law." The assembled bankers "vigorously applauded" in response. In October, O'Connor again asserted before an audience of bankers that guaranty had made postal savings redundant. Postmaster General James A. Farley hastened to assure Americans there was "not a chance" that postal savings would be discontinued. He was not, however, interested in "put[ting] my department into the banking business."[38]

A. P. Giannini—a valued Roosevelt supporter and personal friend of O'Connor—also insisted that guaranty made postal savings superfluous. Giannini had founded the Bank of Italy in San Francisco in 1904, after marrying the daughter of a wealthy real estate investor. The fledgling institution prospered following the Great 1906 San Francisco Earthquake. Giannini had removed its records and assets before the ensuing fire destroyed most of the city. Meanwhile, San Francisco's other banks did not dare to open their fire-proof vaults before they had cooled out of fear that the contents would ignite if a fresh supply of oxygen was introduced. Giannini's bank consequently was able to operate during a pivotal period while his competitors remained closed. He subsequently established an extensive branching system by circumventing California law in order to purchase smaller institutions and incorporate them into his growing network of banks. The nation's chief proponent of branching, Giannini wanted to expand his Bank of America nationwide, and he claimed that guaranty would "make postal savings banking unnecessary."[39]

No one was better positioned to profit from more permissive branching laws than the leading banker of the West. Giannini claimed that the new law "is the forerunner of legislation which eventually will extend branch banking to a nationwide basis." The spread of branching that Giannini envisioned already was apparent just months after Roosevelt signed the new law. "Extension of branch banking . . . has been marked since the passage of the federal bank act," *Trust Companies* reported. By 1936 only nine states prohibited branch banks.[40]

An appreciative American people derived immediate, substantial benefit from the Banking Act of 1933. Its regulatory safeguards helped to usher in a period of unequaled economic stability. Banking panics had been a recurrent feature of American life for over a century. And bank failures had occurred regularly. Yet, suddenly, banking crises no longer precipitated severe economic downturns. Americans no longer lived with a foreboding sense of anxiety over the safety of their savings. The American people came to enjoy a new sense of security.[41]

The private banking system was another beneficiary of the Roosevelt administration's actions. In 1934 Utah banker Marriner S. Eccles noted that "had it not been for the Government support given to the banking system by the Roosevelt Administration, there would be no private banking system in operation today." "We were close to so-cial revolution in the Spring of 1933," the wealthy department store owner Edward A. Filene averred. Years later, the gravity of this histori-cal moment remained palpable. Financier Sidney J. Weinberg—"Mr. Wall Street"—acknowledged that "Roosevelt saved the system.... We were on the verge of something. You could have had a rebellion; you could have had a civil war." Astute political observers—who were not uncritical of the New Deal—arrived at analogous conclusions. Farley stated that Roosevelt "saved our free enterprise system, he saved the banks." In 1932 James Michael Curley's familiarity with the distress in the nation's cities had led him to contend that the "very future of the Republic is problematical." "Few people realize how close America was to a revolution in 1932," he later observed.[42]

While the Roosevelt administration's financial reforms salvaged the existing economic order, it had taken extraordinary measures to do so. Financial orthodoxy had understood guaranty to be unthink-able and viewed the gold standard as inviolable. Paradoxically, re-pudiating sacrosanct articles of orthodox financial doctrine bolstered the private banking system. Representative Marion A. Zioncheck (D-WA) alleged that the Banking Act of 1933 "gives the bankers a greater stranglehold upon the legitimate governmental business of banking and currency and control of credit, and will make it more difficult for us to bring about a safe and sane national banking system owned and operated for and in the interest of the people of the United States." Georgia banker Eugene R. Black recognized, "We bankers got off pretty light in the Banking Act of 1933." But bankers were not out of the woods just yet. The American Federation of Labor anticipated government banking in the future. "If banking does not put its house in order so as to serve the nation honestly and well a Government banking system is almost inevitable."[43]

9

Government Programs and Mutual Aid

"Why Privately Owned Banks, Anyhow?"

In 1934 the pioneering stock market analyst Roger W. Babson remarked that "bankers are already 'getting theirs' . . . [and] it would appear that they deserve what has come to them." Such unabashed criticism from a prominent financial figure portended further reform. The Banking Act of 1933 had not quieted popular demands to transform the nation's financial system. A local of the Operative Plasterers' and Cement Finishers' International Association in Jersey City, New Jersey, "urge[d] the President . . . to continue . . . in his efforts to nationalize our money, to control our finances and to restore silver." Many working people were convinced it was imperative to annul the power that bankers exercised over the nation. "The lives of the people of this country," an Ohio union steelworker stated, "are at the mercy of a small group of economic and financial masters without social vision."[1]

Farmers and workers continued to propose government banking as the solution to this state of affairs. At the close of 1933, the Idaho State Grange and Idaho State Federation of Labor both resolved "that the government be authorized and instructed to take over all banking activities of the United States." Bankers escalated their public relations efforts in response to the challenge this political moment presented. But government provided the greatest assistance to the bankers' cause. The New Deal attended to a number of the nation's most pressing financial issues when it established programs to aid depositors, farmers, and homeowners. This development reduced public pressure for far-reaching reform of the private banking system. Simultaneously, popular interest in financial questions increasingly was directed toward the credit union movement, which attracted the efforts of more and more working people who devoted their energy to establishing these cooperative institutions, rather than pressing for broader financial reforms.[2]

"Scarcity of Money"

Following President Roosevelt's inauguration, one financial policy initiative after another endeavored to help bring about recovery. Such New Deal programs as the Home Owners Loan Corporation relieved debt burdens. A host of new financing agencies—from the Commodity Credit Corporation to the Electric Home and Farm Authority—provided liquidity to money markets. Western silverites secured the Silver Purchase Act of 1934, which expanded the monetary base through the issuance of silver certificates. The Gold Reserve Act of 1934 established a bullion standard where the gold value of the dollar was fixed at $35 per troy ounce, and only foreign governments and central banks could convert dollars into gold. This law authorized Roosevelt to reduce the dollar's gold value 41 percent, which gave foreign investors more dollars in exchange for their gold. The Department of the Treasury used the large gold inflow that resulted from devaluation to increase the money supply. However, the private banking system seemed to be undermining these efforts. In January 1934, Federal Reserve System member banks had accumulated $866 million in excess of their required reserves. One year later, their excess reserves stood at over $2 billion. Lorena A. Hickok, an investigator for the Federal Emergency Relief Administration, instructively reported that the banks in Maine "have nothing but money, and they are afraid to lend it."[3]

"We have enough money in the banks," Senator William E. Borah affirmed in January 1934. The question, he contended, was how to "put more money into circulation among the people?" The southern periodical *Progressive Farmer* predicted: "If the banks don't awaken to their responsibilities pretty soon, the government will likely go into the banking business on a permanent basis." Chairman of the Reconstruction Finance Corporation Jesse H. Jones said as much in February, when he observed that "because the banker has the power to extend or withhold credit, he has greater responsibility in the recovery program . . . than any, save President Roosevelt himself." Jones then warned: "If the banker fails to grasp his opportunity and to meet his responsibility, there can be but one alternative—government lending." His threat had public support. "I think the main trouble is with the bankers," affirmed one New Jersey railroad clerk who had been denied a loan, "and that we won't have the remedy until Uncle Sam goes into the banking business."[4]

Demands to reform the control and distribution of money and credit were heard frequently in 1934. The Farmers Union local in Cleveland County, Oklahoma, stated that it was "paramount to all other measures that the money and credit of the nation be nationalized and taken completely out of private hand[s]." The Oregon State Grange resolved that it wanted "the United States Treasury to coin and issue money and prohibit any private person or corporation from fulfilling this great public function." The seasoned agrarian firebrand Milo Reno had been an organizer for the National Farmers' Alliance in Iowa prior to emerging as a leader of the state's Farmers Union and the National Farmers' Holiday Association. He believed that "as long as we permit . . . the Wall Street bankers to control our currency as they see fit, we can never hope for permanent prosperity."[5]

Practitioners of banking politics saw scarce money as the primary obstacle to recovery. "There is scarcity of money," the Reverend Charles E. Coughlin declared, "a man-made, bookkeeping scarcity

. . . so that the money-lenders and changers can profit and the non-money-changers can suffer." He argued this circumstance made it imperative to displace the "great central bankers" who dominated the banking system. Coughlin's objection to financial monopoly provided coherence to the evolving collection of heterodox reforms he promoted, which included "establishment of a Government Bank of Control" to "issue both currency and credit," and "complete nationalization of all credit." Unlike the varying reforms Coughlin advanced, Representative Wright Patman maintained a consistent focus on the Federal Reserve System in his denunciations of financial monopoly. He contended that the influence "Mr. Mellon, Mr. Morgan, and Mr. Mitchell" exercised over the Federal Reserve Bank of New York gave them "more weight and influence in the control, issuance, and distribution of money and credit than all the rest of the people in the Nation combined." In 1934 Patman told his fellow Texans that the Federal Reserve Bank of Dallas was not furnishing adequate credit to business. "The Federal Reserve officials of this Nation should be ashamed of themselves," he concluded. "Federal Reserve Banks should be taken over by the Government."[6]

When Coughlin and Patman discussed central banking, they dwelt on troubling questions of unaccountable, concentrated power. Coughlin afforded small banks slight notice, once even alluding to "honest little local bankers." The threat that financial monopoly posed to an ideal of community life was his foremost concern. Coughlin's radio addresses regularly depicted inaccessible financial institutions where shadowy figures manipulated the levers of the economy. The impact of "bigness" on local communities sustained Patman's preoccupation with finance as well. A staunch advocate of local business, he led the decade's political battle against the proliferation of chain stores. Patman's interest in banking partly arose from his commitment to ensuring that small businesses had sufficient access to credit. He called small banks that actively granted loans—rather than collecting profits through "just buying Government bonds" and levying deposit account fees—"a great asset in a community." Patman's financial criticisms targeted "the present system of a few bankers controlling the volume, issuance, and distribution of money."[7]

"Nationalization of Banking"

Although public criticism of finance often focused on large banks, the entire banking fraternity was in a precarious position. "Even 25 years ago such a word as 'bankster' would have been blasphemous," *Time* commented. "But not now. . . . If keepers of other people's money continue to lose caste at the present rate, 'banker' may some day be an insult." One Tennessee woman stated that "most of the bankers . . . [have] been crooked, that is how they became wealthy, by cheating the honest man." A Michigan carpenter, union leader, and former state representative intemperately proposed a "law giving an eight day holliday [*sic*] on Bankers," which, he clarified, "means an open season."[8]

Government banks continued to appeal to an American public that was thoroughly disparaging of bankers. "Nationalizing banks is nothing . . . radical in any way," contended an Italian-American chemical worker in Ellwood City, Pennsylvania. "Congress has the power to coin + regulate money." A German-American farmer in Spink County, South Dakota, believed that "private control of money must be changed to public control." He proposed to achieve this transformation through the "repeal of all private banking laws and the establishment of a United States government-owned-and-controlled bank; controlled 100% by the government in the interest of all people." Oakland union electrician John J. Young asked: "Why privately owned banks, anyhow? The R.F.C. itself performs many of the functions of the bank, why not go a step further and inaugurate federal owned and controlled banks for commercial banking, and also extend the postal savings system to receive unlimited deposits?"[9]

Worker and farmer organizations pressed the public demand for government banking. The American Federation of Teachers wanted federal legislation that would empower local governments to establish municipal banks. Plans for inaugurating state banks circulated as well. In 1934 the Farmer-Labor Party of Minnesota, the Montana Farmers Union, and the Oregon State Grange all resolved in favor of establishing government banks in their respective states. Most public banking proposals focused on federal banks. A number of farmer organizations in the Midwest and the West threw their support behind nationalization. The Washington State Grange "favor[ed] the ownership and operation of all banks in our country by the Federal Government." The state Farmers Unions of Iowa, Missouri, and Montana also demanded that the national government own and operate the banking system. This enthusiasm for public banking led the National Farmers Union to adopt a legislative program that sought "Government ownership of banking and credit."[10]

Labor organizations expressed similar interest in government banking. After censuring bankers for attempting "to control government through their power to withhold credit," the American Federation of Teachers resolved that the federal government should operate its own banking system. The Oregon State Federation of Labor concluded the Banking Act of 1933's promotion of branching meant that "only those who are on the inside with the banking groups will be able to get accommodations from the banks," and therefore declared "in favor of the government ownership of all banking institutions in the United States." The state Federations of Labor in Montana, Oklahoma, and Washington resolved in favor of nationalization as well. The Amalgamated Association of Iron, Steel and Tin Workers of North America wanted to nationalize the banking system "so the people may have a safe place to deposit their money and be able to get loans at a reasonable rate of interest for the purchase of homes and other legitimate needs." The demands of workers and farmers for public banking merged in Minnesota's vibrant third-party movement. The Farmer-Labor Party's 1934 platform declared: "We advocate nationalization of banking with government monopoly of money and credit, operated without profit."[11]

While calls for government banking often denied any wish to abolish the existing economic order, these demands did consistently reveal a desire for financial institutions that fostered a more equitable society and were more responsive to democratic controls. The Indiana State Federation of Labor, for example, contended that in order for organized labor "to continue under capitalism," it needed to "turn every effort toward public ownership and operation of our banking system to the end that credit can be extended for the benefit of all classes." The labor federation, therefore, wanted the national government to initiate a process that would culminate in federal ownership and operation of banks "as a public service." In the meantime, the organization insisted the Postal Savings System should be "free from all dictates of the banker's association and permitted to carry on all services usual to a bank."[12]

Support for sweeping reform of the banking system led a number of Americans to criticize the Roosevelt administration. One Farmers Union member recalled that "in his inaugural he [Roosevelt] said something about 'driving the money changers out of the Temple.'" This Kentuckian had found the president's subsequent actions disappointing. "If they were ever driven out, they must have been called back." Prominent figures, including Father Coughlin and Milo Reno, encouraged this viewpoint. In 1934 Senator Bronson M. Cutting (R-NM) publicly called failing to nationalize banking during the bank holiday "President Roosevelt's great mistake." Like Roosevelt, Cutting was born into a wealthy New York family and educated at Groton School and Harvard College. Because he suffered from tuberculosis, Cutting headed for the high desert air, establishing himself as a newspaper publisher in Santa Fe, New Mexico. Following service during World War I, he helped finance and organize the American Legion. He also amassed a political following among his adopted state's Hispanos. Cutting was sympathetic to the plight of disadvantaged people. In 1934 he introduced legislation to establish a "Federal Monetary Authority" that would control the supply of credit in the interest of promoting full employment and price stability.[13]

A magazine article Cutting published in 1934 calling for government to control banking generated thousands of supportive letters. "Here is a power controlling the very destinies of the nation," Cutting wrote. "Yet the people of the nation have no word in the selection of the men who control credit." The senator elaborated over the NBC radio network on his future plans for reforming the banking system. "The creation of a national bank which will eventually have a monopoly of the issuance of credit is . . . the most vital need of the country today." Cutting foresaw a lengthy and grueling campaign. "The fight against the abolition of the credit power of private banks will be a savage one, for their power as a unit is without equal in the country." Advocates of a more democratic banking system were spoiling for a showdown. "Push the bill the People are with you," one supporter shakily scrawled on a postcard.[14]

"Mold Public Opinion"

In the fall of 1933, the American Bankers Association still maintained that the sole problem with banking was the unwarranted intrusion of government. "The belief exists . . . that the banking system failed. That is not true. It was the political authority over banking that failed." The organization, therefore, insisted that "the demand for stricter regulation of the banking business is based upon a premise that is wholly false." Not all bankers were this self-justifying. In 1932 one Nebraska banker had implicitly questioned the wisdom of banker self-regulation. "There are too many incompetent men who manage our banking institutions," he conceded. "'Incompenent' [*sic*] takes in a mighty big territory, and would include as I see it, 'unscrupulous.'"[15]

Although bankers were not unanimous in denying culpability for the banking crisis, the banking fraternity was inclined to interpret its predicament as a public image problem. In the past, bankers had regarded advertising primarily as a means to attract business. Following the bank holiday, they increasingly viewed advertising as a device for improving the private banking system's public image. Ray A. Ilg, vice president of National Shawmut Bank, instructed his fellow bankers that "bank advertising does not have new business as its main objective. . . . Bank advertising today must mold public opinion. . . . This great mass must be considered as one of the main objectives in advertising programs." H. A. Lyon, manager of Bankers Trust Company, similarly enjoined bankers to make public relations a priority. "The public must be convinced of their own interest in banking and their individual bank. . . . [I]t requires a conscious continuing policy."[16]

Beginning in 1933, the Financial Advertisers Association began concentrating on influencing public opinion. The "theme" of its annual convention that year was "that bankers must educate the public . . . aggressively in all financial matters, and particularly in the knowledge that banks and trust companies are in reality engaged in a great public service in which the community, rather than the government, is the natural partner." Bankers were inclined to take this obligation seriously. "In the current discussion of new banking legislation," *Commercial West* acknowledged, "it is frequently said that 'control of banking, money and credit must be a government function.'" In 1934 the president of the Financial Advertisers Association advised that "good public relations—and that is largely advertising and publicity—is the surest way to combat the threat of socialized banking." Bankers were bracing for the worst. *Southern Banker* admitted: "It may be necessary to swallow some bitter pills but, if in so doing, the lethal alternative of complete government domination can be avoided, the battle may be counted won."[17]

New Deal Programs

Government action ultimately did more to relieve criticism of the private banking system than the efforts of bankers. Ironically, after bitterly opposing the Banking Act of 1933's deposit guaranty feature, bankers discovered this program improved their image. Comedian W. C. Fields's mistrust of banks led him to spread his savings across approximately three dozen different institutions. But the prospect of guaranty inspired Fields's confidence. He established new bank accounts in fifteen of the nation's largest cities at exactly the amount that government guaranteed. *North Pacific Banker* observed that shortly after guaranty's implementation, Spokane's bankers were "already report[ing] that the deposit insurance plan is bringing money back to banks." Guaranty was not the only program instituted in the first hundred days that helped relieve the political pressure on financial interests. The Roosevelt administration inaugurated important measures to protect farmers and homeowners from foreclosure and provide these groups with permanent supplies of reliable, low-cost credit.[18]

In 1936 an Iowa farmer expressed his profound sense of gratitude to Roosevelt during a presidential visit to the state. "God bless you, you saved my farm," he shouted out at the passing motorcade. Roosevelt had moved quickly to aid rural Americans. On April 3, 1933, the president sent a message to Congress requesting legislation that would "provide for the refinancing of mortgage and other indebtedness . . . which in many instances are . . . unconscionably high . . . to give sufficient time to farmers to restore to them the hope of ultimate free ownership of their own land." The resulting Emergency Farm Mortgage Act shielded farmers and ranchers from foreclosure. It authorized Federal Land Banks to issue $2 billion of bonds for refinancing farm mortgages held by financial institutions. Farmers would pay no more than 4.5 percent interest for five years, with no payment due on the principal during this period. The law also directed the Reconstruction Finance Corporation to provide $200 million for loans to help foreclosed farmers redeem their farms. Federal Land Banks disbursed over $2 billion to refinance more than 760,000 farms over the following three years.[19]

The Emergency Farm Mortgage Act provided immediate relief to hard-pressed farmers, but the Roosevelt administration also reorganized the federal agricultural credit program. On March 27, the president issued an executive order consolidating all government agricultural credit operations in the newly created Farm Credit Administration. Subsequently, the Farm Credit Act of 1933 institutionalized this arrangement, dividing the nation into a dozen regions with specialized entities for making short-term, intermediate, and long-term loans to farmers, and for providing credit to agricultural cooperatives. Federal Land Banks handled mortgages, Intermediate Credit Banks discounted financial institutions' agricultural paper, Production

Credit Corporations organized farmers into lending associations and subsequently provided for their supervision, and Banks for Cooperatives furnished credit to local agricultural cooperatives. The legislation also established the Central Bank for Cooperatives to finance larger cooperatives.[20]

The national government's mechanisms for extending agricultural credit had been restructured but not remade. William I. Myers served as governor of the Farm Credit Administration. Raised on a substantial dairy farm in Chemung County, New York, Myers was a George F. Warren protégé who had taught agricultural economics at Cornell University. Myers thought agriculture should operate with businesslike efficiency. During the 1920s, he had lobbied to get bankers to "consider farmers as business men who deserve credit." Myers worried that the Depression might lead to radical economic change and concluded that it was necessary "to save for future generations the American system of free business initiative." His efforts as a New Deal official sought to bolster the existing agricultural credit system. "The *one* thing I want to emphasize is this," he explained, "generally speaking the Farm Credit Administration is not lending Government money. . . . On the contrary, its object is to set up machinery through which farmers may obtain funds for financing their farm businesses from the investment markets at the lowest possible cost." This deliberate moderation defined the New Deal's agricultural credit program. Many farmers had hoped to transform the credit system. One Ohioan, for example, wanted "cancellation of farm mortgages," and for "the government [to] go into the banking business, giving us money at cost." But farmers noted what the New Deal achieved. Average farm mortgage rates had not dropped below 6 percent during the previous two decades. In 1934 farm mortgage rates declined to 5.8 percent, and by 1937 they were under 5 percent.[21]

Roosevelt also asked Congress to pass legislation that would protect homeowners. "The broad interests of the Nation," he declared, "require that special safeguards . . . be thrown around home ownership as a guaranty of social and economic stability." The administration sought legislation along "the general lines of the farm mortgage refinancing bill." Congress enacted the Home Owners Refinancing Act to fund the purchase of defaulted mortgages from private lending institutions. This law created the Home Owners Loan Corporation (HOLC), which redeemed foreclosed homes, advanced money for tax payments and home repairs, and refinanced mortgages. The agency extended almost $3.1 billion in loans to assist over one million homeowners. "I was saved by the Home Owners' Loan Corporation," attested the grateful owner of "a very humble home." One deeply affected woman claimed that the assistance the program provided "saved my life. I would have killed myself if I would have lost my house."[22]

Homeownership had proven elusive to generations of workers. Almost twenty years previously, two labor leaders serving in Congress had pursued home financing reform. Representatives John Ignatius Nolan (R-CA) and J. Frank Buchanan (D-IL) both supported the single tax and approached workers' housing needs with a similarly heterodox perspective. Nolan was an iron molder by trade who had served as secretary of the San Francisco Labor Council before being elected to Congress in 1912 on Theodore Roosevelt's Bull Moose ticket. His 1914 legislation proposed extending low-cost government loans to workers purchasing or constructing homes. Buchanan served as president of the International Structural Iron Workers' Union before winning election to Congress in 1910 with the aid of William Jennings Bryan's support. Prior to the election, Buchanan had played a central role in the establishment of a union-controlled bank in Chicago. His 1915 bill proposed that the Postal Savings System extend loans at 3 percent to prospective homeowners, farmers, and government—from the local to federal level—for funding public works projects.[23]

Progressive Era concerns about home lending still remained relevant in the early 1930s. In 1931 William Green noted that the existing home finance system had proven "exceedingly difficult for a wage earner." The typical mortgage was between only one and five years with a sizable lump-sum payment due at its conclusion. This arrangement could place borrowers in an especially unfavorable position if the money supply was tight upon their mortgage's expiration.

The HOLC better adapted home mortgage practices to the needs of Americans of modest means. The agency made homeownership easier to achieve by restructuring the defaulted mortgages it purchased from private lenders and by promoting the issuance of long-term mortgages with uniform payments over the life of the loan.[24]

The HOLC's establishment was followed one year later by the National Housing Act of 1934, which created the Federal Housing Administration (FHA). This legislation was the product of a committee the administration appointed to formulate housing policy. The head of this group was corporate lawyer Frank C. Walker who wanted to preserve private lending. Fellow committee member Marriner S. Eccles agreed: "I wanted the housing program to be private in character," the Utah banker stated. The FHA accordingly insured the loans of private mortgage lenders, which reduced their risk. Borrowers, as a consequence, benefited from lower interest rates and smaller down payments. The FHA reinforced practices that the HOLC had advanced by guaranteeing loans of twenty-five or thirty years and structuring mortgages around uniform payments over the full term of the mortgage. "Never in history has home ownership been so accessible to the average family," John S. Fitzpatrick, president of the New York State League of Savings and Loan Associations, stated in 1938. During the first quarter century of the FHA's operation, the percentage of American families living in their own homes increased from 45 percent to 62 percent. By providing farmers and homeowners with more affordable credit, the Roosevelt administration had reduced their incentive to push for sweeping reform of the financial order.[25]

Credit Unions

Government measures to make the private financial system more responsive to the needs of working people were joined by their own mutual aid efforts. During the 1930s, the civic energy of workers and farmers focused increasingly on the credit union movement. The establishment of labor banks during the 1920s had prefigured this push. Labor banks pioneered such services for working people as un-

secured small personal loans, low-minimum-balance checking accounts, and extended operating hours. But the banking crises of the
Great Depression dealt a severe blow to labor banking: between October 1929 and June 1933, eighteen labor banks closed, merged, or sev-
ered their affiliation with organized labor. By this latter date, only four
labor banks remained, prompting union members to question the
wisdom of operating them. After the American Flint Glass Workers
Union's bank closed during the Toledo bank crash of 1931, a member
of the union said, "Leave the banks to the bankers."[26]

As labor banking declined, however, credit unions swelled in
number and financial resources. Credit unions were more limited in
their operations than labor banks. They focused on providing their
members with opportunities for thrift and affordable small loans. The
nation's first credit union—St. Mary's Co-operative Credit Association—received its charter from the state of New Hampshire in 1909.
The state's bank commissioners anticipated the new institution would
"afford them [members] a means of protection from the exactions of
the loan shark." These abusive lenders advanced short-term, high-
interest loans to workers who lived payday to payday. All too often,
borrowers became ensnared in a cycle of usurious debt payments. A
1907 study of New York City families revealed that almost half of those
with annual incomes under $700 required small loans. "There are
times when a poor man must borrow money," explained one Brotherhood of Locomotive Engineers member. "The poor man with nothing
but his salary, or his household furniture as collateral, has been forced
to go to the loan sharks."[27]

Roy F. Bergengren Sr. stressed the lending function of credit
unions, charging that "the genus 'loan shark' . . . is a pariah, exploiting
human necessity, getting fat on human misery." "There is no place for
him in a civilized society," he avowed. The son of a Swedish immigrant
doctor, Bergengren could have used his Harvard Law School degree
to pursue a lucrative legal career. Instead, he returned to his hometown of Lynn, Massachusetts, and represented working-class clients
beset by chronic underemployment, crowded tenements, and ruth-

less loan sharks. Bergengren's interest in urban reform led him to campaign successfully for election as the city's commissioner of finance. In 1917 Bergengren's municipal activism brought him to the attention of the wealthy social reformer Edward A. Filene, the department store owner who bankrolled the credit union movement. Following Bergengren's military service during World War I, Filene hired the tenacious attorney to head the Credit Union National Extension Bureau, which fostered the growth of credit unionism nationwide.[28]

The cooperative financial structure of credit unions provided members with the opportunity to secure significantly cheaper loans than were otherwise available. They charged only 12 percent on average, while the next most favorable source of credit—Morris Plan companies—charged over 17 percent. Some pawnbrokers demanded interest payments as high as 120 percent. There were even lenders who legally charged $1 for a one-week $5 loan. Thoroughly respectable credit sources extracted exorbitant interest payments as well. A study of black-owned banks found that borrowers frequently paid more than 50 percent on small loans. The credit union provided a mechanism for combating such usury. "Credit Unions are the people's bank," affirmed a union local. "They kill the loan shark."[29]

Credit unions provided their members with a haven during the financial storm of the early 1930s. Not one closed in thirty-five of the thirty-eight states where they operated. "In these times when people are frantic about the present, let alone the future," James Michael Curley observed, "the Credit Union has been a godsend and a blessing to the great mass of humanity which goes on and on in life, meeting exigencies as they present themselves, and at that with extreme difficulty." In 1929 there were 974 credit unions with 264,908 members; by 1934 these numbers had risen to 2,489 and 427,097, respectively. Frederic J. Haskin of the eponymous information bureau stated that "Americans have not waited for official action but have begun the work of socializing banking themselves." The impressive record credit unions achieved during this difficult period inspired Bergengren to conclude they had become a permanent feature of the nation's financial landscape. "The credit union is an established fact," he reflected. "From this point on—we may advance more rapidly and with greater confidence."[30]

Credit unions appealed to farmer organizations because they provided a means for establishing farmer-controlled financial institutions. Grangers had founded banks as early as the 1870s. More recently, the Pennsylvania State Grange established eighteen banks in the Keystone State and two in New York State between 1906 and 1909. In 1927 there were ten Farmers Union–controlled banks in Kansas. During the Great Depression, farmer organizations embraced the credit union movement. A representative of the Missouri Farmers Union reported: "A lot of interest has developed in the Credit Unions. . . . [I]t is time we started handling our own money." In 1933 eight Farmers Union credit unions were operating in Nebraska. "Why shouldn't a farmer who wants to make a small loan borrow it from his own neighbors," a Nebraska farmer asked, "rather than get it from some bank or loan company whose stockholders are the money grabbers of Wall Street?" The Farm Bureau also was promoting credit unions: by 1935 the organization had established them in twenty-five Indiana counties.[31]

It was urban America, however, where credit unions achieved spectacular growth. The Post Office Department provided notable support to the fledgling institutions by encouraging its employees to form credit unions. In 1923 eight postal workers in Brockton, Massachusetts, pooled $18.50 to establish the first postal credit union. By the end of 1930, 40,574 postal workers were members of 245 credit unions holding over $3.3 million in assets. Some private-sector employers opposed credit unions, but some encouraged them, because they aligned with the company's paternalistic welfare program. Armour and Company was particularly notable in its support, with sixty-five employee credit unions serving 11,895 members in July 1933.[32]

Organized labor promoted credit unionism as well. In 1930 the American Federation of Labor's journal encouraged the formation of credit unions by publishing multiple articles authored by Bergengren. Amalgamated Clothing Workers of America locals in New York City, Rochester, and Cincinnati all operated credit unions. Union representatives who attended the National Negro Labor Conference endorsed these cooperative institutions as a means to defend "Negro workers . . . victimized by loan sharks." The Los Angeles local of the Dining Car Cooks and Waiters Union had just established "the first credit union among Negro workers in the West." The banking crisis imparted added urgency to workers' efforts to organize credit unions. The Wisconsin State Federation of Labor resolved that "labor unions should establish credit unions wherever possible." "Certainly need one with the unstable banking conditions," observed a member of the National Association of Letter Carriers in Youngstown, Ohio.[33]

Bergengren hoped that a federal credit union law would consolidate the movement's rapid gains. By the end of 1933, thirty-eight states—containing 95 percent of the national population—had passed laws enabling the organization of credit unions. The enactment of a credit union measure for the District of Columbia in 1932 had served as a trial balloon for federal legislation. "We had a good deal of difficulty due to the opposition of banks and the private money lenders," Bergengren reported. In the spring of 1934, legislation that Senator J. Morris Sheppard (D-TX) had introduced to establish a federal credit union system began receiving earnest consideration. Sheppard called attention to credit unionism's cardinal principle of mutual aid: "The bill involves no Government loans, no subsidy, no appropriations of money. Credit unions pay their own way." And Bergengren emphasized that credit unions served a financial niche that banks neglected: small low-interest loans. He insisted, therefore, that credit unions posed no competitive threat to banks. "It is not a competitor of a bank. Never has been and never will be." The legislation passed the Senate in May and went to the House.[34]

President Roosevelt had sponsored New York's original credit union legislation two decades earlier as a state senator. Now his intervention ensured that federal legislation received the House's attention before adjournment that summer. Wright Patman—the measure's chief advocate in the House—stressed that credit unions protected "the poorest people of our Nation" from predatory lenders and noted the toll such lending practices exacted on the depressed national economy. "Between two and three billion dollars' purchasing power each year is destroyed by reason of excessive interest rates." Roosevelt signed the Federal Credit Union Act on June 26, 1934. By 1935 there were 641,797 members of 3,372 credit unions holding $50 million in assets. The following year, the assets of 5,241 credit unions serving close to 1.2 million members totaled almost $83 million. The rapid emergence of credit unions had inspired James P. Warbasse, president of the Cooperative League of the U.S.A., to claim "the day will come . . . when the people will know Roy F. Bergengren and Mr. Morgan will be forgotten."[35]

When workers and farmers established their own banking institutions, they recognized their own financial competence and power. During the bank holiday, Filene observed that credit unions had demonstrated "an unexcelled record for stability, despite the fact they are managed not by bankers, but by railroad clerks, letter carriers, farmers, telephone linemen, factory hands, and others." Bergengren pointed out that "the credit union requires of men and women who never had much of anything to . . . learn how to manage money honestly and efficiently and how to put it to work for the good of all the people in the group." At the same time that many workers and farmers were achieving a new feeling of financial authority, the provisions of the Banking Act of 1933 that divorced banks from their investment affiliates and privileged prudence over risk-taking imparted an impression that the "money power" had been defanged. "It begins to look as if the power of a Morgan to tap his favorites on the shoulder, to place upon them the accolade of financial knighthood, is at an end," surmised the Bricklayers, Masons and Plasterers International Union of America. "The jig, it seems, is about up." The San Francisco Labor Council proclaimed: "It can be said with great certainty that Wall Street banking is dead." "Control of credit passes more and more out of Wall Street's hands each week," its journal gleefully observed. "The common people will yet have their chance to do a jig on the coffin of entrenched privilege."[36]

The power of finance appeared to be in full retreat following the Banking Act of 1933. A large section of the American public expressed open hostility toward the "banksters" and pressed for whole-sale change. The establishment of government banks was a distinct possibility. The Chicago Federation of Labor pronounced the banking fraternity would no longer command deference from the American people. "The people don't go creeping around in such awe of bankers. ASKING them favors. We near the time when bankers won't be asked; they'll be TOLD." But simultaneous crosscutting developments were blunting pressure for banking and monetary reform. Government programs addressed particular grievances of depositors, farmers, and homeowners. And the vibrancy of the credit union movement attracted an increasing share of the finite energy that reformers could devote to financial issues. The political culture of the New Deal would further arrest the movement for reform.[37]

10

The New Deal for Farmers and Workers

"The Responsibilities That Go with Status"

In the fall of 1933, the labor press dismissively remarked that "the bankers and their banks just can't cut the mustard." Critical appraisals of finance were heard less frequently by the end of the decade. Watershed legislation such as the National Labor Relations Act and Agricultural Adjustment Act attested to the new standing labor and agriculture enjoyed during the 1930s. But labor unions and farmer organizations relinquished a measure of political autonomy in exchange for this influence. New Deal policymakers sought to foster partnership between competing economic interests. The adversarial nature of banking politics clashed with this effort to mediate the inherent conflicts that existed between various groups. Banking politics was ill suited for helping organized labor and agriculture forge alliances with New Deal policymakers.[1]

The New Deal encouraged farmer and worker organizations to participate in discrete policy areas, defined by boundaries established during the process of professionalization that created agricultural and labor expertise. This arrangement limited the range of policy questions deemed to fall under their purviews. Demands for broader economic reform did not conform to this policymaking structure. Unions learned to concentrate their political efforts on established labor issues, while farmer organizations focused on well-defined agricultural questions. Organized agriculture and labor began to withdraw from banking and monetary issues. As a result, banking politics soon lacked sustaining institutional support, and by the end of the decade was in eclipse.[2]

A Seat at the Table

New Deal programs for depositors, farmers, and homeowners combined with government support for credit unionism to give workers and farmers new confidence that financial policies served the public interest. The Roosevelt administration's policymaking approach further strengthened the sense of ordinary Americans that government was responsive to their economic concerns. The New Deal broke new ground when government officials brought representatives of labor and agriculture into the policymaking process. Workers and farmers thought this practice contrasted favorably with the preceding administration. "Mr. Hoover's first loyalty appeared to be linked with the selfishness of the money interests," attested the St. Paul Trades and Labor Assembly's journal. "Repeated solicitations for a parley were met with smirks of indifference and disdain." Whereas, according to the *Farmers Union Herald*, "President Roosevelt's brain trust was recruited from college professors and economists who urged that the best brains of organized labor and agriculture be brought around the council table together with the financiers and business men."[3]

Administration officials explicitly articulated these intentions. In 1933 Secretary of Labor Frances Perkins informed "every wage earner" that they "should feel that the [labor] department is at his or her service at all times on every matter affecting the working conditions of wage earners." Organized labor and agriculture found the administration's embrace of workers and farmers gratifying. At the outset of the last Democratic administration, Grange leader Carey B.

Kegley had protested that Woodrow Wilson failed to grant farmers adequate representation. Kegley stated that it was "difficult to tell the disappointment" of Grangers that the president had not appointed a "genuine farmer" to serve as secretary of agriculture. "The Secretary-ship of Agriculture is a farmer's job and the farmer's pride in himself is wounded to the quick when an outsider is selected."[4]

Roosevelt made a concerted effort to cultivate worker and farmer organizations. In January 1933, William Green reported the president-elect "was determined to work with and . . . have the cooperation of the American Federation of Labor for the next four years." Roose-velt's first encounter with the Farm Bureau's Edward A. O'Neal oc-curred at the New York State Fair while he was still governor of the Empire State. "I want you to advise me," Roosevelt assured O'Neal. In March 1932, Roosevelt wrote John A. Simpson: "I wish that I could meet you personally and talk with you about many matters on which I need information and advice." The two men met for the good por-tion of an afternoon shortly thereafter. And immediately following the 1932 election, Roosevelt reached out to Master of the National Grange Louis J. Taber. Roosevelt reminded Taber that he held membership in the Grange. "I, like you, rejoice in the fact that our great organization is to be represented at the Capital."[5]

Nevertheless, Roosevelt's cabinet selections demonstrated that he did not intend to implement the particular policy agendas of specific organizations. A farmer organization leader was not appointed sec-retary of agriculture, and no union leader was appointed secretary of labor. There had been a movement for Simpson to head the De-partment of Agriculture, but Simpson himself said it would be "very unusual for a man with as radical views as I have to be placed in a President's cabinet." Representative J. Marvin Jones (D-TX) recalled that Grangers "probably would have liked to have someone [named] from their own organization," but Roosevelt settled on Iowa farm journal editor Henry A. Wallace. O'Neal and Taber both approved of this selection. Simpson withheld immediate judgment. "He would not be eligible for membership in our organization because he isn't a farmer," the Farmers Union leader pointed out. "Maybe he will make a good secretary anyhow." Still, New Deal official William I. Myers recalled, "there was general approval that we had a man with an agricultural background. . . . In general, the secretaries of agriculture before Wallace had not been known for their knowledge of agriculture." According to one large circulation weekly agricultural newspaper: "There is no question of his [Wallace] sympathy with agriculture and his knowledge of the situation with which farmers are confronted."[6]

Organized labor initially expressed disapproval of Roosevelt's selection to head the Department of Labor. When former commissioner of the New York State Department of Labor Frances Perkins was chosen instead of a union leader, Green protested bitterly that "labor can never become reconciled to the selection made." He dismissed her as "some college professor who learned about labor from textbooks." Perkins was the first woman to serve in the cabinet. "He wouldn't have been so excited if it had been a man not from the ranks of labor," she later remarked. John P. Frey recalled: "I didn't think that a person who had given over her life to social work knew enough about . . . the employer-employee end of the industrial game to be sound." Green actually instructed labor officials not to meet with Perkins. He shortly changed his tune, however, and within two months of Perkins's appointment was presiding over a banquet held in her honor.[7]

"Cooperation and Not Conflict"

The inclusion of agriculture and labor in New Deal policymaking imparted these groups with stature. "Labor has improved its status tremendously," Perkins observed. This new standing also created the expectation that organized labor would serve as a cooperative partner of government. "Organized labor's responsibilities today are greater than they ever have been in the entire history of Unionism," mayor of Buffalo George J. Zimmerman (D) instructed. "The eyes of the nation are upon labor at this time and . . . labor must play a dignified, harmonious part." This role was one that unions largely embraced. "Organized labor owes a responsibility to itself and to our government today that we never owed before," stated Van A. Bittner of the United Mine

Workers of America. "We have a place in the counsels of our government."[8]

The ascendancy of farmer organizations was less marked—because through the farm bloc agriculture had attained a notable degree of influence in the early 1920s—but similarly consequential. J. Marvin Jones, chairman of the House Committee on Agriculture, reported that "when Albert Goss [Grange] and Ed O'Neal [Farm Bureau] wanted hearings, they got hearings on any bill of importance that affected the farmers, because they represented a great number of farmers." The major farmer organizations—with the notable exception of the Farmers Union—reciprocated by seeking to cooperate with government policies. "All farmers," the Indiana Farm Bureau Federation enjoined, "should be alert and ready to cooperate in the New Deal for agriculture."[9]

The New Dealers strove to mediate between interest groups. In the words of Assistant Secretary of Commerce John S. Dickinson: "What this administration is trying to do is to look at our economic and social life as a process in which all have a partnership." Roosevelt established this tone early in his first term when he referred to "a partnership between Government and farming and industry and transportation." Opposite ends of the political spectrum represented within Roosevelt's "brain trust" agreed with this premise. Raymond C. Moley explained that the administration "conceives of the relationship of worker and employer, debtor and creditor, State and people as a common effort to unify the people of this country." And Rexford G. Tugwell claimed that "cooperation and not conflict is the better organizing principle."[10]

The oppositional consciousness that animated banking politics clashed with the New Deal's emphasis on partnership. Forms of politics that evoked conflict made Wallace apprehensive. He had responded to "this fighting element in the Farmers Union" by concluding that the organization was "just a little wild." Perkins's similar outlook on conflict was consistent with her background in social welfare reform. Social reformers sought to resolve the tensions between workers and employers. Their approach to labor questions did not focus on using worker-controlled institutions to challenge directly the power of employers. "The most important things that we do for labor," Perkins stated, "are the mass protections that come out of law, out of legislation." Union leaders recognized the distinction between how organized workers and social reformers addressed labor issues. Jacob S. Potofsky of the Amalgamated Clothing Workers Union identified Perkins as "a great social worker" rather than a "labor leader," because she "would be more the soft type who would just try to appease and settle things in a nice way."[11]

Both Perkins and Wallace had come of age at the turn of the century and shared the anxiety about social conflict characteristic of Progressives. Wallace understood the "great modern problem" of the new "age of abundance" to be how "to distribute the fruits of science in a just way." He believed addressing this issue "require[d] a new degree of tolerance among competing economic groups." Wallace worried publicly about the potential for "discord . . . to break us up into warring groups with hatred continually breeding hatred with no prospect of a constructive outcome." Perkins similarly claimed that "in the cooperation of the various apparently conflicting interests lies . . . the heart of a sound program of stabilization of industry in this country." She pursued policies that sought to maintain "industrial peace for the benefit of employers and workers." Thus, the New Deal addressed the labor question by erecting legal mechanisms that allowed workers to resolve their differences with employers within established confines. Worker and farmer organizations generally adapted to this mediatory framework. Perkins congratulated labor that its "challenge to accept the responsibilities that go with status has been made and met on the whole."[12]

"Took Their Counsel"

Organized agriculture and labor reaped legislative benefits from foregoing oppositional politics and focusing on discrete policy issues. The first comprehensive agricultural legislation enacted as part of the New Deal was the Agricultural Adjustment Act. This measure awarded farmers payments for restricting their production so that commodity prices would rise. "The passage of this bill represents one of the greatest legislative victories which organized agriculture ever achieved," O'Neal stated. "It is the first fundamental farm relief measure advocated by organized agriculture which has ever been enacted into law." He referred to the new law as "the Magna Charta of American agriculture." Roosevelt claimed: "The measures to which we turned to stop the decline and rout of American agriculture originated in the aspirations of the farmers themselves expressed through the several farmer organizations. I turned to these organizations and took their counsel and sought to help them to get these purposes embodied in the law of the land."[13]

Leaders of farmer organizations appraised their relationship with the administration in similar terms. "Certainly, more than any Secretary of Agriculture that I have ever known," O'Neal stated in 1936, "Secretary Wallace has conferred and advised with the farm organizations' leaders." O'Neal believed the administration's agricultural legislation was the product of its solicitous attitude toward farmer organizations. "I'd say the Farm Bureau was primarily responsible for the contents of the AAA bill," he later claimed. Taber had a similar perspective on the relationship between farmer organizations and New Deal agricultural reforms. "During '33 we had as much influence as we cared for both with Henry Wallace and the President," he recalled. "We were consulted on all moves." For example, the National Grange took special interest in agricultural credit issues, and Taber attested that the organization was "much consulted" during the drafting of the Farm Credit Act.[14]

Union leaders felt similarly affirmed by their association with the Roosevelt administration. Perkins recalled that shortly after Green impulsively objected to her selection as secretary, there was "really great cooperation" between herself and the labor leader. "It was very simple for him to come . . . to see me whenever he wanted to, or to call up." Unions strongly supported the labor legislation enacted during these years. When Section 7(a) of the National Industrial Recovery Act guaranteed labor's right to organize for collective-bargaining purposes, John L. Lewis, president of the United Mine Workers of America, proclaimed: "There has been no legal instrument comparable with it since President Lincoln's Emancipation Proclamation." Green believed this law offered "the greatest opportunity which has ever been presented to the workers to organize and to bargain collectively." He urged organized labor to be "alert, prepared and ready . . . to take advantage of every opportunity which presents itself, through this legislative proposal, to organize, bargain collectively, increase wages and reduce the hours of employment."[15]

Section 7(a) profoundly altered unions' efforts to organize workers. Within months, the ranks of the American Federation of Labor increased by almost 800,000. Workers had faced numerous barriers to organizing—including egregious instances of physical intimidation and violence. In Aliquippa, Pennsylvania, for example, anyone engaging in union activity was subject to being summarily fined and even assaulted. Borough police and the private security force employed by Jones & Laughlin Steel Corporation jointly imposed the company's will. A steelworker who played in a union baseball league elicited a typically outrageous response: "Some cops come over [into his home] and threw me out of bed and wanted to blackjack me." "They had that kind of power. . . . Jesus Christ, they had power to do anything they wanted," he remembered. One union organizer who dared to distribute pamphlets in Aliquippa was severely beaten by two men, fined by a borough official, and menacingly shadowed as he fled town. Louis Leonard of the Amalgamated Association of Iron, Steel and Tin Workers stated that "prior to the adoption of the NRA . . . it was foolish for a representative of the Amalgamated Association to go into the midst of the steel towns." Leonard recalled an instance when he was "notified . . . that the Chamber of Commerce had met . . . and had decided by unanimous vote that I should be ridden out of town that night on a rail."[16]

When steelworkers learned of the National Industrial Recovery Act, they began to organize. The threat of violence could no longer forestall union activity. The Amalgamated Association chartered 129 new locals in a matter of months. One member of a newly formed

local expressed exhilaration over the labor movement's future prospects: "We can not fail, when the President of the United States has
told us many times he is with us. What more courage do we need?"
The Supreme Court later invalidated the National Industrial Recovery
Act, but the National Labor Relations Act of 1935 restored the right to
organize, and Green referred to this legislation as "the Magna Charta
of Labor of the United States."[17]

Drawing an implicit comparison with the Hoover administration, Roosevelt claimed that his administration had "put the power of
government behind not only railroads and banks, but the industrial
workers of the nation, the farmer, the small home owners, the unemployed, and the young people who suffered from utter lack of opportunity." Although the institutional base of banking politics enjoyed
new influence under the Roosevelt administration, farmer organizations and labor unions directed their efforts where they could realize
immediate gains: explicitly agricultural and labor-related issues. They
did not emphasize financial questions.[18]

The Farmers Union

Political activity that did not seek to overcome conflicts of interest
between opposing groups countered New Deal efforts to foster economic partnership. Therefore, organizations that maintained an adversarial political posture or emphasized issues outside of their proper
policy sphere saw their influence suffer. From the earliest days of the
Roosevelt administration, the Farmers Union was on the margins
of agricultural policymaking, unlike the other major farmer organizations. According to Wallace: "The Farm Bureau felt that it had a
voice—the Grange felt that it had a voice . . . the Farmers Union felt
more or less out of it." Likewise, O'Neal recalled that the Farmers
Union's "voice wasn't very strong." While elements of both the Farm
Bureau and Grange were critical of bankers and urged financial reforms, the national organizations did not engage in the combative
brand of banking politics that the National Farmers Union practiced.
Its leaders promoted sweeping financial reforms and regularly excori-

ated bankers. Years later, Wallace remained apprehensive about the firebrands who had led the Farmers Union during the early years of the Great Depression: he characterized John A. Simpson and Milo Reno as "demagogues."[19]

The Farmers Union persisted in pressing financial issues even after the Banking Act of 1935 that was enacted in August of that year ostensibly resolved these questions. In October, the Kansas Farmers Union demanded "that control of credit and currency be taken from the very small group of bankers and vested in the whole people — the Government of the United States." And in November, the National Farmers Union adopted a program that proposed the issuance of greenbacks, remonetization of silver, and enactment of legislation "to nationalize our currency and credit money through a central bank, owned, operated and controlled exclusively by the government."[20]

The National Farmers Union courted further controversy by backing the Frazier-Lemke refinance bill. In May 1936, the ever-determined Representative William Lemke successfully filed a discharge petition that forced a vote on his measure to provide government refinancing of farm mortgages at 3 percent. Father Charles E. Coughlin's National Union for Social Justice and a handful of state Granges and Farm Bureaus also supported this effort to liquidate farm debt at a reduced interest rate. But the Roosevelt administration opposed the idea as inflationary, and the American Farm Bureau Federation and National Grange did not endorse it. When the final roll call vote was tallied, administration pressure had defeated the legislation.[21]

National Farmers Union leaders regularly challenged financial and political orthodoxy. Secretary Edward E. Kennedy forthrightly stated that banking and monetary issues inherently provoked conflict. "Now, you can put patches on banking systems until Gabriel blows his horn," he declared. "I am going to say to you that, no matter how hard we try to solve our problems right, they will never be solved through compromise, just as the slavery question was faced by fifty years of compromise, when it finally had to come to the issue." But Farmers Union members were arriving at the unhappy conclusion that the sea change they had hoped for was not imminent. The 1935 national convention passed a resolution stating: "Any further attempt at gaining monetary justice by petitioning the Congress of the United States is hopeless and futile." The National Farmers Union resolved, therefore, to "carry the Federal Reserve Bank Act and National Bank Act to the United States Supreme Court to be tested as to constitutionality."[22]

A changing of the guard in 1936 and 1937 reoriented the National Farmers Union's political efforts. New leadership placed greater emphasis on cooperative enterprise rather than political activity and was more supportive of the New Deal agricultural program. Confrontational figures such as Simpson and Reno (who had both passed away) no longer typified its leadership. "It wasn't until about 1936 or '37 that the Farmers Union became really friendly," Wallace recalled. The Farmers Union's new leaders focused on issues that fell within the established parameters of organized agriculture's sphere of influence, such as commodity prices, and downplayed controversial questions related to banking and monetary reform. The organization thereby assimilated itself to accepted New Deal political practices. In 1938 the National Farmers Union adopted a new, more constricted, legislative program that organized its lobbying efforts around specific agricultural commodities.[23]

These internal organizational changes coincided with a reordering of established agricultural policymaking patterns in Washington. Over the course of Roosevelt's second term, an opening emerged that allowed the Farmers Union to exert greater influence over farm policy: there was a divergence between the Department of Agriculture and the Farm Bureau. Wallace later inferred there had been "a [political] shift both ways." "The depression emergency had passed," he observed, "and Ed O'Neal returned to his [conventional] ways, and I went on." Subsequently, a debate over the status of the Farm Credit Administration allowed the Farmers Union to assume the unfamiliar role of partner to the Roosevelt administration. Characteristic positions suddenly were reversed, as the administration and Farmers Union joined forces in opposition to the Farm Bureau and Grange.[24]

In April 1939, as part of a major reorganization of the executive branch, Roosevelt announced his intention to incorporate the

Farm Credit Administration into the Department of Agriculture. He thought the New Deal's agricultural program would benefit from having "the activities of the Farm Credit Administration . . . coordinated with other activities designed to improve the economic position of farmers." But the agency continued to operate as if it retained independent standing. The Farmers Union opposed this prolongation of the status quo and, in November 1939, resolved in favor of the Department of Agriculture exercising its newly granted authority. Farm Credit Administration officials opposed the change. "We liked our independence," the agency's head F. F. "Frosty" Hill recalled, saying, "[we] had a reputation for operating a good program, well administered and not allowing political considerations to influence decisions in making loans." Wallace asked Hill for his resignation.[25]

Hill's successor brought a fresh perspective on how the agency should operate. Albert G. Black wanted the Farm Credit Administration to consider the social implications of its lending practices. Black thought the agency had a "duty . . . to help farmers become landowners." He accordingly announced that a "broad social view" would now govern the agency, which entailed the abandonment of "strict banking procedure" in favor of "extreme leniency in cases where farmer borrowers are deemed to have a chance eventually of meeting their obligations." Black hoped this policy change would reduce farm foreclosures.[26]

The actual procedure under which Farm Credit Administration loans were issued was also a concern. Farmers never received 5 percent of their loan—although they paid interest on the full amount—because this portion went toward purchasing stock in the lending borrower association. One farm woman in Lancaster County, Nebraska, protested requiring borrowers to purchase stock that they "would never get any benefit from." "Now we were under the impression," she related, "that in case the time ever came when we were unable to meet the interest [on the loan] this money could be used up for same." Farmers Union officials supported abolishing this stock purchase requirement "shakedown." "At that time," Wallace recalled, "there was a real sense of injustice on the part of the farmers [over this issue]."[27]

The Farm Bureau and the Grange objected to the Farm Credit Administration's loss of independence and proposals to alter its lending policies. Both organizations represented the interests of farmers who were generally more affluent than those the Farmers Union spoke for, and who consequently found the agency's existing policies less burdensome. Moreover, because much of the Farm Bureau's influence derived from its connection with county extension agents, the organization routinely opposed centralizing authority over agricultural programs. The American Farm Bureau Federation insisted that "future legislation must be directed toward the objective of maintaining a farmer-owned and farmer-controlled credit system, with administration thoroughly decentralized—not centered in one man in Washington."[28]

In December 1939, the American Farm Bureau Federation resolved that the Farm Credit Administration status quo "must not be compromised in any matter." While Wallace was conciliatory—he emphasized the importance of "avoiding many, sudden, and drastic actions"—the administration proved unreceptive to the intransigent attitude of its erstwhile partner. Indeed, Wallace publicly joined forces with the Farmers Union. He even traveled to St. Paul to headline a Farmers Union rally that addressed the issue. Thus, the Farmers Union played the heretofore unlikely role of administration ally, while the other two national farmer organizations assumed the mantle of the opposition. By the end of the 1930s, the Farmers Union had relinquished its combative banking politics and positioned itself to enjoy the administration's support in a policy debate related to a financial issue that was explicitly agricultural.[29]

Symbolic Banking Politics

Institutional retreat from banking politics did not entail wholesale abandonment. Banking politics was too deeply embedded in the political culture. It provided Americans with a means for apprehending how structures of power operated. Worker and farmer organizations found ways to use banking politics—and the broader understanding of power relations that it imparted—to their advantage while remaining within accepted New Deal parameters. John L. Lewis notably deployed the language of banking politics to seize the unprecedented opportunities that the New Deal presented labor.[30]

Giving voice to banking politics helped Lewis organize the mass-production industries. When Lewis called for iron and steel workers to participate in the Committee of Industrial Organization's campaign to organize their industry, he rhetorically stepped outside of the accepted parameters and invoked the adversarial language of banking politics. In a 1936 address delivered over the NBC network, Lewis referred to labor's opponents as "the 'Money Trust,' or 'The Invisible Government.'" He explicitly aligned the organizing drive with such outspoken past practitioners of banking politics as "Fighting Bob" La Follette and Charles A. Lindbergh Sr. The labor leader could have been delivering a speech on the need for financial reform when he explained to his radio listeners that "there has . . . developed a highly concentrated control over the money, banking, and credit facilities of the country. Its power . . . has been shown to rest in the hands . . . of New York private bankers and financiers symbolized and dominated by the New York banking house of J. P. Morgan and Company."[31]

However, Lewis evocatively employed the compelling argument of banking politics to encourage workers to organize. He was not promoting reform of the financial system. His words addressed the conflict between concentrated economic power and democratic principles that banking politics had long confronted. But Lewis focused on increasing the countervailing power of workers. He did not aim to curb directly the undue influence of bankers. The Amalgamated Association had adopted a similar approach, observing that "the Banker plays many games—profitable for him." "Workers can take a leaf from his book," exhorted the union. "That is—get together, organize for a definite purpose, for economic justice and refuse to be further squeezed financially by the financiers and bankers."[32]

In 1939 striking farmworkers in Kern County, California, aimed to do just that. Workers manning the picket line sang a song that called on their fellow cotton pickers to support the strike. "You'd better come down and join the Union," the singing strikers urged. "Every body else is joining." The song identified two adversaries that had benefited from organization: growers and bankers. "Associated Farmers started a Union, Most of the Farmers joined. . . . The bankers started a Union, Most of the Bankers joined." While intractable cotton growers were the striking workers' direct opponents in this confrontation, and farmworkers had struggled against the virulently antiunion Associated Farmers of California for years, bankers were not the strikers' immediate antagonists, rather they were potent symbols of the wealth, power, and privilege that workers hoped to overcome by uniting. The farmworkers' song resonated profoundly. In representation and in rhetoric, banking politics was rooted deeply within American popular consciousness.[33]

The New Deal transformed American political culture when it brought previously marginalized groups into the policymaking process. This attempt to establish a national climate of unity diminished space for political actors who underscored the existence of mutually incompatible interests. Because banking politics was predicated on the inherent opposition between private banking interests and the broader public, New Deal policymaking practices undermined this dynamic strand of American political culture. Organized agriculture and labor rapidly adapted to this new political framework and seized opportunities the New Deal afforded to enhance their position within existing political and economic parameters. The institutional foundation of banking politics was eroding.

.

11

The Banking Act of 1935

"A New Coat of Paint"

In 1934 Wall Street financier James P. Warburg perceived that "the private banking system is at this very moment on trial for its life." During the following winter, policymakers began preparing financial reform legislation. Practitioners of banking politics would attempt to seize the opportunity this moment presented. "The [1933] law, providing a federal guarantee for deposits, was proof that the government should handle the banking business," Colorado State Grange master John Morris insisted. "And, since it has gone half way, it should take over the banking business." Roosevelt administration policy, however, accepted the existing private system. In his first Fireside Chat of 1935, President Roosevelt called "the reestablishment of public confidence in the banks . . . one of the most hopeful results of our efforts . . . to reestablish public confidence in private banking."[1]

But Roosevelt also thought further financial reform was necessary. He wanted to ensure that the Federal Reserve System could conduct what is now called "countercyclical" monetary policy. The abiding demand of workers and farmers for government banking assisted the efforts of the administration and its congressional allies to increase the Federal Reserve System's independence from the banking fraternity. Throughout the legislative process that produced the Banking Act of 1935, banker opposition to the measure was uncharacteristically restrained. The popular appeal of banking politics also helped marginalize the bankers' longtime champion Carter Glass, who exerted comparatively diminished influence over this reform. Although bankers winced at the idea of publicly appointed officials initiating monetary policy, the alternative of government banking posed a more forbidding prospect.

Marriner S. Eccles

In 1935 there were movements to establish state banks in California, Iowa, Kansas, Massachusetts, Minnesota, Montana, Nebraska, New Jersey, Oregon, South Dakota, Washington, and Wisconsin. A Swedish-American house painter in Vineland, New Jersey, testified to the widespread demand for public banking. "If congress will not repeal all the bank acts, thereby restoring control of money to the government where it belongs," he urged, "the people should take the issue to the supreme court." A laundryman persevering through a winter of unemployment in Kalispell, Montana, expressed his hope that reform would remove "the yoke of the money changers . . . from our necks" so "it [could] become a Nation for and by the People as intended by our Forefathers." A shared judgment motivated calls for banking reform. An oil driller in Beaumont, Texas, succinctly expressed this verdict: "The private banking system has failed and it is time for a change."[2]

The president agreed that further financial reform was necessary. "Twenty years of experience with this [Federal Reserve] system . . . have shown by experience definite possibilities for improvement." Marriner S. Eccles would lead the administration's campaign for central banking legislation. Eccles became known to the Roosevelt administration through economics writer Stuart Chase, who had brought the banker to the attention of Rexford G. Tugwell. Eccles had assumed authority over his Mormon family's extensive business interests at the age of twenty-two. During the 1920s, he expanded the family's financial holdings by purchasing additional Utah banks and organizing them into a holding company—the First Security Corporation. The Great Depression had led Eccles to question economic orthodoxy, and he emerged as an advocate of the federal government using deficit spending to stimulate the economy. His reformist stance on economic issues made him a notable rarity among bankers. "The orthodox capitalistic system of uncontrolled individualism . . . will no longer serve our purpose," he testified.[3]

Eccles's reform efforts would command the support of millions of Americans who were certain that Roosevelt championed the interests of the nation's working people. One union member in Toledo proclaimed: "Our confidence in the future should lie in the fact that we have as our leader an honorable, upright, honest, lovable citizen like our President, Franklin D. Roosevelt, a friend of the worker." A union stationary engineer in Oakland illustrated the widespread confidence that Roosevelt was committed to reining in the banks when he commented that "the agents of international bankers are trying to discredit President Roosevelt's progressive and humanitarian plans." Many Americans were convinced the president was advancing a banking politics agenda. "I would vote for Roosevelt because every banker is against him," avowed one resident of Homestead, Pennsylvania.[4]

In January 1934, Secretary of the Treasury Henry Morgenthau Jr. invited Eccles to come work in his department. The resignation of the governor of the Federal Reserve Board that June gave rise to talk of Eccles occupying that important position. Eccles was interested, but "only if fundamental changes were made in the Federal Reserve System." He believed that "the preservation of our capitalistic economy . . . depends upon our capacity to prepare ourselves adequately to prevent a recurrence of the disasters which all but destroyed us in the recent past." In early November, Eccles drafted a memorandum to Roosevelt outlining reforms to the Federal Reserve System that would enhance its ability to implement countercyclical monetary policy. Eccles stated that too often "banker interest, as represented by the individual Reserve Bank Governors, has prevailed over the public interest, as represented by the Board." He believed the Federal Reserve Board's effectiveness was hampered by "its lack of authority to <u>initiate</u> open-market policy, and . . . the complete independence of the Reserve Bank Governors." He was convinced, therefore, that it was "essential that the authority of the Federal Reserve Board should be strengthened." Eccles was appointed governor one week after submitting his memorandum. Roosevelt thought the reforms Eccles proposed were "necessary," but predicted enacting them would require "a knock-down and drag-out fight."[5]

In February 1935, an administration-backed central banking bill was introduced in Congress. The legislation was divided into three parts. Title I dealt with deposit guaranty. Notably, it inaugurated the permanent Federal Deposit Insurance Corporation and reduced the assessments levied on banks to fund this program. Title III included a number of technical amendments to banking laws. Of particular importance to bankers was an extension of the time period for repaying personal loans that their institutions had granted them prior to the Banking Act of 1933's prohibition of the practice. Title II broadened the securities that member banks could discount with Federal Reserve Banks to include "any sound asset" and gave national banks new authority to make real estate loans. Eccles hoped these two reforms would promote recovery by encouraging banks to extend credit. Title II also included a controversial feature: centralization of control over the money supply in Washington, DC. The publicly appointed Federal Reserve Board would be empowered to determine discount rates and member bank reserve requirements. Existing policy only allowed the board to modify reserve requirements in emergencies. And a new five-person committee consisting of three Federal Reserve Board members—including the governor who would serve as chairman—and two Federal Reserve Bank governors would direct open market operations.[6]

Senator Glass recently had claimed there was no need for additional banking reform. He also resented Eccles personally, perceiving the younger man as a threat. Shortly after being appointed to the Federal Reserve Board, Eccles wrote Glass to express his "great respect" for the senator. This gesture was not reciprocated. Back in 1933, Senator Peter Norbeck had observed that Glass was "quite given to being irritable." The passage of time had not discouraged this tendency. Journalist Marc A. Rose described the aged Virginian as "cantankerous . . . [and] immensely proud of his reputation as the outstanding authority in the Senate on all banking matters." The self-anointed "Father of the Federal Reserve System" was enraged that he had not been consulted about Eccles's appointment or the proposed banking legislation. Glass launched a campaign to defeat Eccles's confirmation by soliciting information that could be used to discredit the nominee. Glass asserted that Eccles was "utterly unfit to be a member of the Board of Governors of the Federal Reserve System, and I shall do my best to defeat his confirmation." "I must go on the Eccles Banking Bill and do my best to wreck it," he privately explained. "I have some hope also of wrecking Eccles," he added vindictively.[7]

That winter, Glass held up Eccles's confirmation by failing to appear at the requisite committee hearings. By early spring, Roosevelt was growing increasingly impatient with the delay. The president asked the Senate Banking and Currency Committee's chairman, Duncan U. Fletcher (D-FL), "is there some way you can get Eccles confirmed?" Hearings finally convened a couple of weeks later, the delay being, according to Glass, unavoidable and "much to my regret." The committee recommended the appointment without dissent shortly thereafter. Glass was not present for this vote. The Senate confirmed Eccles the following day. While the petulant Virginian maintained his grip on the chairmanship of the Subcommittee on Monetary Policy, Banking, and Deposit Insurance, Fletcher had weakened Glass's hold over that body by appointing members who were generally supportive of New Deal reforms, including Bronson M. Cutting. Recognizing that his influence was waning, Glass groused that in regard to banking legislation, "as so frequently happens now, my sound opinions did not count for much." The fact that Eccles was closely associated with the proposed measure provoked a transparently jealous reaction from Glass. "I call it the Eccles bill because that is what it is. . . . Eccles dictated its terms and directed its preparation." Major banking reforms of the past—such as the Federal Reserve Act and Banking Act of 1933—had borne Glass's name: these laws often were referred to as the Glass-Owen Act and the Glass-Steagall Act. Glass would sustain his embittered attack on the administration's central banking legislation to the very end.[8]

Title II

While banking politics had compelled the White House to accept reforms it had not wanted—notably the Federal Deposit Insurance Corporation—popular involvement with financial issues also aided administration efforts to achieve reforms it did want. In 1935 public support for financial heterodoxy helped the administration advance its central banking legislation. The bill's primary aim of reducing the control that bankers exerted over the money supply aligned with a long-standing tenet of banking politics. Because adherents of banking politics sought to erect a financial system that promoted the economic well-being of working people, they wanted the publicly accountable government to exercise authority over the money supply. In 1932 a union steelworker in Granite City, Illinois, explained: "Unless the power to control the money supply is taken from Wall Street, the money masters will produce another panic in ten years." During the debate over Title II, the administration promoted a principle that practitioners of banking politics had prepared the way for over many years.[9]

Eccles later explained that the administration adopted a legislative "strategy of tying something the bankers didn't want [Title II] to something they wanted very much [Titles I and III]." Glass had been forced to concede Eccles's confirmation, but he still hoped to split the central banking bill into its three constituent parts, so that Titles I and III could be enacted and Title II blocked. Glass claimed that "our existing banking system will be wrecked by Mr. Eccles and his academic advisers. Indeed, the whole banking fraternity of this country should bestir itself." But bankers had emerged from the depths of the Great Depression somewhat chastened. The American Bankers Association shrewdly recognized that adopting a posture of unbridled opposition toward the bill would prove counterproductive. "In the first place, it would surely have revived the cry that bankers were back at their old game of selfish obstructionism," the organization's journal explained. "Also it would have solidified and strengthened the determination of those in Washington who are interested in putting through banking legislation far more radical." A dismayed Warburg remarked upon "the amazing reticence on the part of the banking profession to appear and discuss this bill."[10]

Despite such hesitance, bankers supported Glass's attempt to impede the legislation: the American Bankers Association endorsed both Titles I and III, while urging changes to Title II. The banking fraternity opposed enlarging public authority over the financial system. Robert March Hanes, president of the Wachovia Bank and Trust Company, explained: "We feel strongly that the Federal Reserve Board should not be controlled by any administration, and it should in no way be affected by politics." However, bankers wanted Title III enacted promptly for pressing personal reasons. The Banking Act of 1933 required them to repay any loans they had received from their banks by June 16, 1935, and Title III included a provision that extended this deadline. Rudolf S. Hecht, president of the American Bankers Association, stressed this issue in his congressional testimony. "I wish to call your special attention to the fact that the time element is an essential factor." The bankers aired an additional concern following the legislation's passage in the House. Title I had been amended to raise Federal Deposit Insurance Corporation assessments from one-twelfth of 1 percent of a bank's deposits to one-eighth of 1 percent. Hecht protested: "Our approval [of Title I] was based on the original provision." A. P. Giannini called "one-eighth percent an unjustifiable burden to place upon the earnings of banks" and proposed reducing the assessment to one-sixteenth of 1 percent. Another banker came to the point when he asked his senator to "make Federal Deposit Insurance Corporation assessments as small as possible."[11]

The banking fraternity affirmed its opposition to Title II in May, when the American Bankers Association declared the necessity of

fighting "political control." The organization particularly wanted to remove the secretary of the treasury and the comptroller of the currency
from the central bank's board. According to Hecht: "The suggestion is
based wholly on a matter of principle, namely, to reduce numerically
governmental influence in the board." The American Bankers Association further declared that it was "bound to stand upon the position"
that Federal Reserve Banks "should have an effective vote with respect
to open market operations, discount rates and reserve requirements."
The U.S. Chamber of Commerce similarly attacked the legislation for
proposing a "concentration of power over reserve and commercial
banking" that would yield a "political dictatorship" over credit. The
American Liberty League likewise denounced the bill for increasing
public control over the financial system. This corporate-funded, anti–
New Deal organization claimed the measure "makes our monetary
and banking structure subject to the whims of political influence."[12]

"Nationalize the Banking System"

Bankers recognized that numerous reform proposals posed significantly greater threat to their interests than the administration's bill.
"During the last year," Warburg acknowledged, "this country has
been flooded with propaganda to 'nationalize the banking system' to
'socialize credit,' and so forth." *Coast Banker* expressed concern over
the imminent possibility of "government ownership of banks and all
credit agencies." The banking journal observed that "the pressure of
radical thought trend[s] so powerfully in that direction that the country may be driven to this goal irresistibly. It is an ominous prospect."
Guy Emerson, vice president of Bankers Trust Company of New York,
noted: "There is much talk of a central bank, in the form of a completely government-controlled institution." Some bankers inferred
that such an outcome was probable. "It is not beyond the realm of conversation among sound-thinking bankers of the East today," *Southern
Banker* reported, "to discuss the mutualization of banks under government ownership."[13]

Contemporary political events suggested that heterodox bank-

ing reform would make progress. The banking fraternity's opposition to the World War I veterans' bonus during the intense debate
over the issue that spring further embittered veterans toward bankers. One veteran explained that he joined Father Charles E. Coughlin's National Union for Social Justice after becoming "fed up with the
banking group of this country." Veterans also featured prominently
among the large numbers of Americans attracted to Senator Huey P.
Long's Share Our Wealth Society. Long's supporters frequently expressed interest in financial reforms, including issuing greenbacks,
remonetizing silver, and abolishing the private banking system. By
1935 the similarities between the Coughlin and Long movements had
led observers to conclude they would join forces, while individual
advocates of Francis E. Townsend's old-age pension plan were blend-
ing that popular proposal with the other two programs. A number
of leading organizational proponents of banking politics already had
taken steps to coordinate their efforts. In January 1935, representatives of the National Union for Social Justice, the National Farmers
Union, former senator Robert L. Owen Jr.'s Sound Money League,
and other organizations gathered in the nation's capital to discuss financial issues. The resulting National Monetary Conference resolved
that Federal Reserve Banks should "be converted into a new central
bank, government-owned and government-operated . . . for the Federal issue and control of all credit and currency."[14]

Legislators also were pushing for the national government to assume authority over money and credit. In the words of Arthur Krock,
the *New York Times* Washington bureau chief, the Congress that took
office in January 1935 was "a radical body at heart." The insurgent faction of House members pushing an agenda of "economic and social
justice"—who were called "Mavericks" in honor of their spokesman
F. Maury Maverick (D-TX)—endorsed federal regulation of money
and credit. In the Senate, Cutting reintroduced his Federal Monetary
Authority legislation, and Wright Patman introduced a companion
measure in the House. Representative T. Alan Goldsborough presented bills to establish a central bank capitalized at $4 billion with the
ability to issue $40 billion in currency. A seven-member board would

govern this institution, consisting of three presidential appointees and two appointees each from the House and Senate. Senator Elmer Thomas introduced legislation to have the national government take over the Federal Reserve System and control the money supply. Representative Andrew L. Somers submitted a bill to create a "national bank of the United States."[15]

When Representative William Lemke had attempted to establish the Bank of the United States immediately after the bank holiday, his measure never made it out of committee. Lemke remained determined nevertheless. In 1935 he secured Senator Lynn J. Frazier's (R-ND) support for the idea, and they jointly introduced legislation to set up a public central bank governed by an elected forty-eight-member board of directors representing every state in the Union. "This bill," Lemke reminded the House, "would create the Bank of the United States, owned, operated, and controlled by the people of the United States." The North Dakota House of Representatives passed a resolution that blamed the private banking system for the nation's "deplorable financial condition" and commended the proposed Bank of the United States. Grangers in Idaho submitted resolutions to Congress backing Lemke's legislation. Edward E. Kennedy, secretary of the National Farmers Union, declared: "To pass this bill is perhaps the only power that Congress now has that is a greater power over the lives and welfare of the people of the United States than that now possessed by the international bankers."[16]

The National Union for Social Justice's banking reform legislation garnered significant congressional and public attention. This bill proposed to replace the Federal Reserve System with the "Bank of the United States of America," which would control the money supply by issuing all currency and requiring banks to maintain the total sum of checking account funds in reserve. A board, also comprising forty-eight members elected from each state, would govern this public institution. A representative of the Union testified to Congress that the Federal Deposit Insurance Corporation, Federal Land Banks, Home Owners Loan Corporation, Reconstruction Finance Corporation, and U.S. Treasury provided the necessary constituents for such a bank. "There is no reason in the world why we cannot combine all of that into a central bank." The National Farmers Union endorsed Coughlin's legislation, and Long lent additional support in the manuscript of the book he drafted outlining his political agenda.[17]

"A Distinct Shock"

The central banking legislation the House passed on May 9 moved further toward public control than the original measure by assigning responsibility for open market operations to the Federal Reserve Board itself. Government banking then received surprising encouragement from the Roosevelt administration. Secretary of the Treasury Morgenthau was dissatisfied over the Federal Reserve System's lack of support for administration policies. "The Open Market Committee have done nothing in the interest of the government." He feared that budget deficits would produce runaway inflation and thought the central bank should do more to help the federal government borrow cheaply. Morgenthau unexpectedly testified in favor of the national government owning all the stock of the Federal Reserve Banks. The president indicated sympathy for Morgenthau's position. "I think it would solve a great many questions if we did," Roosevelt remarked. Startled bankers found the administration's statements deeply troubling. Hecht acknowledged that Morgenthau's testimony "came as a distinct shock."[18]

The administration had encouraged an idea the banking fraternity deemed verboten. Warburg claimed that government banking constituted "the device of those who seek . . . to destroy the foundations of western civilization." The ownership and control of business enterprise by private corporations and individuals evidently was fused in his mind with medieval cathedrals and ancient Greek philosophers. "If we pass the sentence of death upon the private banking system and go in for a system of Government owned and operated banks," he asserted, "we shall have passed the sentence of death upon all private business." Warburg's prediction of Judgment Day for capitalism included citing Vladimir Ilyich Lenin as identifying "the nationalization of banks" to be "the first step . . . toward communism." Other voices in financial circles sounded similarly apocalyptic. "The creation of a [government] central bank is a threat that towers above all others like a pall which numbs the senses," *Southern Banker* confessed. "Carried to its ultimate conclusion, it would mean certainly the acquisition by the government of all the capital stock of all Federal Reserve banks, and it is even hinted that such a policy would lead in natural sequence to government ownership of all banking capital. How to prevent either of these consummations is the burning question of the hour."[19]

Bankers continued to emphasize the ostensible threat of politics lurking in increasing public authority over the central bank. "It is almost certain," Hecht contended, "that a central bank owned by the government would be conducted to serve the strategic requirements of politics." Such criticisms failed to convince a resident of King George County, Virginia, who objected that "a shout to political control seems to me to be just a bogy raised by privileged interests to frighten us plain people but a good many of us are not a bit afraid."[20]

During 1935, the Postal Savings System remained a threat to financial interests even as bankers grew increasingly anxious about central banking reform. Representative George J. Schneider (P-WI) introduced yet another measure to increase the postal savings deposit limit. And Representative John Henry Hoeppel (D-CA) proposed establishing a service that would furnish postal savings depositors with no-fee money instruments similar to a checking account. "My bill is not favorably looked upon by the banking fraternity," he acknowledged. The American Bankers Association worried that postal savings was "stronger than ever." Representative Claude A. Fuller (D-AR) wanted to "put the Government out of the banking business," so he introduced legislation prohibiting citizens from utilizing the Postal Savings System in locations deemed to have "adequate banking facilities." He may have considered Eureka Springs, Arkansas, where he was a bank president, to be one of those communities.[21]

"Decent Rather Harried Faces"

Not all bankers opposed the administration's central banking bill. Notably, A. P. Giannini wrote Eccles's secretary to inform him "of our willingness and desire to be of service to you and the Governor whenever we can." The California banker's backing of the Roosevelt administration was not unrelated to the assistance it was providing his relentless effort to expand the Bank of America. Ninety-nine new branch offices received official sanction by the fall of 1936. "I take no stock in the 'political domination' argument against the Banking bill," Giannini publicly asserted. He pointed out that Federal Reserve Board members served terms of "twelve years, or eight years beyond the Presidential term . . . with no provision for removal of members except for malfeasance." Moreover, Giannini identified a reason for bankers to welcome greater government involvement in banking. "Private banking is sufficiently on the defensive without having to bear the onus of blame for the mistakes of those few bankers who are in a position to determine monetary policy."[22]

As Giannini's statement indicates, public opinion in 1935 unnerved bankers. In Minnesota, for example, the Farmer-Labor Association stated that "the only trouble with the Eccles bill is that it does not go far enough. . . . [T]he nation's banking system has been operated for private profit with no attention to the effect of that policy upon the people of the nation." A Minneapolis union electrician charged that "the banks seem to be 'getting the breaks.'" "The issuance of currency and the control of credit have been left in the hand of the banking interests instead of being restored to the hand of the government," he objected. "The Federal Reserve Banks have been left as privately owned and operated institutions, instead of being put under government ownership and control." Farmer-Labor Party activist Sander O. Sanderson found his belief that "the money-changers rule the temple with greater power than ever before" so disillusioning that he urged "the common people (who by the sweat of their brows have produced the wealth of the nation) to make an uncompromising demand upon Congress to defeat the 'Banking Act of 1935.'"[23]

Widespread popular enthusiasm for Father Coughlin's financial program attests to the strength of public interest in far-reaching reform. Coughlin protested that the central banking bill "directly opposes the full nationalization of the Federal Reserve Banks. . . . [T]his is most disappointing." In early May, Coughlin attacked the legislation before an audience of almost 25,000 in Cleveland. The Federal Reserve System, he remonstrated, "is a private corporation owned by a group of private individuals for the purpose of privately printing and controlling the money of the United States for the private profit of the profiteers." Coughlin's declaration that the National Union for Social Justice's efforts would focus on establishing a government central bank was met with cries of approval and applause. Two weeks later, Coughlin spoke at Madison Square Garden before a full house, which the *New York Herald Tribune* described as "little people. . . . Their faces were decent rather harried faces. . . . They came from small cluttered flats in Brooklyn, from ramshackle semi-detached houses in Queens, from the far reaches of the Bronx and Staten Island." Thousands who had been unable to purchase tickets listened from the building's basement. The crowd roared its approval of his proposed central bank. The *Herald Tribune* journalist perceived that "each clause in each point [of the proposal] seemed . . . to be a part of the emotional life of most of the audience."[24]

Members of Congress spoke to popular discontent with the administration's legislation. "You know the banking bill that we have before us at this time is just a new coat of paint over the corroded, rotten system that we have had heretofore to fool the public," stated Lemke. "It is just an effort to cover up the corrosion. But you cannot paint over corrosion because the paint will not stick." Representative Charles V. Truax pointed out that the national government first had propped up, and then resuscitated, the financial system. "Had it not been for Government guaranty of deposits the banks would be the most unsound financial institutions in our midst today. If it is a sound credit system for the farmer it is because of the Government's activities to provide funds by separate lending agencies. . . . If the credit system today is sound for owners of homes, then it is only sound through

Government activity." "I cannot support the bill," he avowed. "I will support—today, tomorrow, or at any time in the future—a real, honest bill that proposes to nationalize the banks . . . and destroy once and forever the throttling of the racketeering bankers." Eccles's secretary was well aware of such sentiments. He claimed that if the bankers "should foolishly permit Title II to be defeated, they are very likely to get something much more drastic after the next presidential election." Influential members of Congress were searching for a mechanism that would establish government banking. Senator William E. Borah stated: "I shall support any measure for the creation of a government owned and controlled bank of issue." Borah believed that "restoration of prosperity among the masses" demanded such an institution.[25]

The Senate Bill

Glass remained unrelenting in his hostility to the principle underlying Title II. He abhorred the prospect of publicly appointed officials "having no pecuniary interest whatsoever [in the banking system]" exercising control over "the banking reserves of the country." The annual commencement season was a busy one for Glass; he received honorary degrees that year from Princeton University, Tufts College, Wesleyan University, the College of William and Mary, and Yale University. His viewpoint on the proper role of elected officials was on full display during this tour, as he used these forums to disparage popular democracy. "Mobocracy" had been a recurring theme of his vituperations over the years. "With the theory that a United States Senator is only a public servant, I utterly disagree," Glass announced at Tufts. "His function does not mean servility to every passing whim of popular opinion." The senator added that one occupying his elected position should "always [be] holding fast to a firm determination not to be swayed by the momentary clamor of the multitude." But Glass could still depend on encouragement from comfortable segments of society that had long admired his economic views. One resident of New York's Fifth Avenue asked the senator to block the administration's bill, because "it is going to be very bad for the holders of bank stock."[26]

While Glass was preoccupied with the receipt of academic acco-
lades, important deadlines which Titles I and III addressed had been
approaching rapidly. Time was growing short. Bankers were required
to repay loans from their banks by June 16, and the Temporary Federal Deposit Insurance Fund was scheduled to expire on July 1. Morgenthau voiced apprehension about the legislative delay. He naturally
"felt considerable responsibility in the situation as Secretary of the
Treasury," and no longer courted controversy by raising the question
of government ownership of Federal Reserve Bank stock. Congress
hastily granted temporary extensions to both the deposit guaranty
program and the repayment period for bankers.[27]

An amended version of the bill finally was reported to the Senate on July 2. Glass registered his disapproval of expanding public authority over monetary policy by incorporating the bankers' wish that
the secretary of the treasury and comptroller of the currency be removed from the Federal Reserve Board. The bill also now required
that a supermajority of the central bank's board cast affirmative votes
before reserve requirements could be altered and proposed an open
market committee consisting of the seven board members and five
representatives of the Federal Reserve Banks. In response to the banking fraternity's appeals, the Senate bill also returned Federal Deposit
Insurance Corporation assessments to one-twelfth of 1 percent of
deposits. Glass initiated a new controversy as well. He proposed to
stimulate industrial stock issues by granting commercial banks limited authority to underwrite corporate securities. The partners of J. P.
Morgan & Company hoped desperately for the success of this provision.[28]

Debate in the Senate began on July 23, with the administration's
supporters committed to advancing the legislative process. Gerald P.
Nye (R-ND) offered an amendment that sought to establish the National Union for Social Justice's Bank of the United States of America.
His effort proved futile. Robert M. La Follette Jr. recorded his "regret"
at voting against Nye's amendment because he thought "we must have
complete control of credit and monetary policies in the public interest." But La Follette was both unwilling to endorse all of the mea-

sure's provisions, and prepared to compromise in order to secure increased public authority over monetary policy. Senator Frederick Steiwer (R-OR) reported that "the whole situation crystalized into . . . a gentlemen's agreement to accept the bill as it was reported from the Committee." The Senate passed the bill on July 26, and it was sent to a conference committee. "This, in my judgment, will be a difficult conference," related House conferee Goldsborough. According to the *New York Times*: "On all sides it was agreed that the real fight on this will come in the conference."[29]

Banking Act of 1935

Almost immediately, Glass brought the conference committee's proceedings to a complete halt. Goldsborough had stated "that a systematic effort has begun on the part of the great bankers of New York to coerce the House to in turn coerce its conferees into adopting the Senate bill." He was decidedly opposed to ceding ground to the upper chamber and claimed: "You will find in the Senate bill from the first page to the last the same handwriting, the same sinister influence, the same hand of that class which has control of the people's money . . . of that class whose manipulation of the people's money destroyed the country in 1929." Glass claimed these comments constituted an affront to his honor and demanded Goldsborough apologize publicly. "The old man said I insulted him and that he won't meet again until I make a public apology." In order to salvage the bill, Goldsborough dutifully took to the floor of the House and delivered an indifferent expression of regret. "I desire to say that I intended no reflection on the steadfast patriotism, the absolute integrity, and the high purpose of any Member of the United States Senate. On the actual issues involved, in the statement I made . . . I adhere absolutely to what I then said."[30]

Glass's pride thus assuaged, the conference could resume. Roosevelt "wholly opposed" Glass's attempt to restore investment banking powers to commercial banks. "Old abuses would come back if underwriting were restored in any shape, manner or form," Roosevelt insisted. The president's personal intervention eliminated this provision.

Another nonmember of the committee also had a hand in its deliberations. Eccles took steps to ensure that the reforms he deemed most important would emerge intact from the conference. He prepared a list of provisions for Goldsborough's use that ranked the relative importance of each point, and regularly met with the congressman during the proceedings to formulate strategy. Eccles's most contested proposed reform remained centralizing control over Federal Reserve System monetary policy. "The conception of the Senate was that the operations of the open-market committee should be controlled by the banks," Goldsborough explained. "The theory of the House was that the operations of the open-market committee . . . was a public function." After days of horse-trading, the House conferees prevailed on this principle.[31]

Roosevelt signed the Banking Act of 1935 into law on August 23. It reduced FDIC assessments, maintaining the Senate bill's rate of one-twelfth of 1 percent of deposits. The new law placed control over the nation's money supply under the Federal Reserve System's governing authority—the rechristened Board of Governors. The secretary of the treasury and comptroller of the currency were no longer members of the board. The Board of Governors was authorized to adjust reserve requirements and direct Federal Reserve Banks to change their discount rates. A committee composed of the publicly appointed seven-member Board of Governors plus five Federal Reserve Bank officials replaced the old Federal Open Market Committee (which had consisted of representatives from each of the twelve Federal Reserve Banks). The new committee had full authority over the central bank's government bond purchases. Individual Federal Reserve Banks could no longer decline to participate in open market operations. Additional reforms included expanding the range of acceptable securities that Federal Reserve Banks could discount for members banks beyond commercial paper to include any satisfactory asset and permitting national banks to engage in long-term real estate lending.[32]

Both Glass and Eccles were pleased with the outcome. Glass had received the gestures of obeisance he craved, while Eccles had achieved the central reform he sought. "Senator Glass got what he wanted most—recognition," observed journalist Marc A. Rose. "Ignored when the bill was first submitted . . . [Glass] played his favorite role of the peppery venerable sage in the spotlight before a deferential Senate, and carried off the plaudits." "Considering the objectives and purposes of the legislation as originally proposed and as finally enacted," Eccles stated, "I am very well satisfied with the outcome." Eccles had sought to ensure that "a recovery does not result in an undesirable inflation . . . [and] that a recovery is not followed by a depression." The Federal Reserve System was now empowered to use monetary policy to stabilize the economy.[33]

Given the unfavorable political climate bankers faced, they accepted the new law. According to *Southern Banker*, the reform process had "opened with odds better than even that the banking system would pass under government control or domination inside of six months." The American Bankers Association conceded that "legislation of this sort is inevitably the result of compromises and adjustments," and granted a restrained endorsement: "We feel that the new law is basically sound." Comptroller of the Currency J. F. T. O'Connor reported the organization's leaders were "pleased with the Bank Bill." Bankers found the low FDIC assessment gratifying. And the banking fraternity had succeeded in removing the secretary of the treasury and comptroller of the currency from the Board of Governors.[34]

The latent import of removing these public officials from the board was not immediately evident. The Federal Reserve System became increasingly responsive to elected officials, despite the board's altered composition. The disrepute that attached to the incumbent banking system impaired the ability of leading bankers to influence policy decisions. Moreover, the leader of the Federal Reserve System supported the policies that public officials were executing to stimulate the economy. Eccles believed the Depression required monetary policy to accommodate expansionary fiscal policy. The Federal Reserve System assumed a subordinate role by supporting administration and congressional policies rather than acting autonomously. At the same time, New Deal policies and programs vested the Department of the Treasury and other government agencies with tremendous influence over the supply and cost of credit. The administration's pursuit of monetary expansion dominated Depression-era monetary policy.[35]

The private banking system had faced potential extinction yet survived. Banking politics had reached its high-water mark, and the influence of its advocates would recede rapidly. But the dynamic banking politics that characterized the Great Depression had left an indelible mark on the nation's financial system. Proponents of banking politics may not have established a transparent financial system that was publicly accountable and responsive to democratic controls, but the idea of banker autonomy had been utterly rejected. Banks across the nation displayed the seal of the FDIC, the House of Morgan was effectively defunct, and initiative over monetary policy had shifted from New York City to Washington, DC. But the continued effectiveness of laws and regulations that serve working people depends on a vigilant public. Without civic engagement, hostile courts, antagonistic regulators, and an indifferent legislature can negate the spirit that underwrote legislation. The potential for covert repeal of the achievements of banking politics was to rise over the following decades.

12

The Decline of Banking Politics

"The Distinguished Company of Experts"

"The past year has been another very difficult one for us all," acknowledged Boston banker Frederic H. Curtiss in 1936. "Our old guides have been changed or have disappeared." Curtiss articulated a prevalent sentiment among bankers, who found both the rapid pace and broad scope of recent changes in financial policy distressing. "We are living in another economic world," he concluded. The banking fraternity was unnerved by New Deal economic reforms and harbored deep forebodings over the future. Postmaster General James A. Farley observed that during President Roosevelt's 1936 campaign, "bankers were against him solidly because they disliked his bank reform program." Much to their relief, Roosevelt's second term would present a respite for banking interests.[1]

The apprehensions of bankers were apparent in 1938, when Senator Claude D. Pepper (D-FL) introduced legislation to establish regional government banks for the purpose of making credit more available to small businesses. His proposal addressed the dissatisfaction of such business owners as a Boston grocer who complained that "the small business man is without a bank. . . . I can borrow money, plenty of it at 18% but not a dime at 6%." The chairman of the American Bankers Association's Federal Legislative Committee, A. L. M. Wiggins, was duly alarmed. "Such a system of government banks in this country would . . . mean the end of private banking," he gasped. The banking fraternity's recent ordeal had provoked an inordinate response. The private banking system was more secure than it had been for years.[2]

The vitality of banking politics ebbed over the course of the 1930s. Enduring popular interest in financial issues was not matched by commensurate support from farmer and worker organizations. Simultaneously, many working people shifted their focus toward furthering the credit union movement. Moreover, a number of the most formidable spokesmen of banking politics departed the scene, leaving a void that would not be filled. But banking politics retained influence, nonetheless, and its argument appeared to be emerging victorious.

Persisting Influence

In the fall of 1936, a resident of upstate New York found challenges to financial orthodoxy so unsettling that he solicited reassurance from his congressman. Supporters of the Townsend Plan who contended that the Federal Reserve System operated "in the interest of the rich man" had shaken his faith in conventional economic ideas. The Sherman resident sought affirmation that his trust in the existing financial system was not misplaced. Bankers were keenly aware that they remained under siege. American Bankers Association President Rudolf S. Hecht acknowledged to Marriner S. Eccles at the close of 1935 that "there were and still are many in Washington who quite frankly favor a much more radical program than you ever proposed."[3]

The continuing influence of banking politics prompted Eccles to surreptitiously aid the Federal Reserve System's congressional supporters in their defense of the institution. In 1937 longtime Federal

Reserve critic Representative William Lemke could still be heard over the NBC network urging "a Government bank—a bank owned, operated and controlled by the people." A former railroad worker who now farmed in New Mexico stressed the inherent conflict of interest between bankers and the public, arguing that under the existing financial order, bankers used depositors' money to exert undue political power. "We are putting up money for them, the Banks to fight us with." Exhortations to combat the anti-democratic influence of bankers were abiding. Methodist minister William E. Marvin of Detroit revealed that "my prayers for liberation from the banking octopus are among those most often and most earnestly offered."[4]

A number of farmer and worker organizations did continue to push for sweeping financial reforms. In 1935 Oregon State Grange master Ray W. Gill had remarked: "I do not think that we will ever be satisfied with our banking system until it is owned and operated by the Government." The following year, the organization resolved in favor of "restoration" of Congress's authority over "the money and credit of the Nation" and establishment of a "United States Bank, to be managed by an Executive board elected from all the states." James T. Phillips, master of the Missouri State Grange, endorsed the need for government banking, testifying that "so long as we perpetuate . . . the present ownership . . . of the money of this Nation and of the banks, the farmers of the Nation can make up their minds to remain . . . in debt forever." The Indiana State Federation of Labor sought an economic order that would provide "cost of production plus a fair profit to the farmer" and "a living and a just annual wage" for workers. This arrangement would "enable every citizen willing and capable of working to maintain and educate his family on an increasing . . . standard of living." In order to accomplish this end, these union members wanted to establish the "Bank of the United States of America," which would be an "agency of the Congress."[5]

Despite such stirrings, however, institutional support for banking politics was waning. In 1939 the National Grange ratified a traditional principle rather than advancing a programmatic vision by "urging that

Congress assume its constitutional responsibility to coin money and regulate the value thereof." This action failed to measure up to the élan of those Grangers who tirelessly advanced banking politics. Annual conventions of the Veterans of Foreign Wars once had provided forums where Senator Elmer Thomas called for "more money to be placed in circulation," and Representative Wright Patman contended that the Federal Reserve System "should be taken over by the Government and operated in the interests of the people." But although the VFW post in Miles City, Montana, resolved in favor of a greenback-based monetary system in 1939, payment of the bonus in 1936 meant that financial heterodoxy no longer commanded the attention of veterans' organizations.[6]

Bankers remained vigilant, nonetheless. They had not forgotten their recent trial. Shortly after passage of the Banking Act of 1935, Hecht urged his fellow bankers to "put up a strong fight against the tendency toward increased government control of banking and credit." He also declared that "a serious effort should . . . be made . . . to at least modify, if not abolish, the law governing the Postal Savings System." Wall Street banker Winthrop W. Aldrich insisted that "there is no further reason for the Postal Savings bank." The American Bankers Association prepared a study that was designed to demonstrate that postal savings served no useful purpose. Bankers still faced strong public opposition on this issue. The National Grange resolved that it "reaffirms its support of our system of postal savings, and demands its continuance and enlargement." One Indianan unequivocally denounced an attempt to decrease the interest rate on postal savings to 1 percent. "The proposal should be defeated. Instead of hamstringing the postal savings banks, Congress should open them up so that the people may use them more freely." Representative John M. Coffee (D-WA) was responsive to such demands. He introduced a bill to inaugurate checking accounts at the post office. Representative Lyle H. Boren's (D-OK) sense of public opinion on the issue led him to conclude that abolishing postal savings "might be an impossible task."[7]

The ability of bankers to wage their battle against government banking was not aided by any notable improvement in their public image as the 1930s unfolded. Working people continued to see bankers as political opponents. A black voter in Homestead, Pennsylvania, explained that he backed the president in the 1936 election because "Roosevelt is for the worker and the poor classes while [Republican nominee Alfred M.] Landon is a tool for the bankers and those who have money." Many Americans remained convinced that bankers bore responsibility for the Depression itself. A migrant farmworker in California concluded that "if we listen to the big bankers . . . we will always be in the ditch." One St. Louis banker's callous observation about Depression-era hardship served to confirm commonly held perceptions about his colleagues' lack of concern with the public welfare. "No doubt there's a lot of suffering," he remarked. "But there is no use getting sentimental about it. The relief problem is going to be with us for a long time." Bankers were less dismissive of their abiding political vulnerability. As the decade came to a close, a Bank of America executive acknowledged the continuing potency of "pressure on banks from various sources."[8]

"No One on the Horizon"

Over the course of the 1930s, the demise of leading spokesmen sapped the vibrancy of banking politics. In March 1934, John A. Simpson had collapsed in the Senate Office Building. He died shortly thereafter. In May 1935, Senator Bronson M. Cutting had died en route to Washington, DC, when the Transcontinental and Western Air flight he boarded in Albuquerque crashed in Missouri. A political opponent murdered Senator Huey P. Long that September in the corridors of the Louisiana State Capitol. Five months after that, William H. "Coin" Harvey passed away at his Ozark Mountain resort at the age of eighty-five. Milo Reno died of a heart attack at a hotel in Missouri a few months later. A number of other figures found their energies directed elsewhere. The Congress of Industrial Organizations' rise prompted the

committed craft unionist John P. Frey to focus on combating the rival
labor federation. Any further efforts to shape banking policy were left
undone. And following the disappointing 1936 general election showing of the Union Party he had played an instrumental role in organizing, Father Charles E. Coughlin devolved into anti-Semitism, to the
neglect of financial issues. In the words of the managing editor of his
newspaper: "A change of policy in our publication has necessitated the
elimination of hammering on the money question." Coughlin's popular support withered, and church superiors ultimately censored the
"radio priest."[9]

There were still veteran practitioners of banking politics who remained active—including Jacob S. Coxey Sr. and Karl F. M. Sandberg.
Echoing the call he made thirty years earlier, a pamphlet Sandberg
published in 1942 advocated "a complete change of our financial system, from a bankers' system for their private profit, to a national system for the good of the nation." A handful of energetic new leaders
joined these established voices. One particularly notable figure was
Representative H. Jerry Voorhis (D-CA). The son of an automobile
company executive, Voorhis was Ivy League educated and idealistic.
The Social Gospel's call to apply Christian ethics to social problems
so influenced Voorhis while he was a college student that he prepared
for the Episcopal ministry. Following his graduation, however, Voorhis worked as a laborer, organized an orphanage, and taught college
before Upton Sinclair's 1934 End Poverty in California (EPIC) campaign inspired his initial foray into electoral politics. In 1936 Voorhis
successfully ran for Congress as a New Deal Democrat.[10]

In January 1937, the freshman congressman joined a sizable contingent in the House who maintained interest in reforming the banking and monetary system. Shortly after taking his seat in Congress,
Voorhis delivered a floor speech calling for "us to buy back the Federal Reserve banks from their present private banker owners and create a real national banking system that will work for the people and
not against them." Such appeals resonated with Americans like Peter
Paul Lucenti of the Bronx, who commended Voorhis: "Allow me to

congratulate you on your comments against the credit manipulators and for your courage."[11]

Banking politics was also clearly alive and well in the person of Representative Charles G. Binderup (D-NE), who had entered Congress in 1935. This self-educated, Denmark-born farmer and creamery operator took great interest in financial questions, advocating such causes as bimetallism and the Frazier-Lemke refinance bill. While his study of monetary issues had taken him to England, France, Denmark, and Sweden, Binderup adhered to long-established lines of American vernacular thought when he lambasted the power a financial elite exercised over the nation's producers, railing against "the power of capital and predatory money monopoly, centralized in the modern Frankenstein, the Federal Reserve Banking System, privately owned, against the toiling masses, the great producers of all wealth."[12]

In March 1937, Binderup and Patman organized a steering committee of seventy Democratic House members representing thirty-two states who supported government ownership of the Federal Reserve Banks. Patman asked Voorhis to serve as secretary of the group. Patman drafted legislation on behalf of the steering committee to have the national government assume ownership of the Federal Reserve System. His bill made notable headway by the end of the year, having gained the support of 150 Democratic members of the House. Their position reflected a strong current of public opinion, expressed ardently by a middle-aged Oklahoman with a fourth-grade education who urged his congressman to "mak[e] a Special Effort to tak[e] over the federal Reserve Banks and op[e]rate them in the interest of the People." "[W]e Believe that money should be controlled By our congress + senet instid of the money clas[s] we have a lot of folks hear Believe just lik[e] us." Elected officials heard such appeals. "The sentiment for the Patman Bill," reported Representative Boren, "seems to be gaining strength daily in the Congress." "This is becoming quite a hot potato!" Roosevelt acknowledged.[13]

Bankers, of course, adamantly opposed the measure. The American Bankers Association's journal condemned the legislation as "not only unnecessary but altogether unwise." The secretary of the Oklahoma Bankers Association reported that the state's bankers felt passionately about the subject. "I wish I had the language to convey to you the interest our bankers manifest in their opposition to the Patman Bill." The Roosevelt administration was comparatively indifferent about the issue. The president evidently saw no pressing need for further banking legislation, having "rehabilitated" the private banking system. And following passage of the Banking Act of 1935, he claimed that henceforth it would be possible "to prevent that disastrous expansion and contraction of credit which in the past has made our economic life a succession of unhealthy booms and disastrous depressions." Within the administration, Eccles was an ally of the Patman bill's opponents. He hoped that active government fiscal policy would preclude further structural economic reforms. Eccles dismissed the measure as "bad legislation" and advised Roosevelt not to lend his support.[14]

The House Banking and Currency Committee held hearings on the legislation, and a large contingent of members committed to vote for it. In April 1938, Representative Joseph A. Gavagan (D-NY) entreated Roosevelt to support the pending measure. "In this wise only may the country have at all times an adequate currency regulated and controlled by the peoples' representatives." Binderup persistently pressed banking and monetary issues with Roosevelt. But the president's interest in the subject was limited. "Groans! I suppose it must be done some day," Roosevelt responded to one memorandum about scheduling a meeting with Binderup. Meanwhile, congressional critics of economic reform had used the onset of a recession in late 1937 to push back against measures they claimed would damage business "confidence." The legislation never received a floor vote. The 1938 election subsequently dealt a significant blow to financial reform efforts in Congress. A number of the members who had supported heterodox banking reform in the past had decided not to seek reelection, and others were defeated at the polls. Surveying the election's aftermath, Voorhis concluded there was "no one on the horizon who appeared inclined to put into legislative form a well-rounded sound program." The voice of banking politics in the nation's capital fell strangely silent.[15]

"End Bankerism"

The prospects for banking politics appeared brighter in California. The Retirement Life Payments Association—popularly known as Ham and Eggs—was a state-level organization that sprang to life in 1937 by promoting an old-age pension program analogous to the Townsend Plan. Ham and Eggs sought both to provide the elderly with financial security and to stimulate the moribund economy. The central role that banking politics played in its campaign demonstrates continuing popular interest in financial questions. The Ham and Eggs movement operated well outside of the New Deal's embrace. Roosevelt dismissed the plan, counseling "against those who advocate short cuts to Utopia or fantastic financial schemes." Ham and Eggs, therefore, was not beholden to the New Deal policymaking framework.[16]

Ham and Eggs proposed increasing purchasing power through payments of "$30-every-Thursday" in self-liquidating $1 scrip certificates to Californians over the age of fifty who were not in the labor force. For these $1 certificates to remain valid, each week scrip holders would have to purchase a 2¢ stamp from a special state bank and affix it to the certificate. This requirement was designed to encourage consumption by keeping the scrip circulating. After one year, the state government—having collected $1, plus 4¢ to cover administrative fees—would redeem the scrip at face value. California's business and political establishment waged an intense campaign against this "impractical and dangerous program." One man living in a Farm Security Administration migratory labor camp near Bakersfield observed that "the money Gods say it wont [work]." Henry King encouraged other working people to pay these "dirty rich liars" no heed. "Ham and Eggs wont work if the rich can help it," he reasoned. "The rich got the first and they want you to take the last." The California Bankers Association announced that the state's banks would refuse to handle the scrip. Ham and Eggs countered with a proposal to establish the "Credit

Clearings Bank of the People of California," which would administer the program. A proposition to enact the Ham and Eggs program met with defeat in 1938, though the vote was unexpectedly close.[17]

This setback did not deter Ham and Eggs supporters. By May 1939, over 1.1 million people had signed petitions favoring the program. Governor Culbert L. Olson (D) opposed Ham and Eggs but equivocated in the face of strong public support for it. He agreed to give Californians another opportunity to vote on the plan. Supporters wanted an election to be held no later than August 15. On July 1, Olson announced the special election would be in November. Delaying the vote until the fall afforded opponents an opportunity to organize, while the enthusiasm of supporters might wane. During the campaign, Ham and Eggs supporters positioned the plan in direct opposition to the state's bankers. The organization's newspaper proclaimed that the essence of the program was that the plan's payments "WILL NOT PAY INTEREST TO BANKERS." "There, in a nutshell," the newspaper declared, "is the story which must be told to every voter in the State." The movement further emphasized that the plan's bank would be "a banking institution of, by, and for the people." "For the first time," the organization stressed, "the people of California will service themselves by operating their own friendly, courteous banking institution."[18]

Ham and Eggs regularly promoted its program as a means to counteract the power of bankers. This intention was poignantly expressed by a picture in its newspaper of an evicted woman, whose possessions were piled on the side of the street in front of her foreclosed home. "Ill, impoverished, Miss Hollie Holman of Stockton couldn't keep up payments," the caption explained. The organization declared that adoption of the Ham and Eggs program would "break the banks' stranglehold on California." "End Bankerism. Don't Be Fooled! Vote YES." Supporters rallied to this call. "The bankers know that $30 every Thursday will work," insisted one Sacramentan, "and that they will lose their grip on the money system." The mutual denunciations between Ham and Eggs and the bankers motivated the movement's supporters. San Franciscans who attended a rally at the Dreamland Auditorium responded particularly enthusiastically because of bankers' recent attacks. "The bankers have the state by the throat," protested one Santa Barbara plasterer. "For too long the people . . . have allowed the bankers to monopolize their chief asset—their credit. We are striving to change the system."[19]

Ham and Eggs was speaking to a still vital set of political ideas. "Work precedes production of goods," proclaimed a Chula Vista resident. "It is the worker and not the banker who really advances credit." Another Californian also voiced producerism. "What do the bankers produce that they can live on the fat of the land while we who produce everything have almost nothing of what we produce?" he demanded. A Stockton resident expressed long-held sentiments about the greed of bankers. "When the bankers say our plan won't work what they mean is that they can't work it to their own selfish advantage." One San Diegan indicted the alleged results of such self-serving behavior. "The banks have deliberately combined to bring on a depression for the express purpose of foreclosing on the homes and farms of the people." "Our people's real enemies are within our own borders, the crooked banking system," an Oaklander avowed.[20]

Yet Californians rejected the Ham and Eggs plan at the polls in November 1939. The *Christian Science Monitor* pronounced the fierce campaign opponents waged against the measure to be "amazing and unprecedented." But while the movement had suffered a defeat that it never would recover from, in the words of one supporter, "a solid phalanx of a million voters" had demonstrated that they "fiercely desired freedom from bankerism." Supporters took pride in their challenge to the state's powerful financial interests. "The bankers have been lavishly subsidized for 75 years," observed a produce salesman, "and we cannot expect to overthrow their entrenched power at once." "Keep up the good work," urged an Azusa resident. "Let us show the bankers that their domination of California and her citizens is at an end." Regardless of what the future held for Ham and Eggs, a married San Francisco couple believed they had achieved a transcendent personal victory. They felt empowered as citizens. They summed up a transformative experience that they shared with many other Americans who had advocated banking politics over the years. "We have learned more about the money system under which we live and real democracy in the past two years . . . than in all our former lifetimes."[21]

"Gone Forever"

While institutional support for banking reforms had grown muted, Voorhis kept pushing, and his efforts continued to meet with public approbation. An article in the Indio Migratory Labor Camp's newspaper commended his pamphlet on the "money question," lauding Voorhis for his "fighting" position on financial issues. "This is what we should remember when Jerry is a candidate again." In March 1939, Voorhis introduced a bill that sought to convert the Federal Reserve Banks into a government-owned central bank. The annual session of the California State Grange resolved in support of this measure. Voorhis insisted that "the very future of free and democratic government in the world depends upon our doing the right thing about the monetary system." He would continue to introduce similar legislation in succeeding congresses.[22]

While the Independent Bankers Association felt compelled to proclaim on its letterhead that it was "unalterably opposed to the socialization of credit," the victories that banking politics had achieved in the 1930s dampened pressure for reform during the 1940s. Traditional nodes of financial power did not manifest the level of influence they had in the past. Following the Banking Act of 1933, the lords of finance on Wall Street appeared to have been toppled from their thrones. In 1941 Harvard University economist Paul M. Sweezy observed: "In the short space of a single decade he [the investment banker] has suffered a dramatic eclipse." Sweezy surmised that "such power as he still retains is largely rooted in a past that is gone forever." Moreover, the private nature of the Federal Reserve System appeared less problematic during World War II, because its leadership deferred to public officials. Federal Reserve monetary policy revolved around financing the war effort by keeping the cost of government borrowing low. In this way, the nation's central bank supported policies that elected officials had established.[23]

The popular response to Voorhis's reform efforts indicates that banking politics still resonated with many Americans well into the 1940s. In 1943 the annual convention of the Minnesota State Federation of Labor endorsed Voorhis's bill to nationalize the Federal Reserve Banks. Oil Workers International Union official Harlan L. Savage's activism during the 1940s revealed him to be a steadfast, energetic banking politics advocate. No stranger to tough fights, Savage had cut his teeth in organized labor as sergeant-at-arms of a fledgling union local in El Dorado, Kansas. He had to guard the door of the farmhouse where union meetings were held with a Colt .45 in order to protect the membership from hired company goons. At his union's 1943 convention, Savage called for an endorsement of Voorhis's bill. "I want to impress upon your minds that only . . . organized working people can ever save our democratic ideal of government." The following year, he convinced his union to wire Voorhis its support of his "great efforts." And the union's 1946 convention, at Savage's prodding, endorsed Voorhis's legislation.[24]

Yet institutional support for Voorhis's bill also indicates the diminishing vitality of banking politics. In 1939 Binderup had expressed the frustration of watching victory slip from his grasp. "If the people will only think," he enjoined, "our great Nation can yet be saved for Democracy, and the current money and banking system will be choked to death by its own iniquities." Public discussion of banking and monetary issues was in decline, and organizations like the Minnesota State Federation of Labor and Oil Workers International Union merely endorsed legislation that Voorhis championed, rather than advancing their own programs. When Representative Lemke repeatedly introduced his bill to establish the Bank of the United States throughout the 1940s, it was a reaffirmation of political faith, not a vital legislative project.[25]

The California State Grange's actions reveal that reduced institutional support for banking reform did not necessarily entail abandonment of financial issues. In 1940 it resolved in favor of legislation providing for government ownership and operation of all banks. Similarly, its 1942 annual convention favored a federal banking system. But, instructively, the organization also endorsed credit unions, which, Master George Sehlmeyer urged, "should be organized wherever possible and those already in operation should expand their activities." In ensuing years, the California State Grange placed new emphasis on credit unionism. It established a standing Credit Union Committee in 1944, separate from its Committee on Banking and Finance. By the following year, the latter committee was gone.[26]

Nationwide, working people increasingly strove to develop a parallel network of credit unions. In 1936 Kenneth W. Hones, president of the Wisconsin Farmers Union, enjoined that greater attention be devoted to organizing them. "We condemn the private banking system, but are too indifferent about building one to take its place." A. Philip Randolph, president of the Brotherhood of Sleeping Car Porters, contended: "It is important and necessary for the workers to control their own savings in their own credit unions." Roy F. Bergengren claimed the credit union movement could transform finance, and he employed the language of banking politics to make this point: "We shall, in credit unions, drive the usurious money lender from the temple."[27]

Banking interests were taking note of the credit union movement's rapid advance. "These little credit unions, in themselves, would not appear to amount to so much, individually, as banking competition," remarked *Commercial West*, "but take them in toto throughout the nation and they reach a volume that must be reckoned with." The movement made remarkable progress over the following decade. There were more than twice as many credit unions in 1945 as there had been ten years previously. And the number of Americans who held membership in them had more than quadrupled to over 2.8 million. The growth of credit union assets was even more phenomenal, increasing over eightfold to $430 million. Credit unionism now occupied the center of working people's financial efforts.[28]

Bretton Woods

Postwar peace ushered in a new international financial order. Its framework upheld the principle of government-managed monetary policy that banking politics promoted. This international accord was formulated during the summer of 1944, when representatives of the Allied nations gathered at the Mount Washington Hotel in Bretton Woods, New Hampshire, to secure stable international economic relations in the postwar world. The resulting monetary regime enshrined the American dollar as the international currency. The Bretton Woods agreements organized a gold exchange standard based on fixed exchange rates in which nations tied their currencies to the dollar. The U.S. government in turn committed to maintaining the value of the dollar at $35 per troy ounce of gold. The International Monetary Fund would facilitate smooth operation of the new order by providing nations with the credit necessary to address balance-of-payment issues. The conference also sought to stimulate postwar recovery by making funds available through the International Bank for Reconstruction and Development. The Bretton Woods financial order sanctioned the ability of states to control international capital movements, which reduced the power of private financial interests over national policymaking. At the close of the conference, Henry Morgenthau Jr. declared the new financial framework would "drive . . . the usurious moneylenders from the temple of international finance."[29]

The Bretton Woods agreements met with broad public acceptance. "Bretton Woods is a milestone of economic understanding amongst nations," Studs Terkel told his radio listeners. "Here is true international banking at its best, for the good and welfare of the peoples of those nations." Both labor federations and the three major farmer organizations all testified before Congress in favor of the agreement. The Congress of Industrial Organizations urged its members to discuss Bretton Woods "in your community or in your church," and to contact their congressional representatives in support of this reform. It even produced a fifteen-minute radio program promoting the agreement that was broadcast over the ABC network. Russell Smith, legislative secretary of the National Farmers Union, reported that "Bretton Woods was thoroughly discussed" within the educational departments of state unions. But involvement with the issue did not transgress the political boundaries workers and farmers had acquiesced to over the previous decade. "We have made no attempt to appraise the agreements, detail by technical detail," Smith explained. "Our view is that if the fundamentals are sound, then the details may safely be left to the distinguished company of experts."[30]

And yet, traditional battle lines were still drawn. Bankers and their organizations spearheaded political opposition to the Bretton Woods system, while persisting spokesmen of banking politics condemned the banking fraternity. "There is an international banking ring with headquarters in this country that is opposing this legislation with all their power and might," Patman stated. "In every way possible they are opposing it. It is against their selfish, greedy interest, for this bill to become a law." Not all practitioners of banking politics agreed, however. Andrae B. Nordskog, who had been the Liberty Party's 1932 vice-presidential nominee, feared the enshrinement of a supranational banking elite. He wrote President Harry S. Truman that approval of the Bretton Woods agreements would mean "you will be elevating the operators thereof above all of the laws of the world; above all of the laws of the United States." But Nordskog's dissent was exceptional. Voorhis articulated the prevailing view. "I believe it represents a most important forward step," he said. "Bretton Woods recognizes that international monetary movements should be controlled by the cooperative action of representatives of the governments and not by private individuals for private gain."[31]

Voorhis approvingly noted that "the whole machinery of Bretton Woods will be in the hands of governmental representatives of the nations." A Brotherhood of Railroad Trainmen official concurred that this new financial order would not serve as handmaiden to the bankers. "I am willing to stand on the product of the best minds of 44 nations' representatives who represented the peoples of those nations rather than the bankers." Public support for Bretton Woods was strong. One woman in Tulsa, Oklahoma, worried that absent Bretton Woods "war-torn helpless nations" would be left "to the mercy of the money lenders," which held the potential to "create an intolerable situation for the safety of us all." Many Americans hoped the accord would help realize future peace and security. The Bretton Woods system presented a promising harbinger to opponents of the power of finance, suggesting that private banking power was passing further under public control. Indeed, by 1945 historian Charles A. Beard concluded: "Bankers have become in large measure mere agents of the Government in Washington." The clamor of voices that had long characterized banking politics was muffled yet appeared to be woven into the very fabric of the postwar economic order.[32]

13

The Fall of Banking Politics

"Wish a Buck Was Still Silver"[1]

On May 1, 1944, ninety-year-old Jacob S. Coxey Sr. stood on the steps of the U.S. Capitol and delivered the address the police had prevented him from giving fifty years earlier. There was no army of unemployed in sight. His audience consisted of two hundred assorted journalists and curious onlookers. Coxey had come full circle, and he marked the occasion by reciting a "little jingle" to illustrate the point he had dedicated his life to making.

> Rags make paper,
> Paper makes money,
> Money makes banks,
> Banks make loans,
> Loans make poverty,
> Poverty makes rags.

Half a century had passed, yet Coxey remained a committed proselytizer of his financial reform program. "You can't give up," he insisted.

"You don't educate people that way." When Coxey had attempted to deliver a speech from the Capitol steps in 1933, he represented a threat to the power structure, and again had been barred from speaking. But the ensuing years had altered the political situation in ways that made granting the tenacious campaigner a forum in the nation's capital a benign gesture. Established interests no longer deemed Coxey threatening. Rather implausibly, he had been enshrined as an elder statesman.[2]

As this altered conception of Coxey indicates, banking politics abruptly receded from popular consciousness in the postwar era. The world looked very different to Americans in the middle of the twentieth century than it had in previous decades. Banking politics had helped to secure the New Deal financial regulations that established a foundation for the economic stability and relatively broadly shared prosperity that Americans began to take for granted. Mass affluence, diminished inequality, and the financial security that a social safety net provided reduced popular interest in the questions of wealth distribution and concentrated economic power in a democracy that banking politics confronted. Banking politics lacked institutional support, as newly empowered agricultural and labor interests focused on a narrowed range of economic issues. Moreover, overtly economic concerns were out of step with postwar liberalism's increasing focus on rights.

By the end of the twentieth century, the fact that banking politics no longer served as a counterweight to the private power of finance was proving increasingly consequential. The national economy was growing ever more dependent on the financial sector and experienced periods of crisis with greater frequency. Bankers exercised unprecedented political power and enjoyed wealth commensurate with a level of economic inequality that harkened back to pre–New Deal levels. In important respects, the nation looked much as it had at the beginning of the century, when banking politics had been voiced so vigorously in the wake of the Panic of 1907.

An Era of Consensus

Political ideas require both sustaining institutions and continuing popular appeal to endure. Millions of Americans benefited from unprecedented mass prosperity during the postwar years. And they enjoyed their newly comfortable material circumstances amid a remarkably stable economic environment. Banking politics did not speak to their lived experience. One business school professor reflected the contemporary view that this exceptional moment was the new norm when he proclaimed that the "future . . . will be characterized by a high degree of economic stability." This unprecedented economic context fostered a complacent popular attitude toward financial issues. The concept of the "money power" faded from the cultural imagination. New Deal home lending and agricultural credit reforms promoted a general feeling that the nation's banking system served the public interest. And the Federal Deposit Insurance Corporation allayed popular distrust of banks. "It is highly improbable that a panic could ever get started," Paul A. Samuelson pronounced in the era's standard economics textbook. The banking fraternity seemed to no longer exercise the undue influence it once had.[3]

The Sin of Harold Diddlebock—a 1947 Preston Sturges comedy starring Harold Lloyd—provides an early illustration of how conflict over banking issues had diminished in the postwar era. In the film, Diddlebock drunkenly places a winning bet on a long shot in a horse race and uses the windfall to purchase a bankrupt circus. After sobering up, he attempts to unload this unwanted asset on a series of bankers, making the sales pitch that operating a big top will do wonders for their public image. His sidekick, "Wormy," freely voices his distaste over the prospect of dealing with bankers. "I hate bankers," he announces three separate times. For good measure, Wormy then observes that "everybody hates them." Diddlebock opens each conversation with these bankers by reminding them of the low esteem in which they are universally held. "As you know . . . you are loathed by everyone." "As you know . . . you are abominated by everybody." "As you know . . . you are despised, reviled, and detested by all normal human beings." One particularly curmudgeonly banker matter-of-factly responds: "I don't want to be popular. I don't like nobody and nobody likes me." In the end, however, the bankers bid furiously for the circus in a farcical attempt to bolster their public image.

What is striking about this film is its portrayal of bankers as ineffectual. They are unpleasant, greedy, and cold-hearted, and, indeed, everyone does loathe them. Although bankers are fully aware of how people feel about them, they have such little regard for the public that they harbor no intention of truly changing, but will seek to improve their reputation in non-genuine ways when such opportunities arise. Still, these bankers no longer pose a threat. While this depiction reveals that bitterness toward bankers persisted among audiences, this portrayal in a Hollywood comedy indicates that banking had ceased to be an issue that was charged with explosive potential.[4]

Banking politics did not vanish. In 1964 National Farmers Union president James G. Patton still proclaimed the producerist rhetoric that played such an integral role in banking politics. He observed that "the family farmer is a working man" while "the wealthy banker," even though he may purchase a farm—likely "as a tax dodging device"—never would be. "They are not workingmen," Patton avowed. "They do not sweat over plows or lathes. In fact many of them have never sweated honestly over any tools." But this argument did not tap into a strong current of public opinion, given the era's relative economic equality and security. The language of banking politics that Patton used notwithstanding, institutions that traditionally had been political opponents of bankers relinquished this stance, and banking politics continued to atrophy.[5]

The prevailing postwar mood of political consensus was at variance with the adversarial framework of banking politics. Unions and farmer organizations took pride in the role they played in administering the national economy during this period. Union leaders disciplined members whose actions threatened to disturb the era's harmonious ethos. The stature that organized labor and agriculture possessed reduced their incentive to push for financial reform. In 1953 Harlan L. Savage of the Oil Workers International Union still held hope that he could convince labor leader Walter P. Reuther to champion banking reform as part of the political program of the Congress of Industrial Organizations. There was little likelihood of organized labor taking up the issue. In 1951 the Federal Reserve System had repudiated the support for government borrowing that it had furnished since World War II, and unions exhibited little concern with the policy struggle that preceded this new monetary regime's inception.[6]

Even an attempt to link banking politics with the anti-communism so characteristic of the Cold War political landscape fell flat. In 1953 a resolution was presented at the California State Grange convention to conduct a study of the control that banks exercised over the money supply. Its framers contended that addressing this issue would strengthen the national economy and thereby help the United States "maintain its position of world leadership against the forces of communism." Just one decade earlier, California's Grangers had endorsed the establishment of a government banking system. But this modest resolution went nowhere.[7]

The Washington State Grange was a notable exception in this time, as it endorsed government banking into the early 1960s. Developments within the Minnesota State Federation of Labor, however, were more representative of contemporary trends. In 1945 the organization had resolved in favor of the national government owning and operating the Federal Reserve System. Resolutions on banking and monetary issues subsequently disappeared from the federation's conventions until 1955, though neither of that year's finance-related resolutions addressed financial reform. One called on state officials to permit the St. Paul Postal Employees Credit Union to serve postal workers throughout the state. The other resolution concerned banks as employers, not financial institutions. It urged union members to assist the Office Employees International Union's campaign to organize bank employees by "apply[ing] direct economic pressures" in their role as depositors.[8]

Banking politics declined as a subject of lay self-education as well. While the production of literature propounding banking politics had long constituted a thriving cottage industry, there was now a dearth of new texts. In 1964 a Bakersfield, California, resident urged Andrae B. Nordskog to republish his works from the 1930s in order "to again enlighten the American people on our monetary + financial system." Unhelpfully, Nordskog had been dead for nearly two years. Likewise, banking politics was virtually absent from the electoral arena. A nominal Greenback Party still managed to eke out a symbolic existence in postwar America. In both 1952 and 1956, it nominated a septuagenarian Washington State grocer for president. Campaign expenses in 1952 totaled a mere $12.50. Party conventions were out of the question. "I'm not really doing much campaigning outside the neighborhood," the grocer acknowledged in 1956. "I get thoroughly disgusted with the colossal ignorance of the public," he confessed. "They don't understand and don't want to."[9]

Chairman Patman

Amid declining public engagement with financial issues, Wright Patman assumed the chairmanship of the House Banking and Currency Committee in 1963. A pleased eighty-one-year-old Texan informed Patman that he had "watched your fight on the control of our money by the large private banks for all these years." This man recently had spoken to a group of college students who had not been exposed to the financial policy debates of previous decades. He distributed a monetary pamphlet to help impart his message—one that Jerry Voorhis had published in the 1940s.[10]

During his chairmanship, Patman energetically attacked the unaccountable power of the financial elite. Patman generally directed his strongest criticism toward the Federal Reserve System, which had asserted its autonomy from public officials in 1951 when the central bank's leadership began to direct monetary policy independently of fiscal policy. President Dwight D. Eisenhower subsequently had publicly affirmed the Federal Reserve System's independence. "I personally believe it would be a mistake to make it definitely and directly responsible to the political head of state." Patman denied the central bank was apolitical. When he confronted the president of the Federal

Reserve Bank of New York in a committee hearing, he charged: "You have the power to veto what the Congress does, and the fact is that you have done it in the past."[11]

Patman's willingness to challenge powerful financial interests stood in stark contrast to the tractable attitude of his colleagues. "They're afraid of big banks," he contended. "The banks have built-in intimidation . . . against every member of Congress." But even Patman had drifted toward a more circumspect position. Murray A. Seeger of the *Los Angeles Times* observed: "Truly radical proposals . . . are rarely heard. Wright Patman's proposals are limited to such things as making the Fed chairman's four-year term coincide with each President's term, subjecting the bank to congressional audits and appropriations hearings and reducing the terms of governors."[12]

The AFL-CIO and National Farmers Union both subscribed to central features of Patman's position on financial issues: they opposed tight money policies and sanctioned reforms intended to reduce the influence bankers exerted over the Federal Reserve System. And controversial monetary policy decisions still elicited scattered grassroots responses. In 1965 the central bank's leadership became concerned about potential inflation and failed to notify the Johnson administration before raising the discount rate to its highest level in thirty-five years. The Farmers Union local in Roundup, Montana, immediately protested this action would "impose further hardship upon the family farm group," and called for legislation "to curb and correct such irresponsible power." A few months later, the Montana Farmers Union agreed that the Federal Reserve System lacked sufficient public accountability and backed Patman's agenda. Senator Lee Metcalf (D-MT) approvingly responded: "Supporting Patman's recommendations with respect to the Federal Reserve is like supporting the Ten Commandments."[13]

For most Americans, however, banking politics had grown unfamiliar by the 1960s. Banking interests, Representative James C. Wright Jr. (D-TX) recalled, depicted Patman "as a quaint relic of a bygone era." One member of the *New York Times'* editorial board expressed little tolerance for the veteran congressman. He found Patman's "loud" and "furious" political manner jarring, and his aggressive approach to banking issues disconcerting, objecting that the Texan's "overzealousness" had provoked an "all-out war against the Federal Reserve System." The *Saturday Evening Post* felt free to dismiss Patman as a "Texas gadfly" on an "oddball crusade," whom most congressmen considered a "'funny money' windbag" peddling "patent-medicine cure-alls."[14]

The Death of Postal Savings

While the financial establishment was successfully resisting Patman's push for reform, the Postal Savings System's days were numbered. In 1952 Senator Wallace F. Bennett (R-UT)—a former president of the National Association of Manufacturers and bank director—introduced the first in a series of bills seeking to do away with the institution. The American Bankers Association stated that postal savings was "in direct competition with private industry" and "no longer serves a needful purpose." Bennett quickly discovered this Progressive Era achievement of banking politics retained supporters. "Are you a banker or interested in some bank," demanded one indignant Chicagoan. Bennett acknowledged that his initial attempt to discontinue postal savings met with "a rough time in the Committee," but he remained "hopeful that conditions may change."[15]

Although the Postal Savings System had endured perpetual attacks from bankers, it now faced active opposition from within the Post Office Department itself. In 1953 President Eisenhower had selected Michigan automobile dealer and Republican Party operative Arthur E. Summerfield to serve as postmaster general. Summerfield's ideological commitment to diminishing the role of public institutions is indicated by his announcement that he was "concerned about the future of the private enterprise system in America which is so heavily influenced by our governmental activities." Upon assuming his post, Summerfield appointed a team of business executives to key positions throughout the department. His selection to head the Bureau of Finance—which was responsible for the Postal Savings System—was Albert J. Robertson, an Iowa banker, who Summerfield revealed had been "recommended to us by the American Bankers Association." Robertson openly opposed the continued existence of postal savings. "I think it would be desirable," he testified, "if it would dry up." In 1957 Summerfield issued an unequivocal call for the abolition of postal savings, arguing, "it is desirable that the Government withdraw from competitive private business at every point."[16]

Public use of the government's savings bank had begun to decline after 1947, when deposits peaked at $3.4 billion. The establishment of the Federal Deposit Insurance Corporation had eliminated a source of competitive advantage for postal savings over banks. But the government's savings bank also was significantly handicapped by its low interest rate, which remained statutorily frozen at 2 percent. In 1962 average deposit rates at private savings institutions surpassed 4 percent. The United Federation of Postal Clerks proposed increasing the postal savings interest rate to 4 percent and raising the deposit limit to match the $10,000 that the FDIC covered. Neither happened. Postal savings also suffered from a severe lack of public exposure. The service had never been publicized. During Summerfield's tenure, postmasters were instructed to remove the program's only publicity: a poster in the lobbies of those post offices that already served as depositories. "If there is one basic reason why the Postal Savings System has not . . . increased in accounts," Representative Arnold Olsen (D-MT) contended, "it is the obvious fact that the Post Office Department has made no effort to encourage new accounts."[17]

In early 1966, a postal union official noted there were "1 million Americans who are, as a matter of right and free choice, depositors in the Postal Savings System." Vigorous public support had allowed the service to survive more than a half century of unrelenting attacks. But such civic activism had lessened considerably as banking politics disappeared from the political landscape. In 1964 the prominent liberal Carey McWilliams had asked President Lyndon B. Johnson to consider whether his War on Poverty might benefit from "some upward adjustment in the interest rates on postal savings." With banking politics no longer a vital force, Johnson responded that the Postal Savings System was "no longer fully adapted to modern needs."[18]

For decades, postal savings had inspired the imaginations of a diverse spectrum of Americans. But by the mid-1960s, financial interests could be politically audacious. Labor unions representing postal workers mounted the only organized advocacy on the service's behalf. "Why is the American Bankers Association being allowed to dictate to the Post Office Department and to the very able Congress of these United States," protested the legislative director of the California Federation of Postal Clerks. In the spring of 1966, the bankers finally succeeded in extinguishing the Postal Savings System.[19]

The Death of Bretton Woods

The death of postal savings reveals the extent to which banking politics had atrophied by the 1960s. Moreover, the popular indifference that allowed bankers to triumph demonstrates how complacent Americans had grown about the private banking system. Even the *Nation* was nonchalant, calling postal savings "a good idea in its time, but good ideas sometimes run their course." Public criticism of banks had not ceased, however. Toward the end of the decade, financial institutions began to draw some political attention as a result of their discriminatory lending policies. Arising from concerns rooted in group identity, rather than more broadly defined economic questions, this development was consonant with the arc of contemporary liberalism. The barriers facing women and blacks seeking access to credit were understood to constitute yet another instance of the discrimination that plagued society in general and were addressed accordingly. Reform of the private banking system itself was not perceived to be relevant. Specific remedies intended to aid disadvantaged groups within the existing financial system were promoted instead.[20]

Banks faced direct protest in the turbulent late 1960s. But protesters did not seek financial reform. Opponents of the apartheid regime that ruled South Africa targeted Chase Manhattan Bank and National City Bank as part of their divestment campaign. Protesters staged demonstrations at their branches, picketed their annual meetings, and pressured institutional shareholders to sell stockholdings in the two banks. Other confrontations proved more volatile. Months of turmoil among college students in Isla Vista, California, culminated in a night of property destruction that included torching the local Bank of America branch. There was no clear explanation for why the bank had been burned down. Grievances over banking and monetary issues had not inspired the recent student unrest, and the disorder that night was a spontaneous response to an instance of police brutality. "It was there . . . the biggest capitalist establishment thing around," one young man reasoned. Dozens of the bank's branches fell victim to explosive and incendiary attacks over the ensuing months. These strikes were uncoordinated but not isolated: a recent wave of attacks had been directed toward numerous corporate, military, and other targets. "There is a new value system emerging in America, starting with the youth but becoming one of the new facts of life for the rest of us to deal with," stated one Bank of America executive. These startling instances of property destruction clearly proved unnerving to bankers but did not alter their business practices.[21]

Less sensational developments would shatter established postwar financial arrangements. In 1950 the United States held almost half of the world's monetary reserves. Subsequent outflows of dollars through American foreign aid and military spending, however, as well as overseas investment by corporations headquartered in the United States, placed the dollar in a precarious position. This situation was underscored in 1965, when the zealous French nationalist Charles de Gaulle announced that the world needed "an indisputable monetary base." The French president resented the preeminent position the Bretton Woods system accorded the United States. "In truth," he contended, "one does not see how one could really have any standard criterion other than gold." The French government began converting large amounts of its dollar holdings into gold bars, which flowed out of the United States Bullion Depository at Fort Knox across the Atlantic Ocean to Paris via Air France. This episode further undermined confidence in the dollar.[22]

By the close of the decade, the international monetary regime established at Bretton Woods was tottering. Gold holdings at Fort

Knox had eroded to the "minimum strategic reserve" of $10 billion. In 1971 President Richard M. Nixon ended the ability of foreign nations to convert their dollars into gold at $35 per ounce. With the 1972 election approaching, he anticipated that devaluation of the dollar would make American exports more competitive, thereby generating new employment. Nixon, fittingly, had first won election to Congress by defeating Jerry Voorhis, with the support of New York financial interests that threatened local businessmen's access to credit if they publicly endorsed Voorhis's reelection. One large bank outright instructed its employees not to vote for Voorhis. The Voorhis campaign spent less than $2,000; a very conservative estimate of Nixon's expenditures ranges from $24,000 to $32,000. One banker alone acknowledged making a $10,000 contribution. During debate over ratification of the Bretton Woods agreements, Voorhis had expectantly envisioned further public controls over global movements of capital. Decades later, the man who defeated him initiated a transformation of the international financial order that countermanded any such progress.[23]

In 1970 Voorhis still upheld the belief that "the issue of money should be in the hands of a government agency, created and controlled by the Congress, and . . . in accord with national need." The American officials charged with forging a replacement for the Bretton Woods system, however, had a very different perspective. They were ideologically opposed to central features of Bretton Woods, such as government adjustment of exchange rates and the capital controls that limited the flow of money across national borders. Nineteen seventy-three witnessed the emergence of a more volatile monetary order predicated on floating exchange rates. This system enabled destabilizing international movements of capital. The trading of national currencies as commodities in foreign exchange markets directly contradicted government authority over money. The growth of Eurodollars—dollars on deposit in banks outside of the United States—proceeded to increase at a rate of around 25 percent annually.[24]

Organized labor recognized the threat that capital mobility posed to American workers. In 1971 AFL-CIO president George Meany apprehensively observed increasing amounts of imported manufactured goods and escalating levels of foreign investment by U.S.-headquartered corporations. He further noted the associated growth of "a vast global network of branches of U.S. banks, which moves funds easily from one country to another, beyond the reach of the monetary policies of any government, including our own." The AFL-CIO Executive Council urged "Congress to direct the Federal Reserve . . . to curb the flow of credit for such activities as conglomerate takeovers, land speculation and foreign subsidiaries." "A Congressional review of the entire Federal Reserve System and the nation's monetary policy is long overdue," the labor federation declared.[25]

But organized labor's belated efforts did not signal a revival of banking politics, which remained largely restricted to the exceptional voice of Patman. In 1972 a resident of Menlo Park, California, facing high mortgage payments, contacted Patman about his concerns. "I appeal to you because yours is the only audible and strong voice raised against the most privileged American Establishment; namely, The Bankers." This view of Patman's virtue was not the prevailing one. Journalist Murray Seeger observed that Patman "is written off as an aging crank and bore." As his position became ever more anomalous, Patman could only deplore the fact that "the United States has become a country of illiterates in the subject of money and banking."[26]

Bankers' Discipline

Americans would pay dearly for their growing ignorance about banking issues. Following the Bretton Woods system's collapse, the dictates of financial institutions and the threat of capital flight increasingly circumscribed the ability of governments to execute policies that citizens voted to implement. For example, during the postwar years New York City's bankers had been politically weak. In the 1970s, however, the bankers were able to reassert significant influence over city policies. New York faced a budgetary crisis following a severe recession that decreased city tax revenues, as well as federal and state assistance. The city had an increasing need to borrow as a consequence. When the American Bankers Association held its 1975 convention in Manhattan, "New York [C]ity can go straight to hell," said one attendee. "Let it get all those bums off the welfare rolls." A financial journalist reported that this reaction "pretty well summed up" bankers' attitudes on the subject: Decrease public services, or else.[27]

New York banks responded to the city's plight by divesting from municipal debt. The resulting financial difficulties allowed Chase Manhattan Bank president David Rockefeller Sr. to instruct the mayor that public expenditures had to be reduced in order to get access to the bond market. City officials implemented the budgetary cuts that bankers demanded. By the early 1980s, New York had eliminated 20 percent of its police officers, almost half of its sanitation workers, and 19,000 public school teachers. Deferred maintenance left 40 percent of drinking fountains in city parks and playgrounds unusable. One-quarter of the city's bus fleet was inoperable on a daily basis, and breakdowns in the subway system had tripled. The city announced plans to close four public hospitals, and tuition was imposed at the City University of New York. From the perspective of one former Chase Manhattan Bank executive: "The city learned that it could not escape the discipline of the marketplace."[28]

The role that bankers played during New York's fiscal crisis did not go unnoticed. Municipal employee unions protested the bankers' agenda. Union leader Victor H. Gotbaum denounced the chairman of National City Bank for drawing a sizable salary while urging wage cuts for city workers. Public employee unions withdrew their deposits from the institution. In 1975 the unions called on their members to boycott the bank and staged a rally in front of its building on Wall Street. Almost 10,000 union members rallied to the cause. Protesting workers carried signs reading "Down With The Banks." "We are here to show that banks can not put themselves above the people of New York and to demonstrate that people are a hell of a lot more important than profits," Gotbaum explained. And yet unions did not mount a campaign to reform the private banking system.[29]

New York's financial elite did not confront a sustained popular challenge to its power. But bankers did grapple briefly with Speaker of the New York State Assembly Stanley Steingut's (D) proposal to

establish a state-owned bank. Steingut declared that banks were failing to "meet their social and economic responsibilities," and his special assistant, William F. Haddad, reported the proposed public bank
had "No. 1 priority." Legislation to establish the "New York State Public Bank Corporation" secured the support of sixty co-sponsors in the
Assembly. The New York State Bankers Association, the New York
Chamber of Commerce and Industry, and the New York Stock Exchange opposed the bill. James J. Needham, chairman of the stock
exchange, pronounced: "Once government encroaches upon the private enterprise system, the free economy begins to erode." A grassroots movement did not arise to support the state bank: the principal
supporters were political and academic figures, including consumer
advocate Ralph Nader and economist Eliot Janeway. The bill passed
the Assembly, but the political influence that bankers wielded in the
Senate won the day, and the legislation advanced no further.[30]

Movements to establish state banks also were stirring on the West
Coast. In Oregon, state representative George W. Starr (D) mounted
a campaign for one. Starr was a railroad conductor and veteran union
activist who had lobbied successfully for railroad safety regulations
prior to his election to the legislature. "If we can get a good return on
Oregon's money, provide tax relief and assist socially worthwhile projects," he argued, "then we have a duty to investigate the possibilities."
But Oregon bankers prevented Starr's measure from advancing. The
Washington Bankers Association also thwarted legislation promoting
a state bank modeled on the Bank of North Dakota.[31]

In California, Voorhis succeeded in securing the support of former
governor Edmund G. "Pat" Brown Sr. (D) for a state bank. Voorhis
claimed that "the people and government of the state of California
would in the course of time be many millions of dollars ahead if they
had a banking institution of their own." In 1977 the state legislature
began investigating the idea. Counterculture activist Thomas E. Hay-
den backed the concept because he objected that public employee
pension funds were "reinvested in cheap labor pools abroad or are
propping up foreign dictatorships." He thought that placing this
money in a state bank would "create more jobs and better living con-

ditions for Californians." The California Bankers Association testified against a state bank, while the California Labor Federation came out in favor of the idea. But as in New York, a handful of political figures and academics spearheaded the campaign. One ally of Voorhis's proposal surmised that bankers had "made a mystique of money" that "so befuddled the public that the average man is afraid even to think about changing the system." The measure was killed in committee. The fate of these proposed state banks demonstrates how enfeebled banking politics had become due to a lack of civic engagement with financial issues. The absence of a grassroots push for public banking allowed bankers to fend off challenges to the financial status quo. Thus, the private banking system remained securely entrenched.[32]

Deindustrialization and Foreclosure

The comparatively unregulated mobility of capital under the new post–Bretton Woods financial regime not only empowered bankers to command influence over public policy, it also facilitated a shift from productive economic activity to speculation. Prior to the dismantling of the Bretton Woods system, 90 percent of international financial transactions had occurred either for long-term investment or trade purposes, and only 10 percent had been speculative. Twenty years later, 90 percent of such transactions were conducted for speculative purposes. Long-term investment in plant and equipment suffered as financial resources were employed in corporate asset transfers.[33]

Absent banking politics, the Federal Reserve System was freer to pursue policies that privileged private financial interests. During the early 1980s, the Federal Reserve's drastic constriction of the money supply to combat inflation exacerbated the productive economy's decline. Real interest rates soared to record highs, acting as a magnet for foreign capital, which presented bankers with profitable new business opportunities. But the resulting increase of the dollar's value in relation to foreign currencies hurt the competitive position of American industrial production. Exports as a percentage of gross domestic product (GDP) dropped from 9 percent in 1979, to 7.2 percent in

1986. "There's going to be a day when the blue-collar worker is not the mainstay of the nation anymore," predicted a local union president in Syracuse. The strong dollar and high interest rates also contributed significantly to the 1980s farm crisis. Agricultural exports declined by over 40 percent between 1983 and 1986. And as farm incomes fell, the value of farmland decreased, which further reduced the ability of farmers to obtain affordable credit. "We were just in the wrong place at the wrong time," observed one man following the auction of his family's upstate New York farm.[34]

The farm crisis and deindustrialization left an indelible mark on much of the nation. During the 1980s, the number of Americans living on farms fell 31 percent. Foreclosure and bankruptcy became notable characteristics of rural life, and increasingly resulted in alcoholism, clinical depression, and even suicide. At the same time, the destruction of the manufacturing base hit American industrial workers hard. As a result of the steel industry's decline, the unemployment rate in Beaver County, Pennsylvania, reached Great Depression levels of 29.6 percent in 1983. Workers experiencing unemployment and underemployment faced loss of savings, homes, and personal possessions, and not infrequently physical and mental health issues.[35]

The impact of deindustrialization was not restricted to only those individuals who lost their jobs. It was a communal experience. Buffalo was one of many cities decimated by the decline of American industry: between 1977 and 1987, 31 percent of its manufacturing jobs vanished. The rapid annihilation of the city's economic base compelled its elected officials to seek out funds for redevelopment efforts. Growing up in Buffalo during the 1930s and 1940s had imprinted banking politics on Mayor James D. Griffin. First elected in 1977, he was an outspoken big-city Irish-American mayor in the mold of James Michael Curley. "I felt the more power bankers had," Griffin once stated, "the less my constituents had." Griffin initially excoriated bankers for declining to invest in his city, voicing a time-honored sentiment when he posited that bankers "have hearts the size of caraway seeds." But the combative Griffin soon mended fences with the bankers and had their full support by the time he faced reelection in 1981. Considering

Buffalo's economic plight, bankers' leverage over the city appeared to necessitate deference.[36]

As industry and agriculture suffered, the relative place of finance in the nation's economy rose. The financial sector comprised 15 percent of GDP in 1980 but had risen to more than 20 percent by 2003. Concurrently, manufacturing's share plummeted from over 20 percent to only 12 percent. Bankers also were reaping increasing financial rewards. For three decades following World War II, the earnings of employees in the banking sector tracked comparable positions in the private sector as a whole. Compensation subsequently exploded: in 2008, 1,626 JPMorgan Chase & Company employees were handed bonus checks that exceeded $1 million. Banking politics had celebrated productive labor and understood finance as a means to facilitate the production of goods and provision of services, rather than as existing for its own sake. Such a perspective condemned the accrual of wealth through financial profiteering. The decay of this aspect of American political culture eliminated a source of opposition to the declining emphasis on productive economic activities and rising inequality that has characterized the United States since the 1970s.[37]

Deregulation

The absence of banking politics created a political vacuum that allowed banking interests to brazenly push for financial deregulation. After decades of relative financial stability, bankers achieved political victories that ushered in a more volatile economic order. Deregulatory reforms encouraged bankers to take speculative risks, rather than exercise prudence. Two major financial crises followed in the wake of deregulation: the savings and loan crisis of the 1980s and 1990s and the 2008 financial crisis. For years, Patman had blocked the banking fraternity's attempts to enact deregulatory legislation. But his death in 1976 removed the chief legislative brake on the bankers' political ambitions. Shortly thereafter, the Depository Institutions Deregulation and Monetary Control Act of 1980 repudiated New Deal regulation. This law phased out interest rate ceilings on savings deposits, permitted interest payments on checking accounts, and allowed savings and loan associations to enter the world of commercial and consumer finance. Meanwhile, Congress took no action in response to the increase in foreign ownership of banks, which made them less accessible to American regulators.[38]

During the early 1980s, savings and loan associations were further deregulated. Thrift institutions traditionally issued low-interest mortgage loans and were finding it difficult to compete for deposits because of record-high real interest rates. The industry successfully lobbied for loosening of ownership requirements, interest rate deregulation, net worth reductions, expanded investment opportunities, and the ability to offer a greater range of financial products. Numerous thrift institutions recklessly took advantage of this deregulated environment. The ensuing crisis witnessed the failure of 1,295 savings and loans holding $621.1 billion in assets. In 1989 the Federal Savings and Loan Insurance Corporation was driven to insolvency. Only massive government intervention averted a still more serious crisis. "If we let the high rollers who have driven the American economy into a wall of debt and insolvency, get away with this holdup with barely a peep," Ralph Nader observed, "it will be a historic collapse in our two hundred year attempt to practice democracy."[39]

Even though estimates of the savings and loan bailout reached $1.4 trillion over forty years, the public reaction was curiously subdued. Banking politics had further atrophied, and no grassroots campaign emerged to curb finance's growing economic and political influence. The result was that large financial interests continued to advance their legislative agenda with impunity. A few short years after the culmination of the savings and loan crisis, the Interstate Banking Act of 1994 abolished prohibitions on interstate branch banking. A. P. Giannini's dream was realized. Large banks could grow even larger. Over 30 percent of the nation's financial institutions ceased to exist during the 1990s.[40]

The bankers' foremost legislative achievement of the decade, however, was nullification of the Banking Act of 1933's separation of investment and commercial banking. J. Pierpont Morgan surely would have been gratified. In 1987 President Ronald Reagan named Alan Greenspan chairman of the Board of Governors of the Federal Reserve System. A disciple of the increasingly influential anti-democratic novelist Ayn Rand, Greenspan proceeded to promote a deregulatory financial agenda. In 1989 Greenspan permitted a commercial bank—J. P. Morgan & Company—to underwrite a corporate bond issue for the first time since the Great Depression. He had served on the bank's board of directors for a decade. The imperative need to authorize banks of deposit to participate in other sectors of the financial industry was a mantra among bankers. In 1990 E. Gerald Corrigan, president of the Federal Reserve Bank of New York, declared that the American banking system was "out of step with the realities of the marketplace." He testified in favor of large financial institutions handling commercial banking, securities, and insurance. Following Corrigan's departure from the central bank in 1993, he took an executive position at Goldman, Sachs & Company.[41]

Financial interests had breached the regulatory dam and remained determined to void the Banking Act of 1933. Nader protested that repealing this landmark law would result in "'too big to be allowed to fail' institutions." "The taxpayers will be left to pick up enormous tabs for bailouts," he warned. Bankers mounted a prolonged lobbying campaign, deluging Congress with $300 million over two decades. Opponents of their deregulatory agenda chaired key congressional committees, however. Representatives John D. Dingell Jr. (D-MI) and Henry B. Gonzalez (D-TX) retained memories of the 1930s banking crisis and staunchly opposed repealing the law. "I saw people evicted from their homes," Dingell explained. "I remember the consequences of the irresponsible behavior in the securities and banking industries." But Republican Party victories in 1994 congressional elections ended their tenures as chairmen, thereby removing these obstacles to bankers' deregulatory ambitions.[42]

Citigroup played a particularly prominent role in the campaign for repeal. This mammoth corporate entity was formed in 1998 by the merger of the bank Citicorp—formerly National City Bank—with financial conglomerate Travelers Group. Citigroup subsequently led a final push for the passage of legislation that would legalize its own existence. Secretary of the Treasury Robert E. Rubin aided the financial behemoth's efforts. The former Goldman Sachs executive would become an executive at Citigroup following his time in the Clinton administration. Industry lobbyists were afforded a privileged position during the legislative process. They reviewed all prospective drafts of the legislation prior to their final introduction in Congress. The resulting Financial Services Act of 1999 authorized a single institution to act as a bank, a securities firm, and an insurance company. "We will, in 10 years['] time," predicted Senator Byron L. Dorgan (D-NPL-ND), "look back and say: We should not have done that . . . we forgot the lessons of the past; those lessons represent timeless truths that were as true in the year 2000 or 2010 as they were in the year 1930." "We will look back at this and wonder how the country was so asleep," Nader affirmed. "It's just a nightmare."[43]

The massive banks that resulted from the late twentieth-century deregulatory push adopted the risk-taking culture of investment banking, rather than the prudence that is supposed to guide commercial banks. And the "too big to fail" character of these institutions served to further encourage reckless practices. Large banks increasingly made risky home loans and converted them into securities that were sold to unsuspecting investors. This securitization of high-risk mortgages helped inflate a menacing housing bubble. When the crash occurred in 2007–2008, homeowners lost $8 trillion of wealth, curtailing consumption and prompting a severe recession. The ensuing credit crisis was further worsened by the inability of financial institutions to cover losses resulting from risky financial instruments—notably derivatives—that bankers had lobbied hard against regulating.[44]

In the fall of 2008, private financial interests insisted that for the sake of the world's economy, an immediate, massive, largely unrestricted government bailout was imperative. "Let's play Wall Street Bailout," protested Representative Marcia C. Kaptur (D-OH). "Disarm the public through fear. Warn that the entire global financial system will collapse and the world will fall into another Great Depression." Such critical voices were soon overwhelmed, however; finance exercised unprecedented political power. The bankers received a blank check, which they cashed for as much as $16 trillion. "Too big to fail" financial institutions had managed to shift their liabilities onto the American public. "For 30 years in one financial scandal after another," Kaptur observed, "Wall Street game masters have kept billions of dollars of their gain and shifted their losses to American taxpayers." The financial crisis and ensuing bailout aroused public indignation that became outspoken anger when the enormous bonuses that Wall Street continued to award itself became widely known. But the immediate popular response to this episode was muted in comparison to the aftermath of the 1933 Norbeck-Pecora investigation and other past revelations of bankers' transgressions.[45]

The economic fallout from the crisis the bankers had created forced another industry to seek government aid. The recession combined with a frozen credit market to push General Motors and Chrysler toward bankruptcy, compelling them to plea for a federal bailout. President Barack H. Obama chuckled, "The only thing less popular than putting money into banks is putting money into the auto industry." The national government begrudgingly offered a comparatively much smaller, more restrictive bailout package to save the American automobile industry. "You have all kinds of funding available to banks that are apparently too big to fail," observed Brian P. Fredline, president of a United Auto Workers local in Michigan. "But when it comes to auto manufacturing and middle-class jobs and people that don't matter on Wall Street, there are certainly different standards." Media coverage frequently emphasized the allegedly excessive compensation of unionized autoworkers, who found themselves forced to defend the very idea of blue-collar workers earning a middle-class living standard. "In 2007, average wage and benefit costs per employee at Goldman Sachs were $661,490," pointed out Robert Weissman, president of Public Citizen. "Even using misleading and wildly inflated auto industry claims, UAW workers cost $150,000 a year."[46]

In a remarkable turn of events, the banking politics of the twentieth century had been flipped on its head. The paper profiteering of bankers had jeopardized the livelihood of workers who labored to produce a tangible product. Yet it was these autoworkers who were villainized for being unproductive and overcompensated. "When the titans of Wall Street came up," observed columnist Mark S. Shields, "there were no questions about pay." But Shields noted the autoworkers' plight elicited a very different response. "A guy who packs a lunch and punches a clock, I mean, you'd think they were raiding the public treasury. . . . [T]hey were treated like Daddy Warbucks." The nation appeared to have turned its back on the producerism that had inspired banking politics.[47]

Epilogue

"Money Changers in This Temple Will Not Stand"

"My administration is the only thing between you and the pitchforks," President Obama apprised a contingent of Wall Street bankers following the 2008 financial crisis. But where was the uprising? Grassroots engagement with financial issues had fallen to the point that anti-government ideas imported by European émigrés—notably Friedrich A. von Hayek, Ludwig von Mises, and Ayn Rand—underpinned some of the more conspicuous criticisms of the banking system. During the late twentieth century, wealthy right-wing individuals had bankrolled an ambitious political effort that aimed to annul the reformed economy that Americans had established in response to the first Gilded Age. This political faction's promotion of free banking and the gold standard contradicted the central demand of banking politics that finance be democratically responsive. In 1970 one Hawaii resident expressed the various impulses of individuals who were receptive to anti-government financial ideas in a letter to her senator that demanded "a return to the gold standard" and investigation of the "UNCONSTITUTIONAL" Federal Reserve System, before outlining her opposition to labor unions, the "Communist dominated" United Nations, government welfare programs, and "compulsory fluoridation" of tap water.[1]

Although the lack of popular engagement with banking issues at the dawn of the twenty-first century was unmistakable, Americans were ensnared in home mortgages, student debt, credit cards, car loans, and numerous other forms of indebtedness. Moreover, as working people confronted rising economic insecurity, they relied on credit. Millions of Americans found themselves virtual prisoners of their creditors, trapped in a cycle of debt. And increasingly a mere handful of large banks presided over these financial fetters. The six largest banking corporations held assets equivalent to 55 percent of GDP in 2006, up from 17 percent in 1995. Following the massive 2008 financial bailout, the assets these six companies held rose to 63 percent.[2]

Early twentieth-century practitioners of banking politics had envisioned a very different financial system. They privileged the economic security of working people. They hoped to establish an economy that was less susceptible to boom and bust. They opposed the centralized private financial power that is irreconcilable with democratic principles. They condemned the pecuniary values that compelled wealthy financiers' exploitation of the laboring majority. Adherents of banking politics privileged higher values than the pursuit of riches, believing American culture should not honor moneymaking for its own sake. They sought a financial order that helped people realize modest economic achievements over their lifetimes, such as owning a decent home, having a comfortable family life, and enjoying the basic trappings of security. A poem from a 1913 union journal extolled this value system:

> I want not wealth—the yellow gold,
> That chills the soul like Arctic cold,
> That turns to ice the warmest heart,
> And withers all its better part;
> I want not wealth:

Only enough to soothe distress,
To cool the brow of wretchedness,
To bring glad smiles to eyes that weep,
And all my live ones safely keep–
This wealth, I want, and nothing more.

Repudiations of acquisitive capitalistic cultural values were heard frequently during the heyday of banking politics. A maxim published in another union journal in 1930 succinctly captured this sentiment. "In dollars and cents don't count your wealth," its author cheerily advised. "But sum it up in good friends and health."[3]

Banking politics dissented from a social order in which the power that money bestows permits a wealthy few to direct the lives of others. The tenets of equality and democracy inspired popular criticism of the existing financial order. Practitioners of banking politics upheld human values. They did not envisage economic activity limited to the artificially constricted social space that orthodox economic thought assumed. Advocates of banking politics saw that the decisions of human actors were responsible for prevailing economic conditions; that the economy was not isolated from other spheres of human endeavor; and that economic decisions have crucial social consequences, and therefore must be responsive to democratic controls. President Franklin D. Roosevelt spoke to the guiding principles of banking politics in his 1933 inaugural address. "The money changers have fled their high seats in the temple of our civilization," he famously observed. "We may now restore the temple to the ancient truths." But Roosevelt went on to say: "The measure of the restoration lies in the extent to which we apply social values more noble than mere monetary profit." Contemporary developments can lend old words new relevance. Stirrings of a banking politics reawakening may now be under way.[4]

In the fall of 2011, simmering anger at large banks erupted when the Occupy Wall Street movement rapidly emerged as a national phenomenon. Its participants united around such slogans as "We are the 99 percent," "Wall Street is destroying America," and "Banks got bailed out, we got sold out!" Although Occupy dissipated that winter, the pressing issues these activists raised found dramatic expression in Senator Bernie Sanders's (I-VT) campaign for the 2016 Democratic presidential nomination. His urgent call for reform of Wall Street helped Sanders win an enthusiastic following despite the steadfast opposition of the party's leadership. "If a bank is too big to fail, it is too big to exist," he declared. "[A] handful of huge financial institutions simply have too much economic and political power over this country." These two dynamic political insurgencies demonstrated revived public interest in banking issues. The dangers of financial monopoly had become such a salient concern that both the 2016 Democratic and Republican platforms proclaimed disapprobation of "too big to fail" banks.[5]

The producerist argument that traditionally justified popular criticism of finance has been heard again as well. In 2012 Bruce Springsteen, long the preeminent cultural spokesman of the nation's white working class, released the album *Wrecking Ball*. Rising to the top of the charts, it voiced our nation's rich legacy of banking politics. His lyrics celebrated the worth of labor—"I always loved the feel of sweat on my shirt"—and asserted the virtuous influence of manual work—"a shovel in the dirt keeps the devil gone." Springsteen juxtaposed his high appraisal of the nation's producers with his estimation of the unearned wealth of bankers. "It's still fat and easy up on banker's hill." And he called attention to the opposing class positions of moneylenders and working people that featured prominently in banking politics. "The banker man grows fat, working man grows thin." Finally, Springsteen affirmed the time-honored hope of practitioners of banking politics. "Jesus said the money changers, in this temple will not stand."[6]

Recent manifestations of public anger over the present financial order recall the banking politics that long provided a counterweight to the power that bankers exercise over a capitalist society. This grassroots political force advanced a series of hard-fought reforms over the first half of the twentieth century that helped establish a postwar era that was remarkably devoid of financial crises. It was a time of exceptional economic stability—as well as of diminished inequality and reduced banker power. Subsequently, the decline of banking politics enabled a political and economic transformation that has created a more unequal, less democratic nation. But the absence of vigorous popular protest of the economic power structure during the postwar years is an anomaly in the grand sweep of American history.

ACKNOWLEDGMENTS

I thank everyone who contributed to this book. It would not have been possible without the work of all those who staff the libraries and archives where I conducted the research. My trip to the Franklin D. Roosevelt Presidential Library and Museum was funded by the Roosevelt Institute. The "Spider of Wall Street" image in chapter 7 is reproduced courtesy of the International Association of Machinists and Aerospace Workers.

Some of this book's arguments appeared previously in "'Tired of Being Exploited': The Grassroots Origin of the Federal Farm Loan Act of 1916," *Agricultural History* 92, no. 4 (2018): 512–40; "'Banks of the People': The Life and Death of the U.S. Postal Savings System," *Journal of Social History* 52, no. 1 (2018): 121–52; "'We Must Deflate': The Crime of 1920 Revisited," *Enterprise & Society* 17, no. 3 (2016): 618–50; and "'The Man in the Street Is for It': The Road to the FDIC," *Journal of Policy History* 27, no. 1 (2015): 36–60. Donald T. Critchlow, Matthew B. Karush, Kimberly Phillips-Fein, Andrew Popp, Albert G. Way, and the anonymous readers of these articles offered critical feedback.

Anna Armentrout, Tracy C. Becker, Kira Blaisdell-Sloan, William Ciarlone, Walter Cohen, Fiona Cundy, Rebecca Darby, Beatrice D. Gurwitz, Ana Mileva, Andrej Milivojevic, Elissa Mondschein, Joseph Lam Nejad-Duong, Zachary S. Ramirez, Daniel M. Robert, Ariel Ron,

Leslie Kristina Salas, Carla Siegel, Michelle K. Trinh, David J. Vogel, and J. O. K. Walsh all contributed to this project in various ways.

During research trips I enjoyed the hospitality of Miles E. Becker, Joseph Bohling, Candace Chen, Dylan J. Esson, Maria Gould, Stephen G. Gross, Tiffany Jo Merrill, Radhika Natarajan, Paul S. Paulson, Padraig Riley, Keith C. Sendziak, Barbara Ramsay Shaw, Robert W. Shaw Jr., and Theodore J. Varno Jr. I am particularly indebted to Todd M. Scriber in this regard.

Paul F. Ramirez offered helpful suggestions. Ryan M. Acton has been a steadfast academic compatriot. John G. Ackerman, Osamah F. Khalil, Kate E. Marshall, Mark A. Peterson, and James Vernon gave valuable advice. John Richard is a generous supporter who provides an inspiring example of perseverance and social commitment.

I am very thankful that Timothy Mennel handled the publication process. He has been an exemplary editor. Erin DeWitt expertly copyedited the manuscript. The anonymous reviewers, including Jeffrey Sklansky (who has since revealed himself), provided extremely helpful comments. Their perceptive criticisms made this book a better one.

Three men who made direct contributions to this project did not live to see its completion. "Facts do not speak for themselves," Lawrence Goodwyn would admonish. He was always provocative, yet consistently supportive. My research began in 2006 under the thoughtful guidance of Jon Gjerde. I miss his sage advice and quiet enthusiasm. Roger S. Erickson played an avuncular role in my life for as long as I can remember.

Christina D. Romer generously offered her keen insight on economic matters. Jan de Vries supported this project from its inception and lent his intellectual rigor throughout. Charles Postel consistently provided both discerning comments on specific details and penetrating feedback on general themes. Robin L. Einhorn has modeled dedication to pursuing and sharing historical knowledge. She has been an advocate who always could be relied on for honest criticism, incisive comments, and insightful advice.

Paulina Hartono provided critical assistance at key moments. I owe her a special debt. I have been blessed with a supportive family.

I am grateful that Timothy P. O'Carroll, Katy Shaw, Judy Jensvold, and Harry E. Shaw believed in what I was doing.

Alvin W. Jensvold impressed upon me the power that finance has over people's lives. A Norwegian Lutheran, Great Depression survivor, World War II veteran, and union electrician, my grandfather also was an engaged citizen, prairie populist, and credit union president and treasurer who spent a lifetime studying finance. We saw Wall Street for the first time together. Although I was only five years old, he wanted me to grasp the gravity of the chaos unfolding below the observation deck of the New York Stock Exchange. I dedicate this book to his memory.

NOTES

Introduction

1. The epigraph is from Woody Guthrie's 1939 song "The Ballad of Pretty Boy Floyd."

2. *New York Times*, April 15, 1913, 3.

3. *Organized Labor* 14, no. 15 (1913): 8. On contemporary interpretations of Jesus as politically radical, see David Burns, *The Life and Death of the Radical Historical Jesus* (New York, 2013). On Morgan's involvement with religion, see Edwin P. Hoyt Jr., *The House of Morgan* (New York, 1966), 274–78.

4. Joseph F. Dinneen, *The Purple Shamrock: The Hon. James Michael Curley of Boston* (New York, 1949), 119.

5. Dinneen, *Purple Shamrock*, 134–37; James Michael Curley (with John Henry Cutler), *I'd Do It Again: A Record of All My Uproarious Years* (Englewood Cliffs, NJ, 1957), 220–21.

6. Curley, *I'd Do It Again*, 222.

7. Kent L. Steckmesser, "The Oklahoma Robin Hood," *American West* 7, no. 1 (1970): 38–41; Paul G. Kooistra, *Criminals as Heroes: Structure, Power and Identity* (Bowling Green, KY, 1989), 132–37; Mark Allan Jackson, *Prophet Singer: The Voice and Vision of Woody Guthrie* (Jackson, MS, 2007), 180–87. On social banditry, see E. J. Hobsbawm, *Primitive Rebels: Studies in Archaic Forms of Social Movements in the 19th and 20th Centuries* (New York, 1965), 13–29; Graham Seal, *Outlaw Heroes in Myth and History* (London, 2011).

8. Negative appraisals of moneylenders have long been widespread. See David R. Graeber, *Debt: The First 5,000 Years* (Brooklyn, 2011). For an insightful examination of such grievances, see R. H. Tawney, "Introduction," in *A Discourse upon Usury*, by Thomas Wilson (New York, 1925), 17–30.

9. Paul Michael Taillon, *Good, Reliable, White Men: Railroad Brotherhoods,*

1877–1917 (Urbana, IL, 2009); Steve B. Leikin, *The Practical Utopians: American Workers and the Cooperative Movement in the Gilded Age* (Detroit, 2005); Herbert G. Gutman, *Work, Culture, and Society in Industrializing America* (New York, 1976); Heath W. Carter, *Union Made: Working People and the Rise of Social Christianity in Chicago* (New York, 2015).

10. Daniel T. Rodgers, *The Work Ethic in Industrial America, 1850–1920* (Chicago, 1978); Marvin Meyers, *The Jacksonian Persuasion: Politics and Belief* (Stanford, CA, 1957); Richard White, *Railroaded: The Transcontinentals and the Making of Modern America* (New York, 2011); Steven L. Piott, *The Anti-Monopoly Persuasion: Popular Resistance to the Rise of Big Business in the Midwest* (Westport, CT, 1985); Gretchen Ritter, *Goldbugs and Greenbacks: The Antimonopoly Tradition and the Politics of Finance in America* (New York, 1997); David Montgomery, *Beyond Equality: Labor and the Radical Republicans, 1862–1872* (New York, 1967); Charles McArthur Destler, *American Radicalism, 1865–1901* (New London, CT, 1946); Charles Postel, *The Populist Vision* (New York, 2007); Lawrence C. Goodwyn, *Democratic Promise: The Populist Moment in America* (New York, 1976); Edward T. O'Donnell, *Henry George and the Crisis of Inequality: Progress and Poverty in the Gilded Age* (New York, 2015); John L. Thomas, *Alternative America: Henry George, Edward Bellamy, Henry Demarest Lloyd and the Adversary Tradition* (Cambridge, MA, 1983).

11. Richard W. Judd, *Socialist Cities: Municipal Politics and the Grass Roots of American Socialism* (Albany, NY, 1989); James R. Green, *Grass-Roots Socialism: Radical Movements in the Southwest, 1895–1943* (Baton Rouge, LA, 1978); Robert D. Johnston, *The Radical Middle Class: Populist Democracy and the Question of Capitalism in Progressive Era Portland, Oregon* (Princeton, NJ, 2003); Kevin Mattson, *Creating a Democratic Public: The Struggle for Urban Participatory Democracy during the Progressive Era* (University Park, PA, 1998).

12. For an illuminating exposition of capitalism, see Robert L. Heilbroner, *The Nature and Logic of Capitalism* (New York, 1985).

13. Charles A. Vogenitz to Elmer Thomas, January 20, 1933, box 5, Elmer Thomas Papers, Carl Albert Congressional Research and Studies Center, University of Oklahoma, Norman.

14. *Watson's Jeffersonian Magazine* 3, no. 3 (1909): 213.

15. These publicly appointed officials have not always produced public accountability. See William Greider, *Secrets of the Temple: How the Federal Reserve Runs the Country* (New York, 1989).

16. D. E. Moggridge, *Maynard Keynes: An Economist's Biography* (New York, 1992), 452. On increasing organizational complexity during the first Gilded Age, see Olivier Zunz, *Making America Corporate, 1870–1920* (Chicago, 1990); Stephen Skowronek, *Building a New American State: The Expansion of National Administrative Capacities, 1877–1920* (New York, 1982); Alan Trachtenberg, *The Incorporation of America: Culture and Society in the Gilded Age* (New York, 1982); Alfred D. Chandler Jr., *The Visible Hand: The Managerial Revolution in American Business*

(Cambridge, MA, 1977); Robert H. Wiebe, *The Search for Order, 1877–1920* (New York, 1967).

17. On the "financial turn" in historical study, see Jeffrey Sklansky, "Labor, Money, and the Financial Turn in the History of Capitalism," *Labor* 11, no. 1 (2014): 23–46. On popular interest in financial issues during the eighteenth and nineteenth centuries, see Sklansky, *Sovereign of the Market: The Money Question in Early America* (Chicago, 2017); Nicolas Barreyre, *Gold and Freedom: The Political Economy of Reconstruction*, trans. Arthur L. Goldhammer (Charlottesville, VA, 2015); Robert E. Shalhope, *The Baltimore Bank Riot: Political Upheaval in Antebellum Maryland* (Urbana, IL, 2009); R. Terry Bouton, *Taming Democracy: "The People," the Founders, and the Troubled Ending of the American Revolution* (New York, 2007); Woody Holton, *Unruly Americans and the Origins of the Constitution* (New York, 2007); Ritter, *Goldbugs and Greenbacks*; Goodwyn, *Democratic Promise*; Walter E. Hugins, *Jacksonian Democracy and the Working Class: A Study of the New York Workingmen's Movement, 1829–1837* (Stanford, CA, 1960); Robert P. Sharkey, *Money, Class, and Party: An Economic Study of Civil War and Reconstruction* (Baltimore, 1959); Arthur M. Schlesinger Jr., *The Age of Jackson* (Boston, 1945).

18. For banker-centric interpretations of American financial history, see Charles W. Calomiris and Stephen H. Haber, *Fragile by Design: The Political Origins of Banking Crises and Scarce Credit* (Princeton, NJ, 2014); Jill M. Hendrickson, *Regulation and Instability in U.S. Commercial Banking: A History of Crises* (New York, 2011); Charles W. Calomiris, *U.S. Bank Deregulation in Historical Perspective* (New York, 2000); Lynne Pierson Doti and Larry E. Schweikart, *Banking in the American West: From the Gold Rush to Deregulation* (Norman, OK, 1991); George J. Benston, *The Separation of Commercial and Investment Banking: The Glass-Steagall Act Revisited and Reconsidered* (New York, 1990); Richard H. Timberlake Jr., *The Origins of Central Banking in the United States* (Cambridge, MA, 1978).

19. Karl Marx and Frederick Engels, *Karl Marx and Frederick Engels: Selected Correspondence*, ed. S. W. Ryazanskaya, trans. I. Lasker (Moscow, 1965), 343; Joseph A. Schumpeter, *Capitalism, Socialism, and Democracy* (New York, 1950), 331; Max Weber, *The Protestant Ethic and the Spirit of Capitalism*, trans. Talcott Parsons (New York, 1952), 55; Werner Sombart, *Why Is There No Socialism in the United States?*, trans. Patricia M. Hocking and C. T. Husbands (White Plains, NY, 1976), 20; Thorstein Veblen, *Absentee Ownership and Business Enterprise in Recent Times* (New York, 1923), 118. Historical studies that present America's capitalistic nature include Joyce Appleby, *The Relentless Revolution: A History of Capitalism* (New York, 2010); Douglas F. Dowd, *U.S. Capitalist Development since 1776: Of, By, and For Which People?* (Armonk, NY, 1993); Gordon S. Wood, *The Radicalism of the American Revolution* (New York, 1992); Jack P. Greene, *Pursuits of Happiness: The Social Development of Early Modern British Colonies and the Formation of American Culture* (Chapel Hill, NC, 1988); Carl N. Degler, *Out of Our Past: The Forces That Shaped Modern America* (New York, 1959); Ray Allen Billington, *West-*

ward Expansion: A History of the American Frontier (New York, 1949); Louis M. Hacker, *The Triumph of American Capitalism* (New York, 1940). For a concise debunking of the "free market," see Dean Baker, *The Conservative Nanny State: How the Wealthy Use the Government to Stay Rich and Get Richer* (Washington, DC, 2006).

20. Christopher Lasch, *The True and Only Heaven: Progress and Its Critics* (New York, 1991), 445–65; C. Vann Woodward, *Tom Watson, Agrarian Rebel* (New York, 1955), 416–50; Alan Brinkley, *Voices of Protest: Huey Long, Father Coughlin, and the Great Depression* (New York, 1982), 269–73; Mary Christine Athans, *The Coughlin-Fahey Connection: Father Charles E. Coughlin, Father Denis Fahey, C.S.Sp., and Religious Anti-Semitism in the United States, 1938–1954* (New York, 1991), 163–207; Norman R. C. Cohn, *Warrant for Genocide: The Myth of the Jewish World Conspiracy and the Protocols of the Elders of Zion* (New York, 1967), 233–36. The anti-Semitism of Father Coughlin and Tom Watson intersected with their Anglophobia. For examples of anti-Semitism among elite financial figures, see Gerald D. Nash, *A. P. Giannini and the Bank of America* (Norman, OK, 1992), 124–25; Wayne A. Wiegand, *Irrepressible Reformer: A Biography of Melvil Dewey* (Chicago, 1996), 255; Ronald Chernow, *The House of Morgan: An American Banking Dynasty and the Rise of Modern Finance* (New York, 1991), 90; Susie J. Pak, *Gentlemen Bankers: The World of J. P. Morgan* (Cambridge, MA, 2013), 130–36. Anti-Semitic prejudices within financial circles support Carey McWilliams's contention that "anti-Semitism in the United States, if it is to be understood, must be studied from the top down and not from the bottom up" (McWilliams, *A Mask for Privilege: Anti-Semitism in America* [Boston, 1948], 124). Practitioners of banking politics included outspoken southern Negrophobes like Tom Watson and Cyclone Davis, who are associated with the region's poor white farmers and laborers. Anti-black racism was diffused throughout the southern white class hierarchy. See Jack M. Bloom, *Class, Race, and the Civil Rights Movement* (Bloomington, IN, 1987), 18–73. Racial prejudice was not associated with any particular position on financial questions. The patrician and pro-banker Carter Glass aggressively promoted white supremacy. See J. Douglas Smith, *Managing White Supremacy: Race, Politics, and Citizenship in Jim Crow Virginia* (Chapel Hill, NC, 2002), 25–26, 147–54, 253–55; Andrew Buni, *The Negro in Virginia Politics, 1902–1965* (Charlottesville, VA, 1967), 17–18, 84, 143–44.

21. Relevant works here include Robert A. Dahl, *Who Governs? Democracy and Power in an American City* (New Haven, CT, 1961); L. Grant McConnell, *Private Power and American Democracy* (New York, 1966); G. William Domhoff, *Who Rules America?* (Englewood Cliffs, NJ, 1967); C. Wright Mills, *The Power Elite* (New York, 1956); Peter B. Evans, Dietrich Rueschemeyer, and Theda Skocpol, eds., *Bringing the State Back In* (New York, 1985); Harold J. Laski, *The State in Theory and Practice* (New York, 1935); Ralph Miliband, *The State in Capitalist Society* (New York, 1969); Frances Fox Piven and Richard A. Cloward, *Poor People's Movements: Why They Succeed, How They Fail* (New York, 1977).

22. On the New Deal's achievements, see Alan Brinkley, *Liberalism and Its Discontents* (Cambridge, MA, 1998), 34–36.

23. David A. Moss, "An Ounce of Prevention: Financial Regulation, Moral Hazard, and the End of 'Too Big to Fail,'" *Harvard Magazine*, September/October 2009, 24–29; Andrew J. Jalil, "A New History of Banking Panics in the United States, 1825–1929: Construction and Implications," *American Economic Journal: Macroeconomics* 7, no. 3 (2015): 295–330; Samuel Rezneck, *Business Depressions and Financial Panics: Essays in American Business and Economic History* (Westport, CT, 1971).

Chapter One

1. *Congressional Record* [hereafter *CR*], March 17, 1908, 3451–52; anonymous to Theodore Roosevelt, December 5, 1907, box 79, Thomas E. Watson Papers, Southern Historical Collection, University of North Carolina, Chapel Hill. Accounts of the Panic of 1907 focus on financial events in Manhattan. See Mary A. O'Sullivan, *Dividends of Development: Securities Markets in the History of U.S. Capitalism, 1866–1922* (New York, 2016), 205–29; Robert F. Bruner and Sean D. Carr, *The Panic of 1907: Lessons Learned from the Market's Perfect Storm* (Hoboken, NJ, 2007); William L. Silber, *When Washington Shut Down Wall Street: The Great Financial Crisis of 1914 and the Origins of America's Monetary Supremacy* (Princeton, NJ, 2007), 42–57; Elmus R. Wicker, *Banking Panics of the Gilded Age* (New York, 2000), 83–113; Robert Sobel, *Panic on Wall Street: A History of America's Financial Disasters* (New York, 1968), 297–321.

2. *Equity Journal* 1, no. 1 (1907): 5; *Brotherhood of Locomotive Firemen and Enginemen's Magazine* 44, no. 3 (1908): 377.

3. *Bankers' Magazine* 76, no. 4 (1908): 480; *Public Ledger* (Philadelphia), March 19, 1908, 14; Theodore Roosevelt, *The Letters of Theodore Roosevelt*, ed. Elting E. Morison, 8 vols. (Cambridge, MA, 1951–54), 5:856.

4. For Pierre Bourdieu, orthodox ideas accord with the opinions of the "dominant classes." Orthodoxy, therefore, "exists only in the objective relationship which opposes it to heterodoxy" (Bourdieu, *Outline of a Theory of Practice*, trans. Richard Nice [New York, 1977], 169).

5. Isaac F. Marcosson, *Anaconda* (New York, 1957), 94–96; Ida M. Tarbell, *The History of the Standard Oil Company*, 2 vols. (New York, 1904), 2:225. On the influence that Amalgamated Copper—later the Anaconda Copper Mining Company—exerted over Montana, see Dennis L. Swibold, *Copper Chorus: Mining, Politics, and the Montana Press, 1889–1959* (Helena, MT, 2006); Joseph Kinsey Howard, *Montana: High, Wide, and Handsome* (New Haven, CT, 1943); Christopher P. Connolly, *The Devil Learns to Vote: The Story of Montana* (New York, 1938). On the Standard Oil Gang, see John T. Flynn, *God's Gold: The Story of Rockefeller and His Times* (New York, 1932), 344–48; Allan Nevins, *Study in Power: John D. Rockefeller, Industrialist and Philanthropist*, 2 vols. (New York, 1953), 2:279–87.

On Gilded Age business practices, see Matthew Josephson, *The Robber Barons: The Great American Capitalists, 1861-1901* (New York, 1934).

6. Reno H. Sales, *Underground Warfare at Butte* (Butte, MT, 1964), 9; *McClure's Magazine* 29, no. 1 (1907): 2; Sarah McNelis, *Copper King at War: The Biography of F. Augustus Heinze* (Missoula, MT, 1968), 17. On the apex law, see H. W. MacFarren, *Mining Law for the Prospector, Miner, and Engineer* (San Francisco, 1911), 138–45. Forrest L. Foor, "The Senatorial Aspirations of William A. Clark, 1898-1901: A Study in Montana Politics" (PhD diss., University of California, Berkeley, 1941), 189; C. B. Glasscock, *The War of the Copper Kings: Builders of Butte and Wolves of Wall Street* (New York, 1935), 263–65; *McClure's Magazine* 29, no. 2 (1907): 224; *Current Literature* 44, no. 1 (1908): 34; Marcosson, *Anaconda*, 132–33.

7. *New York Tribune*, January 9, 1907, 10; *Wall Street Journal*, October 12, 1906, 6; McNelis, *Copper King at War*, 157–58; *San Francisco Chronicle*, October 17, 1907, 1; *New York World*, October 17, 1907, 1. The most extended account of the Panic of 1907 ignores any connection between the Standard Oil Gang and this event (Bruner and Carr, *Panic of 1907*). Other studies maintain Heinze's business opponents did play a role in precipitating this financial crisis. See Michael P. Malone, *The Battle for Butte: Mining and Politics on the Northern Frontier, 1864-1906* (Seattle, 1981), 194; Sobel, *Panic on Wall Street*, 308–11; McNelis, *Copper King at War*, x, 167; Connolly, *Devil Learns to Vote*, 306–7; Glasscock, *War of the Copper Kings*, 304.

8. *Chicago Daily Tribune*, October 20, 1907, 2; *Washington Post*, October 20, 1907, 3. A spurned female friend of Heinze later claimed that he had "spilled all his secrets in the United Copper deal" to a "Titian-haired beauty" that the Standard Oil Gang employed to "obtain advance information" on business affairs. See *St. Louis Post-Dispatch*, August 30, 1910, 1; August 28, 1910, II-3.

9. Saul Engelbourg, "Behind the Throne: A Non-Morgan View of the Panic of 1907," *Revue Internationale d'Histoire de la Banque* 4 (1971): 141–57; *New York Times*, October 8, 1902, 7; Flynn, *God's Gold*, 344–45; Maury N. Klein, *The Life and Legend of E. H. Harriman* (Chapel Hill, NC, 2000), 163; Harold van B. Cleveland and Thomas F. Huertas, *Citibank, 1812-1970* (Cambridge, MA, 1985), 34–35; John K. Winkler, *The First Billion: The Stillmans and the National City Bank* (New York, 1934), 60–61; *New York Times*, April 11, 1910, 1; Anna Robeson Burr, *The Portrait of a Banker: James Stillman, 1850-1918* (New York, 1927), 232; McNelis, *Copper King at War*, 163; *New York World*, October 20, 1907, 1. New York City banks formed the first clearinghouse association in 1853 to settle account balances between member banks. Over time, clearinghouses began to police the operations of member banks in order to ensure their financial soundness. These associations also coordinated mutual action in times of financial stress, including extending loans to members. In cases of extreme crisis, clearinghouses issued scrip to circulate among the public. See James Graham Cannon, *Clearing Houses* (Washington, DC, 1910).

10. Vincent P. Carosso with Rose C. Carosso, *The Morgans: Private International Bankers, 1854–1913* (Cambridge, MA, 1987), 535–36; *New York Times*, October 22, 1907, 1; October 23, 1907, 2; *New York World*, October 23, 1907, 2.

11. *New York Times*, October 26, 1907, 5; *New York Tribune*, October 24, 1907, 1; October 26, 1907, 1; *New York World*, February 15, 1908, 1; Boyden Sparkes and Samuel Taylor Moore, *The Witch of Wall Street: Hetty Green* (New York, 1935), 280–88.

12. *New York Times*, October 24, 1907, 1; *New York World*, October 24, 1907, 2; *Brooklyn Daily Eagle*, October 24, 1907, 2; *New York World*, October 25, 1907, 2; *Washington Post*, October 29, 1907, 1; James Stillman to George Cortelyou, November 4, 1907, box 6, James Stillman Papers, Rare Book & Manuscript Library, Columbia University, New York City.

13. Eugene Nelson White, *The Regulation and Reform of the American Banking System, 1900–1929* (Princeton, NJ, 1983), 65–74; Margaret G. Myers, *The New York Money Market*, 4 vols. (New York, 1931–32), 1:240–50; *Oakland Tribune*, November 7, 1907, 6; Wesley Clair Mitchell, *Business Cycles and Their Causes* (Berkeley, 1950), 79; *Cortland (NY) Democrat*, November 15, 1907, 4; James Graham Cannon, *Clearing House Loan Certificates* (New York, 1910); *Seattle Sunday Times*, February 16, 1908, 8; F. Cyril James, *The Growth of Chicago Banks*, 2 vols. (New York, 1938), 2:761.

14. *Nevada State Journal* (Reno), October 25, 1907, 1; *Tulsa (OK) Daily World*, November 1, 1907, 1; *Morning Olympian* (Olympia, WA), October 30, 1907, 1; *San Francisco Call*, October 31, 1907, 1; *Morning Oregonian* (Portland), November 4, 1907, 5; James H. Gilbert, "The History of Banking in Oregon," in *History of the Willamette Valley, Oregon*, by Robert Carlton Clark, 3 vols. (Chicago, 1927), 1:772–76; *Morning Oregonian* (Portland), December 14, 1907, 10; *San Francisco Chronicle*, November 20, 1907, 2; December 18, 1907, 3; *Los Angeles Times*, December 22, 1907, I-1.

15. *Michigan Farmer* 52, no. 26 (1907): 454; *California Cultivator* 29, no. 22 (1907): 524; *Daily Picayune* (New Orleans), November 24, 1907, 8; *Weekly Market Growers Journal* 1, no. 14 (1907): 2; *Berkeley Independent*, October 30, 1907, 1.

16. Richard E. Sylla, "Federal Policy, Banking Market Structure, and Capital Mobilization in the United States," *Journal of Economic History* 29, no. 4 (1969): 656–86; William E. Laird and James R. Rinehart, "Deflation, Agriculture, and Southern Development," *Agricultural History* 42, no. 2 (1968): 115–24; Thomas Dionysius Clark, "The Furnishing and Supply System in Southern Agriculture since 1865," *Journal of Southern History* 12, no. 1 (1946): 24–44; Vincent P. Carosso, *Investment Banking in America: A History* (Cambridge, MA, 1970).

17. Comptroller of the Currency, *Annual Report, 1907* (Washington, DC, 1907), 9; Sharon Ann Murphy, *Other People's Money: How Banking Worked in the Early American Republic* (Baltimore, 2017), 157–61; Cleveland and Huertas, *Citibank*, 44–46; *Financier*, January 23, 1905, 326–27.

18. Comptroller of the Currency, *Annual Report, 1907*, 34; George E. Barnett,

State Banks and Trust Companies (Washington, DC, 1911); Ross M. Robertson, *The Comptroller and Bank Supervision: A Historical Appraisal* (Washington, DC, 1968), 64–66; Richard E. Sylla, *The American Capital Market, 1846–1914* (New York, 1975), 52–53; Carl W. Thompson, *Costs and Sources of Farm-Mortgage Loans in the United States*, Department of Agriculture, Bulletin No. 384 (1916): 9–13; Clay Herrick, *Trust Companies* (New York, 1909), 47–51; John Moody, *The Masters of Capital* (New Haven, CT, 1919), 120–21. National banks found ways to circumvent the prohibition on real estate lending. See Richard H. Keehn and W. Gene Smiley, "Mortgage Lending by National Banks," *Business History Review* 51, no. 4 (1977): 474–91.

19. Weldon Welfling, *Mutual Savings Banks: The Evolution of a Financial Intermediary* (Cleveland, 1968); Senate, *Special Report from the Banks of the United States*, 61st Cong., 2nd Sess. (1909), S. Doc. 225, 58, 44–46; Comptroller of the Currency, *Annual Report, 1907*, 50–51; Raymond W. Goldsmith, *A Study of Saving in the United States*, 3 vols. (Princeton, NJ, 1955–56), 1:725: Suzanne M. Zukowski, "From Peasant to Proletarian: Home Ownership in Milwaukee's Polonia," *Polish American Studies* 66, no. 2 (2009): 5–44. On the financial strategies of savings bank depositors, see R. Daniel Wadhwani, "Banking from the Bottom Up: The Case of Migrant Savers at the Philadelphia Savings Fund Society during the Late Nineteenth Century," *Financial History Review* 9, no. 1 (2002): 41–63.

20. Alfred O. Crozier, "The Recent Panic and the Present Deadly Peril to American Prosperity," *Arena* 39, no. 220 (1908): 273; *Michigan Alumnus* 40, no. 14 (1934): 236; New York State Banking Department, *Annual Report, Relative to Savings Banks, Trust Companies, Safe Deposit Companies and Miscellaneous Corporations, 1901* (Albany, 1902), 20; idem, *Annual Report, Relative to Savings Banks, Trust Companies, Safe Deposit Companies and Miscellaneous Corporations, 1907* (Albany, 1908), 15; idem, *Annual Report, 1901* (Albany, 1902), ix; idem, *Annual Report, 1907* (Albany, 1908), vi; Myers, *New York Money Market*, 1:251–53; *Trust Companies* 5, no. 6 (1907): 821.

21. Winkler, *First Billion*, 170–71; Lewis Corey, *The House of Morgan: A Social Biography of the Masters of Money* (New York, 1930), 345; Burr, *Portrait of a Banker*, 233–34; Upton Sinclair, *The Brass Check: A Study of American Journalism* (Pasadena, CA, 1919), 80–81. Sinclair later revealed that James B. Dill and Samuel Untermyer were the two attorneys (Upton Sinclair, interviewed by Ronald G. Hesman, Oral History Research Office, Columbia University, 1963, 33). *St. Louis Post-Dispatch*, February 9, 1908, 2. Morgan subsequently denied statements he made in this interview; the journalist submitted an affidavit affirming its accuracy (*St. Louis Post-Dispatch*, February 16, 1908, 3). Jon R. Moen and Ellis W. Tallman, "Clearinghouse Membership and Deposit Contraction during the Panic of 1907," *Journal of Economic History* 60, no. 1 (2000): 145–63; Silber, *When Washington Shut Down*, 48; Joseph French Johnson, "The Crisis and Panic of 1907," *Political Science Quarterly* 23, no. 3 (1908): 465; Jon R. Moen and Ellis W. Tallman, "The Bank Panic of 1907: The Role of Trust Companies," *Journal of Economic History*

52, no. 3 (1992): 611–30; *New York World*, October 28, 1907, 2; *Los Angeles Times*, October 28, 1907, I-2.

22. Sinclair, *Brass Check*, 81; Herbert Quick, "Lessons from Former Panics," *Moody's Magazine* 4, no. 11 (1907): 559; *San Francisco Call*, August 22, 1907, 8; *New York World*, October 21, 1907, 2.

23. Lloyd Wendt and Herman Kogan, *Bet a Million! The Story of John W. Gates* (Indianapolis, 1948), 256–92; Justin Fuller, "History of the Tennessee Coal, Iron, and Railroad Company, 1852–1907" (PhD diss., University of North Carolina, Chapel Hill, 1966), 156–66; Sobel, *Panic on Wall Street*, 317–20; Frederick Lewis Allen, *The Lords of Creation* (New York, 1935), 135–37.

24. *Wall Street Journal*, November 7, 1907, 3; Harvey O'Connor, *Steel—Dictator* (New York, 1935), 54–57; Kenneth Warren, *The American Steel Industry, 1850–1970: A Geographical Interpretation* (Oxford, 1973), 186; *Wall Street Journal*, November 8, 1907, 2; *News and Observer* (Raleigh, NC), November 8, 1907, 4. U.S. Steel shortly came under antitrust scrutiny. See Walter Adams and James W. Brock, *The Bigness Complex: Industry, Labor, and Government in the American Economy* (New York, 1986), 139–41; Thomas W. Ramage, "Augustus Owsley Stanley: Early Twentieth Century Kentucky Democrat" (PhD diss., University of Kentucky, 1968), 64–130; House, *Investigation of United States Steel Corporation*, 62nd Cong., 2nd Sess. (1912), H. Rept. 1127.

25. John P. Altgeld, *The Cost of Something for Nothing* (Chicago, 1904), 61–62; *Locomotive Engineers Journal* 42, no. 6 (1908): 518.

26. *United Mine Workers Journal* 18, no. 43 (1908): 6; *Wilkes-Barre (PA) Times Leader*, April 2, 1917, 3; David Jones, *Memorial Volume of Welsh Congregationalists in Pennsylvania, U.S.A.* (Utica, NY, 1934), 352–54; *Philadelphia Inquirer*, September 8, 1869, 4.

27. *Wilkes-Barre (PA) Times*, May 15, 1905, 11; Jones, *Memorial Volume*, 352–54; *Wilkes-Barre (PA) Times Leader*, July 21, 1909, 9; January 16, 1913, 3; *Wilkes-Barre (PA) Times*, January 6, 1903, 4; *Wilkes-Barre (PA) Leader*, September 18, 1878, 3; *Scranton (PA) Tribune*, January 10, 1894, 1; *Wilkes-Barre (PA) Times*, October 27, 1894, 8; May 7, 1906, 11; *Weekly Patriot* (Harrisburg, PA), September 23, 1869, 3. On the Avondale disaster, see Ronald L. Lewis, *Welsh Americans: A History of Assimilation in the Coalfields* (Chapel Hill, NC, 2008), 159–67. Avondale led to new mine safety legislation. See Alexander Trachtenberg, *The History of Legislation for the Protection of Coal Miners in Pennsylvania, 1824–1915* (New York, 1942), 37.

28. *Wilkes-Barre (PA) Times Leader*, January 16, 1913, 3; *United Mine Workers Journal* 18, no. 50 (1908): 2; idem, 19, no. 1 (1908): 6; *Implement Age* 38, no. 23 (1911): 18; *United Mine Workers Journal* 21, no. 37 (1911): 7; idem, 18, no. 43 (1908): 6.

29. [Finley Peter Dunne], *Dissertations by Mr. Dooley* (New York, 1906), 303–5.

30. *Boston Daily Globe*, November 2, 1907, 6; *Wall Street Journal*, November 7,

1907, 1; *Morning Oregonian* (Portland), November 8, 1907, 8; *Washington Post*, October 26, 1907, 6.

31. *Bricklayer and Mason* 10, no. 12 (1907): 177; *La Crosse (WI) Tribune*, October 31, 1907, 3; *Berkeley Independent*, November 7, 1907, 2.

32. Woodward, *Tom Watson*; *Watson's Jeffersonian Magazine* 1, no. 12 (1907): 1133–34.

33. O'Sullivan, *Dividends of Development*, 230; *CR*, December 3, 1907, 71; Edwin W. Kemmerer, "Seasonal Variations in the New York Money Market," *American Economic Review* 1, no. 1 (1911): 41–42; *Wallaces' Farmer* 32, no. 52 (1907): 1523; *Morning Oregonian* (Portland), November 4, 1907, 1; Gilbert, "History of Banking in Oregon," 1:774; *Capital Journal* (Salem, OR), November 5, 1907, 2. On the sub-treasury plan, see William P. Yohe, "An Economic Appraisal of the Sub-Treasury Plan," in Goodwyn, *Democratic Promise*, 571–81.

34. Richard T. McCulley, "The Origins of the Federal Reserve Act of 1913: Banks and Politics during the Progressive Era, 1897–1913" (PhD diss., University of Texas, Austin, 1980), 116–37. The gold standard was premised on a theoretically self-correcting mechanism whereby national outflows of gold resulting from balance-of-payments deficits produced deflation, while inflows of gold generated inflation. For a succinct historical overview of American paper currency, see Bureau of Engraving and Printing, *Currency Notes* (Washington, DC, 2004).

35. *Statutes at Large* 31 (1900): 49; Michael K. Kuehlwein, "The National Bank Note Controversy Reexamined," *Journal of Money, Credit, and Banking* 24, no. 1 (1992): 111–26; Robert Craig West, *Banking Reform and the Federal Reserve, 1863–1923* (Ithaca, NY, 1977), 42–46. Asset currency had been advocated since the 1890s. See Indianapolis Monetary Convention, *Report of the Monetary Commission* (Chicago, 1898), 231–36; Department of the Treasury, *Annual Report, 1894* (Washington, DC, 1894), lxvii–lxxxiii; Comptroller of the Currency, *Annual Report, 1894* (Washington, DC, 1894), 31–36; American Bankers Association, *Twentieth Annual Convention* (New York, 1894), 69–72.

36. *Watson's Magazine* 4, no. 1 (1906): 118; House Banking and Currency Committee, *Hearings and Arguments on Proposed Currency Legislation*, 60th Cong. (Washington, DC, 1908), 73.

37. *Washington Post*, January 1, 1908, 4; Paolo E. Coletta, "Greenbackers, Goldbugs, and Silverites: Currency Reform and Policy, 1860–1897," in *The Gilded Age: A Reappraisal*, ed. H. Wayne Morgan (Syracuse, NY, 1963); Milton Friedman, "Bimetallism Revisited," *Journal of Economic Perspectives* 4, no. 4 (1990): 85–104; William Jennings Bryan, "The Government Should Issue Notes and Guarantee Bank Deposits," *Journal of Accountancy* 5, no. 5 (1908): 370. For Bryan's position on financial issues, see Paolo E. Coletta, "William Jennings Bryan and Currency and Banking Reform," *Nebraska History* 45, no. 1 (1964): 31–57. Prior to the Coinage Act of 1873, the United States operated under a policy of bimetallism: United States Mints would coin all silver bullion brought to them into dollars without charge. Following enactment of this law, silver was effectively demonetized, and

in practice the nation was on the gold standard. A deflationary slide extending from the 1870s into the 1890s prompted demands for inflation that included political efforts to remonetize silver. This movement culminated in the 1896 Bryan presidential campaign that supported resumption of free and unlimited coinage of the silver dollar.

38. Ritter, *Goldbugs and Greenbacks*; Postel, *Populist Vision*, 280–81; Goodwyn, *Democratic Promise*, 152–53; Kirk H. Porter and Donald Bruce Johnson, eds., *National Party Platforms, 1840–1956* (Urbana, IL, 1956), 91; Worth Robert Miller, *Oklahoma Populism: A History of the People's Party in Oklahoma Territory* (Norman, OK, 1987), 159; John G. Blocker, *The Guaranty of State Bank Deposits* (Lawrence, KS, 1929), 8–9; T. Bruce Robb, *The Guaranty of Bank Deposits* (Boston, 1921), 20–21; Michigan Federation of Labor, *Official Year Book, 1906–7* (Detroit, 1907), 327.

39. John D. Hicks, *The Populist Revolt: A History of the Farmers' Alliance and the People's Party* (Minneapolis, 1931), 186–204; *Atlanta Journal*, November 5, 1907, 2; Senate, S. Res. 27, 60th Cong., 1st Sess. (1907); *CR*, December 16, 1907, 343; *Indianapolis Star*, November 15, 1907, 8; *Watson's Jeffersonian Magazine* 2, no. 1 (1908): 25; *Washington Post*, November 26, 1907, 1; *Atlanta Constitution*, December 10, 1907, 1; *Wall Street Journal*, December 12, 1907, 7; *Atlanta Constitution*, January 12, 1908, 1B; *CR*, December 9, 1907, 220.

40. *New York Times*, November 10, 1907, 1; *International Wood-Worker* 17, no. 12 (1907): 29. On Coxey, see Embrey B. Howson, "Jacob Sechler Coxey: A Biography of a Monetary Reformer, 1854–1951" (PhD diss., Ohio State University, 1973). On Coxey's Army, see Carlos A. Schwantes, *Coxey's Army: An American Odyssey* (Lincoln, NE, 1985); Benjamin F. Alexander, *Coxey's Army: Popular Protest in the Gilded Age* (Baltimore, 2015).

41. *Chicago Record-Herald*, November 18, 1907, 3; Margaret A. Haley, *Battleground: The Autobiography of Margaret A. Haley*, ed. Robert L. Reid (Urbana, IL, 1982), 20, 12; *Equity Farm Journal* 1, no. 5 (1908): 5.

42. Robert W. Larson, *Populism in the Mountain West* (Albuquerque, NM, 1986); *Nevada State Journal* (Reno), November 4, 1907, 4; *Salt Lake (UT) Herald*, January 17, 1908, 1; *Goodwin's Weekly* 12, no. 5 (1907): 1; *Buffalo Evening Times*, February 4, 1908, 9; *Plain Dealer* (Cleveland), February 18, 1908, 4. Census records available at HeritageQuest Online yielded information about some of the more obscure individuals in this work, including Thomas Murphy.

43. *Houston Daily Post*, November 18, 1907, 4; National Grange, *Thirty-First Session* (Mechanicsburg, PA, 1897), 185–86; Farmers' National Congress, *Seventeenth Annual Session* (n.p., 1897), 60; American Federation of Labor, *Thirteenth Annual Convention* (n.p., 1893), 37; Knights of Labor, *Ninth Regular Session* (n.p., 1885), 12; *St. Louis Labor* 6, no. 354 (1907): 4; *Chicago Record-Herald*, November 18, 1907, 5. The Social Democracy of America—precursor to the Socialist Party of America—had endorsed postal savings at its 1897 founding convention. See Ira A. Kipnis, *The American Socialist Movement, 1897–1912* (New York, 1952), 52.

44. *Public Ledger* (Philadelphia), October 27, 1907, 1; *Postal Clerk* 6, no. 12 (1907): 4–6. On the Old Guard Republican membership of Philadelphia's Union League, see Maxwell Whiteman, *Gentlemen in Crisis: The First Century of the Union League of Philadelphia, 1862–1962* (Philadelphia, 1975). Meyer was not the first postmaster general to promote postal savings: John Wanamaker had been a notable advocate. See Herbert Adams Gibbons, *John Wanamaker*, 2 vols. (New York, 1926), 1:284–87.

45. Wayne A. Wiegand, *Patrician in the Progressive Era: A Biography of George von Lengerke Meyer* (New York, 1988), 41, 56–57; *Postal Clerk* 6, no. 12 (1907): 4–6; Post Office Department, *Report of the Postmaster-General, 1907* (Washington, DC, 1907), 8; *Chicago Record-Herald*, November 9, 1907, 1. Savings bank dividend rates from 1900 to 1910 averaged 3.80 percent (Sidney Homer and Richard E. Sylla, *A History of Interest Rates* [Hoboken, NJ, 2005], 361).

46. *Bankers' Magazine* 75, no. 6 (1907): 870, 789; George von L. Meyer to W. Murray Crane, November 20, 1907, box 10, George von L. Meyer Papers, Massachusetts Historical Society, Boston; George von L. Meyer, "The Need of Postal Savings-Banks," *American Review of Reviews* 39, no. 1 (1909): 48.

47. *Shoe Workers' Journal* 8, no. 12 (1907): 31; *Brotherhood of Locomotive Firemen and Enginemen's Magazine* 44, no. 1 (1908): 120, 123; *Typographical Journal* 31, no. 6 (1907): 648; *Chicago Daily Tribune*, November 18, 1907, 2; *Imperial Valley (CA) Press* 7, no. 36 (1907): 4; *Equity Journal* 1, no. 1 (1907): 14; *Bellingham (WA) Herald*, November 15, 1907, 4.

48. Farmers' National Congress, *Official Proceedings, 1907* (n.p., 1907), 25; National Grange, *Forty-First Annual Session* (Concord, NH, 1907), 113; American Federation of Labor, *Twenty-Seventh Annual Convention* (Washington, DC, 1907), 335, 342; *Journal of the Knights of Labor* 27, no. 7 (1908): 1; *Evening Star* (Washington, DC), November 14, 1907, 9. On the AFL's engagement with financial reform, see Joyce Goldy Skeels, "The Early American Federation of Labor and Monetary Reform," *Labor History* 12, no. 4 (1971): 530–50.

49. *Outlook* 87, no. 15 (1907): 795; *Collier's* 40, no. 7 (1907): 28. Postal savings supporters regularly noted the prevalence of post office savings banks internationally. See Sheldon M. Garon, *Beyond Our Means: Why America Spends While the World Saves* (Princeton, NJ, 2012), 107–8. *Ohio Farmer* 112, no. 21 (1907): 412; *Breeder's Gazette*, 52, no. 19 (1907): 946; *Morning Oregonian* (Portland), November 9, 1907, 11.

50. In 1893 then-congressman Bryan introduced legislation to guarantee national bank deposits (*CR*, September 22, 1893, 1700). There was nineteenth-century precedent for guaranty: New York State had established the Safety Fund System in 1829 to pay the debts of failed banks. The fund's resources were strained following the Panic of 1837, and the law was amended to guarantee only banknotes. See Robert E. Chaddock, *The Safety-Fund Banking System in New York State, 1829–1866* (Washington, DC, 1910). Vermont, Indiana, Michigan, Ohio, and Iowa set up guaranty programs prior to the Civil War. All of them had ceased to

exist by 1866. See Carter H. Golembe and Clark A. Warburton, *Insurance of Bank Obligations in Six States during the Period 1829–1866* (Washington, DC, 1958); Golembe, "Origins of Deposit Insurance in the Middle West, 1834–1866," *Indiana Magazine of History* 51, no. 2 (1955): 113–20. *Commoner* 7, no. 44 (1907): 3; New York State Grange, *Thirty-Fifth Annual Session* (Syracuse, 1908), 141–42; *National Stockman and Farmer* 31, no. 37 (1907): 25; United Mine Workers of America, *Nineteenth Annual Convention* (Indianapolis, 1908), 298.

51. FDIC, *The First Fifty Years: A History of the FDIC, 1933–1983* (Washington, DC, 1984), 29; *CR*, January 9, 1908, 563; January 15, 1908, 715; *St. Louis Daily Globe-Democrat*, January 18, 1908, 9; *American Review of Reviews* 36, no. 6 (1907): 650; *Farm Journal* 32, no. 4 (1908): 173.

52. *Shoe Workers' Journal* 8, no. 12 (1907): 9; *Berkeley Independent*, December 7, 1907, 2; *Equity Journal* 1, no. 1 (1907): 14.

53. *Sacramento (CA) Evening Bee*, November 30, 1907, 11.

Chapter Two

1. Peter H. Buckingham, *Rebel against Injustice: The Life of Frank P. O'Hare* (Columbia, MO, 1996), 52; Andrew Carnegie, "The Worst Banking System in the World," *Journal of Accountancy* 5, no. 5 (1908): 357–61; *New York Tribune*, February 6, 1908, 2.

2. *Chicago Daily Tribune*, October 23, 1907, 2; Adolph Edwards, *The Roosevelt Panic of 1907* (New York, 1907); Kathleen Dalton, *Theodore Roosevelt: A Strenuous Life* (New York, 2002), 331–32; *St. Louis Post-Dispatch*, February 9, 1908, 2; Kathleen Dalton, "Theodore Roosevelt, Knickerbocker Aristocrat," *New York History* 67, no. 1 (1986): 55–58; William Henry Harbaugh, *Power and Responsibility: The Life and Times of Theodore Roosevelt* (New York, 1961), 309–11; *New York Times*, August 21, 1907, 1; *Los Angeles Times*, January 28, 1908, 11.

3. Roosevelt, *Letters*, 6:872, 908; *Oakland Examiner*, November 23, 1907, 1; *San Francisco Examiner*, November 25, 1907, 3; Corey, *House of Morgan*, 372.

4. Roosevelt, *Letters*, 5:843; *Washington Post*, December 10, 1907, 4; *Sunday Oregonian* (Portland), November 24, 1907, 1; *New York Times*, November 29, 1907, 1.

5. Roosevelt, *Letters*, 5:826; *Inter-Ocean* (Chicago), December 14, 1907, 2.

6. Majority leader was not yet an official position; Aldrich performed an equivalent function. Nathaniel Wright Stephenson, *Nelson W. Aldrich: A Leader in American Politics* (New York, 1930), 268–73; Blair Bolles, *Tyrant from Illinois: Uncle Joe Cannon's Experiment with Personal Power* (New York, 1951), 19–22; William Rea Gwinn, *Uncle Joe Cannon: Archfoe of Insurgency* (New York, 1957), 9–10; Scott William Rager, "Uncle Joe Cannon: The Brakeman of the House of Representatives, 1903–1911," in *Masters of the House: Congressional Leadership Over Two Centuries*, ed. Roger H. Davidson et al. (Boulder, CO, 1998), 68; *Los Angeles Times*, December 20, 1907, 14; *CR*, February 10, 1908, 1756. Aldrich was a highly valued benefactor of the American Sugar Refining Company. The appreciative

Sugar Trust provided the senator with a sizable loan to purchase, extend, and electrify horse-drawn trolley lines in Providence. This deal secured millions of dollars for Aldrich without the expenditure of a cent on his part. See Jerome L. Sternstein, "Corruption in the Gilded Age Senate: Nelson W. Aldrich and the Sugar Trust," *Capitol Studies* 6, no. 1 (1978): 32–34.

7. *Bulletin of Yale University* 29, no. 3 (1932): 35; *Washington Post*, February 16, 1908, III-8; *New York Times*, May 28, 1932, 15; Bolles, *Tyrant from Illinois*, 94.

8. Minnesota Bankers Association, *Twenty-Fourth Annual Convention* (n.p., 1913), 38; Douglass C. North, *Growth and Welfare in the American Past: A New Economic History* (Englewood Cliffs, NJ, 1966), 149–59.

9. James C. Livingston, *Origins of the Federal Reserve System: Money, Class, and Corporate Capitalism, 1890–1913* (Ithaca, NY, 1986); Naomi R. Lamoreaux, *The Great Merger Movement in American Business, 1895–1904* (New York, 1985); William G. Roy, *Socializing Capital: The Rise of the Large Industrial Corporation in America* (Princeton, NJ, 1997); Gerald P. Berk, *Alternative Tracks: The Constitution of American Industrial Order, 1865–1917* (Baltimore, 1994); Robert H. Wiebe, *Businessmen and Reform: A Study of the Progressive Movement* (Cambridge, MA, 1962), 62–65.

10. *Sun* (New York), November 12, 1907, 2; *Chicago Record-Herald*, January 4, 1908, 5; Leslie Mortier Shaw, *Current Issues* (New York, 1908), 281–83. On Shaw's tenure at the Department of the Treasury, see Richard H. Timberlake Jr., "Mr. Shaw and His Critics: Monetary Policy in the Golden Age Reviewed," *Quarterly Journal of Economics* 77, no. 1 (1963): 40–54. Livingston, *Origins of the Federal Reserve*, 150–54; *CR*, June 26, 1902, app. 511; White, *Regulation and Reform*, 14–15; American Bankers Association, *Twenty-Eighth Annual Convention* (New York, 1902), 132–33; Andrew Jay Frame, *Andrew J. Frame: A Sketch of His Life; With Some of His Public Addresses and Writings* (n.p., 1931), 51. There had been previous advocacy on behalf of branch banking from influential quarters. See Indianapolis Monetary Convention, *Report*, 376–86; Comptroller of the Currency, *Annual Report, 1896* (Washington, DC, 1896), 1:103–5.

11. American Bankers Association, *Twenty-Seventh Annual Convention* (New York, 1901), 118; Department of the Treasury, *Annual Report, 1901* (Washington, DC, 1901), 77; *Sun* (New York), December 22, 1901, 1; New York State Chamber of Commerce, *Report by the Special Currency Committee* (n.p., 1906), 9–11; American Bankers Association, *Thirty-Second Annual Convention* (New York, 1906), 147–48; Livingston, *Origins of the Federal Reserve*, 160–65; *Berkeley Independent*, January 4, 1908, 2; Carl H. Chrislock, *The Progressive Era in Minnesota, 1899–1918* (St. Paul, MN, 1971), 23–24; Wiebe, *Businessmen and Reform*, 74.

12. Edwin R. A. Seligman, ed., *The Currency Problem and the Present Financial Situation* (New York, 1908), 149, 17; *Wall Street Journal*, December 17, 1907, 1; Sereno S. Pratt, "The Remedy for Our Currency Ills," *World's Work* 15, no. 3 (1908): 9817; *Commercial West* 13, no. 3 (1908): 22-b; George E. Roberts, "Financial Legislation," *North American Review* 185, no. 614 (1907): 34–43; Roberts, "The

Need of a Central Bank," *Annals of the American Academy of Political and Social Science* 31 (1908): 45–54; Comptroller of the Currency, *Annual Report, 1907*, 75. The academy played a supporting role during the banking reform debate by facilitating dialogue within financial circles and frequently lending an imprimatur to bankers' positions. By the early twentieth century, economists largely buttressed the existing economic order. See Mary O. Furner, *Advocacy and Objectivity: A Crisis in the Professionalization of American Social Science, 1865–1905* (Lexington, KY, 1975).

13. House Banking and Currency Committee, *Hearings and Arguments on Proposed Currency Legislation*, 256; Andrew J. Frame to Nelson Aldrich, January 20, 1908, reel 25, Nelson W. Aldrich Papers, Manuscript Division, Library of Congress, Washington, DC. Frame proposed a "National Reserve Bank," see "Diagnosis of the World's Elastic Currency Problems," *Annals of the American Academy of Political and Social Science* 31 (1908): 95–97.

14. House Banking and Currency Committee, *Hearings and Arguments on Senate Bill No. 3023*, 60th Cong. (Washington, DC, 1908), 154; *Commoner* 7, no. 43 (1907): 2; Chauncey Depew, "Our Currency," *Government* 2, no. 3 (1907): 155.

15. Alexander Dana Noyes, "A Year after the Panic of 1907," *Quarterly Journal of Economics* 23, no. 2 (1909): 211; *Public Ledger* (Philadelphia), February 21, 1908, 2; Leah Hannah Feder, *Unemployment Relief in Periods of Depression: A Study of Measures Adopted in Certain American Cities, 1857 through 1922* (New York, 1936), 202; Ida M. Tarbell, *The Life of Elbert H. Gary: The Story of Steel* (New York, 1925), 213–14; Gustavus Myers, *History of the Great American Fortunes* (New York, 1936), 627–28.

16. *Chicago Record-Herald*, April 12, 1908, 1; *American Industries* 6, no. 6 (1907): 21; *St. Louis Post-Dispatch*, February 9, 1908, 2; *Chicago Record-Herald*, February 11, 1908, 2; *Detroit News*, February 27, 1908, 13.

17. Margaret E. Byington, *Homestead: The Households of a Mill Town* (New York, 1910), 135; David Brody, *Steelworkers in America: The Nonunion Era* (Cambridge, MA, 1960), 106; David E. Cassens, "The Bulgarian Colony of Southwestern Illinois, 1900–1920," *Illinois Historical Journal* 84, no. 1 (1991): 21; John E. Bodnar, *Immigration and Industrialization: Ethnicity in an American Mill Town, 1870–1940* (Pittsburgh, 1977), 88; *Buffalo Evening News*, February 1, 1908, 1; *Buffalo Evening Times*, February 1, 1908, 7; *Buffalo Times*, March 21, 1933, 10; *Chicago Daily Tribune*, December 29, 1907, 1; *Harper's Weekly* 52, no. 2673 (1908): 12; Mike L. Wallace, *Greater Gotham: A History of New York City from 1898 to 1919* (New York, 2017), 94.

18. *Cincinnati Enquirer*, January 10, 1908, 12; *St. Louis Post-Dispatch*, January 14, 1908, 1; *Boston Daily Globe*, January 20, 1908, 1; *New Britain (CT) Daily Herald*, January 20, 1908, 1; *Detroit News*, January 28, 1908, 1; *Seattle Post-Intelligencer*, January 21, 1908, 1. On Swift, see William O. Reichert, "The Melancholy Political Thought of Morrison I. Swift," *New England Quarterly* 49, no. 4 (1976): 542–58.

19. *Cincinnati Enquirer*, January 29, 1908, 7; *Sun* (Baltimore), February 10,

1908, 9; *Dallas Morning News*, February 27, 1908, 9; *Sun* (Baltimore), February 24, 1908, 9. On How, the "millionaire hobo," see Nels Anderson, *On Hobos and Homelessness* (Chicago, 1998), 90–94. On hobo intellectual culture, see Frank Tobias Higbie, *Indispensable Outcasts: Hobo Workers and Community in the American Midwest, 1880–1930* (Urbana, IL, 2003), 191–93, 205–6.

20. *New York Times*, February 28, 1908, 1; *CR*, February 28, 1908, 2688; *Washington Post*, February 27, 1908, 2; *Chicago Daily Tribune*, February 27, 1908, 4.

21. *Washington Post*, November 25, 1907, 1; *Atlanta Constitution*, January 12, 1908, 1B; *CR*, January 30, 1908, 1322; *Chicago Record-Herald*, January 22, 1908, 1; *Nashville Tennessean*, February 10, 1908, 1; Senate, S. 3023, 60th Cong., 1st Sess. (1908); *Cincinnati Post*, January 9, 1908, 3; *Public Ledger* (Philadelphia), January 29, 1908, 1.

22. House Banking and Currency Committee, *Hearings and Arguments on Senate Bill No. 3023*, 7, 73, 117, 196; Carl H. Bennett to Knute Nelson, January 9, 1908, box 13, Knute Nelson Papers, Minnesota Historical Society, St. Paul. For the widespread opposition to Aldrich's bill, see *Chicago Daily Tribune*, April 13, 1908, 4; House Banking and Currency Committee, *Hearings and Arguments on Senate Bill No. 3023*, 276–77.

23. *CR*, March 17, 1908, 3449; March 19, 1908, 3574. On La Follette and Wisconsin Progressivism, see John D. Buenker, *The Progressive Era, 1893–1914*, vol. 4 of *The History of Wisconsin*, ed. William Fletcher Thompson (Madison, WI, 1998), 455–568; David P. Thelen, *The New Citizenship: Origins of Progressivism in Wisconsin, 1885–1900* (Columbia, MO, 1972), 290–308; Robert S. Maxwell, *La Follette and the Rise of the Progressives in Wisconsin* (Madison, WI, 1956).

24. *CR*, February 11, 1908, 1819; *Washington Post*, March 18, 1908, 4; Robert M. La Follette, *La Follette's Autobiography: A Personal Narrative of Political Experiences* (Madison, WI, 1913), 461–64; *CR*, March 27, 1908, 4018.

25. Millard L. Gieske and Steven J. Keillor, *Norwegian Yankee: Knute Nelson and the Failure of American Politics, 1860–1923* (Northfield, MN, 1995); Martin W. Odland, *The Life of Knute Nelson* (Minneapolis, 1926), 265; *CR*, March 12, 1908, 3199; March 25, 1908, 3857; March 26, 1908, 3965; March 27, 1908, 4025.

26. *CR*, January 8, 1908, 549; *Plain Dealer* (Cleveland), November 4, 1907, 3; *Boston Herald*, January 17, 1908, 2; *Sun* (Baltimore), January 9, 1908, 7. Fowler's bill won the support of Andrew Carnegie. See *Bulletin* (San Francisco), February 27, 1908, 12. Fowler had espoused guaranty before. See *CR*, March 15, 1897, 21; February 1, 1898, 1340.

27. *Bankers' Magazine* 76, no. 2 (1908): 222; New York State Bankers Association, *Fifteenth Annual Convention* (New York, 1908), 16; *Commercial West* 13, no. 3 (1908): 7; A. Barton Hepburn to Nelson Aldrich, January 15, 1908, reel 25, Aldrich Papers; *CR*, February 29, 1908, 2720; *Boston Post*, February 29, 1908, 9.

28. Edgar A. Hornig, "Campaign Issues in the Presidential Election of 1908," *Indiana Magazine of History* 54, no. 3 (1958): 243–44; Robert W. Cherny, *A Righteous Cause: The Life of William Jennings Bryan* (Boston, 1985), 112; *Kansas City*

(MO) Times, August 28, 1908, 2; *Chicago Record-Herald*, March 31, 1908, 1; *Evening Bulletin* (Philadelphia), February 25, 1908, 8; Porter and Johnson, *National Party Platforms*, 156.

29. Norbert R. Mahnken, "William Jennings Bryan in Oklahoma," *Nebraska History* 31, no. 4 (1950): 247–74; Robert D. Lewallen, "'Let the People Rule': William Jennings Bryan and the Oklahoma Constitution," *Chronicles of Oklahoma* 73, no. 3 (1995): 278–307; *Guthrie (OK) Daily Leader*, December 18, 1907, 1; State of Oklahoma, *Session Laws of 1907–1908* (Guthrie, 1908), 145–52; *Outlook* 88, no. 2 (1908): 55.

30. *Commoner* 8, no. 6 (1908): 3; E. G. Leipheimer, *The First National Bank of Butte: Seventy-Five Years of Continuous Banking Operation, 1877 to 1952* (Butte, MT, 1952), 22; Thomas P. Kane, *The Romance and Tragedy of Banking: Problems and Incidents of Governmental Supervision of National Banks* (New York, 1923), 464–65; Carosso, *Morgans*, 289. In 1908 federal examiners found legal violations in 75 percent of the banks examined over a three-month period. See Edwin H. Sutherland, *White Collar Crime* (New York, 1949), 11.

31. Paul W. Glad, *The Trumpet Soundeth: William Jennings Bryan and His Democracy, 1896–1912* (Lincoln, NE, 1960), 92; *Commoner* 7, no. 43 (1907): 2; *Buffalo Evening Times*, February 12, 1908, 1; *Daily Picayune* (New Orleans), November 29, 1907, 1; *Dallas Morning News*, January 10, 1908, 2; *Kansas City (MO) Star*, November 25, 1907, 8.

32. *Seattle Daily Times*, January 3, 1908, 20; *CR*, March 25, 1908, 3854; *Dallas Morning News*, January 10, 1908, 2; Bricklayers and Masons International Union of America, *First Biennial and Forty-First Convention* (Indianapolis, 1908), 133; *Nashville Tennessean*, February 10, 1908, 3; *Evansville (IN) Journal-News*, December 23, 1907, 3; *CR*, April 9, 1908, 4573; May 6, 1908, 5773.

33. *CR*, April 2, 1908, 4267; December 5, 1907, 173; May 7, 1908, 5856; Richard B. Roeder, "Thomas H. Carter, Spokesman for Western Development," *Montana: The Magazine of Western History* 39, no. 2 (1989): 23–29; Thomas H. Carter to Dudley Axtell, March 24, 1910, reel 7, Thomas H. Carter Papers, Manuscript Division, Library of Congress, Washington, DC. On the other leading postal savings bills proposed that winter, see *Chicago Daily News*, January 9, 1908, 18.

34. House Banking and Currency Committee, *Hearings and Arguments on Senate Bill No. 3023*, 17, 42, 123, 202, 246, 274, 284; New York State Chamber of Commerce, *Fiftieth Annual Report* (New York, 1908), 1:128–29; *CR*, April 20, 1908, 4995; *Bankers' Magazine* 76, no. 2 (1908): 158; *Buffalo Evening News*, February 12, 1908, 1; *CR*, March 19, 1908, 3569.

35. *Public Ledger* (Philadelphia), April 10, 1908, 1; *New York Times*, April 18, 1908, 1; *Wall Street Journal*, April 21, 1908, 7; *CR*, April 28, 1908, 5327; *New York Tribune*, April 14, 1908, 3; *New York Times*, May 9, 1936, 15; *Washington Post*, November 25, 1907, 1; Bolles, *Tyrant from Illinois*, 11.

36. House Banking and Currency Committee, *H.R. 20835 to Amend the National Banking Law (so-called the Vreeland Bill)*, 60th Cong. (Washington, DC,

1908), 39; Gilbert L. Janson, "The Aldrich-Vreeland Act: A Chapter in the History of Currency Legislation in the United States" (master's thesis, Leland Stanford Junior University, 1918), 67; *New York Times*, May 16, 1908, 4; House, H.R. 21414, 60th Cong., 1st Sess. (1908); *New York Times*, April 23, 1908, 1; *Boston Evening Transcript*, April 21, 1908, 2; *New York Tribune*, May 5, 1908, 1; *Washington Post*, May 6, 1908, 1. For detail on the enactment of the Emergency Currency Act, see Stanley Markowitz, "The Aldrich-Vreeland Bill: Its Significance in the Struggle for Currency Reform, 1893–1908" (master's thesis, University of Maryland, 1965), 104–37.

37. *CR*, May 27, 1908, 7072–73; Fred C. Brenckman, *History of the Pennsylvania State Grange* (Harrisburg, PA, 1949), 103, 105; *Danville (PA) Intelligencer*, August 24, 1906, 1.

38. Alfred O. Crozier, *The Magnet* (New York, 1908); *Cincinnati Enquirer*, May 31, 1908, 2; *Journal of the Knights of Labor* 28, no. 1 (1908): 8; Belle Case La Follette and Fola La Follette, *Robert M. La Follette*, 2 vols. (New York, 1953), 1:245–56.

39. *CR*, May 30, 1908, 7260; *Statutes at Large* 35 (1908): 546–53; *Journal of the American Bankers' Association* 1, no. 1 (1908): 3; Nelson Aldrich to Andrew J. Frame, June 18, 1908, reel 27, Aldrich Papers. Emergency currency was issued at the outbreak of World War I in response to fear of a banking crisis. See Silber, *When Washington Shut Down*, 66–85.

40. *Washington Post*, December 23, 1907, 1; December 27, 1907, 4; *Bankers' Magazine* 76, no. 6 (1908): 822.

Chapter Three

1. *Breeder's Gazette* 52, no. 22 (1907): 1104; *Cleveland Press*, January 6, 1908, 7; Post Office Department, *Report of the Postmaster-General, 1908* (Washington, DC, 1908), 13, 293.

2. California State Federation of Labor, *Tenth Annual Convention* (n.p., 1909), 32; Arthur D. Hittner, *Honus Wagner: The Life of Baseball's "Flying Dutchman"* (Jefferson, NC, 1996), 239–40; *Chicago Daily Tribune*, September 16, 1906, 3.

3. *Arizona Republican* (Phoenix), December 29, 1908, 15; Wayne E. Fuller, *The American Mail: Enlarger of the Common Life* (Chicago, 1972), 182–84; M. Clyde Kelly, *United States Postal Policy* (New York, 1932), 168–69; House Committee on the Post Office and Post Roads, *Postal Savings Bank*, 60th Cong., 2nd Sess. (Washington, DC, 1909), 8; Wayne E. Fuller, *RFD: The Changing Face of Rural America* (Bloomington, IN, 1964), 3.

4. *St. Louis Post-Dispatch*, September 1, 1908, 3; Roosevelt, *Letters*, 6:1132–33; *Chicago Daily Tribune*, June 15, 1908, 1; *Washington Post*, June 17, 1908, 2. James B. Forgan claimed he convinced Roosevelt guaranty was an unsound policy in *Recollections of a Busy Life* (New York, 1924), 191.

5. *Chicago Daily Tribune*, June 16, 1908, 2; *Berkeley Independent*, February 7,

1908, 8; M. A. DeWolfe Howe, *George von Lengerke Meyer: His Life and Public Services* (New York, 1920), 376; Roosevelt, *Letters*, 6:1076–77; *Chicago Daily Tribune*, June 18, 1908, 2; Porter and Johnson, *National Party Platforms*, 159, 147; *San Francisco Call*, July 8, 1908, 2.

6. American Federation of Labor, *Twenty-Eighth Annual Convention* (Washington, DC, 1908), 88–89; *Shoe Workers' Journal* 9, no. 6 (1908): 7. Farmers' National Congress, *Twenty-Eighth Annual Convention* (n.p., 1908), 83; National Farmers Union, *Minutes, 1908* (Little Rock, AR, 1908), 61; National Grange, *Forty-Second Annual Session* (Concord, NH, 1908), 127, 134. On labor and the injunction, see William E. Forbath, *Law and the Shaping of the American Labor Movement* (Cambridge, MA, 1991), 59–97.

7. American Bankers Association, *Thirty-Fourth Annual Convention* (New York, 1908), 42, 286, 290, 304; Wiebe, *Businessmen and Reform*, 115–16; National Association of Manufacturers, *Thirteenth Annual Convention* (n.p., 1908), 255.

8. *Pacific Banker* 13, no. 33 (1908): 5; *Boston Daily Globe*, January 20, 1910, 7; Minnesota Bankers Association, *Twentieth Annual Convention* (n.p., 1909), 76–91; American Bankers Association, *Thirty-Fifth Annual Convention* (New York, 1909), 248; *CR*, December 15, 1908, 257–58.

9. The attorney general ruled against national banks belonging to state guaranty programs. See James A. Finch, ed., *Official Opinions of the Attorneys-General of the United States* (Washington, DC, 1909), 37–42, 272–84. Country Life Commission Meeting, December 5, 1908, box 24, Liberty Hyde Bailey Papers, Division of Rare and Manuscript Collections, Cornell University, Ithaca, NY; *Commoner* 10, no. 28 (1910): 14; A. Blodgett Jr. to Knute Nelson, February 18, 1908, box 13, Nelson Papers; William Jennings Bryan and Mary Baird Bryan, *Speeches of William Jennings Bryan*, 2 vols. (New York, 1909), 2:161; Z. Clark Dickinson, *Bank Deposit Guaranty in Nebraska: An Historical and Critical Study* (Lincoln, NE, 1914), 17; Avery Luvere Carlson, *A Monetary and Banking History of Texas: From the Mexican Regime to the Present Day, 1821–1929* (Fort Worth, TX, 1930), 62.

10. *Guthrie (OK) Daily Leader*, January 8, 1908, 4; *Chicago Daily Tribune*, September 20, 1908, 6. On banker support for guaranty, see Joseph M. Grant and Lawrence L. Crum, *The Development of State-Chartered Banking in Texas from Predecessor Systems Until 1970* (Austin, TX, 1978), 77–78; Robert S. La Forte, "The Bank Depositor's Guaranty Law of Kansas, 1909: Some Aspects of State Progressivism," in *Essays on Kansas History—In Memoriam: George L. Anderson, Jayhawker—Historian*, ed. Burton J. Williams (Lawrence, KS, 1977), 71; W. E. Kuhn, *History of Nebraska Banking: A Centennial Retrospect* (Lincoln, NE, 1968), 108; Thomas Robert Nelson, "The Guaranty Fund System of Texas" (master's thesis, University of Texas, 1922), 13–14.

11. *Norfolk (NE) Weekly News-Journal*, October 2, 1908, 6; H. C. Van Horne to E. F. Swinney, September 17, 1908, reel 94, William Howard Taft Papers, Manuscript Division, Library of Congress, Washington, DC; University of Nebraska, *Nebraska Party Platforms, 1858–1940* (Lincoln, 1940), 321, 324, 327; *Omaha (NE)*

Daily Bee, February 15, 1909, 1; Dickinson, *Bank Deposit Guaranty in Nebraska,* 17-18.

12. *Dallas Morning News,* February 4, 1909, 2; State of Kansas, *Proceedings of the House of Representatives, January 16 to February 4, 1908* (Topeka, 1908), 28-29; *Kansas City (MO) Star,* January 16, 1908, 1; George L. Anderson, *Essays on the History of Banking* (Lawrence, KS, 1972), 201; La Forte, "Bank Depositor's Guaranty Law," 72-73.

13. *Austin (TX) Statesman,* February 13, 1909, 2; *Dallas Morning News,* February 17, 1909, 6; *Austin (TX) Statesman,* February 5, 1909, 8; August 13, 1908, 1; *Dallas Morning News,* April 17, 1909, 1; January 26, 1909, 7; September 18, 1948, 1; April 12, 1909, 1, 17.

14. In 1911 the Supreme Court found state guaranty laws constitutional. See Noble State Bank v. Haskell, 219 U.S. 104 (1911). State of Nebraska, *The Revised Statutes of the State of Nebraska, 1913* (Lincoln, 1914), 151-57; C. F. W. Dassler, *General Statutes of Kansas, 1909* (Topeka, 1910), 129-35; State of Texas, *General Laws of the State of Texas Passed by the Thirty-First Legislature* (Austin, 1909), 406-29; *Christian Science Monitor,* June 23, 1909, 6; South Dakota Legislature, *South Dakota Legislative Manual, 1909* (Pierre, 1909), 590, 594; *Daily Argus-Leader* (Sioux Falls, SD), February 13, 1909, 2; George W. Kingsbury, *History of Dakota Territory,* 5 vols. (Chicago, 1915), 4:639; *Daily Argus-Leader* (Sioux Falls, SD), February 19, 1909, 1; State of South Dakota, *The Compiled Laws, 1910,* vol. 2 (Pierre, 1910), 166a-67; John E. Wickstrom, "A History of the Depositors Guaranty Law in the State of South Dakota" (master's thesis, University of South Dakota, 1951), 18-19; George H. Shibley, *History of Guaranty of Bank Deposits in the States of Oklahoma, Texas, Kansas, Nebraska, and South Dakota, 1908-1914* (Washington, DC, 1914), 9; Robb, *Guaranty of Bank Deposits,* 162; *Daily Capital-Journal* (Pierre, SD), June 23, 1909, 1; June 25, 1909, 1. South Dakota subsequently enacted a mandatory guaranty law in 1915. See Wickstrom, "History of the Depositors Guaranty Law," 28-37.

15. *Wall Street Journal,* March 27, 1909, 8; *Dallas Morning News,* February 18, 1909, 1; February 19, 1909, 1, 3; *Plain Dealer* (Cleveland), February 19, 1909, 2; *Dallas Morning News,* February 20, 1909, 1; Arizona Bankers' Association, *Proceedings of the Arizona Bankers' Association,* vol. IV (n.p., 1910), 77; American Bankers Association, *Thirty-Fifth Annual Convention,* 253. By 1917 eight states had guaranty laws: Oklahoma, Kansas, Nebraska, Texas, Mississippi, South Dakota, North Dakota, and Washington.

16. Merwin R. Swanson, "The American Country Life Movement, 1900-1940" (PhD diss., University of Minnesota, 1972), 64-66; D. Jerome Tweton, "The Attitudes and Policies of the Theodore Roosevelt Administration toward American Agriculture" (PhD diss., University of Oklahoma, 1964), 129-30; *Morning Oregonian* (Portland), November 30, 1908, 2; *Detroit Free Press,* February 14, 1909, 6; Thomas H. Carter, "Postal Savings Banks," *Independent* 66, no. 3137 (1909): 74;

CR, June 9, 1910, 7693; A. M. Somers to Country Life Commission, December 5, 1908, box 22, Bailey Papers.

17. Howe, *George von Lengerke Meyer*, 412; *New York Times*, August 27, 1909, 1; *Sun* (Baltimore), August 5, 1909, 2; American Bankers Association, *Thirty-Fifth Annual Convention*, 90, 259.

18. Henry F. Pringle, *The Life and Times of William Howard Taft: A Biography*, 2 vols. (New York, 1939), 1:517–20; *CR*, December 7, 1909, 32; *New York Times*, December 10, 1909, 1. Taft had taken an interest in postal savings while serving as governor-general of the Philippines, site of the earliest U.S. involvement with the concept. See Edwin W. Kemmerer, "The Philippine Postal Savings Bank," *Annals of the American Academy of Political and Social Science* 30 (1907): 46; Theresa Ventura, "American Empire, Agrarian Reform, and the Problem of Tropical Nature in the Philippines, 1898–1916" (PhD diss., Columbia University, 2009), 186–219.

19. *Journal of the American Bankers' Association* 2, no. 7 (1910): 265; House Committee on the Post Office and Post Roads, *Postal Savings Bank*, 60th Cong., 154; *Coast Banker* 2, no. 7 (1909): 273.

20. William Howard Taft, *The Collected Works of William Howard Taft*, ed. David H. Burton, 8 vols. (Athens, OH, 2001–4), 3:163; *Boston Daily Globe*, August 26, 1909, 1; *Bankers' Magazine* 78, no. 2 (1909): 183; idem, 79, no. 5 (1909): 753; *New York Tribune*, January 22, 1910, 1; William Howard Taft to Knute Nelson, January 1, 1910, reel 499, Taft Papers.

21. On early twentieth-century efforts to promote thrift, see Andrew L. Yarrow, *Thrift: The History of an American Cultural Movement* (Amherst, MA, 2014). George von L. Meyer, "Postal Savings Banks," *Independent* 64, no. 3083 (1908): 11; Post Office Department, *Report of the Postmaster-General, 1908*, 14; *Commercial West* 10, no. 12 (1906): 16; Jane Addams, *Twenty Years at Hull-House* (New York, 1911), 302; Florence Kelley, "Postal Savings Banks," *Charities and the Commons* 21, no. 17 (1909): 717–19; George von L. Meyer, "Postal Savings-Banks," *North American Review* 188, no. 633 (1908): 248.

22. House Committee on the Post Office and Post Roads, *Postal Savings Bank*, 61st Cong., 2nd Sess. (Washington, DC, 1910), 121–22; Senate, *Reports of the Immigration Commission*, 61st Cong., 3rd Sess. (1910), S. Doc. 753, 216; Jared N. Day, "Credit, Capital and Community: Informal Banking in Immigrant Communities in the United States, 1880–1924," *Financial History Review* 9, no. 1 (2002): 65–78. For examples of dishonest immigrant bankers, see Gunther W. Peck, *Reinventing Free Labor: Padrones and Immigrant Workers in the North American West, 1880–1930* (New York, 2000), 174; Mark Wyman, *Round-Trip to America: The Immigrants Return to Europe, 1880–1930* (Ithaca, NY, 1993), 57, 60.

23. Andrew T. Kopan, "Greek Survival in Chicago," in *Ethnic Chicago: A Multicultural Portrait*, ed. Melvin G. Holli and Peter d'A. Jones (Grand Rapids, MI, 1984), 133; Franklin D. Scott, "The Causes and Consequences of Emigration in Sweden," *Chronicle* 2, no. 1 (1955): 9; House Committee on the Post Office and

Post Roads, *Postal Savings Bank*, 61st Cong., 121; Meyer, "Postal Savings Banks," 11; *Morning Oregonian* (Portland), June 24, 1910, 10.

24. Wisconsin State Grange, *Thirty-Eighth Annual Session* (n.p., 1909), 8; California State Federation of Labor, *Eighth Annual Convention* (n.p., 1908), 12; Michigan State Grange, *Thirty-Fifth Annual Session* (Jackson, 1907), 82.

25. *Chicago Record-Herald*, November 18, 1907, 3; *Chicago Daily Tribune*, January 22, 1918, 19; H. Shelton Stromquist, *Reinventing "The People": The Progressive Movement, the Class Problem, and the Origins of Modern Liberalism* (Urbana, IL, 2006), 77–79; Roy Everett Littlefield III, *William Randolph Hearst: His Role in American Progressivism* (Lanham, MD, 1980), 226; Irwin Yellowitz, *Labor and the Progressive Movement in New York State, 1897–1916* (Ithaca, NY, 1965), 201–2; Porter and Johnson, *National Party Platforms*, 153–54.

26. *Equity Farm Journal* 2, no. 9 (1908): 19; *National Co-operator and Farm Journal* 30, no. 21 (1909): 8; Benjamin Horace Hibbard, "Farm Tenancy in the United States," *Annals of the American Academy of Political and Social Science* 40 (1912): 30; *Wenatchee (WA) Daily World*, February 17, 1910, 2.

27. New Hampshire State Grange, *Twenty-Fourth Annual Session* (Concord, 1908), 95; United Mine Workers of America, *Nineteenth Annual Convention* (Indianapolis, 1908), 298.

28. *Progressive Farmer* 25, no. 7 (1910): 161; *Journal of the Knights of Labor* 29, no. 9 (1910): 8; *Ohio Farmer* 125, no. 8 (1910): 240; *Flint (MI) Daily Journal*, January 14, 1910, 14; *Olympia (WA) Daily Recorder*, January 3, 1910, 4; *Nashville Tennessean*, March 1, 1910, 10; *CR*, January 27, 1910, 1061; January 31, 1910, 1252; Claude E. Barfield Jr., "The Democratic Party in Congress, 1909–1913" (PhD diss., Northwestern University, 1965), 246–48; Taft, *Collected Works*, 3:456; *Indianapolis Star*, March 1, 1910, 1; *Sun* (Baltimore), March 1, 1910, 2.

29. *La Follette's Weekly Magazine* 2, no. 10 (1910): 7; *American Agriculturist* 85, no. 10 (1910): 390; *Miners Magazine* 11, no. 350 (1910): 4; *CR*, March 2, 1910, 2621; March 5, 1910, 2765, 2760–61, 2780. On "frenzied finance," see Louis Filler, *Crusaders for American Liberalism* (Yellow Springs, OH, 1950), 177–83.

30. On the fall of Cannonism, see Bolles, *Tyrant from Illinois*, 213–24; Kenneth W. Hechler, *Insurgency: Personalities and Politics of the Taft Era* (New York, 1940), 63–82. *Boston Evening Transcript*, March 9, 1910, 10; *Wall Street Journal*, March 11, 1910, 7; April 18, 1910, 2; *Philadelphia Inquirer*, April 20, 1910, 6; *St. Louis Post-Dispatch*, May 7, 1910, 3; May 4, 1910, 1; May 1, 1910, 5B; *St. Louis Globe-Democrat*, May 5, 1910, 13.

31. *Brooklyn Daily Eagle*, May 13, 1910, 4; *CR*, June 7, 1910, 7585; June 13, 1910, 7926, 7928; June 9, 1910, 7768; June 21, 1910, 8640; June 22, 1910, 8741; *Chicago Daily Tribune*, June 21, 1910, 5; *New York Tribune*, June 21, 1910, 3; *Washington Post*, June 22, 1910, 1; *New York Tribune*, June 22, 1910, 3. The centrality of postal officials to the establishment of postal savings is emphasized by Daniel P. Carpenter, *The Forging of Bureaucratic Autonomy: Reputations, Networks, and Policy*

Innovation in Executive Agencies, 1862–1928 (Princeton, NJ, 2001), 149–63. On the important role of legislators who represented agricultural regions, see Jean Reith Schroedel and Bruce D. Snyder, "People's Banking: The Promise Betrayed?," *Studies in American Political Development* 8, no. 1 (1994): 173–93. Taft's influence is stressed by Hechler, *Insurgency*, 158–62. For more on the Postal Savings Bank Act's path through Congress, see Donald Sham, "The Origin and Development of the United States Postal Savings System" (PhD diss., University of California, Berkeley, 1942), 203–68.

32. *Statutes at Large* 36 (1910): 814–19; American Bankers Association, *Thirty-Sixth Annual Convention* (New York, 1910), 524, 47; *Shoe Workers' Journal* 11, no. 7 (1910): 26. On the Postal Savings System's history, see Christopher W. Shaw, "'Banks of the People': The Life and Death of the U.S. Postal Savings System," *Journal of Social History* 52, no. 1 (2018): 121–52.

33. On farmers' long-standing credit plight, see Jeffrey Ostler, *Prairie Populism: The Fate of Agrarian Radicalism in Kansas, Nebraska, and Iowa, 1880–1892* (Lawrence, KS, 1993), 12–22; Goodwyn, *Democratic Promise*, 26–31, 115–20; Fred A. Shannon, *The Farmer's Last Frontier: Agriculture, 1860–1897* (New York, 1945), 183–90; Everett N. Dick, *The Sod-House Frontier, 1854–1890* (New York, 1937), 95–97. Senate, *Industrial Relations*, 64th Cong., 1st Sess. (1916), S. Doc. 415, 9096; *New York Times*, December 9, 1903, 3; *CR*, December 8, 1903, 32; December 7, 1905, 219; December 9, 1907, 210; March 25, 1909, 260; *New York Times*, March 13, 1904, financial supplement, 2. On the commercial loan theory, see Lloyd W. Mints, *A History of Banking Theory in Great Britain and the United States* (Chicago, 1945), 9–10.

34. Carl W. Thompson, *Factors Affecting Interest Rates and Other Charges on Short-Time Farm Loans*, Department of Agriculture, Bulletin No. 409 (1916); Department of Agriculture, *Annual Report, 1912* (Washington, DC, 1913), 26; *Rural New-Yorker* 72, no. 4184 (1913): 13; William I. Myers, *Cooperative Farm Mortgage Credit, 1916–1936* (Washington, DC, 1936), 4; *Wallaces' Farmer* 41, no. 8 (1916): 14.

35. *Atlanta Journal*, January 9, 1908, 4; Senate, *Report of the Country Life Commission*, 60th Cong., 2nd Sess. (1909), S. Doc. 705, 14; Tweton, "Attitudes and Policies," 156–58; Swanson, "American Country Life Movement," 55.

36. L. Grant McConnell, *The Decline of Agrarian Democracy* (Berkeley, 1959), 30–31; William L. Bowers, *The Country Life Movement in America, 1900–1920* (Port Washington, NY, 1974), 19–20; *Second Annual Conference of the Committees on Agricultural Development and Education of the State Bankers' Associations* (n.p., 1912), 290; J. H. Johnson to George von L. Meyer, October 19, 1908, box 14, Meyer Papers; *Cleveland Plain Dealer*, December 12, 1897, 8; Myron T. Herrick, "Banks for the Farmer," *Moody's Magazine* 14, no. 3 (1912): 185–89; Herrick, "The Farmer and Finance," *Atlantic Monthly* 111, no. 2 (1913): 170–78; Stuart W. Shulman, "The Origin of the Federal Farm Loan Act: Agenda-Setting in the Progressive Era Print

Press" (PhD diss., University of Oregon, 1999), 414–16. The educational campaign that wealthy California businessman David Lubin conducted further promoted private agricultural lending. See Daniel T. Rodgers, *Atlantic Crossings: Social Politics in a Progressive Age* (Cambridge, MA, 1998), 336–37.

37. Department of State, *Preliminary Report on Land and Agricultural Credit in Europe* (Washington, DC, 1912), 3–7; National Grange, *Forty-Sixth Annual Session* (Concord, NH, 1912), 147; Howard W. Allen, *Poindexter of Washington: A Study in Progressive Politics* (Carbondale, IL, 1981), 148; *Texas Farm Co-operator* 35, no. 52 (1912): 3.

38. On Aldrich's domination of the National Monetary Commission, see Andrew L. Gray, "Who Killed the Aldrich Plan?," *Bankers Magazine* 154, no. 3 (1971): 63, 73.

39. *New York Times*, November 24, 1908, 6; *New York Tribune*, July 21, 1908, 3; Nelson Aldrich to J. P. Morgan, June 19, 1908, reel 27, Aldrich Papers; Herbert L. Satterlee, *J. Pierpont Morgan: An Intimate Portrait* (New York, 1939), 493; *Evening Star* (Washington, DC), August 4, 1908, 4; Stephenson, *Nelson W. Aldrich*, 334–35; Thomas W. Lamont, *Henry P. Davison: The Record of a Useful Life* (New York, 1933), 143.

40. *New York Times*, November 19, 1908, 3; Stephenson, *Nelson W. Aldrich*, 365; *Watson's Jeffersonian Magazine* 3, no. 3 (1909): 191; idem, 3, no. 10 (1909): 769. An overview of the commission's publications is in Wesley Clair Mitchell, "The Publications of the National Monetary Commission," *Quarterly Journal of Economics* 25, no. 3 (1911): 563–93.

41. *New York Times*, August 18, 1909, 8; *Wall Street Journal*, August 24, 1909, 8; *Nashville Tennessean*, March 1, 1910, 10; *Moody's Magazine* 9, no. 1 (1910): 2; Allen, *Lords of Creation*, 175–77; *World's Work* 20, no. 4 (1910): 13235; *Journal of the Knights of Labor* 29, no. 8 (1910): 5.

42. *McClure's Magazine* 37, no. 4 (1911): 418; *St. Louis Post-Dispatch*, June 12, 1910, 7B; *La Follette's Weekly Magazine* 2, no. 24 (1910): 15; Frank A. Vanderlip with Boyden Sparkes, *From Farm Boy to Financier* (New York, 1935), 190. For contemporary magazine coverage of centralized financial power, see *World's Work* 19, no. 4 (1910): 12618–25; *Everybody's Magazine* 23, no. 3 (1910): 291–98; idem, 23, no. 4 (1910): 449–60; idem, 23, no. 5 (1910): 646–56; *McClure's Magazine* 37, no. 1 (1911): 73–87; idem, 37, no. 2 (1911): 185–202; idem, 37, no. 4 (1911): 418–28. On the collaborative business practices of leading investment banking firms, see Carosso, *Investment Banking*, 100–101.

43. Lamont, *Henry P. Davison*, 96–97; James P. Warburg, interviewed by Dean Albertson and Wendell H. Link, Columbia University Oral History Research Office, Columbia University, 1952, 34; Vanderlip, *From Farm Boy to Financier*, 216; Stephenson, *Nelson W. Aldrich*, 381; J. Laurence Laughlin, *The Federal Reserve Act, Its Origins and Problems* (New York, 1933), 16. Accounts of the Jekyll Island meeting are in Vanderlip, *From Farm Boy to Financier*, 210–19; Lamont, *Henry P. Davison*, 96–102; Stephenson, *Nelson W. Aldrich*, 373–79; Paul M. Warburg, *The Federal*

Reserve System: Its Origins and Growth, 2 vols. (New York, 1930), 1:58–60; B. C. Forbes, "Men Who Are Making America," *Leslie's* 123, no. 3189 (1916): 423.

44. California Bankers Association, *Seventeenth Annual Convention* (San Francisco, 1911), 42; Senate, *Suggested Plan for Monetary Legislation, Submitted to the National Monetary Commission by Hon. Nelson W. Aldrich*, 61st Cong., 3rd Sess. (1911), S. Doc. 784. On the Aldrich plan as foundational to the Federal Reserve System, see Elmus R. Wicker, *The Great Debate on Banking Reform: Nelson Aldrich and the Origins of the Fed* (Columbus, OH, 2005).

45. American Bankers Association, *Thirty-Seventh Annual Convention* (New York, 1911), 380–81; *Chicago Daily Tribune*, May 3, 1911, 12; *Banking Law Journal* 26, no. 12 (1909): 942; *Journal of the American Bankers' Association* 4, no. 3 (1911): 147; *Collier's* 47, no. 12 (1911): 34.

46. *Moody's Magazine* 13, no. 4 (1912): 274; idem, 9, no. 4 (1910): 275; Wisconsin Bankers Association, *Seventeenth Annual Convention* (n.p., 1911), 187–88; Wiebe, *Businessmen and Reform*, 77; *Commercial West* 20, no. 7 (1911): 20.

47. *National Grange Monthly* 8, no. 9 (1911): 4; *Philadelphia Inquirer*, November 24, 1911, 16; National Farmers Union, *Seventh Annual Meeting* (Texarkana, TX, [1911]), 65; *Commoner* 11, no. 21 (1911): 1; La Follette, *La Follette's Autobiography*, 475.

48. National Board of Trade, *Forty-First Annual Meeting* (Philadelphia, 1911), 187; New York State Chamber of Commerce, *Fifty-Third Annual Report* (New York, 1911), 1:151; J. Laurence Laughlin, ed., *Banking Reform* (Chicago, 1912), 419–20; Henry Parker Willis, *The Federal Reserve System: Legislation, Organization and Operation* (New York, 1923), 149.

49. Henry Pratt Judson to J. Laurence Laughlin, June 1, 1911, box 3, J. Laurence Laughlin Papers, Manuscript Division, Library of Congress, Washington, DC; *Banking Reform* 1, no. 12 (1912): 1–3, 6; idem, 1, no. 13 (1912): 3; Laughlin, *Federal Reserve Act*, 45–46; A. D. Welton, "The Educational Campaign for Banking Reform," *Annals of the American Academy of Political and Social Science* 99 (1922): 32; J. Laurence Laughlin to Nelson Aldrich, June 2, 1911, reel 45, Aldrich Papers; Alfred H. Bornemann, *J. Laurence Laughlin: Chapters in the Career of an Economist* (Washington, DC, 1940), 50–51; *Coast Banker* 8, no. 7 (1912): 451; *Commercial West* 21, no. 1 (1911): 7.

50. Lynn Haines and Dora B. Haines, *The Lindberghs* (New York, 1931), 55; Bruce L. Larson, *Lindbergh of Minnesota: A Political Biography* (New York, 1973); Richard B. Lucas, *Charles August Lindbergh, Sr.: A Case Study of Congressional Insurgency, 1906–1912* (Uppsala, Sweden, 1974); *CR*, February 27, 1912, app. 61. On Lindbergh's courage, see Haines and Haines, *Lindberghs*, 279–94.

51. Larson, *Lindbergh of Minnesota*, 128–29; *CR*, February 27, 1912, app. 61; Charles A. Lindbergh to John H. Rich, February 26, 1912, box 10, Charles A. Lindbergh and Family Papers, Minnesota Historical Society, St. Paul; *Agricultural Grange News* 1, no. 5 (1913): 15.

52. Winkler, *First Billion*, 200; McCulley, "Origins of the Federal Reserve Act,"

299–303; Cleveland and Huertas, *Citibank*, 62–66; Fritz Redlich, *The Molding of American Banking: Men and Ideas*, 2 vols. (New York, 1940–51), 2, pt. 2:392–93; *CR*, July 8, 1911, 2751; Larson, *Lindbergh of Minnesota*, 106–27.

53. McCulley, "Origins of the Federal Reserve Act," 303–18; *New York Times*, November 4, 1911, 12; *Journal of Commerce*, November 21, 1911, 1; Cleveland and Huertas, *Citibank*, 67; Senate, *Legality of Certain Agreements Concerning Holdings of National Bank Stock*, 72nd Cong., 1st Sess. (1932), S. Doc. 92; Winkler, *First Billion*, 203–7.

54. Senate, *National Monetary Commission*, 62nd Cong., 2nd Sess. (1912), S. Doc 243, 15; *Texas Farm Co-operator* 35, no. 36 (1912): 11; *Portland (OR) Labor Press* 11, no. 46 (1912): 7; *New York Tribune*, February 2, 1912, 2; *Cincinnati Enquirer*, February 2, 1912, 14; *American Co-operative Journal* 7, no. 6 (1912): 474. On hobo workers, see Higbie, *Indispensable Outcasts*; Todd A. DePastino, *Citizen Hobo: How a Century of Homelessness Shaped America* (Chicago, 2003). On the farmers' elevator movement, see Hal S. Barron, *Mixed Harvest: The Second Great Transformation in the Rural North, 1870–1930* (Chapel Hill, NC, 1997), 107–52; Steven J. Keillor, *Cooperative Commonwealth: Co-ops in Rural Minnesota, 1859–1939* (St. Paul, MN, 2000), 191–211.

55. *CR*, December 4, 1911, 13; *Journal of Commerce*, December 18, 1911, 6; *Journal of the Knights of Labor* 31, no. 9 (1912): 8; *Washington Post*, January 21, 1912, 4.

56. *Commercial West* 21, no. 4 (1912): 7; *Railway Carmen's Journal* 16, no. 11 (1911): 627.

57. *Commoner* 12, no. 3 (1912): 1; *CR*, January 29, 1912, 1511; *Los Angeles Times*, March 23, 1913, VI3; *Charlotte (NC) Daily Observer*, April 19, 1908, 3; *United Mine Workers Journal* 22, no. 40 (1912): 4. On the Standard Oil indictments, see Robert C. Cotner, *James Stephen Hogg* (Austin, TX, 1959), 436–39.

58. *Sun* (Baltimore), February 9, 1912, 1; *New York Times*, February 8, 1912, 1; *New York World*, February 8, 1912, 7; *CR*, February 24, 1912, 2382

59. *CR*, February 24, 1912, 2383, 2392, 2393.

60. *CR*, February 24, 1912, 2419, 2412; *New York Times*, March 6, 1912, 5; *Wall Street Journal*, December 28, 1911, 7. On the plutocratic networks of leading bankers, see Pak, *Gentlemen Bankers*, 47–106.

61. *Washington Post*, April 23, 1912, 4; *New York Times*, April 23, 1912, 7; *CR*, April 22, 1912, 5163; April 25, 1912, 5346; O'Sullivan, *Dividends of Development*, 256; *Trust Companies* 14, no. 5 (1912): 357.

62. House Committee on Banking and Currency, *Money Trust Investigation*, 62nd Cong., 2nd Sess. (Washington, DC, 1913), 4:300–302, 3:241–42; O'Sullivan, *Dividends of Development*, 258–61; Pak, *Gentlemen Bankers*, 29–35; Edward Tuck to George F. Baker Sr., March 1, 1913, box 1, Baker Family Papers, Special Collections, Harvard Business School, Boston, MA.

63. *St. Louis Post-Dispatch*, June 9, 1912, 1; *New York Times*, June 8, 1912, 1; *Chicago Daily Tribune*, June 8, 1912, 1; *San Francisco Examiner*, June 8, 1912, 1; *Philadelphia Inquirer*, June 7, 1912, 1; *Daily Picayune* (New Orleans), June 7, 1912, 1; *Wis-*

consin Equity News 5, no. 7 (1912): 1; *Sun* (Baltimore), June 26, 1912, 2; Porter and Johnson, *National Party Platforms*, 185, 171, 179.

64. *Journal of the Knights of Labor* 31, no. 11 (1912): 11; David M. Pletcher, *Rails, Mines, and Progress: Seven American Promoters in Mexico, 1867-1911* (Ithaca, NY, 1958), 106-48; *Pacific Banker* 18, no. 21 (1912): 1.

65. *Journal of the American Bankers' Association* 5, no. 5 (1912): 331; Jacob Gould Schurman to M. S. Wildman, January 23, 1912, reel 22, Schurman to William Barnes Jr., November 11, 1911, box 2, Jacob Gould Schurman Papers, Division of Rare and Manuscript Collections, Cornell University, Ithaca, NY.

Chapter Four

1. *Bankers' Magazine* 76, no. 1 (1908): 2. On Populist caricature, see Roger A. Fischer, "Rustic Rasputin: William A. Peffer in Color Cartoon Art, 1891-1899," *Kansas History* 11, no. 4 (1988): 222-39. "Whiskers" Peffer—the famously bearded Populist leader—proposed a government central bank that would lend to individuals at low interest. See William Alfred Peffer, "Government Banking," *North American Review* 191, no. 650 (1910): 17

2. On the influence of financial and business interests on the Federal Reserve System's establishment, see Wiebe, *Businessmen and Reform*; Gabriel Kolko, *The Triumph of Conservatism: A Reinterpretation of American History, 1900-1916* (New York, 1963); West, *Banking Reform*; McCulley, "Origins of the Federal Reserve Act"; Livingston, *Origins of the Federal Reserve*; J. Lawrence Broz, *The International Origins of the Federal Reserve System* (Ithaca, NY, 1997). On the influence of leading political figures on the Federal Reserve Act, see Arthur S. Link, *Wilson*, 5 vols. (Princeton, NJ, 1956), 2:202-38; Wicker, *Great Debate*.

3. House Committee on Banking and Currency, *Money Trust Investigation*, 62nd Cong., 3rd Sess. (Washington, DC, 1913), 14:984; La Follette, *La Follette's Autobiography*, 464; *American Review of Reviews* 46, no. 2 (1912): 207.

4. *National Cyclopaedia of American Biography*, 63 vols. (New York, 1891–1984), 38:234; Odd S. Lovoll, *A Century of Urban Life: The Norwegians in Chicago before 1930* (Urbana, IL, 1988), 269-70; Karl F. M. Sandberg, *The New Rebellion: A Revolt against Our Financial Slavery* (Chicago, 1913), 18; Woodward, *Tom Watson*, 405-8; *Watson's Magazine* 4, no. 5 (1910): 366; idem, 16, no. 2 (1912): 116.

5. *Kansas City (MO) Star*, September 9, 1911, 2; September 10, 1911, 4; *Brooklyn Daily Eagle*, September 3, 1911, 4; *New York Times*, January 8, 1912, 10.

6. *Texas Farm Co-operator* 35, no. 8 (1912): 3; *Farm Journal* 36, no. 9 (1912): 488; *Colman's Rural World* 66, no. 1 (1913): 14; American Federation of Labor, *Thirty-Second Annual Convention* (Washington, DC, 1912), 379; *Painter and Decorator* 27, no. 10 (1913): 481, 668.

7. Sandberg, *New Rebellion*, 23; Eleanor J. Stebner, *The Women of Hull House: A Study in Spirituality, Vocation, and Friendship* (Albany, NY, 1997), 79; *American Co-operative Journal* 8, no. 4 (1912): 291; idem, 6, no. 12 (1911): 991; Charles O.

Boring, *The Psychology of Prohibition* (Chicago, 1908); Jo Conners, ed., *Who's Who in Arizona, 1913* (Tucson, 1913), 1:369; *Arizona Republican* (Phoenix), February 6, 1913, 2; *Coast Banker* 10, no. 2 (1913): 160.

8. Furner, *Advocacy and Objectivity*; Wiebe, *Search for Order*, 159–63; Theodore Roosevelt, *The New Nationalism* (New York, 1910), 112. For Progressivism's stress on ameliorating class conflict, see Stromquist, *Reinventing "The People."*

9. *CR*, December 6, 1912, 206; Walter Lippmann, *Drift and Mastery: An Attempt to Diagnose the Current Unrest* (New York, 1914), 54.

10. *Commercial West* 24, no. 16 (1913): 7.

11. A. Cash Koeniger, "'Unreconstructed Rebel': The Political Thought and Senate Career of Carter Glass, 1929–1936" (PhD diss., Vanderbilt University, 1980). On Glass's central role in voter disenfranchisement, see Harold S. Wilson, "The Role of Carter Glass in the Disfranchisement of the Virginia Negro," *Historian* 32, no. 1 (1969): 69–82; Harry E. Poindexter, "From Copy Desk to Congress: The Pre-Congressional Career of Carter Glass" (PhD diss., University of Virginia, 1966), 462–501. Carter Glass, *An Adventure in Constructive Finance* (New York, 1927), 35; Carter Glass to Woodrow Wilson, November 7, 1912, box 6, Carter Glass Papers, Special Collections, University of Virginia, Charlottesville; Willis, *Federal Reserve System*, 134.

12. Carter Glass to Victor Morawetz, November 21, 1912, box 17, Glass Papers; Carter Glass, "Banking and Currency Reform," *Nation's Business* 1, no. 10 (1913): 7; *Courier-Journal* (Louisville, KY), February 4, 1913, 1; Willis, *Federal Reserve System*, 142–45.

13. Carter Glass to Woodrow Wilson, November 7, 1912, box 6, Glass Papers; Glass, *Adventure in Constructive Finance*, 81–82; Richard Hofstadter, *The American Political Tradition and the Men Who Made It* (New York, 1948), 330–36; William Diamond, *The Economic Thought of Woodrow Wilson* (Baltimore, 1943), 73–74, 82; *American Review of Reviews* 75, no. 4 (1927): 347; Arthur S. Link, ed., *The Papers of Woodrow Wilson*, 69 vols. (Princeton, NJ, 1966–94), 23:157; Lester V. Chandler, "Wilson's Monetary Reform," in *The Philosophy and Politics of Woodrow Wilson*, ed. Earl Latham (Chicago, 1958); Willis, *Federal Reserve System*, 146; Carter Glass to Henry Parker Willis, January 3, 1913, box 1, Henry Parker Willis Papers, Rare Book & Manuscript Library, Columbia University, New York City.

14. Glass, *Adventure in Constructive Finance*, 84–85; West, *Banking Reform*, 100–101; Carter Glass to Henry Parker Willis, December 14, 1912, box 1, Willis Papers.

15. *Historical and Biographical Annals of Columbia and Montour Counties, Pennsylvania*, 2 vols. (Chicago, 1915), 2:676–78; House Committee on Banking and Currency, *Banking and Currency Reform*, 62nd Cong., 3rd Sess. (Washington, DC, 1913), 9:493–94, 496, 498–500, 502, 504; Porter and Johnson, *National Party Platforms*, 171; *CR*, January 4, 1913, 1044; *Plain Dealer* (Cleveland), January 5, 1913, 1B.

16. Link, *Wilson*, 2:204–5; House Committee on Banking and Currency, *Bank-*

ing and Currency Reform, 1:3; Link, *Papers of Woodrow Wilson*, 27:79; *Washington Post*, March 20, 1913, 1.

17. Robert L. Owen, *The Federal Reserve Act* (New York, 1919), 70–72; Kenny L. Brown, "Robert Latham Owen, Jr.: His Careers as Indian Attorney and Progressive Senator" (PhD diss., Oklahoma State University, 1985); Edward B. Dickinson, *Proceedings of the Democratic National Convention, 1896* (Logansport, IN, 1896), 71–72; *New York Times*, April 2, 1913, 1; *Evening Star* (Washington, DC), April 12, 1913, II-1; *Washington Post*, April 21, 1913, 3. Owen presented legislation that provided for greater public oversight of the proposed central bank than Glass's bill allowed. See Willis, *Federal Reserve System*, 1697–706.

18. Willis, *Federal Reserve System*, 1554–73; Link, *Wilson*, 2:206; William Jennings Bryan dictated to Mrs. Bryan, July 6, 1913, box 29, William Jennings Bryan Papers, Manuscript Division, Library of Congress, Washington, DC; Owen, *Federal Reserve Act*, 72–79; William G. McAdoo, *Crowded Years: The Reminiscences of William G. McAdoo* (Boston, 1931), 232; Robert L. Owen, "The Origin, Plan, and Purpose of the Currency Bill," *North American Review* 198, no. 695 (1913): 568; Frank A. Vanderlip to James Stillman, May 12, 1913, Part B, Series 1, box 5, Frank A. Vanderlip Papers, Rare Book & Manuscript Library, Columbia University, New York City.

19. Joseph P. Tumulty, *Woodrow Wilson as I Know Him* (Garden City, NY, 1921), 178–80; Link, *Papers of Woodrow Wilson*, 27:21, 413; Link, *Wilson*, 1:488–93, 2:212; Melvin I. Urofsky and David W. Levy, eds., *Letters of Louis D. Brandeis*, 5 vols. (Albany, NY, 1971–78), 3:114; Carter Glass to Woodrow Wilson, June 18, 1913, box 8, Glass Papers; Paolo E. Coletta, *William Jennings Bryan*, 3 vols. (Lincoln, NE, 1964–71), 2:130; Michael Kazin, *A Godly Hero: The Life of William Jennings Bryan* (New York, 2006), 223. Brandeis's views are outlined in *Other People's Money and How the Bankers Use It* (New York, 1914).

20. Willis, *Federal Reserve System*, 1595–613; Peter James Hudson, *Bankers and Empire: How Wall Street Colonized the Caribbean* (Chicago, 2017); Robert S. Mayer, "The Origins of the American Banking Empire in Latin America: Frank A. Vanderlip and the National City Bank," *Journal of Interamerican Studies and World Affairs* 15, no. 1 (1973): 60–76; Frank A. Vanderlip to O. M. Smith, June 19, 1913, Part B, Series 1, box 5, Vanderlip Papers. While Vanderlip approved of much of the legislation, he objected that the central bank would be too "political." See O'Sullivan, *Dividends of Development*, 267–69.

21. *CR*, June 26, 1913, 2173, 2216; *Outlook* 104, no. 9 (1913): 400; Minnesota Bankers Association, *Twenty-Fourth Annual Convention*, 37–41; Lester V. Chandler, *Benjamin Strong, Central Banker* (Washington, DC, 1958), 35; O'Sullivan, *Dividends of Development*, 266–69; *Trust Companies* 17, no. 1 (1913): 1.

22. *CR*, June 23, 1913, 2143; *New York Times*, June 7, 1913, 10; *Christian Science Monitor*, July 2, 1913, 8; *Indianapolis Star*, July 10, 1913, 1.

23. *New York Times*, July 24, 1913, 2; *Cosmopolitan* 55, no. 6 (1913): 798; *Washington Post*, July 25, 1913, 1. On congressional southern Democrats and the era's

economic reforms, see Arthur S. Link, "The South and the 'New Freedom': An Interpretation," *American Scholar* 20, no. 3 (1951): 314–24; David Sarasohn, *The Party of Reform: Democrats in the Progressive Era* (Jackson, MS, 1989); M. Elizabeth Sanders, *Roots of Reform: Farmers, Workers, and the American State, 1877–1917* (Chicago, 1999).

24. *Daily Picayune* (New Orleans), July 28, 1913, 1; *Journal of the Knights of Labor* 33, no. 2 (1913): 9; *Journal of Commerce*, August 1, 1913, 1; *Sun* (Baltimore), July 31, 1913, 2; *New York World*, August 2, 1913, 4; *Charlotte (NC) Daily Observer*, August 6, 1913, 1; Glass, *Adventure in Constructive Finance*, 134.

25. Littlefield, *William Randolph Hearst*, 309; *Pullman (WA) Herald*, November 2, 1917, 2; Carlos A. Schwantes, "Farmer-Labor Insurgency in Washington State: William Bouck, the Grange, and the Western Progressive Farmers," *Pacific Northwest Quarterly* 76, no. 1 (1985): 2–3; Robert D. Saltvig, "The Progressive Movement in Washington" (PhD diss., University of Washington, 1966), 118–19; Washington State Grange, *Twenty-Fifth Annual Session* (Olympia, 1913), 37.

26. Minnesota Bankers Association, *Twenty-Fourth Annual Convention*, 41; George M. Reynolds to Carter Glass, July 7, 1913, box 16, Glass Papers. On the advisory council's origin, see Kolko, *Triumph of Conservatism*, 232. *Nation's Business* 1, no. 13 (1913): 5; *Journal of Commerce*, August 2, 1913, 1; J. Laurence Laughlin to Wallace D. Simmons, January 15, 1914, box 2, Laughlin Papers; *Wall Street Journal*, August 11, 1913, 8.

27. *Dallas Morning News*, August 12, 1913, 2; *Washington Post*, August 13, 1913, 3; August 14, 1913, 1; *Evening Star* (Washington, DC), August 13, 1913, 1.

28. *Texas Farm Co-operator* 36, no. 41 (1913): 14; Senate Committee on Banking and Currency, *Banking and Currency*, 63rd Cong., 1st Sess. (Washington, DC, 1913), 1:673–74.

29. *Wall Street Journal*, August 23, 1913, 1; *New York World*, August 23, 1913, 5; *Chicago Daily Tribune*, August 23, 1913, 1; August 24, 1913, 4.

30. *Washington Post*, August 23, 1913, 1; *Commoner* 13, no. 29 (1913): 6; Coletta, *William Jennings Bryan*, 2:135–36; *New York Tribune*, August 26, 1913, 4; *New York World*, August 29, 1913, 7.

31. *Progressive Farmer* 28, no. 38 (1913): 986; *Texas Farm Co-operator* 36, no. 34 (1913): 15; *Cincinnati Enquirer*, August 29, 1913, 1; *Courier-Journal* (Louisville, KY), August 26, 1913, 1.

32. *CR*, September 9, 1913, 4633; *Texas Farm Co-operator* 36, no. 41 (1913): 6; Larson, *Lindbergh of Minnesota*, 161–63; *CR*, September 11, 1913, 4734, 4749–50; September 18, 1913, 5129.

33. American Bankers Association, *Thirty-Ninth Annual Convention* (New York, 1913), 88–90; Kolko, *Triumph of Conservatism*, 238–41; Robert H. Treman to Carter Glass, August 30, 1913, box 19, Glass Papers; *World's Work* 26, no. 6 (1913): 610; Arizona Bankers' Association, *Proceedings of the Arizona Bankers' Association*, vol. VII (n.p., 1913), 46; *Banking Reform* 2, no. 10 (1913): 7.

34. These three Democratic senators were motivated by not only differences

with the legislation itself, but also resentment of the administration's high-handed approach to Congress, and dissatisfaction over the distribution of patronage. See *Dallas Morning News*, October 2, 1913, 2; *New York World*, October 6, 1913, 2; *New York Tribune*, October 9, 1913, 5; *New York Times Magazine*, November 16, 1913, 1. *New York World*, October 10, 1913, 9; *Washington Post*, October 8, 1913, 1; American Bankers Association, *Fortieth Annual Convention* (New York, 1914), 113; Senate Committee on Banking and Currency, *Banking and Currency*, 3:2975; Investment Bankers Association, *Second Annual Convention* (Chicago, 1913), 237.

35. Senate Committee on Banking and Currency, *Banking and Currency*, 3:2968, 2970–71, 2974.

36. *Chicago Daily Tribune*, November 8, 1913, 15; *New York Times*, November 9, 1913, 3; *Washington Post*, November 11, 1913, 1; *New York World*, November 11, 1913, 11; *Boston Evening Transcript*, November 26, 1913, 5; Link, *Wilson*, 2:234–35; *Chicago Daily Tribune*, October 31, 1913, 3; Senate, *House Banking and Currency Bill*, 63rd Cong., 1st Sess. (1913), S. Doc. 242, 91; *Sun* (New York), November 29, 1913, 5; *Atlanta Constitution*, December 1, 1913, 9; *Sun* (New York), November 30, 1913, 10.

37. *CR*, December 19, 1913, 1230; *New York Times*, December 21, 1913, 1; *CR*, December 22, 1913, app. 562; *New York Times*, December 22, 1913, 1; *Pacific Banker* 18, no. 33 (1913): 1; *CR*, December 22, 1913, 1464; December 23, 1913, 1488; *Washington Post*, December 24, 1913, 1; Ferdinand Lundberg, *America's 60 Families* (New York, 1937), 123.

38. *Statutes at Large* 38 (1913): 251–75; Jane W. D'Arista, *Federal Reserve Structure and the Development of Monetary Policy: 1915–1935* (Washington, DC, 1971).

39. American Bankers Association, *Fortieth Annual Convention*, 102; Alexander Dana Noyes, *The Market Place: Reminiscences of a Financial Editor* (Boston, 1938), 202.

40. H. W. Wheeler to Wallace D. Simmons, January 12, 1914, box 2, Laughlin Papers; David F. Houston, *Eight Years with Wilson's Cabinet*, 2 vols. (New York, 1926), 1:84; Senate, *Agricultural Credit*, 63rd Cong., 2nd Sess. (1914), S. Doc. 380; D. C. Mullen to William Borah, March 15, 1914, box 14, William E. Borah Papers, Manuscript Division, Library of Congress, Washington, DC; House Committee on Banking and Currency, *Rural Credits*, 63rd Cong., 2nd Sess. (Washington, DC, 1914), 195; National Grange, *Forty-Seventh Annual Session* (Concord, NH, 1913), 153–54.

41. *CR*, January 19, 1914, 1956; National Grange, *Forty-Eighth Annual Session* (Concord, NH, 1914), 114; House, *Rural Credits*, 228–31, 191; Senate and House Committees on Banking and Currency, *Rural Credits*, 63rd Cong., 2nd Sess. (Washington, DC, 1914), 266; *Progressive Farmer* 28, no. 17 (1913): 558; *Equity News* 6, no. 23 (1914): 360; American Federation of Labor, *Thirty-Fourth Annual Convention* (Washington, DC, 1914), 102–3; *New York Times*, May 13, 1914, 1; Senate, S. 5542, 63rd Cong., 2nd Sess. (1914); *CR*, September 24, 1914, 15615; Link, *Papers of Woodrow Wilson*, 31:462; Gail Radford, *The Rise of the Public Authority:*

Statebuilding and Economic Development in Twentieth-Century America (Chicago, 2013), 53–61; Myron T. Herrick to Woodrow Wilson, May 29, 1914, box A-49, Vanderlip Papers.

42. North Carolina Farmers Union, *Minutes of the Annual Meeting* (Raleigh, 1914), 24; *Fort Worth (TX) Star-Telegram*, December 29, 1914, 7. For a discussion of tenancy, see Jon A. Gjerde, "'Roots of Maladjustment' in the Land: Paul Wallace Gates," *Reviews in American History* 19, no. 1 (1991): 142–53.

43. *Agricultural Grange News* 3, no. 5 (1915): 13; National Farmers Union, *Eleventh Annual Session* (Texarkana, TX, 1915), 29–30, 49.

44. House, *Rural Credits*, 64th Cong., 1st Sess. (1916), H. Doc. 494; Radford, *Rise of the Public Authority*, 57–59.

45. Link, *Wilson*, 4:347–48; S. D. Lovell, *The Presidential Election of 1916* (Carbondale, IL, 1980), 160; *CR*, May 4, 1916, 7412; May 15, 1916, 8017; *Evening Star* (Washington, DC), July 17, 1916, 1; *Statutes at Large* 39 (1916): 360–84; Federal Farm Loan Board, *Tenth Annual Report* (Washington, DC, 1927), 21. On the Federal Farm Loan Act, see Christopher W. Shaw, "'Tired of Being Exploited': The Grassroots Origin of the Federal Farm Loan Act of 1916," *Agricultural History* 92, no. 4 (2018): 512–40.

46. American Bankers Association, *Forty-Second Annual Convention* (New York, 1916), 76; *Journal of the American Bankers' Association* 8, no. 12 (1916): 1059.

47. *Equity News* 8, no. 17 (1916): 269; *Organized Farmer* 2, no. 24 (1916): 4; *CR*, May 31, 1916, 8958; *Journal of the Knights of Labor* 35, no. 11 (1916): 8; American Federation of Labor, *Thirty-Sixth Annual Convention* (Washington, DC, 1916), 273.

48. *Organized Farmer* 2, no. 24 (1916): 5; Louis W. Koenig, *Bryan: A Political Biography of William Jennings Bryan* (New York, 1971), 452; Robert E. Weir, "Solid Men in the Granite City: Municipal Socialism in Barre, Vermont, 1916–1931," *Vermont History* 83, no. 1 (2015): 53.

49. Eleanor Flexner, *Century of Struggle: The Woman's Rights Movement in the United States*, rev. ed. (Cambridge, MA, 1975); Katherine H. Adams and Michael L. Keene, *Alice Paul and the American Suffrage Campaign* (Urbana, IL, 2008); Joseph A. McCartin, *Labor's Great War: The Struggle for Industrial Democracy and the Origins of Modern American Labor Relations, 1912–1921* (Chapel Hill, NC, 1998); Allen F. Davis, *Spearheads for Reform: The Social Settlements and the Progressive Movement, 1890–1914* (New Brunswick, NJ, 1984), 221.

Chapter Five

1. *Agricultural Grange News* 8, no. 13 (1920): 2; *Evening Star* (Washington, DC), October 19, 1896, 2; *Commoner* 21, no. 9 (1921): 4.

2. David R. Weir, "A Century of U.S. Unemployment, 1890–1990: Revised Estimates and Evidence for Stabilization," *Research in Economic History* 14 (1992): 341; Jean Seder, *Voices of Kensington: Vanishing Mills, Vanishing Neighborhoods* (Ardmore, PA, 1982), 53–54; Sture Lindmark, "The Swedish-Americans and the

Depression Years, 1929–1932," *Swedish Pioneer Historical Quarterly* 19, no. 1 (1968): 17; Harpo Marx with Rowland O. Barber, *Harpo Speaks!* (New York, 1961), 281.

3. John A. Simpson, *The Militant Voice of Agriculture* (Oklahoma City, 1934), 112; *American Flint* 23, no. 1 (1931): 13; Montana State Federation of Labor, *Official Year Book, 1932* (n.p., 1932), 6.

4. Department of Agriculture, *Yearbook 1921* (Washington, DC, 1922), 12; Federal Reserve Board, *Seventh Annual Report* (Washington, DC, 1921), 57–59; Christopher W. Shaw, "'We Must Deflate': The Crime of 1920 Revisited," *Enterprise & Society* 17, no. 3 (2016): 618–50; Department of Agriculture, *Yearbook 1922* (Washington, DC, 1922), 8; James H. Shideler, *The Farm Crisis, 1919–1923* (Berkeley, 1957). The farm parity ratio did not recover until World War II. See Bureau of the Census, *Historical Statistics of the United States: Colonial Times to 1970*, 2 vols. (Washington, DC, 1975), 1:483.

5. *Farmers' Union Messenger* 3, no. 10 (1920): 7; *Commoner* 21, no. 10 (1921): 1; Joint Congressional Committee on Short-Time Rural Credits, *Short-Time Rural Credits*, 67th Cong., 2nd Sess. (Washington, DC, 1922), 32.

6. *Saturday Evening Post*, 194, no. 17 (1921): 73; Shideler, *Farm Crisis*, 171–72; Kazin, *Godly Hero*, 271; Woodward, *Tom Watson*, 473–74; *CR*, July 19, 1921, 4031; *Statutes at Large* 42 (1922): 620; Ronald E. Robbins, "Edward H. Cunningham (1869–1930)," in *Biographical Dictionary of the Board of Governors of the Federal Reserve*, ed. Bernard S. Katz (New York, 1992), 66–68.

7. Irving Fisher, *Stabilizing the Dollar* (New York, 1920); David D. Webb, "Farmers, Professors and Money: Agriculture and the Battle for Managed Money, 1920–1941" (PhD diss., University of Oklahoma, 1978), 136–54; Robert Loring Allen, *Irving Fisher: A Biography* (Cambridge, MA, 1993), 160, 164, 166; *CR*, May 25, 1922, 7692; House, H.R. 11788, 67th Cong., 2nd Sess. (1922); *CR*, May 23, 1922, 7507; T. Alan Goldsborough, "The Twilight of Bureaucracy," *Vital Speeches of the Day* 13, no. 16 (1947): 507–11; *Collier's* 122, no. 6 (1948): 20.

8. *Evening Star* (Washington, DC), December 2, 1921, 2; *CR*, August 3, 1921, 4572; Senate, S. 2342, 67th Cong., 1st Sess. (1921); *Granite Cutters' Journal* 45, no. 6 (1921): 6; Jeannette P. Nichols, "Bryan's Benefactor: Coin Harvey and His World," *Ohio Historical Quarterly* 67, no. 4 (1958): 299–325; W. H. Harvey, *Coin's Financial School* (Chicago, 1894); Livingston, *Origins of the Federal Reserve*, 90–94; Frank Luther Mott, *Golden Multitudes: The Story of Best Sellers in the United States* (New York, 1947), 170–71; *Railway Carmen's Journal* 27, no. 4 (1922): 250.

9. House, *Report of the Joint Commission of Agricultural Inquiry*, 67th Cong., 1st Sess. (1921), H. Rept. 408, 2:8; Senate Committee on Banking and Currency, *Rural Credits*, 67th Cong., 4th Sess. (Washington, DC, 1923), 1–3; Senate, *Agricultural Credits*, 67th Cong., 4th Sess. (1923), S. Rept. 1003.

10. Senate Committee on Banking and Currency, *Rural Credits*, 390, 185; *Wall Street Journal*, June 29, 1923, 6; Claude L. Benner, *The Federal Intermediate Credit System* (New York, 1926), 119–20; Robert K. Murray, *The Harding Era: Warren G. Harding and His Administration* (Minneapolis, 1969), 383–84; *Chicago Daily*

Tribune, December 18, 1922, 28; *Statutes at Large* 42 (1923): 1454–82; Federal
Farm Loan Board, *Thirteenth Annual Report* (Washington, DC, 1930), 81; M. H.
Uelsmann, *The Federal Intermediate Credit Banks, 1923–1939* (Washington, DC,
1940), 17. For additional details on the Agricultural Credits Act's enactment, see
Herbert F. Margulies, *Senator Lenroot of Wisconsin: A Political Biography, 1900–
1929* (Columbia, MO, 1977), 363–67.

11. Shaw, "'We Must Deflate'"; Christina D. Romer, "Spurious Volatility in
Historical Unemployment Data," *Journal of Political Economy* 94, no. 1 (1986): 31;
Bureau of the Census, *Historical Statistics*, 1:135; Weir, "Century of U.S. Unem-
ployment," 341; Philip S. Foner, *History of the Labor Movement in the United States*,
9 vols. (New York, 1947–91), 9:3; Peter J. Albert and Grace Palladino, eds., *The
Samuel Gompers Papers*, 12 vols. (Urbana, IL, 1986–2010), 11:444.

12. *AFL Weekly News Letter* 10, no. 31 (1920): 1; Samuel Gompers, "Labor's
Protest against a Rampant Tragedy," *American Federationist* 27, no. 6 (1920): 531;
Illinois Federation of Labor Weekly News Letter 7, no. 22 (1921): 3; Allen M. Wak-
stein, "The Open-Shop Movement, 1919–1933" (PhD diss., University of Illinois,
Urbana, 1961); Irving Bernstein, *The Lean Years: A History of the American Worker,
1920–1933* (Boston, 1960), 146–57; American Federation of Labor, *Forty-Second
Annual Convention* (Washington, DC, 1922), 90.

13. Industrial Relations Section, *The Labor Banking Movement in the United
States* (Princeton, NJ, 1929); *Cleveland Plain Dealer*, November 2, 1920, 18; *Locomotive Engineers Journal* 56, no. 12 (1922): 921–22; Walter V. Moffitt, "The Labor
Banking Movement in the United States: A Study of Its History, Present Devel-
opment and Future Possibilities" (master's thesis, Duke University, 1928), 30–63;
Robert Hunt Lyman, ed., *The World Almanac and Book of Facts for 1929* (New
York, 1929), 161. By the mid-1920s, the Brotherhood of Locomotive Engineers
exited banking because of financial difficulties due to speculative undertakings—
including Florida real estate investments. See Industrial Relations Section, *Labor
Banking Movement*, 248–253.

14. Industrial Relations Section, *Labor Banking Movement*, 191; Victoria M.
Gombert, "Labor Banks: Their Relation to the Labor Movement and the Field
of Banking in General" (master's thesis, Columbia University, 1928), 29; Labor
Research Department of the Rand School of Social Science, *The American Labor
Year Book, 1923–1924* (New York, 1924), 236; *Cleveland Plain Dealer*, January 8,
1922, 4C; Sophie G. Jaffe, "Labor Banking" (master's thesis, Columbia Univer-
sity, 1928), 27; untitled manuscript, January 1928, box 198, Amalgamated Clothing
Workers of America Records, Center for Labor-Management Documentation and
Archives, Cornell University, Ithaca, NY.

15. International Association of Machinists, *Seventeenth Convention* (Washington, DC, 1924), 116; *Tucson (AZ) Citizen*, June 27, 1920, 1; *Philadelphia Inquirer*,
July 26, 1920, 3; *Manufacturers Record* 87, no. 22 (1925): 59; Moffitt, "Labor Banking Movement," 18.

16. Carolyn Robinson, "Labor Banking in the United States" (master's thesis, Columbia University, 1927), 12; *New Freeman* 1, no. 22 (1930): 515–16.

17. Industrial Commission of North Dakota, *The North Dakota Industrial Program* (Bismarck, 1920), 6; Michael J. Lansing, *Insurgent Democracy: The Nonpartisan League in North American Politics* (Chicago, 2015); Robert L. Morlan, *Political Prairie Fire: The Nonpartisan League, 1915–1922* (Minneapolis, 1955); Rozanne Enerson Junker, *The Bank of North Dakota: An Experiment in State Ownership* (Santa Barbara, CA, 1989); Federal Writers' Project of Oklahoma, *Labor History of Oklahoma* (Oklahoma City, 1939), 52; Gilbert C. Fite, "Oklahoma's Reconstruction League: An Experiment in Farmer-Labor Politics," *Journal of Southern History* 13, no. 4 (1947): 535–55; Hugh T. Lovin, "The Nonpartisan League and Progressive Renascence in Idaho, 1919–1924," *Idaho Yesterdays* 32, no. 3 (1988): 2–15; *Idaho Daily Statesman* (Boise), August 24, 1922, 10; Bureau of Public Printing, *South Dakota Legislative Manual, 1923* (Pierre, 1923), 410; Carl J. Hofland, "The Nonpartisan League in South Dakota" (master's thesis, University of South Dakota, 1940); Labor Research Department, *Labor Year Book, 1923–1924*, 158; State Legislature of Arizona, *Journal of the Senate, 1923* (n.p., 1923), 450; *Coast Banker* 30, no. 3 (1923): 342.

18. *Railway Maintenance of Way Employes Journal* 33, no. 3 (1924): 32; Robert Lee Hunt, *A History of Farmer Movements in the Southwest, 1873–1925* (n.p., 1935), 189; Mrs. T. A. Allen to William Borah, December 3, 1923, box 152, Borah Papers.

19. Post Office Department, *Annual Report, 1920* (Washington, DC, 1921), 111; *CR*, August 20, 1921, 5301; House, *Amendment of Law Relating to Postal Savings System*, 67th Cong., 1st Sess. (1921), H. Rept. 489; National Grange, *Fifty-Fourth Annual Session* (Springfield, MA, 1920), 168; idem, *Fifty-Fifth Annual Session* (Springfield, MA, 1921), 153; American Federation of Labor, *Forty-Second Annual Convention*, 325; *CR*, December 9, 1920, 146; House, H.R. 14855, 66th Cong., 3rd Sess. (1920).

20. Martin P. Mayer, *The Bankers* (New York, 1974), 398; Koenig, *Bryan*, 616; *CR*, February 10, 1922, 2387; Porter and Johnson, *National Party Platforms*, 254.

21. On the rise of branch banking, see Robertson, *Comptroller and Bank Supervision*, 100–105. Federal Reserve Committee on Branch, Group, and Chain Banking, *Branch Banking in the United States* (n.p., 1932), 3; J. I. Cook to William Borah, November 23, 1922, box 108, Borah Papers; *Progressive* 1, no. 1 (1929): 4; Jonathan J. Kasparek, *Fighting Son: A Biography of Philip F. La Follette* (Madison, WI, 2006), 90, 104; Cory L. Sparks, "Locally Owned and Operated: Opposition to Chain Stores, 1925–1940" (PhD diss., Louisiana State University, 2000), 137–43; Philip F. La Follette, *Adventure in Politics: The Memoirs of Philip La Follette* (New York, 1970), 137; Louis L. Emmerson, ed., *Blue Book of the State of Illinois, 1925–1926* (Springfield, 1925), 811; *Urbana (IL) Daily Courier*, October 28, 1924, 2; *Federal Reserve Bulletin* 10, no. 12 (1924): 930–31; National Grange, *Fifty-Ninth Annual Session* (Springfield, MA, 1925), 159. In 1930 there were approximately 23,000

banks, 750 of which had branches (Board of Governors of the Federal Reserve System, *Banking and Monetary Statistics* [Washington, DC, 1943], 16; Federal Reserve Committee on Branch, Group, and Chain Banking, *Branch Banking in the United States*, 3).

22. *Statutes at Large* 44 (1927): 1224–34; *CR*, February 11, 1924, 2281; Marquis James and Bessie Rowland James, *Biography of a Bank: The Story of Bank of America N.T. & S.A.* (New York, 1954), 185. On the growth of investment affiliates, see Carosso, *Investment Banking*, 272–79.

23. *CR*, January 13, 1925, 1773; Denison Bingham Hull, *The Legislative Life of Morton Denison Hull* (Chicago, 1948), 116–17; *Commercial West* 50, no. 10 (1926): 33; James and James, *Biography of a Bank*, 188; Carter Glass to Paul M. Warburg, October 18, 1926, box 8, Glass Papers; *Southern Banker* 48, no. 1 (1927): 29.

24. M. H. Jones to Furnifold M. Simmons, January 7, 1927, box 60, Furnifold M. Simmons Papers, Rare Book & Manuscript Library, Duke University, Durham, NC; W. E. Katenkamp to W. Cabell Bruce, December 29, 1926, box 240, Glass Papers; *American Bankers Association Journal* 19, no. 5 (1926): 309; *CR*, February 26, 1927, 4938; *San Francisco Chronicle*, March 1, 1927, 16.

25. Donald L. Barlett and James B. Steele, *America: Who Really Pays the Taxes?* (New York, 1994), 62–67; Harvey O'Connor, *Mellon's Millions: The Biography of a Fortune* (New York, 1933), 124–61; *New York Times*, May 11, 1924, IX-3; Koenig, *Bryan*, 597, 610, 616.

26. William Pencak, *For God and Country: The American Legion, 1919–1941* (Boston, 1989), 197–200; Romain D. Huret, *American Tax Resisters* (Cambridge, MA, 2014), 120–25; Senate Committee on Finance, *Payment of Veterans' Adjusted-Service Certificates*, 71st Cong., 3rd Sess. (Washington, DC, 1931), 55; Herbert C. Hoover, *The Memoirs of Herbert Hoover*, 3 vols. (New York, 1951–52), 3:30; Herman E. Krooss, *Executive Opinion: What Business Leaders Said and Thought on Economic Issues, 1920s–1960s* (Garden City, NY, 1970), 128–29; Lester V. Chandler, *American Monetary Policy, 1928–1941* (New York, 1971), 117–23; *Pittsburgh Post-Gazette*, September 21, 1931, 1; O'Connor, *Mellon's Millions*, 342–44; Elmus R. Wicker, *The Banking Panics of the Great Depression* (New York, 1996), 82–83.

27. John Sherman to Wright Patman, April 28, 1931, Arthur V. Hamman to Patman, January 17, 1932, anonymous to Patman, January 6, 1932, J. B. Smith to Patman, February 11, 1932, box 1511C, Nanette Christy to Patman, January 20, 1933, box 436A, Wright Patman Papers, Lyndon B. Johnson Presidential Library and Museum, Austin, TX.

28. *CR*, January 6, 1932, 1400–1401; Janet Schmelzer, "Wright Patman and the Impeachment of Andrew Mellon," *East Texas Historical Journal* 23, no. 1 (1985): 33–46; Wright Patman Diary, February 25, 1932, box 1705, Patman Papers; Nancy Beck Young, *Wright Patman: Populism, Liberalism, and the American Dream* (Dallas, 2000); Janet Schmelzer, "The Early Life and Early Congressional Career of Wright Patman: 1894–1941" (PhD diss., Texas Christian University, 1978); Robert G. Sherrill, "'The Last of the Great Populists,'" *New York Times Magazine*,

May 16, 1969, 24; Milton Friedman and Anna Jacobson Schwartz, *A Monetary History of the United States, 1867–1960* (Princeton, NJ, 1963), 301–2, 712–13; Senate Committee on Finance, *Payment of Veterans' Adjusted-Service Certificates*, 85.

29. *New York Times*, February 4, 1932, 1; Milton H. Hall to Wright Patman, December 11, 1931, Mrs. Thomas Jenkins to Patman, January 6, 1932, American Legion Post No. 296 to Patman, February 4, 1932, box 1511C, Patman Papers. Mellon would later shut down a Gulf Oil plant located in Patman's district and finance the campaign of a challenger for his seat in 1936 (*San Francisco Chronicle*, April 29, 1936, 11).

30. Robert F. Martin, *Income in Agriculture, 1929–1935* (New York, 1936), 89; Studs Terkel, *Hard Times: An Oral History of the Great Depression* (New York, 1970), 218; Department of Agriculture, *Major Statistical Series of the U.S. Department of Agriculture*, vol. 6, Agriculture Handbook No. 118 (1957), 11; David E. Hamilton, *From New Day to New Deal: American Farm Policy from Hoover to Roosevelt, 1928–1933* (Chapel Hill, NC, 1991), 149; Chandler, *American Monetary Policy*, 233–39; *Farmers Union Herald* 5, no. 18 (1931): 4; Kevin J. Cahill, "Fertilizing the Weeds: The New Deal's Rural Poverty Program in West Virginia" (PhD diss., West Virginia University, 1999), 33. On the credit market's breakdown, see Ben S. Bernanke, "Nonmonetary Effects of the Financial Crisis in the Propagation of the Great Depression," *American Economic Review* 73, no. 3 (1983): 257–76.

31. Krooss, *Executive Opinion*, 134–35; *Nation's Business* 20, no. 4 (1932): 90; *Financial World* 57, no. 11 (1932): 8; Herbert C. Hoover, *Public Papers of the Presidents of the United States: Herbert Hoover, 1932–33* (Washington, DC, 1977), 45, 42; *Arizona Producer* 11, no. 6 (1932): 5. On Hoover's anti-hoarding campaign, see William J. Barber, *From New Era to New Deal: Herbert Hoover, the Economists, and American Economic Policy, 1921–1933* (New York, 1985), 141–44; Edward Robb Ellis, *A Nation in Torment: The Great Depression, 1929–1939* (New York, 1970), 195–97.

32. Webb, "Farmers, Professors and Money," 159–81; Pennsylvania State Grange, *Fifty-Ninth Annual Session* (n.p., 1931), 10; Michigan State Grange, *Fifty-Ninth Annual Session* (n.p., 1932), 75; *Wallaces' Farmer* 56, no. 42 (1931): 3; Oregon State Grange, *Fifty-Ninth Annual Session* (n.p., 1932), 91; *Farmers Union Herald* 5, no. 1 (1930): 4; idem, 6, no. 1 (1931): 9.

33. Everett L. Cooley, "Silver Politics in the United States, 1918–1946" (PhD diss., University of California, Berkeley, 1951), 24–51; John A. Brennan, *Silver and the First New Deal* (Reno, NV, 1969), 27, 47–50; *San Francisco Examiner*, February 16, 1932, 21; *Commonweal* 15, no. 3 (1931): 67.

34. John A. Brennan, "Silver Politics and the Hoover Administration, 1931–1932," *Rendezvous* 6, no. 2 (1971): 33–46; Richard T. Ruetten, "Burton K. Wheeler and the Montana Connection," *Montana: The Magazine of Western History* 27, no. 3 (1977): 2–19; *CR*, January 4, 1932, 1167; January 25, 1932, 2616. John M. Evans (D-MT) introduced a companion measure to Wheeler's bill in the House

(*CR*, January 4, 1932, 1277). Not all members of the silver bloc wanted to foster inflation: Senator Key Pittman (D-NV) simply sought to increase the price of silver. See Fred L. Israel, "The Fulfillment of Bryan's Dream: Key Pittman and Silver Politics, 1918–1933," *Pacific Historical Review* 30, no. 4 (1961): 372–73.

35. Brennan, *Silver and the First New Deal*, 56–57; *CR*, March 5, 1932, 5336; James C. Milligan and L. David Norris, "Organizing Wide-Awake Farmers: John A. Simpson and the Oklahoma Farmers' Union," *Chronicles of Oklahoma* 74, no. 4 (1996–97): 356–83; Gilbert C. Fite, "John A. Simpson: The Southwest's Militant Farm Leader," *Mississippi Valley Historical Review* 35, no. 4 (1949): 563–84; Simpson, *Militant Voice*, 86–87; Colorado State Grange, *Fifty-Eighth Annual Session* (n.p., 1932), 60; Oregon State Grange, *Fifty-Ninth Annual Session*, 128; Washington State Grange, *Forty-Fourth Annual Session* (n.p., 1932), 189; *Bureau Farmer* (Utah) 7, no. 8 (1932): 12.

36. *Wallaces' Farmer* 57, no. 1 (1932): 4; Simpson, *Militant Voice*, 87; Senate Committee on Banking and Currency, *Restoring and Maintaining the Average Purchasing Power of the Dollar*, 72nd Cong., 1st Sess. (Washington, DC, 1932), 1:92–93; George F. Warren, "Stabilization of Measure of Value," *Alameda and Contra Costa Counties Farm Bureau Monthly* 16, no. 2 (1933): 10; Warren, "Depression—What to Do about It—I," *Ohio Farmer* 171, no. 9 (1933): 3; George F. Warren and Frank A. Pearson, *Prices* (New York, 1933); Warren and Pearson, "The Future of the General Price Level," *Journal of Farm Economics* 14, no. 1 (1932): 23–46; Frank A. Pearson and William I. Myers, "The Fact-Finder," *Farm Economics* 208 (1957): 5509; Subcommittee of the House Committee on Banking and Currency, *Stabilization of Commodity Prices*, 72nd Cong., 1st Sess. (Washington, DC, 1932), 1:85; Bernard F. Stanton, *George F. Warren, Farm Economist* (Ithaca, NY, 2007), 356–58. In the fall of 1933, President Roosevelt gave Warren's theory a brief trial. See Scott B. Sumner, "Roosevelt, Warren, and the Gold-Buying Program of 1933," *Research in Economic History* 20 (2001): 135–72. Warren assisted the Committee for the Nation. Business interests formed this right-wing proponent of inflation. See Herbert M. Bratter, "The Committee for the Nation: A Case History in Monetary Propaganda," *Journal of Political Economy* 49, no. 4 (1941): 531–53; Gary Dean Best, *Peddling Panaceas: Popular Economists in the New Deal Era* (New Brunswick, NJ, 2005), 1–85.

37. *Bureau Farmer* 7, no. 7 (1932): 7; Webb, "Farmers, Professors and Money," 181–84; *CR*, May 2, 1932, 9410; Subcommittee of the House Committee on Banking and Currency, *Stabilization of Commodity Prices*, 1:325.

38. *CR*, May 2, 1932, 9432; *Trust Companies* 54, no. 5 (1932): 560; *Wallaces' Farmer* 57, no. 10 (1932): 5; Fred Brenckman et al. to Robert J. Bulkley, May 20, 1932, box 2, John A. Simpson Papers, Western History Collections, University of Oklahoma, Norman; *New York Times*, June 2, 1932, 1.

39. Subcommittee of the House Committee on Banking and Currency, *Stabilization of Commodity Prices*, 1:6; *Bureau Farmer* (Nevada) 7, no. 5 (1932): 11; Simpson, *Militant Voice*, 18.

40. Labor Research Department, *Labor Year Book, 1923–1924*, 238; *American Bankers Association Journal* 23, no. 3 (1930): 187; idem, 23, no. 4 (1930): 384; *New York Times*, January 12, 1931, 1; January 14, 1931, 4.

41. *Wall Street Journal*, April 15, 1931, 15; Benjamin M. Anderson Jr., "Equilibrium Creates Purchasing Power," *Chase Economic Bulletin* 11, no. 3 (1931): 16, 14; *American Labor Banner* 2, no. 26 (1931): 4.

42. Grace Palladino, *Dreams of Dignity, Workers of Vision: A History of the International Brotherhood of Electrical Workers* (Washington, DC, 1991), 148; *AFL Weekly News Service* 21, no. 5 (1931): 1; *Oregon Labor Press* 29, no. 51 (1931): 2; Pennsylvania State Federation of Labor, *Thirty-Second Annual Convention* (n.p., 1933), 47; *Central Labor Council Herald* 1, no. 11 (1931): 1; *United Mine Workers Journal* 42, no. 8 (1931): 6; *New York Times*, September 26, 1931, 2.

43. Ohio State Federation of Labor, *Forty-Eighth Annual Convention* (n.p., 1931), 63; *International Molders Journal* 68, no. 6 (1932): 355; American Flint Glass Workers Union, *Fifty-Sixth Convention* (n.p., 1932), 154.

44. *New York Times*, February 2, 1930, XX1; Alex G. Gottfried, *Boss Cermak of Chicago: A Study of Political Leadership* (Seattle, 1962), 247; *New York Times*, January 23, 1930, 1; *Federation News* 26, no. 17 (1931): 2; *Chicago Herald and Examiner*, June 18, 1932, 1; *Chicago Daily News*, June 2, 1932, 16; Penny Joan Lipkin, "Payless Paydays: Financial Crisis of the Chicago Board of Education, 1930–1934" (master's thesis, Columbia University, 1967), 11–13; Ellis, *Nation in Torment*, 202; John F. Lyons, *Teachers and Reform: Chicago Public Education, 1929–1970* (Urbana, IL, 2008), 31–32; *Federation News* 25, no. 26 (1931): 1.

45. *CR*, January 9, 1932, 1583; *New York Herald Tribune*, June 2, 1932, 20; *Labor* 13, no. 22 (1932): 1.

46. *New York Times*, January 11, 1932, 1; *Wall Street Journal*, January 20, 1932, 11; January 21, 1932, 1; Thomas Kessner, *Fiorello H. La Guardia and the Making of Modern New York* (New York, 1989), 218–19; *American Bankers Association Journal* 24, no. 8 (1932): 187.

47. *New York Times*, December 8, 1932, 1; Kessner, *Fiorello H. La Guardia*, 220; *Nation's Business* 20, no. 12 (1932): 60; *New York Times*, December 30, 1932, 1; *Progressive* 3, no. 55 (1932): 2; *Labor* 14, no. 16 (1932): 1.

48. Frederik F. Ohles, Shirley M. Ohles, and John G. Ramsay, *Biographical Dictionary of Modern American Educators* (Westport, CT, 1997), 201–2; *New York Herald Tribune*, November 8, 1956, A10; American Federation of Teachers, *Sixteenth Annual Convention* (n.p., 1932), 1:52; *American Teacher* 17, no. 2 (1932): 3; *Brooklyn Daily Eagle*, December 18, 1932, 8; *New York Herald Tribune*, December 18, 1932, 19; *New York Times*, December 7, 1932, 18.

49. *Journal of Electrical Workers and Operators* 31, no. 10 (1932): 492; *Shoe Workers' Journal* 33, no. 5 (1932): 3; *Central Labor Council Herald* 1, no. 9 (1931): 3; *Farmer-Labor News* 9, no. 1 (1931): 2.

50. *Tarheel Banker* 10, no. 7 (1932): 23; *Chicago Banker* 72, no. 7 (1931): 9; *Sunshine Banker* 5, no. 7 (1930): 9.

51. *Southern Banker* 56, no. 2 (1931): 24; *American Bankers Association Journal* 24, no. 2 (1931): 124.

52. *Nebraska Union Farmer* 17, no. 10 (1930): 1; *Capital Times* (Madison, WI), March 23, 1933, 18; *Hartford (CT) Courant*, October 7, 1932, 10.

53. *Producer* 13, no. 7 (1931): 17; Oregon State Grange, *Fifty-Eighth Annual Session* (n.p., 1931), 24.

Chapter Six

1. Wicker, *Banking Panics of the Great Depression*; Frederick Lewis Allen, *Only Yesterday: An Informal History of the Nineteen-Twenties* (New York, 1931), 345; *Literary Digest* 114, no. 2 (1932): 37; Robert A. Slayton, *Back of the Yards: The Making of a Local Democracy* (Chicago, 1986), 190; *Chicago Daily Tribune*, June 27, 1932, 13; *Chicago Defender*, March 13, 1932, 15.

2. *Federal Reserve Bulletin* 23, no. 9 (1937): 907; *CR*, May 25, 1932, 11232.

3. Federal Reserve Committee on Branch, Group, and Chain Banking, *Bank Suspensions in the United States, 1892–1931* (n.p., 1933), 26. On incompetent small-town bank management, see Howard, *Montana*, 230; Anderson, *Essays on the History of Banking*, 200; Clarence W. Groth, "Sowing and Reaping: Montana Banking—1910–25," *Montana: The Magazine of Western History* 20, no. 4 (1970): 32; Allan Garfield Gruchy, *Supervision and Control of Virginia State Banks* (New York, 1937), 233. Aaron Hardy Ulm, "When Large City Banks Close," *Barron's* 12, no. 23 (1932): 20–21; Jonathan D. Rose, "Old-Fashioned Deposit Runs," Finance and Economics Discussion Series 2015–111, Board of Governors of the Federal Reserve System (Washington, DC, 2015): 19–23; *Coast Banker* 49, no. 2 (1932): 39; *Commercial West* 61, no. 6 (1931): 6. On the alleged communist sabotage of banks, see Christopher W. Shaw, "'The Story Was Not Printed': The Press Covers the 1930s Banking Crisis," *Journalism History* (forthcoming).

4. Gary Richardson, "Categories and Causes of Bank Distress during the Great Depression, 1929–1933: The Illiquidity Versus Insolvency Debate Revisited," *Explorations in Economic History* 44, no. 4 (2007): 588–607; Oscar Schisgall, *Out of One Small Chest: A Social and Financial History of the Bowery Savings Bank* (New York, 1975), 136; Gerald R. Smith and George M. Basler, *On the Seamy Side of the Street: Colorful Characters from Broome County's History* (Binghamton, NY, 2013), 81–91; Timothy W. Hubbard and Lewis E. Davids, *Banking in Mid-America: A History of Missouri's Banks* (Washington, DC, 1969), 171. On the role of banker criminality in this era's suspensions, see Raymond B. Vickers, *Panic in the Loop: Chicago's Banking Crisis of 1932* (Lanham, MD, 2011); Timothy Messer-Kruse, *Banksters, Bosses, and Smart Money: A Social History of the Great Toledo Bank Crash of 1931* (Columbus, OH, 2004).

5. David E. Hamilton, "The Causes of the Banking Panic of 1930: Another View," *Journal of Southern History* 51, no. 4 (1985): 581–608; John Berry McFerrin, *Caldwell and Company: A Southern Financial Empire* (Nashville, TN, 1969).

6. *New York World*, December 11, 1930, 3; M. R. Werner, *Little Napoleons and Dummy Directors: Being the Narrative of the Bank of United States* (New York, 1933), 203–4; *New York Times*, December 12, 1930, 1; Jewel Bellush, "Roosevelt's Good Right Arm: Lieut. Governor Herbert H. Lehman," *New York History* 41, no. 4 (1960): 433–34.

7. *New York Daily News*, December 14, 1930, 6; Werner, *Little Napoleons*, 62–130; *New York Herald Tribune*, June 24, 1931, 1; *Time* 18, no. 1 (1931): 13. On reckless management at the Bank of United States, see also Paul B. Trescott, "The Failure of the Bank of United States, 1930," *Journal of Money, Credit, and Banking* 24, no. 3 (1992): 384–99; Joseph L. Lucia, "The Failure of the Bank of United States: A Reappraisal," *Explorations in Economic History* 22, no. 4 (1985): 402–16; Peter Temin, *Did Monetary Forces Cause the Great Depression?* (New York, 1976), 90–94.

8. Board of Governors of the Federal Reserve System, *Banking and Monetary Statistics*, 283; Messer-Kruse, *Banksters, Bosses, and Smart Money*, 5–8; *Toledo News-Bee*, June 18, 1931, 1; August 17, 1931, 1; Charles C. Alexander, *Breaking the Slump: Baseball in the Depression Era* (New York, 2002), 16.

9. *Toledo News-Bee*, August 17, 1931, 1; Messer-Kruse, *Banksters, Bosses, and Smart Money*, 111–49; Rena Steinzor, *Why Not Jail? Industrial Catastrophes, Corporate Malfeasance, and Government Inaction* (New York, 2015), 79–80. Prosecutions of bankers following the Caldwell and Company–associated failures also were compromised by the power of the charged individuals. See McFerrin, *Caldwell and Company*, 205–21.

10. *Urbana (IL) Daily Courier*, January 19, 1932, 1; *Time* 19, no. 5 (1932): 10; *Chicago Herald and Examiner*, January 23, 1932, 7; *Chicago Daily Tribune*, January 24, 1932, 12A; *Chicago Daily News*, July 1, 1932, 9; *Chicago Daily Tribune*, July 6, 1932, 5; *Chicago Herald and Examiner*, June 29, 1932, 15; *Chicago Daily Tribune*, July 1, 1932, 20.

11. O. K. Burrell, *Gold in the Woodpile: An Informal History of Banking in Oregon* (Eugene, OR, 1967), 264; Laura A. Friedman, "A Study of One Hundred Unemployed Families in Chicago, January, 1927, to June, 1932" (master's thesis, University of Chicago, 1933), 185; *Federation News* 26, no. 1 (1931): 9; Terkel, *Hard Times*, 430.

12. *Brooklyn Daily Eagle*, September 4, 1931, 17; *New York Herald Tribune*, September 6, 1931, 6; *New York Times*, August 16, 1931, 7.

13. *Detroit Free Press*, August 8, 1932, 1; August 7, 1932, I-2; *Chicago Daily Tribune*, September 11, 1931, 3; *Labor* 13, no. 34 (1932): 4; H. Clay East, interviewed by M. Sue Thrasher, Southern Oral History Program, University of North Carolina, 1973, 37–38.

14. J. B. Clarkson to Peter Norbeck, March 2, 1932, box 1, Peter Norbeck Papers, Archives & Special Collections, University of South Dakota, Vermillion; Washington State Federation of Labor, *Thirty-First Annual Convention* (n.p., 1932), 71; Elna C. Green, ed., *Looking for the New Deal: Florida Women's Letters during the Great Depression* (Columbia, SC, 2007), 30.

15. *Saturday Evening Post* 205, no. 19 (1932): 5; Blocker, *Guaranty of State Bank Deposits*, 23–46; *Morning Oregonian* (Portland), March 19, 1932, 8; *Omaha (NE) World-Herald*, January 9, 1931, 12; *Federation News* 28, no. 2 (1932): 4; *Producer* 14, no. 2 (1932): 10; Michigan State Grange, *Fifty-Ninth Annual Session*, 73; United Mine Workers of America, *Thirty-Second Consecutive Constitutional Convention* (Indianapolis, 1932), 2:717. The fate of Washington State's short-lived voluntary guaranty program was not linked to the agricultural depression. Failure of the program's largest bank as a result of mismanagement depleted the fund. See Howard H. Preston, "A Crisis in Deposit Guaranty in the State of Washington," *Quarterly Journal of Economics* 36, no. 2 (1922): 350–56.

16. FDIC, *Annual Report, 1950* (Washington, DC, 1950), 92–99; House, H.R. 12221, 68th Cong., 2nd Sess. (1925); *CR*, March 7, 1932, 5423; Jack Brien Key, "Henry B. Steagall: The Conservative as a Reformer," *Alabama Review* 17, no. 3 (1964): 198–209; *CR*, April 14, 1932, 8273; April 19, 1932, 8539; House, *To Amend the National Banking Act and the Federal Reserve Act and to Provide a Guaranty Fund for Depositors in Banks*, 72nd Cong., 1st Sess. (1932), H. Rept. 1085, 2.

17. Subcommittee of the House Committee on Banking and Currency, *To Provide a Guaranty Fund for Depositors in Banks*, 72nd Cong., 2nd Sess. (Washington, DC, 1932), 117–34, 251, 154; *Guthrie (OK) Daily Leader*, February 10, 1910, 6; Keith L. Bryant Jr., *Alfalfa Bill Murray* (Norman, OK, 1968), 78. On Oklahoma's Depositors' Guaranty Fund, see Norbert R. Mahnken, "No Oklahoman Lost a Penny: Oklahoma's State Bank Guarantee Law, 1907–1923," *Chronicles of Oklahoma* 71, no. 1 (1993): 42–63.

18. *CR*, May 27, 1932, 11453; Democratic National Convention, *Proceedings of the Democratic National Convention, 1932* (n.p., 1932), 198, 196.

19. *Southern Banker* 58, no. 4 (1932): 18; *American Bankers Association Journal* 25, no. 5 (1932): 41; *New York Herald Tribune*, June 26, 1932, 14.

20. *Sacramento (CA) Bee*, December 26, 1932, 18; H. H. McDonald to Josiah William Bailey, January 8, 1932, box 217, Josiah William Bailey Papers, Rare Book & Manuscript Library, Duke University, Durham, NC.

21. Hoover, *Memoirs*, 3:24; Hoover, *The New Day: Campaign Speeches of Herbert Hoover, 1928* (Stanford, CA, 1928), 31; Elliot A. Rosen, *Hoover, Roosevelt, and the Brains Trust: From Depression to New Deal* (New York, 1977), 43–44; *American Bankers Association Journal* 24, no. 9 (1932): 579. On Hoover's pursuit of limited financial reform, see Rosen, *Hoover, Roosevelt, and the Brains Trust*, 277–79; Susan Estabrook Kennedy, *The Banking Crisis of 1933* (Lexington, KY, 1973), 23–25; Lester V. Chandler, *America's Greatest Depression, 1929–1941* (New York, 1970), 87–88; Arthur M. Schlesinger Jr., *The Age of Roosevelt*, 3 vols. (Boston, 1957–60), 1:474.

22. Chandler, *American Monetary Policy*, 188–89; Hoover, *Memoirs*, 3:115–17; *CR*, February 11, 1932, 3734, 3801; *New York Times*, February 14, 1932, 1; *Statutes at Large* 47 (1932): 56–57.

23. *CR*, December 8, 1931, 25; Gerald D. Nash, "Herbert Hoover and the Origins of the Reconstruction Finance Corporation," *Mississippi Valley Historical Review* 46, no. 3 (1959): 455–68; Subcommittee of the Senate Committee on Banking and Currency, *Creation of a Reconstruction Finance Corporation*, 72nd Cong., 1st Sess. (Washington, DC, 1932), 1:177; *New York Times*, January 23, 1932, 1.

24. *CR*, January 11, 1932, 1742; *Amalgamated Journal* 33, no. 33 (1932): 20; *CR*, April 5, 1932, 7465–67; Thomas R. Amlie to George A. Manupella, June 24, 1932, box 7, Thomas R. Amlie Papers, Wisconsin Historical Society, Madison; *Labor* 13, no. 35 (1932): 4.

25. Subcommittee of the House Committee on Banking and Currency, *Creation of a System of Federal Home Loan Banks*, 72nd Cong., 1st Sess. (Washington, DC, 1932), 107; Thomas B. Marvell, *The Federal Home Loan Bank Board* (New York, 1969), 18; Bureau of the Census, *Historical Statistics*, 2:651; Friedman, "Study of One Hundred Unemployed Families," 185; Franklin J. Havelick and Michael Kwartler, "Sunnyside Gardens: Whose Land Is It Anyway?," *New York Affairs* 7, no. 2 (1982): 71; Subcommittee of the Senate Committee on Banking and Currency, *Home Owners' Loan Act*, 73rd Cong., 1st Sess. (Washington, DC, 1933), 31–32.

26. *Washington Post*, November 14, 1931, 1; *Trust Companies* 54, no. 2 (1932): 187; *Economic Conditions*, December 1931, 182; *American Bankers Association Journal* 24, no. 8 (1932): 519; Subcommittee of the Senate Committee on Banking and Currency, *Creation of a System of Federal Home Loan Banks*, 72nd Cong., 1st Sess. (Washington, DC, 1932), 1:139; *Chicago Daily News*, June 7, 1932, 14; *Advance* 18, no. 2 (1932): 16.

27. Josephine Hedges Ewalt, *A Business Reborn: The Savings and Loan Story, 1930–1960* (Chicago, 1962), 52–54; David L. Mason, *From Building and Loans to Bail-Outs: A History of the Savings and Loan Industry, 1831–1995* (New York, 2004), 60–62; H. Morton Bodfish and A. D. Theobald, *Savings and Loan Principles* (New York, 1938), 58–59; Subcommittee of the Senate Committee on Banking and Currency, *Creation of a System of Federal Home Loan Banks*, 2:285, 3:569–72; Subcommittee of the House Committee on Banking and Currency, *Creation of a System of Federal Home Loan Banks*, 68–70; J. R. Oettinger to Josiah W. Bailey, March 29, 1932, H. L. Cranford to Bailey, June 22, 1932, box 217, Bailey Papers; Truman D. Cameron to Robert F. Wagner, January 9, 1932, box LE 198, Robert F. Wagner Papers, Special Collections, Georgetown University, Washington, DC; John W. Blodgett to John Garner, n.d., box 77, Amlie Papers; J. W. Lambert to Wright Patman, June 15, 1932, box 36A, Patman Papers.

28. *CR*, July 16, 1932, 15756; *Statutes at Large* 47 (1932): 725–41; Wright Patman to W. T. Merchant, January 16, 1933; Patman to James D. Baker, January 11, 1933; J. T. Hawkins to Patman, November 28, 1932, box 36A, Patman Papers. Senator James J. Couzens had submitted a successful amendment that permitted

homeowners to apply for direct loans from the twelve regional banks (*CR*, July 5, 1932, 14584). Yet out of 41,000 applications received only three loans were issued (Marvell, *Federal Home Loan Bank Board*, 23).

29. *Trust Companies* 54, no. 3 (1932): 297; Helen M. Burns, *The American Banking Community and New Deal Banking Reforms, 1933–1935* (Westport, CT, 1974), 53; Harris Gaylord Warren, *Herbert Hoover and the Great Depression* (New York, 1959), 163; J. B. Killian to Hugo Black, December 6, 1932, box 223, Hugo L. Black Papers, Manuscript Division, Library of Congress, Washington, DC.

30. Cedric B. Cowing, *Populists, Plungers, and Progressives: A Social History of Stock and Commodity Speculation, 1890–1936* (Princeton, NJ, 1965), 133–142; Cowing, "Sons of the Wild Jackass and the Stock Market," *Business History Review* 33, no. 2 (1959): 138–55; Patrick J. Maney, *"Young Bob" La Follette: A Biography of Robert M. La Follette, Jr., 1895–1953* (Columbia, MO, 1978), 53–54; Senate Committee on Banking and Currency, *Brokers' Loans*, 70th Cong., 1st Sess. (Washington, DC, 1928), 2; John D. Lyle, "The United States Senate Career of Carter Glass, 1920–1933" (PhD diss., University of South Carolina, 1974), 136–37, 154; *CR*, February 11, 1929, 3206; Carter Glass, "The Federal Reserve System Grossly Misused," *American Review of Reviews* 78, no. 3 (1928): 257–58; *Journal of Commerce*, June 7, 1928, 3. On the role that banks played in fostering the highly speculative 1920s bull market, see John Kenneth Galbraith, *The Great Crash, 1929* (Boston, 1955), 24–27. On the dangers of investment affiliates, see Carosso, *Investment Banking*, 277–78.

31. *CR*, June 17, 1930, 10973; January 21, 1932, 2403; *Southern Banker* 58, no. 3 (1932): 15; Senate Committee on Banking and Currency, *Operation of the National and Federal Reserve Banking Systems*, 72nd Cong., 1st Sess. (Washington, DC, 1932), 1:17; *CR*, March 17, 1932, 6329; *New York Times*, March 18, 1932, 16; D'Arista, *Federal Reserve Structure*, 139–40; Willis H. Booth to George Wingfield, March 23, 1932, box 39, George Wingfield Papers, Nevada Historical Society, Reno.

32. *CR*, April 18, 1932, 8350; *New York Times*, May 1, 1932, N7; *Trust Companies* 54, no. 6 (1932): 682, 755.

33. Carter Glass to H. B. Lear, December 3, 1932, box 297, Glass Papers; *Wallaces' Farmer* 57, no. 16 (1932): 4.

34. Simpson, *Militant Voice*, 111; Milo Reno to Emil Loriks, January 26, 1933, box 1, Milo Reno Papers, Special Collections & University Archives, University of Iowa, Iowa City; *Morning Oregonian* (Portland), July 26, 1931, 12; June 18, 1932, 1; August 25, 1932, 10; Washington State Federation of Labor, *Thirty-First Annual Convention*, 73; Harvey O'Connor, *Revolution in Seattle: A Memoir* (New York, 1964), 222.

35. Howson, "Jacob Sechler Coxey," 324–53; *New York Herald Tribune*, August 26, 1930, 5; American Federation of Labor, *Fiftieth Annual Convention* (Washington, DC, 1930), 302; *CR*, June 4, 1930, 10077; December 15, 1931, 587; *Evening Independent* (Massillon, OH), January 2, 1932, 1; *Chicago Herald and Examiner*, January 25, 1932, 5.

36. *Washington Post*, January 16, 1932, 1; *Detroit Free Press*, June 13, 1932, 4; *Sun* (Baltimore), June 25, 1932, 2; Porter and Johnson, *National Party Platforms*, 333.

37. *New York Times*, August 16, 1931, 24; *Liberty Bell* 1, no. 3 (1932): 2; William Herschel Hughes, "Octogenarian-Nominee of Newborn Party," *Arkansas Historical Quarterly* 22, no. 4 (1963): 291–300; W. H. Harvey, *The Book* (Monte Ne, AR, 1932), 216–22.

38. Thomas H. Coode and John D. Petrarulo, "The Odyssey of Pittsburgh's Father Cox," *Western Pennsylvania Historical Magazine* 55, no. 3 (1972): 217–38; *Pittsburgh Post-Gazette*, January 6, 1932, 1; Elmer Cope to Goldie McCue, January 13, 1932, Elmer Cope, "Father Cox and His Jobless Army," reel 5, Elmer Fern Cope Papers, Ohio Historical Society, Columbus; *Pittsburgh Post-Gazette*, January 18, 1932, 13.

39. *Liberty Bell* 1, no. 3 (1932): 3; *St. Louis Post-Dispatch*, August 17, 1932, 1A; August 18, 1932, 7A; Andrew J. Krupnick, "Father Cox's Campaign for the Presidency of the United States," Archives Service Center, University of Pittsburgh, Pittsburgh; *Pittsburgh Post-Gazette*, September 22, 1932, 1; October 13, 1932, 5; October 19, 1932, 5. The Jobless Party cross-endorsed four successful candidates—three Democrats and one Republican—for the House from western Pennsylvania (Robert A. Diamond, ed., *Congressional Quarterly's Guide to U.S. Elections* [Washington, DC, 1976], 774).

40. *Columbia Law Review* 37, no. 1 (1937): 86–101; Howson, "Jacob Sechler Coxey," 392; *New York Times*, July 6, 1932, 12; July 10, 1932, 24; George H. Mayer, *The Political Career of Floyd B. Olson* (Minneapolis, 1951), 96–102; Franklin D. Roosevelt, *The Public Papers and Addresses of Franklin D. Roosevelt*, ed. Samuel I. Rosenman, 13 vols. (New York, 1938–50), 1:645–46.

41. *New York Times*, November 9, 1932, 17; *St. Louis Post-Dispatch*, August 18, 1932, 7A; Edwin C. Robertson, untitled manuscript, Edwin C. Robertson Papers, Minnesota Historical Society, St. Paul; *Bugle Call* 1, no. 7 (1931): 4.

42. John Bentley and Ralph W. Miller, "Andrae Nordskog," *Jazz Monthly* 5, no. 3 (1959): 8-10; Morrow Mayo, *Los Angeles* (New York, 1933), 234–35; Andrae B. Nordskog, *Spiking the Gold; or, Who Caused the Depression . . . and the Way Out* (Los Angeles, 1932), 119–20; Andrae Nordskog to Knud Wefald, January 24, 1932, box 2, Knud Wefald Papers, Minnesota Historical Society, St. Paul; Andrae Nordskog to W. H. Harvey, December 4, 1931, Nordskog to Harvey, January 21, 1932, box 13, Andrae B. Nordskog Papers, Urban Archive Center, California State University, Northridge; *Liberty Bell* 1, no. 4 (1932): 1; Edwin Robertson to Fritz Nieman, April 14, 1932, Robertson to Murphy and Parker, August 10, 1932, Robertson Papers; J. W. Perrine to Andrae Nordskog, July 16, 1932, box 1, Andrae B. Nordskog Papers, Minnesota Historical Society, St. Paul.

43. *Liberty Bell* 1, no. 12 (1932): 2–3; Diamond, *Congressional Quarterly's Guide*, 775, 304.

44. Porter and Johnson, *National Party Platforms*, 338, 352.

45. Thomas A. Rumer, *The American Legion: An Official History, 1919–1989* (New York, 1990), 179; *New York Times*, February 2, 1931, 1; House Committee on Ways and Means, *Payment of Soldiers' Adjusted Compensation Certificates*, 71st Cong., 3rd Sess. (Washington, DC, 1931), 338; Paul Dickson and Thomas B. Allen, *The Bonus Army: An American Epic* (New York, 2004), 1; W. W. Waters with William C. White, *B.E.F.: The Whole Story of the Bonus Army* (New York, 1933), 125–27.

46. John L. Shover, *Cornbelt Rebellion: The Farmers' Holiday Association* (Urbana, IL, 1965); Roland A. White, *Milo Reno, Farmers Union Pioneer* (Iowa City, 1941), 71; *Chicago Herald and Examiner*, July 2, 1932, 14; Donald R. Murphy, "The Farmers Go on Strike," *New Republic* 72, no. 926 (1932): 66–68; *Time* 20, no. 9 (1932): 13.

47. *Business Week*, September 7, 1932, 9; *Farm News Letter* 1, no. 8 (1932): 1; idem, 1, no. 9 (1932): 3; Charles O. Conrad and Joyce Conrad, *50 Years, North Dakota Farmers Union* (n.p., 1976), 37–38.

48. Lyell D. Henry Jr., *Zig-Zag-and-Swirl: Alfred W. Lawson's Quest for Greatness* (Iowa City, 1991), 17; Frank Graham Sr., *McGraw of the Giants: An Informal Biography* (New York, 1944), 5–10; George Hardie Jr., "The Airline That Might Have Been," *Historical Messenger* 27, no. 1 (1971): 13–21; *Direct Credits for Humanity* 1, no. 2 (1932): 27; *Humanity* 1, no. 1 (1932): 5.

49. Brinkley, *Voices of Protest*; Charles E. Coughlin, *Eight Discourses on the Gold Standard, and Other Kindred Subjects* (Royal Oak, MI, 1933), 64; Charles J. Tull, *Father Coughlin and the New Deal* (Syracuse, NY, 1965), 20.

50. *American Bankers Association Journal* 25, no. 2 (1932): 65; idem, 25, no. 5 (1932): 71; *North Pacific Banker* 41, no. 5 (1932): 6; *Washington State Labor News* 9, no. 50 (1932): 4.

51. Donald A. Ritchie, *Electing FDR: The New Deal Campaign of 1932* (Lawrence, KS, 2007), 115; *Trust Companies* 54, no. 5 (1932): 658; Robert S. McElvaine, "Thunder without Lightning: Working-Class Discontent in the United States, 1929–1937" (PhD diss., State University of New York at Binghamton, 1974), 65. Not all bankers opposed Roosevelt. See Louise Overacker, "Campaign Funds in a Depression Year," *American Political Science Review* 27, no. 5 (1933): 776–77; Thomas Ferguson, "From Normalcy to New Deal: Industrial Structure, Party Competition, and American Public Policy in the Great Depression," *International Organization* 38, no. 1 (1984): 82.

Chapter Seven

1. George E. Anderson, "Are Bankers Intelligent?," *North American Review* 234, no. 4 (1932): 343; *Dallas Morning News*, January 19, 1933, 2; J. H. Davis to Wright Patman, December 14, 1932, box 41B, Patman Papers.

2. Roosevelt, *Public Papers*, 2:12.

3. In 1931 the Wingfield chain held 57.2 percent of the state's total bank

deposits (F. W. Barsalou, "The Concentration of Banking Power in Nevada: An Historical Analysis," *Business History Review* 29, no. 4 [1955]: 355–56). *Time* 20, no. 20 (1932): 47; Sally Springmeyer Zanjani, *Goldfield: The Last Gold Rush on the Western Frontier* (Athens, OH, 1992), 58–61; Barbara C. Thornton, "George Wingfield in Nevada from 1896 to 1932" (master's thesis, University of Nevada, 1967), 47; Ralph Denton, interviewed by Michael S. Green, Special Collections and University Archives, University of Nevada, 2001, 37; John Wesley Noble, *Harolds Club or Bust! The Story of "Pappy" Smith, Nevada Gaming Pioneer* (Reno, NV, 2003), 115; Eric N. Moody and Guy Louis Rocha, "The Rise and Fall of the Reno Stockade," *Nevada* 38, no. 2 (1978): 29; Jerome E. Edwards, "Wingfield and Nevada Politics—Some Observations," *Nevada Historical Society Quarterly* 32, no. 2 (1989): 126–39.

4. *Reno (NV) Evening Gazette*, November 1, 1932, 1; James S. Olson, "Hoover, the R.F.C., and the Banking Crisis in Nevada, 1932–1933," *Western Historical Quarterly* 6, no. 2 (1975): 155–56; Loren Briggs Chan, *Sagebrush Statesman: Tasker L. Oddie of Nevada* (Reno, NV, 1973), 145–46; C. Elizabeth Raymond, *George Wingfield: Owner and Operator of Nevada* (Reno, NV, 1992), 202–4; Jerome E. Edwards, *Pat McCarran: Political Boss of Nevada* (Reno, NV, 1982), 48–49.

5. *Reno (NV) Evening Gazette*, November 22, 1932, 1; *Las Vegas (NV) Age*, November 23, 1932, 2; *Battle Mountain (NV) Scout*, November 4, 1932, 2; Charles H. Russell, interviewed by Mary Ellen Glass, Special Collections and University Archives, University of Nevada, 1967, 1:180; Clark J. Guild, interviewed by Mary Ellen Glass, Special Collections and University Archives, University of Nevada, 1971, 139; George Wingfield to Owen Duffy, April 3, 1933, box 40, Wingfield Papers; Olson, "Hoover, the R.F.C., and the Banking Crisis," 156–57.

6. Marquis W. Childs, "Main Street Ten Years After," *New Republic* 73, no. 946 (1933): 263–64; *American Legion Monthly* 14, no. 2 (1933): 10; Washington State Grange, *Forty-Fourth Annual Session*, 189; *Shoe Workers' Journal* 33, no. 5 (1932): 3; *American Labor Banner* 3, no. 11 (1932): 4; *Washington State Labor News* 8, no. 46 (1932): 2.

7. *American Bankers Association Journal* 25, no. 5 (1932): 71; *Chicago Defender*, March 13, 1932, 15; *Progressive* 1, no. 46 (1930): 4; idem, 3, no. 37 (1932): 3.

8. Andrew S. Greenfield to Fiorello H. La Guardia, September 1, 1931, reel 6, Fiorello H. La Guardia Papers, New York Public Library; Henry C. Cutting, *Liquefied Wealth: A Cure for Financial Racketeering* (Oakland, 1932); *San Francisco Examiner*, October 19, 1932, 13; Sam P. Davis, ed., *The History of Nevada*, 2 vols. (Reno, 1913), 2:1202–3; Charles Albert Hawkins, *Economic Slavery or Freedom: Business Depressions Their Cause and Cure* (San Francisco, 1932); Hawkins, "Our Present Banking Situation and the Remedy," box 1, Official File 230, Franklin D. Roosevelt Presidential Library and Museum, Hyde Park, NY; *San Francisco Chronicle*, July 8, 1932, 1-V; *Fresno (CA) Bee*, November 17, 1952, 15-A; *CR*, February 26, 1932, 4753.

9. Reynold M. Wik, *Henry Ford and Grass-Roots America* (Ann Arbor, MI,

1972); Steven A. Watts, *The People's Tycoon: Henry Ford and the American Century* (New York, 2005); Henry Ford, "Essentials of Sound Banking," *Rotarian* 62, no. 4 (1933): 57; Reynold M. Wik, "Henry Ford and the Agricultural Depression of 1920–1923," *Agricultural History* 29, no. 1 (1955): 19. On Ford's anti-Semitism, see Leo P. Ribuffo, "Henry Ford and *The International Jew*," *American Jewish History* 69, no. 4 (1980): 437–77. More recent works on this subject include Victoria Saker Woeste, *Henry Ford's War on Jews and the Legal Battle against Hate Speech* (Stanford, CA, 2012); Stefan J. Link, "Rethinking the Ford-Nazi Connection," *Bulletin of the German Historical Institute* 49 (2011): 135–50; Neil E. Baldwin, *Henry Ford and the Jews: The Mass Production of Hate* (New York, 2001). For a critical discussion of Baldwin's book, see Ronald R. Stockton, "McGuffey, Ford, Baldwin, and the Jews," *Michigan Historical Review* 35, no. 2 (2009): 85–96.

10. J. Philip Jenkins, *Hoods and Shirts: The Extreme Right in Pennsylvania, 1925–1950* (Chapel Hill, NC, 1997), 117–24; *New York Times*, June 1, 1933, 7; *New York Herald Tribune*, December 17, 1931, 21; *B'nai B'rith Messenger* 38, no. 2 (1934): 4. While hostility toward Jews intensified over the 1930s, anti-Semitism did not attain political respectability. See Leonard Dinnerstein, *Antisemitism in America* (New York, 1994), 105–27, 245.

11. *Omaha (NE) World-Herald*, January 5, 1931, 4; Subcommittee of the Senate Committee on Banking and Currency, *Creation of a Reconstruction Finance Corporation*, 1:169; *Review of Reviews and World's Work* 86, no. 6 (1932): 32.

12. *New York Times*, January 7, 1933, 21; *United Mine Workers Journal* 44, no. 3 (1933): 6; Charles E. Coughlin, *Driving Out the Money Changers* (Royal Oak, MI, 1933), 66.

13. *CR*, December 12, 1929, 574; December 8, 1931, 159; *New York Times*, February 7, 1932, 21; *CR*, January 11, 1932, 1754; Subcommittee of House Committee on Appropriations, *Post Office Appropriation Bill, 1933*, 72nd Cong., 1st Sess. (Washington, DC, 1932), 96; *Washington Post*, January 26, 1932, 2; *Union Postal Clerk* 28, no. 3 (1932): 16. In 1918 the postal savings deposit limit had been raised to $2,500 (*Statutes at Large* 40 [1918]: 754).

14. *Federation News* 26, no. 15 (1931): 10; Washington State Federation of Labor, *Thirty-First Annual Convention*, 18; Kerry E. Irish, *Clarence C. Dill: The Life of a Western Politician* (Pullman, WA, 2000); *CR*, February 23, 1932, 4489; John C. Johnston to Robert F. Wagner, June 6, 1932, Walter A. Koske to Wagner, June 3, 1932, box LE 210, Wagner Papers; Montana State Federation of Labor, *Official Year Book, 1932*, 6; *Oregon Labor Press* 30, no. 23 (1932): 4; *Progressive* 3, no. 61 (1933): 2.

15. *American Federationist* 40, no. 4 (1933): 361; *International Molders Journal* 68, no. 10 (1932): 608; *Ithaca (NY) Journal-News*, March 29, 1933, 9; Barbara Kimberley, interviewed by Gary D. Barber, University Archives, State University of New York at Buffalo, 1976, 4; *New York Times*, April 13, 1933, 20; *Oregon Labor Press* 30, no. 23 (1932): 4; *Scientific American* 148, no. 5 (1933): 265.

16. Vernon L. Brown, "Emergency Currency or Scrip Issued in the United

States during the Depression Years, 1931-1934," box 8, Robert L. Owen Papers, Manuscript Division, Library of Congress, Washington, DC; Loren C. Gatch, "Local Money in the United States during the Great Depression," *Essays in Economic & Business History* 26 (2008): 47-61; *Telegraph-Herald* (Dubuque, IA), January 20, 1933, 1; *Time* 21, no. 7 (1933): 41.

17. On conditions in Detroit during the Depression, see Sidney Fine, *Frank Murphy*, 3 vols. (Ann Arbor, MI, 1975-84), 1:246-52. Department of Commerce, *Statistical Abstract of the United States, 1941* (Washington, DC, 1942), 452; John J. Holland Jr., "The Detroit Banking Collapse of 1933" (PhD diss., New York University, 1972), 95-131; Roy D. Chapin and A. A. Ballantine, "Statement of Interview with Mr. Henry Ford," box 3, Arthur A. Ballantine Papers, Herbert Hoover Presidential Library and Museum, West Branch, IA; Howard R. Neville, "An Historical Study of the Collapse of Banking in Detroit, 1929-1933" (PhD diss., Michigan State University, 1956), 74-79.

18. Neville, "Historical Study of the Collapse," 80-85; Patricia O'Donnell McKenzie, "Some Aspects of the Detroit Bank Crisis of 1933" (PhD diss., Wayne State University, 1963), 111-21, 127-41; G. Walter Woodworth, "The Detroit Money Market," *Michigan Business Studies* 5, no. 2 (1932): 241, 229; Kennedy, *Banking Crisis of 1933*, 80-82; Senate Committee on Banking and Currency, *Stock Exchange Practices*, 73rd Cong., 2nd Sess. (Washington, DC, 1934), 9:4392; F. Gloyd Awalt, "Memorandum for Secretary Mills, November 12, 1932," box 4, F. Gloyd Awalt Papers, Herbert Hoover Presidential Library and Museum, West Branch, IA.

19. Lawrence Sullivan, *Prelude to Panic: The Story of the Bank Panic* (Washington, DC, 1936), 83; Chapin and Ballantine, "Statement of Interview with Mr. Henry Ford"; Harry Barnard, *Independent Man: The Life of Senator James Couzens* (New York, 1958), 224-26, 233; Watts, *People's Tycoon*, 433-34; *Detroit Free Press*, February 15, 1933, 4; February 22, 1933, 1.

20. *Sun* (Baltimore), February 25, 1933, 1; *New York Times*, February 27, 1933, 4; *Akron (OH) Beacon Journal*, February 27, 1933, 1; *Cleveland Plain Dealer*, February 27, 1933, 1; *San Francisco Chronicle*, March 2, 1933, 1; *Los Angeles Times*, March 3, 1933, 2; *San Francisco Chronicle*, March 4, 1933, 17; *New York Times*, March 4, 1933, F23.

21. *Fortune* 5, no. 2 (1932): 81-82; Schisgall, *Out of One Small Chest*, 132-36; *Time* 21, no. 11 (1933): 9; Henry J. Bruère, interviewed by Allan Nevins, Arthur W. MacMahon, Dean Albertson, Oral History Research Office, Columbia University, 1949, 145; *Akron (OH) Beacon Journal*, March 3, 1933, 1.

22. *Christian Science Monitor*, February 17, 1933, 9; *Federal Reserve Bulletin* 19, no. 12 (1933): 744, 779; Lizabeth Cohen, *Making a New Deal: Industrial Workers in Chicago, 1919-1939* (New York, 1990), 273; Walter J. G. Mellon to Carter Glass, March 9, 1933, box 397, Glass Papers; *Detroit Labor News* 18, no. 27 (1931): 1; *News and Observer* (Raleigh, NC), March 11, 1933, 4.

23. *New York Times*, March 4, 1933, 1; *Chicago Daily Tribune*, March 4, 1933, 1. On the New York and Illinois bank holidays, see Allan Nevins, *Herbert H. Lehman*

and His Era (New York, 1963), 135–37; James, *Growth of Chicago Banks*, 2:1059–66. *New York Herald Tribune*, March 5, 1933, C1; Frances Perkins, *The Roosevelt I Knew* (New York, 1947), 139; George McJimsey, ed., *Documentary History of the Franklin D. Roosevelt Presidency* (Bethesda, MD, 2001), 3:15; Raymond Moley, *After Seven Years* (New York, 1939), 146; J. W. Rixey Smith and Norman Beasley, *Carter Glass: A Biography* (New York, 1939), 340–42; Roosevelt, *Public Papers*, 2:24–26.

24. *New York Times*, March 8, 1933, 3; *Oakland Tribune*, March 8, 1933, 2; *Binghamton (NY) Press*, March 11, 1933, 1.

25. The public's amenability to the bank holiday is emphasized by Pamela Webb, "Business as Usual: The Bank Holiday in Arkansas," *Arkansas Historical Quarterly* 39, no. 3 (1980): 247–61; William H. Jervey Jr., "When the Banks Closed: Arizona's Bank Holiday of 1933," *Arizona and the West* 10, no. 2 (1968): 127–52. Will Rogers, *Will Rogers' Daily Telegrams*, ed. James M. Smallwood, 4 vols. (Stillwater, OK, 1978–79), 4:1; *Boston Daily Globe*, March 7, 1933, 5; *Buffalo Courier-Express*, March 7, 1933, 2.

26. *San Francisco Chronicle*, March 6, 1933, 2; State of California, *Journal of the Senate during the Fiftieth Session* (Sacramento, 1933), 690.

27. *Equity News* 28, no. 4 (1933): 1; Roosevelt, *Public Papers*, 2:12; Marquis W. Childs, *I Write from Washington* (New York, 1942), 21.

28. *Business Week*, March 8, 1933, 7; Carter Glass to Franklin D. Roosevelt, February 7, 1933, box 6, Glass Papers; R. L. Rickerd to Milo Reno, January 30, 1933, box 1, Reno Papers; Roosevelt, *Public Papers*, 1:753; Richard T. Ruetten, "Burton K. Wheeler of Montana: A Progressive between the Wars" (PhD diss., University of Oregon, 1961), 116–17; William J. Barber, *Designs within Disorder: Franklin D. Roosevelt, the Economists, and the Shaping of American Economic Policy, 1933–1945* (New York, 1996), 21–22; Eric Rauchway, *The Money Makers: How Roosevelt and Keynes Ended the Depression, Defeated Fascism, and Secured a Prosperous Peace* (New York, 2015), 19–37; Chandler, *America's Greatest Depression*, 166–68.

29. Moley, *After Seven Years*, 148; James P. Warburg, *The Long Road Home: The Autobiography of a Maverick* (Garden City, NY, 1964), 110; Arthur A. Ballantine, "When All the Banks Closed," *Harvard Business Review* 26, no. 2 (1948): 138–39; Kennedy, *Banking Crisis of 1933*, 168–75.

30. *CR*, March 9, 1933, 83; *Washington Post*, March 10, 1933, 1; Moley, *After Seven Years*, 153; *Journal of Commerce*, March 10, 1933, 4. On the Emergency Banking Act, see Frank Freidel, *Franklin D. Roosevelt*, 4 vols. (Boston, 1952–73), 4:214–29.

31. *Statutes at Large* 48 (1933): 1–7; Billy Graham, *Just as I Am* (San Francisco, 1997), 4–5; *New York Herald Tribune*, April 15, 1933, 5. On reopening the banks, see Kennedy, *Banking Crisis of 1933*, 182–202.

32. Rexford G. Tugwell, *In Search of Roosevelt* (Cambridge, MA, 1972), 272; *CR*, March 9, 1933, 63; Robert M. La Follette Jr. and Edward P. Costigan to Franklin D. Roosevelt, March 8, 1933, box 11, series C, La Follette Family Papers,

Manuscript Division, Library of Congress, Washington, DC; John Dewey to Franklin D. Roosevelt, March 8, 1933, reel 11, Howard Y. Williams Papers, Minnesota Historical Society, St. Paul; *Federation News* 32, no. 11 (1933): 1; Carl D. Thompson to Franklin D. Roosevelt, March 9, 1933, box 11, William Lemke Papers, Department of Special Collections, University of North Dakota, Grand Forks. On the administration's adherence to orthodoxy, see James E. Sargent, *Roosevelt and the Hundred Days: Struggle for the Early New Deal* (New York, 1981), 102–3; Burns, *American Banking Community*, 99; Kennedy, *Banking Crisis of 1933*, 168; Barton J. Bernstein, "The New Deal: The Conservative Achievements of Liberal Reform," in *Towards a New Past*, ed. Bernstein (New York, 1968), 267–68.

33. Raymond Moley, *The First New Deal* (New York, 1966), 171; *Nebraska Union Farmer* 19, no. 23 (1933): 4.

34. Louis T. Mortimer Jr., "John Philip Frey: Spokesman for Skilled American Labor" (PhD diss., George Washington University, 1982); *International Molders' and Foundry Workers' Journal* 94, no. 1 (1958): 3–7; John P. Frey to J. A. Gauthier, February 2, 1933, box 2, John P. Frey Papers, Manuscript Division, Library of Congress, Washington, DC; John P. Frey, interviewed by Dean Albertson, Oral History Research Office, Columbia University, 1955, 548.

35. AFL Metal Trades Department, *Twenty-Fourth Annual Convention* (n.p., 1932), 26; John P. Frey, "Bankers' Domination," *American Federationist* 40, no. 2 (1933): 134–44; Hyman Weintraub, *Andrew Furuseth: Emancipator of the Seamen* (Berkeley, 1959); American Federation of Labor, *Fifty-Second Annual Convention* (Washington, DC, 1932), 232.

36. Subcommittee of the Senate Judiciary Committee, *Thirty-Hour Work Week*, 72nd Cong., 2nd Sess. (Washington, DC, 1933), 2:420; Hugo L. Black to John P. Frey, February 10, 1933, Whidden Graham to Frey, January 27, 1933, anonymous to Frey, February 1, 1933, box 2, Frey Papers; *New York Times*, October 28, 1944, 15; *Federation News* 32, no. 8 (1933): 4.

37. Subcommittee of the Senate Judiciary Committee, *Thirty-Hour Work Week*, 2:474; George W. Norris, *Fighting Liberal: The Autobiography of George W. Norris* (New York, 1945), 195–96; Richard Lowitt, *George W. Norris*, 3 vols. (Urbana, IL, 1963–78); *Boilermakers Journal* 45, no. 4 (1933): 83. On visual representations of financial monopoly, see Peter Knight, *Reading the Market: Genres of Financial Capitalism in Gilded Age America* (Baltimore, 2016), 240–49.

38. *CR*, February 23, 1933, 4778–79.

39. Gilbert C. Fite, *Peter Norbeck, Prairie Statesman* (Columbia, MO, 1948); *New York Times*, December 8, 1971, 40; May 21, 1933, VIII-2; *Time* 21, no. 24 (1933): 18. City College's commitment to free higher education facilitated Pecora's ability to attain a college degree. See S. Willis Rudy, *The College of the City of New York: A History, 1847–1947* (New York, 1949), 459–64.

40. *Amherst Graduates' Quarterly* 41 (1921): 82; *Michigan Manufacturer and Financial Record* 27, no. 24 (1921): 11; *American Magazine*, February 1923, 16; James D. Grant, *Bernard M. Baruch: The Adventures of a Wall Street Legend* (New

York, 1983), 235; Edmund Wilson, "Sunshine Charley," *New Republic* 75, no. 969 (1933): 176.

41. *Time* 21, no. 10 (1933) 47–48; Ferdinand Pecora, *Wall Street under Oath: The Story of Our Modern Money Changers* (New York, 1939), 110–12; Subcommittee of the Senate Committee on Banking and Currency, *Stock Exchange Practices*, 72nd Cong., 2nd Sess. (Washington, DC, 1933), 6:1869–70, 1786, 1778, 1814; *New York Times*, March 19, 1933, 1.

42. *CR*, February 22, 1933, 4696; *New Republic* 74, no. 953 (1933): 87; *New York Times*, March 22, 1933, 1.

43. *Catholic World* 137, no. 817 (1933): 102; *Christian Century* 50, no. 10 (1933): 316; *International Engineer* 43, no. 3 (1933): 80.

44. H. J. Hahn, "Jesus' Way Out," box 14, Reverend Herman J. Hahn Papers, University Archives, State University of New York, Buffalo; Louis M. Benjamin, *Freedom of the Air and the Public Interest: First Amendment Rights in Broadcasting to 1935* (Carbondale, IL, 2001), 155–57; Raymond Moley, *27 Masters of Politics: In a Personal Perspective* (New York, 1949), 227–28.

45. Fine, *Frank Murphy*, 1:375; *Nation's Business* 21, no. 4 (1933): 14; *Trust Companies* 56, no. 5 (1933): 557; *Farmers Union Herald* 7, no. 2 (1933): 3; James Maloney to John Frey, February 14, 1933, box 2, Frey Papers.

46. G. T. McElderry to Milo Reno, April 5, 1933, box 2, Reno Papers; Maurice W. Murphy to Ernest Lundeen, March 18, 1933, box 62, Ernest Lundeen Papers, Hoover Institution on War, Revolution, and Peace, Stanford, CA.

47. W. N. Doty to Milo Reno, March 9, 1933, box 1, Reno Papers; *Detroit Labor News* 20, no. 27 (1933): 4; anonymous to John P. Frey, January 28, 1933, box 2, Frey Papers.

Chapter Eight

1. *CR*, March 13, 1933, 298; Karl Polanyi, *The Great Transformation* (Boston, 1957), 25–26; *Public Ledger* (Philadelphia), March 14, 1933, 10; *Stockton (CA) Daily Evening Record*, March 16, 1933, 28.

2. Glass's role in the Banking Act of 1933 is underlined by Kennedy, *Banking Crisis of 1933*, 203–23; Burns, *American Banking Community*, 77–95; Sue C. Patrick, *Reform of the Federal Reserve System in the Early 1930s: The Politics of Money and Banking* (New York, 1993), 17, 165–203. On the importance of the severity of the economic crisis to this law's enactment, see Barry J. Eichengreen, *Hall of Mirrors: The Great Depression, the Great Recession, and the Uses—and Misuses—of History* (New York, 2015), 244–47.

3. *Sacramento (CA) Bee*, March 27, 1933, 16; *Akron (OH) Beacon Journal*, March 4, 1933, 4; *Morning Oregonian* (Portland), March 8, 1933, 4; *Ithaca (NY) Journal-News*, March 15, 1933, 11.

4. *Detroit Labor News* 20, no. 26 (1933): 4; Colorado State Federation of Labor, *Thirty-Eighth Annual Convention* (Denver, 1933), 19; *Federation News* 32,

no. 12 (1933): 2; *Farm Holiday News* 1, no. 2 (1933): 4; *Cooperative Farmer* 5, no. 7 (1933): 3; *Sacramento (CA) Bee*, March 25, 1933, 3.

5. Socialist Party, *The Intelligent Voter's Guide* (New York, 1928), 14; Diamond, *Congressional Quarterly's Guide*, 289; *New York Times*, March 6, 1933, 2. One-half of the Socialist vote may not have been counted. David A. Shannon, *The Socialist Party of America* (New York, 1955), 259.

6. W. A. Swanberg, *Norman Thomas: The Last Idealist* (New York, 1976), 140; *New York Times*, March 15, 1933, 36; Norman Thomas, "A Socialist Program for Banking," *Nation* 136, no. 3533 (1933): 309; Thomas, "An Important Omission," *Nation* 136, no. 3535 (1933): 376; *Houston Post*, March 20, 1933, 4.

7. Edward C. Blackorby, *Prairie Rebel: The Public Life of William Lemke* (Lincoln, NE, 1963); *CR*, March 20, 1933, 647; May 22, 1933, 3907–9. On the proposed Bank of the United States, see William Lemke, *You and Your Money* (Philadelphia, 1938), 69–78.

8. William Lemke to Richard McCarten, March 31, 1933, Lemke to Fred E. Sims, May 2, 1933, box 11, Lemke Papers; *Farmers Union Herald* 7, no. 4 (1933): 1. Lemke had to contend with a longtime political opponent in the administration: J. F. T. O'Connor. See Junker, *Bank of North Dakota*, 7; Blackorby, *Prairie Rebel*, 118, 151–55; Alice Jane Johnson, "The Public Career of J. F. T. O'Connor" (master's thesis, University of North Dakota, 1956), 37–38.

9. *Detroit Free Press*, March 2, 1933, 8; W. D. Haas Jr. to Franklin D. Roosevelt, March 4, 1933, box 1, Official File 230, Roosevelt Library; *Producer* 14, no. 11 (1933): 10; *AFBF Official News Letter* 12, no. 5 (1933): 1; idem, 12, no. 6 (1933): 3.

10. Jay R. Monroe to Carter Glass, February 21, 1933, box 397, Glass Papers; *Sacramento (CA) Bee*, March 2, 1933, 2; Texas Retail Dry Goods Association to Wright Patman, March 4, 1933, box 65B, Patman Papers; *Nation's Business* 21, no. 5 (1933): 29.

11. *Boston Daily Globe*, March 8, 1933, 5; *Buffalo Times*, March 8, 1933, 2; *Ithaca (NY) Journal-News*, March 8, 1933, 2; *Sun* (Baltimore), March 8, 1933, 1; *AFL Weekly News Service* 23, no. 2 (1933): 1; George Norris to William Hughes, April 8, 1933, box 174, George L. Winter to Norris, March 11, 1933, box 173, George W. Norris Papers, Manuscript Division, Library of Congress, Washington, DC; B. T. Falls to Josiah William Bailey, April 12, 1933, box 219, Bailey Papers; Bogdan J. Lukomski and Louis E. Capinski to Franklin D. Roosevelt, April 5, 1933, box 2, Official File 230, Roosevelt Library.

12. *American Bankers Association Journal* 25, no. 10 (1933): 37; *CR*, March 15, 1933, 501; May 15, 1933, 3442; *Minnesota Union Advocate* 37, no. 10 (1933): 1; *Progressive* 3, no. 68 (1933): 2; *Boston Post*, March 10, 1933, 14.

13. *Sacramento (CA) Bee*, March 10, 1933, 22; *Journal of Electrical Workers and Operators* 32, no. 4 (1933): 164; *Saturday Evening Post* 205, no. 39 (1933): 20.

14. *Wall Street Journal*, December 22, 1932, 4. The U.S. Chamber of Commerce supported the bankers' opposition to separating commercial and investment banking. See *Commercial & Financial Chronicle* 136, no. 3524 (1933): 52–53.

CR, December 15, 1932, 480–81; T. Harry Williams, *Huey Long* (New York, 1969); Brinkley, *Voices of Protest*; *San Francisco Chronicle*, January 18, 1933, 11.

15. *CR*, January 5, 1933, 1330, 1332; January 10, 1933, 1459; Williams, *Huey Long*, 620–24.

16. Eric Manheimer, "The Public Career of Elmer Thomas" (PhD diss., University of Oklahoma, 1952); Elmer Thomas to G. C. Frier, February 8, 1933, Jess Larson to Thomas, January 12, 1933, box 4, T. W. Johnson to Thomas, January 12, 1933, box 5, Thomas Papers; *CR*, January 25, 1933, 2517; February 20, 1933, 4553; Rexford G. Tugwell, "Transition: Hoover to Roosevelt, 1932–1933," *Centennial Review* 9, no. 2 (1965): 170; Kennedy, *Banking Crisis of 1933*, 73–74.

17. *CR*, March 11, 1933, 196; *New York Times*, March 14, 1933, 1; *Wall Street Journal*, April 12, 1933, 1; *New York Times*, May 5, 1933, 27; Roosevelt, *Public Papers*, 2:37; Bascom N. Timmons, *Garner of Texas: A Personal History* (New York, 1948), 178–80; Sargent, *Roosevelt and the Hundred Days*, 240; Jesse H. Jones with Edward Angly, *Fifty Billion Dollars: My Thirteen Years with the RFC (1932–1945)* (New York, 1951), 45; Lionel V. Patenaude, "Vice President John Nance Garner: A Study in the Use of Influence during the New Deal," *Texana* 11, no. 2 (1973): 127–28.

18. *CR*, April 17, 1933, 1831, 1842; April 14, 1933, 1742; *Des Moines (IA) Register*, January 22, 1933, G-7; Peter Norbeck to Alan Bogue, April 1, 1933, box 115, Norbeck Papers.

19. Burton K. Wheeler with Paul F. Healy, *Yankee from the West* (Garden City, NY, 1962), 304; Freidel, *Franklin D. Roosevelt*, 4:320–39; *CR*, April 17, 1933, 1844; Rauchway, *Money Makers*, 64–66; *CR*, April 22, 1933, 2170–71; *Washington Post*, April 27, 1933, 1; *CR*, April 28, 1933, 2551–52; *Statutes at Large* 48 (1933): 51–54.

20. William A. Kielman to Robert F. Wagner, May 15, 1933, box LE 217, Wagner Papers; H. B. Crandall, circular letter, May 12, 1933, box 218, Marriner S. Eccles Papers, Special Collections, University of Utah, Salt Lake City; *CR*, May 25, 1933, 4176; *United States Investor* 44, no. 27 (1933): 29; *AFL Weekly News Service* 23, no. 15 (1933): 1.

21. *CR*, May 10, 1933, 3109, 3203; May 17, 3611; May 23, 1933, 4058; *New York Times*, May 14, 1933, 6; *CR*, May 20, 1933, 3840; May 27, 1933, 4427; *Boston Daily Globe*, May 26, 1933, 1; *CR*, May 26, 1933, 4239–41; Bascom N. Timmons, *Jesse H. Jones: The Man and the Statesman* (New York, 1956), 194–95.

22. *CR*, May 25, 1933, 4181–82; House, H.R. 5661 Public Print, 73rd Cong., 1st Sess. (1933); Charles M. Linke, "The Evolution of Interest Rate Regulation on Commercial Bank Deposits in the United States," *National Banking Review* 3, no. 4 (1966): 465–69; Arthur J. Rolnick, "The Benefits of Bank Deposit Rate Ceilings: New Evidence on Bank Rates and Risk in the 1920s," *Quarterly Review* (Federal Reserve Bank of Minneapolis) 11, no. 3 (1987): 2–18; *Federal Reserve Bulletin* 19, no. 9 (1933): 571–74. The Federal Open Market Committee comprised one representative from each Federal Reserve Bank. Individual Federal Reserve Banks were prohibited from independently initiating open market operations, but could abstain from them. The Banking Act of 1935 made the decisions of a new com-

mittee dominated by the Board of Governors regarding open market operations binding upon Federal Reserve Banks.

23. Roosevelt, *Public Papers*, 1:683; *St. Louis Post-Dispatch*, May 27, 1932, 1E; Hiram W. Johnson to John Francis Neylan, March 10, 1933, Part III, box 14, Hiram Johnson Papers, Bancroft Library, University of California, Berkeley.

24. *Chung Sai Yat Po* (San Francisco), March 8, 1933, 1 (translated by M. Paulina Hartono); Steven Fraser, *Every Man a Speculator: A History of Wall Street in American Life* (New York, 2005), 411–39; Robert S. McElvaine, ed., *Down and Out in the Great Depression: Letters from the "Forgotten Man"* (Chapel Hill, NC, 1983), 42; *Central Labor Council Herald* 2, no. 42 (1933): 4; *Federation News* 32, no. 15 (1933): 11; J. L. Hooper to Milo Reno, January 9, 1933, box 1, Reno Papers.

25. *New York Times*, March 8, 1933, 1; Ray Eldon Hiebert, *Courtier to the Crowd: The Story of Ivy Lee and the Development of Public Relations* (Ames, IA, 1966), 206–7; *Journal of Commerce*, March 9, 1933, 1; *Federation News* 32, no. 12 (1933): 1; *United Mine Workers Journal* 44, no. 10 (1933): 13; *Journeymen Plumbers and Steam Fitters Journal* 48, no. 4 (1933): 5; *Bricklayer, Mason and Plasterer* 36, no. 6 (1933): 97; *Detroit Labor News* 20, no. 26 (1933): 4.

26. Willard F. Mueller, "Conglomerates: A 'Nonindustry,'" in *The Structure of American Industry*, ed. Walter Adams, 6th ed. (New York, 1982), 470–71; Christopher W. Shaw, "'The Man in the Street Is for It': The Road to the FDIC," *Journal of Policy History* 27, no. 1 (2015): 36–60; Gaines Thomson Cartinhour, *Branch, Group and Chain Banking* (New York, 1931); Charles Wallace Collins, *Rural Banking Reform* (New York, 1931); Bernhard Ostrolenk, *The Economics of Branch Banking* (New York, 1930); Comptroller of the Currency, *Annual Report, 1929* (Washington, DC, 1930), 1–9; *CR*, May 10, 1932, 9891. Branching proponents' desire to promote branch banks animated their hostility to guaranty. They feared that protecting depositors from loss would impede the growth of larger banks. In 1932 Comptroller of the Currency John W. Pole had called guaranty "the very antithesis of branch banking" (Subcommittee of the House Committee on Banking and Currency, *To Provide a Guaranty Fund for Depositors*, 7).

27. *CR*, July 14, 1932, 15303; *Trust Companies* 56, no. 4 (1933): 508; *American Bankers Association Journal* 25, no. 5 (1932): 41.

28. Kansas State Grange, *Fifty-Ninth Annual Session* (n.p., 1930), 46; *Bureau Farmer* (New York) 8, no. 8 (1933): 9; Harry W. Laidler, *Concentration of Control in American Industry* (New York, 1931), 338–39; *Progressive* 3, no. 68 (1933): 1.

29. Thomas J. Walsh to S. V. Stewart, December 4, 1930, box I:159, Thomas J. Walsh and John E. Erickson Papers, Manuscript Division, Library of Congress, Washington, DC; *San Francisco Examiner*, November 3, 1930, 30; James and James, *Biography of a Bank*, 353; Matthew Josephson, *The Money Lords: The Great Finance Capitalists, 1925–1950* (New York, 1972), 148–50; James, *Growth of Chicago Banks*, 2:1029; James S. Olson, *Saving Capitalism: The Reconstruction Finance Corporation and the New Deal, 1933–1940* (Princeton, NJ, 1988), 18. Charles G. Dawes's Central Republic Bank & Trust Company was the recipient of this siz-

able RFC loan. Dawes abruptly resigned his position as president of this agency less than two weeks before the loan was granted. See Vickers, *Panic in the Loop*, 181–200. On branch banks and large banks not being safer banks during this era, see Carl M. Gambs, "Bank Failures: An Historical Perspective," *Monthly Review* (Federal Reserve Bank of Kansas City) 62, no. 6 (1977): 10–20.

30. William R. Keeton, "Small and Large Bank Views of Deposit Insurance: Today vs. the 1930s," *Federal Reserve Bank of Kansas City Economic Review* 75, no. 5 (1990): 29–30; G. J. Moen to Peter Norbeck, March 14, 1933, box 115, Norbeck Papers; Leake S. Covington to Josiah William Bailey, May 19, 1933, box 219, Bailey Papers. Even among those bankers who were most inclined to support guaranty—small-town bankers—sentiment was overwhelmingly opposed—by a factor of two to one, according to one survey. Another survey—conducted in the unit banking state of Texas—found less than 2 percent of bankers questioned supported guaranty. See *Commercial West* 66, no. 5 (1933): 20; Grant and Crum, *Development of State-Chartered Banking*, 231.

31. *CR*, May 26, 1933, 4399; House, *Banking Act, 1933*, 73rd Cong., 1st Sess. (1933), H. Rept. 254; *CR*, June 13, 1933, 5897, 5862; Walter Wyatt, interviewed by James E. Sargent, Oral History Research Office, Columbia University, 1973, 75–76.

32. Josiah William Bailey to H. G. Connor Jr., May 15, 1933, box 219, Bailey Papers; J. F. T. O'Connor Diary, June 2, 1933, June 7, 1933, J. F. T. O'Connor Diaries and Correspondence, Bancroft Library, University of California, Berkeley; Jones and Angly, *Fifty Billion Dollars*, 45–46; *Central Labor Council Herald* 3, no. 1 (1933): 3; *New York Times*, June 16, 1933, 14; *Statutes at Large* 48 (1933): 162–95; *Commercial West* 65, no. 25 (1933): 6.

33. Wright Patman to J. H. Davis, May 30, 1933, box 41B, Patman Papers; Rauchway, *Money Makers*, 36–44; Roosevelt, *Public Papers*, 2:54–56, 111–14, 141–43; *Statutes at Large* 48 (1933): 112–13; J. Willard Hurst, *A Legal History of Money in the United States, 1774–1970* (Lincoln, NE, 1973), 42.

34. Four years after departing the gold standard, Glass urged that the nation submit to drastic deflation for the purpose of reestablishing this monetary principle. See *New York Times*, June 15, 1937, 33. Freidel, *Franklin D. Roosevelt*, 4:320–21; *CR*, April 27, 1933, 2461; *New York Times*, May 19, 1933, 16; May 3, 1933, 16; *Current History* 38, no. 3 (1933): 330; Chernow, *House of Morgan*, 357–58; Peter Temin and Barrie A. Wigmore, "The End of One Big Deflation," *Explorations in Economic History* 27, no. 4 (1990): 483–502; Christina D. Romer, "What Ended the Great Depression?," *Journal of Economic History* 52, no. 4 (1992): 757–84.

35. *North Pacific Banker* 42, no. 3 (1933): 1; *Chicago Daily Tribune*, September 7, 1933, 23; American Bankers Association to Franklin D. Roosevelt, September 6, 1933, box 2, Official File 230, Roosevelt Library.

36. *Central Labor Council Herald* 3, no. 16 (1933): 4; *Oregon Labor Press* 30, no. 33 (1933): 2; *Federation News* 33, no. 13 (1933): 4; American Federation of Labor, *Fifty-Third Annual Convention* (Washington, DC, 1933), 432.

37. Henry B. Steagall, "Recent Banking Legislation," *Tarheel Banker* 12, no. 4 (1933): 71; *Wall Street Journal*, September 13, 1933, 15; FDIC, *First Fifty Years*, 46.

38. *Coast Banker* 50, no. 5 (1933): 218; *Trust Companies* 57, no. 3 (1933): 316; *New York Herald Tribune*, September 10, 1933, II-1; *Boston Evening Transcript*, October 19, 1933, 5; *Christian Science Monitor*, October 24, 1933, 11; James A. Farley, *Jim Farley's Story: The Roosevelt Years* (New York, 1948), 40. O'Connor was a former bank officer. See Johnson, "Public Career of J. F. T. O'Connor," 101.

39. Felice A. Bonadio, *A. P. Giannini: Banker of America* (Berkeley, 1994), 207–10; Josephson, *Money Lords*, 145–46; Nash, *A. P. Giannini*, 112–13; Philip L. Fradkin, *Stagecoach: Wells Fargo and the American West* (New York, 2002), 166–67; James and James, *Biography of a Bank*, 75–76; *New York Herald Tribune*, September 16, 1933, 17. On Giannini's branch banking ambitions, see James and James, *Biography of a Bank*, 268–92; Allen, *Lords of Creation*, 320–25.

40. *Trust Companies* 57, no. 1 (1933): 8; idem, 57, no. 2 (1933): 197; *Federal Reserve Bulletin* 22, no. 11 (1936): 858.

41. Jalil, "New History of Banking Panics"; John Kenneth Galbraith, *Money: Whence It Came, Where It Went* (Boston, 1975), 197. For international perspective on the "reformed capitalism" of the mid-twentieth century, see E. J. Hobsbawm, *The Age of Extremes: A History of the World, 1914–1991* (New York, 1994), 257–86. On the impact economic instability had on American culture during the nineteenth and early twentieth centuries, see David A. Zimmerman, *Panic! Markets, Crises, and Crowds in American Fiction* (Chapel Hill, NC, 2006); Scott A. Sandage, *Born Losers: A History of Failure in America* (Cambridge, MA, 2005). As the terms "panic" and "depression" betray, these traumatic events were linked to Americans' inner emotional lives. See Stephen W. Nissenbaum, *Sex, Diet, and Debility in Jacksonian America: Sylvester Graham and Health Reform* (Westport, CT, 1980), 128.

42. Marriner S. Eccles to A. P. Giannini, October 12, 1934, box 9, Eccles Papers; Edward A. Filene, address to the International Association of Sales Executives, April 3, 1936, box 25, Records of the Virginia Credit Union League, 1923–1991, Special Collections, University of Virginia, Charlottesville; Terkel, *Hard Times*, 73, 264; *Boston Daily Globe*, June 2, 1932, 7; Curley, *I'd Do It Again*, 242. On Curley and Farley as critics of Roosevelt and the New Deal, see William V. Shannon, *The American Irish* (New York, 1963), 223–25, 349–52.

43. *CR*, May 23, 1933, 4041; Federal Reserve Bank of Boston, *Twelfth Annual Meeting* (n.p., 1934), 19; *AFL Weekly News Service* 23, no. 29 (1933): 1.

Chapter Nine

1. Roger W. Babson, *Washington and the Revolutionists* (New York, 1934), 324; Thomas J. Connolly to Franklin D. Roosevelt, January 15, 1934, box 3, Official File 229, Roosevelt Library; *Amalgamated Journal* 35, no. 22 (1934): 7.

2. Idaho State Grange, *Twenty-Fifth Annual Session* (n.p., 1933), 65; Idaho State Federation of Labor, *Eighteenth Annual Convention* (n.p., 1933), 55.

3. Price V. Fishback, Jonathan D. Rose, and Kenneth A. Snowden, *Well Worth Saving: How the New Deal Safeguarded Home Ownership* (Chicago, 2013); Olson, *Saving Capitalism*; Brennan, *Silver and the First New Deal*; Richard C. K. Burdekin and Marc D. Weidenmier, "The Development of 'Non-Traditional' Open Market Operations: Lessons From FDR's Silver Purchase Program," in *The Origins and Development of Financial Markets and Institutions*, ed. Jeremy Atack and Larry D. Neal (New York, 2009); Chandler, *American Monetary Policy*, 289–91; Romer, "What Ended the Great Depression?"; Board of Governors, *Banking and Monetary Statistics*, 371; Lorena A. Hickok, *One Third of a Nation: Lorena Hickok Reports on the Great Depression*, ed. Richard Lowitt and Maurine Beasley (Urbana, IL, 1981), 43.

4. *CR*, January 24, 1934, 1235; *Progressive Farmer* 49, no. 3 (1934): 6; Jesse H. Jones, "The Banker's Responsibility," box 3M 500, Jesse H. Jones Papers, Center for American History, University of Texas, Austin; *Labor* 16, no. 22 (1935): 4.

5. *Farm Holiday News* 2, no. 3 (1934): 2; Oregon State Grange, *Sixty-First Annual Session* (n.p., 1934), 114; White, *Milo Reno*; Milo Reno to E. P. Copeland, November 5, 1933, box 3, Reno Papers.

6. Charles E. Coughlin, *Eight Lectures on Labor, Capital and Justice* (Royal Oak, MI, 1934), 103, 17, 114; *CR*, March 27, 1933, 891; *Dallas Morning News*, September 15, 1934, 2.

7. Coughlin, *Eight Lectures*, 17; Brinkley, *Voices of Protest*, 144–45; Charles E. Coughlin, *The New Deal in Money* (Royal Oak, MI, 1933), 31; Young, *Wright Patman*, 73–98; Marc R. Levinson, *The Great A&P and the Struggle for Small Business in America* (New York, 2011), 151–66; Mark A. Glick, David G. Magnum, and Lara A. Swensen, "Towards a More Reasoned Application of the Robinson-Patman Act," *Antitrust Bulletin* 60, no. 4 (2015): 279–317; *CR*, May 9, 1935, 7254–55; Wright Patman to George M. Craig, February 27, 1933, box 62B, Patman Papers; Wright Patman, *Bankerteering, Bonuseering, Melloneering* (Paris, TX, 1934), 16. On critics of "bigness," see Ellis W. Hawley, *The New Deal and the Problem of Monopoly* (Princeton, NJ, 1966), 286–89.

8. *Time* 23, no. 4 (1934): 51; Elliott J. Gorn, *Dillinger's Wild Ride: The Year That Made America's Public Enemy Number One* (New York, 2009), 127; Carl Young to James Couzens, January 29, 1934, box 140, James Couzens Papers, Manuscript Division, Library of Congress, Washington, DC.

9. Chauncy A. Fusco Sr. to Bronson Cutting, April 27, 1934, box 19, Bronson Cutting Papers, Manuscript Division, Library of Congress, Washington, DC; *Dakota Farmer* 53, no. 13 (1933): 254; *Journal of Electrical Workers and Operators* 33, no. 2 (1934): 32.

10. American Federation of Teachers, *Seventeenth Annual Convention*, (n.p., 1933), 284; 1934 Farmer-Labor Platform of Minnesota, box 2, Farmer-Labor Association of Minnesota Records, Minnesota Historical Society, St. Paul; *Farmers Union Herald* 8, no. 11 (1934): 4; Oregon State Grange, *Sixty-First Annual Session*, 21; Washington State Grange, *Forty-Sixth Annual Session* (Seattle, 1934), 212; *Iowa*

Union Farmer 16, no. 19 (1934): 4; *Cooperative Farmer* 5, no. 18 (1933): 2; *Farmers Union Herald* 8, no. 11 (1934): 4; idem, 8, no. 12 (1934): 2.

11. American Federation of Teachers, *Eighteenth Annual Convention* (Chicago, 1935), 127–28; Oregon State Federation of Labor, *Thirty-Second Annual Convention* (Portland, 1934), 28; Montana State Federation of Labor, *Thirty-Sixth Convention* (n.p., 1933), 8; *Oklahoma Federationist* 24, no. 12 (1933): 4; Washington State Federation of Labor, *Thirty-Third Annual Convention* (n.p., 1934), 84; Amalgamated Association of Iron, Steel and Tin Workers of North America, *Journal of Proceedings, 1934* (n.p., 1934), 2204; 1934 Farmer-Labor Platform of Minnesota.

12. Indiana State Federation of Labor, *Fiftieth Annual Convention* (n.p., 1934), 74.

13. R. H. Bledsoe to John A. Simpson, February 17, 1934, box 2, Simpson Papers; Coughlin, *New Deal in Money*, 18; Milo Reno, address over WHO, February 1935, box 6, Reno Papers; Bronson Cutting, "Is Private Banking Doomed?," *Liberty* 11, no. 13 (1934): 10; Richard Lowitt, *Bronson M. Cutting: Progressive Politician* (Albuquerque, NM, 1992); Gustav L. Seligmann Jr., "The Political Career of Senator Bronson M. Cutting" (PhD diss., University of Arizona, 1967); Nancy Owen Lewis, *Chasing the Cure in New Mexico: Tuberculosis and the Quest for Health* (Santa Fe, NM, 2016), 1; Pencak, *For God and Country*, 129; *CR*, June 6, 1934, 10557. For further detail on Cutting's legislation, see Ronnie J. Phillips, *The Chicago Plan and New Deal Banking Reform* (Armonk, NY, 1995), 79–84. Wright Patman introduced companion legislation in the House (*CR*, June 6, 1934, 10671).

14. Lowitt, *Bronson M. Cutting*, 389; Cutting, "Is Private Banking Doomed?," 10; *CR*, May 22, 1934, 9226; George Mallette to Bronson Cutting, February 1934, box 19, Cutting Papers.

15. *American Bankers Association Journal* 26, no. 4 (1933): 27; F. R. Kingsley to George Norris, April 1, 1932, box 173, Norris Papers.

16. Roland Marchand, *Creating the Corporate Soul: The Rise of Public Relations and Corporate Imagery in American Big Business* (Berkeley, 1998); Daniel M. Robert, "Courteous Capitalism: Customer Relations, Public Opinion, and the Defense of Utility Monopolies" (PhD diss., University of California, Berkeley, 2016); *American Bankers Association Journal* 26, no. 3 (1933): 16, 71; *Tarheel Banker* 12, no. 1 (1933): 16.

17. Jack A. Garrow, "A History of the Financial Advertisers Association (1915–1947)" (master's thesis, University of Wisconsin, 1970), 124–28; *Trust Companies* 57, no. 3 (1933): 316; *Commercial West* 68, no. 8 (1934): 6; *Trust Companies* 59, no. 3 (1934): 297; *Southern Banker* 63, no. 4 (1934): 24.

18. James R. Curtis, *W. C. Fields: A Biography* (New York, 2003), 358, 484; Robert Lewis Taylor, *W. C. Fields: His Follies and Fortunes* (Garden City, NY, 1949), 211; *North Pacific Banker* 42, no. 7 (1934): 3.

19. Herbert H. Plambeck, "The National Drought Conference in Des Moines: When FDR and Alf Landon Met," *Palimpsest* 67, no. 6 (1986): 196; House, *Refinancing of Mortgage and Other Farm Indebtedness*, 73rd Cong., 1st Sess. (1933),

H. Doc. 14; *Statutes at Large* 48 (1933): 41–51; Myers, *Cooperative Farm Mortgage Credit*, 16.

20. House, *Executive Order Reorganizing the Agricultural Credit Agencies of the United States*, 73rd Cong., 1st Sess. (1933), H. Doc. 7; *Statutes at Large* 48 (1933): 257–73.

21. Douglas P. Slaybaugh, *William I. Myers and the Modernization of American Agriculture* (Ames, IA, 1996); William I. Myers, interviewed by Gould P. Colman and Jonathan Levine, Division of Rare and Manuscript Collections, Cornell University, 1969, 158–59; Bernard F. Stanton, *Agricultural Economics at Cornell: A History, 1900–1990* (Ithaca, NY, 2001), 67; William I. Myers, "Policies of the Farm Credit Administration," *California Banker* 15, no. 7 (1934): 306; Myers, "The Program of the Farm Credit Administration," *Journal of Farm Economics* 16, no. 1 (1934): 36; R. P. King to Milo Reno, November 3, 1933, box 3, Reno Papers; Department of Agriculture, *Major Statistical Series of the U.S. Department of Agriculture*, 6:22. For the New Deal's impact on agricultural credit, see Theodore Saloutos, *The American Farmer and the New Deal* (Ames, IA, 1982), 269.

22. House, *Protect Small Home Owners from Foreclosure*, 73rd Cong., 1st Sess. (1933), H. Doc. 19, 1; *Statutes at Large* 48 (1933): 128–32; Federal Home Loan Bank Board, *Sixth Annual Report* (Washington, DC, 1938), 69; *Labor* 16, no. 22 (1935): 4; McElvaine, *Down and Out in the Great Depression*, 58; Cohen, *Making a New Deal*, 273–74.

23. *Single Tax Review* 14, no. 6 (1914): 78; *Labor Clarion* 21, no. 43 (1922): 3; *San Francisco Chronicle*, November 19, 1922, 61; *CR*, February 25, 1914, 3930; December 14, 1915, 250; House, H.R. 13871, 63rd Cong., 2nd Sess. (1914); *Federation News* 23, no. 17 (1930): 1; *Chicago Daily Tribune*, April 19, 1930, 20; *CR*, March 1, 1915, 5045. When Chicago banks aided employers during a 1905 strike, Buchanan and a number of local union leaders organized a "union labor bank." This experiment lasted for eighteen months. See *Typographical Journal* 30, no. 3 (1907): 280–81; *Chicago Record-Herald*, January 21, 1908, 4.

24. William Green, "Homes for Workers," *North American Review* 231, no. 1 (1931): 35; Federal Home Loan Bank System, *The Federal Home Loan Bank System, 1932–1952* (Washington, DC, 1952), 2–3; Kenneth T. Jackson, *Crabgrass Frontier: The Suburbanization of the United States* (New York, 1985), 196–97; Jonathan D. Rose, "The Incredible HOLC? Mortgage Relief during the Great Depression," *Journal of Money, Credit, and Banking* 43, no. 6 (2011): 1080; Marvell, *Federal Home Loan Bank Board*, 24. For the HOLC's impact on housing and the economy during the 1930s, see Fishback, Rose, and Snowden, *Well Worth Saving*, 7–8.

25. *Statutes at Large* 48 (1934): 1246–65; Paul L. Simon, "Frank Walker, New Dealer" (PhD diss., University of Notre Dame, 1965), 180–89; Marriner S. Eccles, *Beckoning Frontiers: Public and Personal Recollections* (New York, 1951), 149; Sidney Hyman, *Marriner S. Eccles: Private Entrepreneur and Public Servant* (Stanford, CA, 1976), 141–46; Gail Radford, *Modern Housing for America: Policy Struggle in the New Deal Era* (Chicago, 1996), 179–80; Richard O. Reisem, *100 Years of the*

Hard Working Dollar: The History of First Federal Savings and Loan Association of Rochester (Rochester, 1997), 19; Kenneth T. Jackson, "Federal Subsidy and the Suburban Dream: The First Quarter-Century of Government Interventions in the Housing Market," *Records of the Columbia Historical Society* 50 (1980): 426–28. On economic orthodoxy guiding the administration's approach to providing credit to farmers and homeowners, see Olson, *Saving Capitalism*, 84, 91–96; Sargent, *Roosevelt and the Hundred Days*, 148, 224–26.

    26. Mayer, *Bankers*, 330–32; Jacob S. Potofsky, "The Pioneering of Workers' Banks," *American Federationist* 70, no. 5 (1963): 14–16; Bernard L. Yellin, "The Labor Banking Movement in the United States" (master's thesis, Columbia University, 1936), 27–28; *American Flint* 23, no. 5 (1932): 25. On the suspension of the American Flint Glass Workers Union's bank, see Messer-Kruse, *Banksters, Bosses, and Smart Money*, 87.

    27. Edson L. Whitney, *Cooperative Credit Societies (Credit Unions) in America and in Foreign Countries* (Washington, DC, 1922), 16; Board of Bank Commissioners of the State of New Hampshire, *Sixty-Fourth Annual Report* (n.p., 1909), xi; Peter R. Shergold, "The Loan Shark: The Small Loan Business in Early Twentieth-Century Pittsburgh," *Pennsylvania History* 45, no. 3 (1978): 196; *Locomotive Engineers Journal* 46, no. 4 (1912): 359.

    28. Roy F. Bergengren, *Cooperative Banking: A Credit Union Book* (New York, 1923), 263; Charles Morrow Wilson, *Common Sense Credit: Credit Unions Come of Age* (New York, 1962), 38–42; *Credit Union Bridge* 20, no. 10 (1955): 2; Christopher T. Martin, "Edward A. Filene and the Promise of Industrial Democracy" (PhD diss., University of Rochester, 2002), 285–90. Filene encouraged his employees to form one of the nation's pioneer credit unions. See Kim McQuaid, "An American Owenite: Edward A. Filene and the Parameters of Industrial Reform, 1890–1937," *American Journal of Economics and Sociology* 35, no. 1 (1976): 87.

    29. Evans Clark, *Financing the Consumer* (New York, 1931), 119; William Hays Simpson, "Cost of Loans to Borrowers under Unregulated Lending," *Law and Contemporary Problems* 8, no. 1 (1941): 73; Abram L. Harris, *The Negro as Capitalist* (Philadelphia, 1936), 175; *Cigar Makers' Official Journal* 46, no. 6 (1922): 16. The progenitor of industrial loan companies, Morris Plan companies operated on a for-profit lending model that Arthur J. Morris developed in 1910. Creditworthy individual borrowers with two co-signers received installment loans. See Louis N. Robinson, "The Morris Plan," *American Economic Review* 21, no. 2 (1931): 222–35.

    30. J. Carroll Moody and Gilbert C. Fite, *The Credit Union Movement: Origins and Development, 1850–1970* (Lincoln, NE, 1971), 128–29, 359; American Federation of Labor, *Fifty-Seventh Annual Convention* (Washington, DC, 1937), 186; *Bridge* 9, nos. 8–11 (1933): 7, 10; Frederic J. Haskin, "Growth of Socialized Banking," February 12, 1934, box 30, Post Presidential Subject Files, Herbert Hoover Presidential Library and Museum, West Branch, IA; Roy F. Bergengren, *Credit Union, North America* (New York, 1940), 105.

    31. D. Sven Nordin, *Rich Harvest: A History of the Grange, 1867–1900* (Jackson,

MS, 1974), 151; Solon Justus Buck, *The Granger Movement* (Cambridge, MA, 1913), 270-71; National Grange, *Forty-Third Annual Session* (Concord, NH, 1909), 99; *Nebraska Union Farmer* 14, no. 13 (1927): 6; Moody and Fite, *Credit Union Movement*, 134; *Cooperative Farmer* 4, no. 18 (1932): 8; *Nebraska Union Farmer* 19, no. 20 (1933): 9; idem, 21, no. 24 (1935): 3; *Hoosier Farmer* 20, no. 12 (1935): 21.

32. Moody and Fite, *Credit Union Movement*, 94, 144; *Bridge* 7, no. 10 (1931): 5; Harlan J. Randall and Clay J. Daggett, *Consumers' Cooperative Adventures: Case Studies* (Whitewater, WI, 1936), 437-48. On welfare capitalism, see Cohen, *Making a New Deal*; Gerald Zahavi, *Workers, Managers, and Welfare Capitalism: The Shoeworkers and Tanners of Endicott Johnson, 1890-1950* (Urbana, IL, 1988); Stephen Meyer III, *The Five Dollar Day: Labor Management and Social Control in the Ford Motor Company, 1908-1921* (Albany, NY, 1981); Stuart D. Brandes, *American Welfare Capitalism, 1880-1940* (Chicago, 1976); Robert W. Ozanne, *A Century of Labor-Management Relations at McCormick and International Harvester* (Madison, WI, 1967).

33. Roy F. Bergengren, "The Credit Union," *American Federationist* 37, no. 1 (1930): 50-54; Bergengren, "The People's Bank," *American Federationist* 37, no. 4 (1930): 437-41; Bergengren, "The Credit Union," *American Federationist* 37, no. 7 (1930): 825-30; *Advance* 19, no. 12 (1933): 30; Charles Elbert Zaretz, *The Amalgamated Clothing Workers of America: A Study in Progressive Trades-Unionism* (New York, 1934), 277-79; *Federation News* 23, no. 7 (1930): 10; A. Philip Randolph, "National Negro Labor Conference," *American Federationist* 37, no. 9 (1930): 1054-57; *Opportunity* 9, no. 7 (1931): 210; Michigan Federation of Labor, *Forty-Third Annual Convention* (n.p., 1932), 49; Wisconsin State Federation of Labor, *Forty-First Annual Convention* (n.p., 1933), 67; *Postal Record* 46, no. 4 (1933): 210.

34. Roy F. Bergengren, *Crusade: The Fight for Economic Democracy in North America, 1921-1945* (New York, 1952), 220-21; Moody and Fite, *Credit Union Movement*, 134-36, 160; Roy F. Bergengren to John A. Ryan, April 14, 1932, box 4, John A. Ryan Papers, American Catholic History Research Center and University Archives, Catholic University of America, Washington, DC; *CR*, May 11, 1933, 3206; April 25, 1934, 7259; Subcommittee of the Senate Committee on Banking and Currency, *Credit Unions*, 73rd Cong., 1st Sess. (Washington, DC, 1933), 20; *CR*, May 10, 1934, 8459.

35. Freidel, *Franklin D. Roosevelt*, 1:153; Moody and Fite, *Credit Union Movement*, 43, 162-63, 359; *Evening Star* (Washington, DC), June 15, 1934, A-4; *CR*, June 16, 1934, 12225-26; *Statutes at Large* 48 (1934): 1216-22; *Cooperation* 17, no. 9 (1931): 167. On the Federal Credit Union Act, see Moody and Fite, *Credit Union Movement*, 150-66.

36. *Boston Sunday Post*, March 12, 1933, 12; Bergengren, *Crusade*, 99; *Bricklayer, Mason and Plasterer* 36, no. 6 (1933): 97; *Labor Clarion* 32, no. 43 (1933): 5.

37. *Federation News* 33, no. 16 (1933): 4.

Chapter Ten

1. *Labor World* (Duluth, MN) 41, no. 2 (1933): 4; *Central Labor Council Herald* 3, no. 15 (1933): 4.

2. Alan Brinkley argued that during its second term the Roosevelt administration began a retreat from economic reform, which culminated in postwar liberalism deemphasizing economic questions. The decline of banking politics over the course of the 1930s helped pave the way for this development. See Brinkley, *The End of Reform: New Deal Liberalism in Recession and War* (New York, 1995).

3. James MacGregor Burns, *Roosevelt: The Lion and the Fox* (New York, 1956), 192–93; William E. Leuchtenburg, *Franklin D. Roosevelt and the New Deal, 1932–1940* (New York, 1963), 89; *Minnesota Union Advocate* 27, no. 10 (1933): 4; *Farmers Union Herald* 7, no. 8 (1933): 2.

4. *Labor Clarion* 32, no. 49 (1933): 5; Washington State Grange, *Twenty-Fifth Annual Session*, 48.

5. Irving Bernstein, *Turbulent Years: A History of the American Worker, 1933–1941* (Boston, 1970), 9; Edward A. O'Neal, interviewed by Dean Albertson, Oral History Research Office, Columbia University, 1952, 77; Franklin D. Roosevelt to John A. Simpson, March 7, 1932, box 3, John A. Simpson Diary, April 3, 1932, box 5, Simpson Papers; Franklin D. Roosevelt to Louis J. Taber, November 19, 1932, box 8, Louis J. Taber Papers, Division of Rare and Manuscript Collections, Cornell University, Ithaca, NY.

6. I. N. McCollister et al. to Franklin D. Roosevelt, December 15, 1932, box 26, Reuben Dean Bowen Papers, Rare Book & Manuscript Library, Duke University, Durham, NC; William Lemke to Henry Teigan, February 13, 1933, box 11, Henry G. Teigan Papers, Minnesota Historical Society, St. Paul; Peter Norbeck to Franklin D. Roosevelt, February 2, 1933, box 36, Norbeck Papers; Harry B. Cordell to Franklin D. Roosevelt, November 23, 1932, Elmer Thomas et al. to Roosevelt, n.d., C. H. Hyde to Roosevelt, November 22, 1932, James T. Phillips to Roosevelt, January 2, 1933, John A. Simpson to G. W. Bohannan, December 16, 1932, box 4, Simpson Papers; Marvin Jones, interviewed by Dean Albertson, Oral History Research Office, Columbia University, 1953, 538; *New York Times*, February 27, 1933, 2; Myers interview, 147; *Weekly Kansas City (MO) Star*, March 8, 1933, 4.

7. *Washington Post*, February 5, 1933, 1; *New York Herald Tribune*, December 17, 1932, 5; *Boston Daily Globe*, December 17, 1932, 1; *Washington State Labor News* 10, no. 10 (1933): 1; Bernstein, *Turbulent Years*, 11; Frances Perkins, interviewed by Dean Albertson, Oral History Research Office, Columbia University, 1955, 4:298; Frey interview, 555.

8. New York State Federation of Labor, *Seventy-Second Annual Convention* (n.p., 1935), 113; idem, *Seventy-First Annual Convention* (n.p., 1934), 5; West Virginia State Federation of Labor, *1934–1935 Official Year Book* (n.p., 1934), 15.

9. During the spring of 1921, farmer organizations—most notably the recently established American Farm Bureau Federation—helped organize the bipartisan

congressional farm bloc to enact agricultural legislation. See Alice M. Christensen, "Agricultural Pressure and Government Response in the United States: 1919-1929" (PhD diss., University of California, Berkeley, 1936), 55–82. Jones interview, 1101; *Hoosier Farmer* 19, no. 2 (1934): 4. On agricultural opposition to the New Deal, see Jean Choate, *Disputed Ground: Farm Groups That Opposed the New Deal Agricultural Program* (Jefferson, NC, 2002).

10. Rosen, *Hoover, Roosevelt, and the Brains Trust*, 315–25; *New York Times*, May 22, 1933, 1; Roosevelt, *Public Papers*, 2:164.

11. Edward L. Schapsmeier and Frederick H. Schapsmeier, "Henry A. Wallace: New Deal Philosopher," *Historian* 32, no. 2 (1970): 177–90; Henry A. Wallace, address to Farmers Union Convention, September 19, 1928, box 3, Edward E. Kennedy Papers, Special Collections & University Archives, University of Iowa, Iowa City; George W. Martin, *Madam Secretary, Frances Perkins* (Boston, 1976); Davis, *Spearheads for Reform*, 108–12; Melvyn Dubofsky, *When Workers Organize: New York City in the Progressive Era* (Amherst, MA, 1968), 25–26; Perkins interview, 1:57; Richard A. Greenwald, *The Triangle Fire, the Protocols of Peace, and Industrial Democracy in Progressive Era New York* (Philadelphia, 2005), 190–91, 213; Jacob S. Potofsky, interviewed by Dean Albertson, Oral History Research Office, Columbia University, 1957, 291.

12. Stromquist, *Reinventing "The People"*; Henry A. Wallace, "The Value of Scientific Research to Agriculture," *Science* 77, no. 2003 (1933): 479–80; *Indianapolis Star*, November 15, 1933, 4; Theodore D. Rosenof, "The Economic Ideas of Henry A. Wallace, 1933–1948," *Agricultural History* 41, no. 2 (1967): 146; Frances Perkins, "A Cooperative Program Needed for Industrial Stabilization," *Annals of the American Academy of Political and Social Science* 154 (1931): 130; Perkins, "A National Labor Policy," *Annals of the American Academy of Political and Social Science* 184 (1936): 3; New York State Federation of Labor, *Seventy-Second Annual Convention*, 114.

13. R. Douglas Hurt, *Problems of Plenty: The American Farmer in the Twentieth Century* (Chicago, 2002), 69–80; *AFBF Official News Letter* 12, no. 10 (1933): 3; idem, 12, no. 25 (1933): 1; AFBF, *Seventeenth Annual Convention* (n.p., 1935), 11.

14. Christiana McFadyen Campbell, *The Farm Bureau and the New Deal: A Study of the Making of National Farm Policy, 1933–40* (Urbana, IL, 1962), 103; O'Neal interview, 86; Louis J. Taber, interviewed by Dean Albertson, Oral History Research Office, Columbia University, 1952, 284; Jones interview, 746; Taber interview, 289.

15. Perkins interview, 4:301; John L. Lewis, "Labor and the National Recovery Administration," *Annals of the American Academy of Political and Social Science* 172 (1934): 58; William Green to union presidents, May 27, 1933, reel 8, William Green Papers, Ohio Historical Society, Columbus; Craig L. Phelan, *William Green: Biography of a Labor Leader* (Albany, NY, 1989), 64–66.

16. *Today* 1, no. 16 (1934): 3; Philip Taft, *Organized Labor in American His-*

tory (New York, 1964), 420; O'Connor, *Steel—Dictator*, 247–60; James R. Green, "Democracy Comes to 'Little Siberia': Steel Workers Organize in Aliquippa, Pennsylvania, 1933–1937," *Labor's Heritage* 5, no. 2 (1993): 4–27; Rade B. Vukmir, *The Mill* (Lanham, MD, 1999), 307–8; Senate, Subcommittee of the Committee on Education and Labor, *Oppressive Labor Practices Act*, 76th Cong., 1st Sess. (Washington, DC, 1939), 65; American Federation of Labor, *Fifty-Fifth Annual Convention* (Washington, DC, 1935), 564. On the obstacles union organizers faced in steel towns, see David Brody, *Labor in Crisis: The Steel Strike of 1919* (Urbana, IL, 1987), 36, 89–95.

17. Jonathan H. Rees, *Managing the Mills: Labor Policy in the American Steel Industry during the Nonunion Era* (Lanham, MD, 2004), 191–92; *Amalgamated Journal* 35, no. 11 (1933): 11; *New York Times*, June 20, 1935, 1; Melvyn Dubofsky, *The State and Labor in Modern America* (Chapel Hill, NC, 1994), 129–31.

18. AFBF, *Seventeenth Annual Convention*, 10; Gilbert C. Fite, *American Farmers: The New Minority* (Bloomington, IN, 1981), 56–59; Melvyn Dubofsky and Foster Rhea Dulles, *Labor in America: A History*, 8th ed. (Wheeling, IL, 2010), 252–54.

19. Henry A. Wallace, interviewed by Dean Albertson, Oral History Research Office, Columbia University, 1951, 211, 5352; O'Neal interview, 85. Undersecretary of Agriculture M. L. Wilson stated that during the administration's early years the Farm Bureau had the greatest influence, the Grange came next, and the Farmers Union ranked last. See Campbell, *Farm Bureau and the New Deal*, 103. Personal differences colored Wallace's perception of Reno, see Michael W. Schuyler, "The Hair-Splitters: Reno and Wallace, 1932–1933," *Annals of Iowa* 43, no. 6 (1976): 403–29.

20. *Kansas Union Farmer* 28, no. 22 (1935): 1; *National Union Farmer* 14, no. 26 (1936): 2.

21. Blackorby, *Prairie Rebel*, 207–16; Tull, *Father Coughlin*, 106–8; House Committee on Agriculture, *Refinancing of Farm Mortgages*, 74th Cong., 1st Sess. (Washington, DC, 1935), 5; *Sun* (Baltimore), May 14, 1936, 1.

22. Farmers Educational & Cooperative Equity Union of America, State Convention, 1935, reel 3, Farmers Educational and Co-operative Union of America, Wisconsin Division Records, 1924–1969, Wisconsin Historical Society, Madison; *National Union Farmer* 15, no. 1 (1936): 3.

23. *Farmers Union Herald* 10, no. 12 (1936): 1; idem, 11, no. 12 (1937): 1; Gladys Talbott Edwards, *The Farmers Union Triangle* (Jamestown, ND, 1941), 43–45; Wallace interview, 211; *National Union Farmer* 18, no. 16 (1939): 2.

24. Campbell, *Farm Bureau and the New Deal*, 156–78; Wallace interview, 5481.

25. *CR*, April 25, 1939, 4711; Franklin D. Roosevelt to Carl E. Ladd, December 20, 1939, Henry A. Wallace to Roosevelt, December 13, 1939, F. F. Hill to Roosevelt, December 13, 1939, box 1, Official File 27, Roosevelt Library; *Washington Post*,

December 14, 1939, 1; *National Union Farmer* 18, no. 20 (1939): 1; *New York Times*, December 15, 1939, 29; Forest F. Hill, interviewed by Laurie Konigsburg Todd, Division of Rare and Manuscript Collections, Cornell University, 1984, 30, 32.

26. *Washington Post*, February 25, 1940, 2; Conrad and Conrad, *50 Years*, 75.

27. Mrs. P. J. Enright to George Norris, May 14, 1940, box 135, Norris Papers; *Washington Post*, May 11, 1940, 3; Wallace interview, 5497.

28. Wallace interview, 5493; *Washington Post*, April 3, 1940, 1; *National Grange Monthly* 37, no. 2 (1940): 14; idem, 37, no. 6 (1940): 8; *AFBF Official News Letter* 19, no. 10 (1940): 2.

29. *AFBF Official News Letter* 18, no. 26 (1939): 1; H. A. Wallace to Nelson G. Kraschel, January 2, 1940, reel 21, Henry A. Wallace Papers, Special Collections & University Archives, University of Iowa, Iowa City; *Farmers Union Herald* 14, no. 5 (1940): 1. Contention over the Farm Credit Administration being part of the Department of Agriculture continued until the Farm Credit Act of 1953 made it an independent agency again. See W. Gifford Hoag, *The Farm Credit System: A History of Financial Self-Help* (Danville, IL, 1976), 251–52.

30. On Lewis's organizing drive, see Melvyn Dubofsky and Warren R. Van Tine, *John L. Lewis: A Biography* (New York, 1977), 203–79.

31. *New York Times*, July 6, 1936, 8; "Industrial Democracy in Steel," July 6, 1936, reel 1, John L. Lewis Papers, Center for Labor-Management Documentation and Archives, Cornell University, Ithaca, NY.

32. *Amalgamated Journal* 36, no. 33 (1935): 24. On tactical reasons for Lewis to assail banks, see Leon Fink, *Progressive Intellectuals and the Dilemmas of Democratic Commitment* (Cambridge, MA, 1997), 230–31.

33. *Tow-Sack Tattler*, October 28, 1939, 15. On this strike, see James N. Gregory, *American Exodus: The Dust Bowl Migration and Okie Culture in California* (New York, 1989), 157–64; Devra Weber, *Dark Sweat, White Gold: California Farm Workers, Cotton, and the New Deal* (Berkeley, 1994), 189–99. On the Associated Farmers, see Carey McWilliams, *Factories in the Field: The Story of Migratory Farm Labor in California* (Boston, 1939), 231–39.

Chapter Eleven

1. James P. Warburg, "Public-Spirited Bank Policies," *California Banker* 15, no. 10 (1934): 401; Colorado State Grange, *Sixty-First Annual Session* (n.p., 1935), 16; Roosevelt, *Public Papers*, 4:139.

2. T. P. Cramer Jr., "Some States Tried Banking," *Banking* 27, no. 12 (1935): 29; *Progressive* 4, no. 138 (1935): 2; J. P. Howard to Gridiron Pub. Co., January 29, 1935, box 30, Nordskog Papers, CSUN; J. H. Carroll to Elmer Thomas, February 8, 1935, box 17, Thomas Papers.

3. Roosevelt, *Public Papers*, 4:140; Eccles, *Beckoning Frontiers*, 113–15; Hyman, *Marriner S. Eccles*; Dean L. May, "Sources of Marriner S. Eccles's Economic Thought," *Journal of Mormon History* 3 (1976): 85–99; Senate Committee on

Finance, *Investigation of Economic Problems*, 72nd Cong., 2nd Sess. (Washington, DC, 1933), 706; Arch O. Egbert, "Marriner S. Eccles and the Banking Act of 1935" (PhD diss., Brigham Young University, 1967), 27–39.

4. McElvaine, "Thunder without Lightning," 76–80; *Journal of Electrical Workers and Operators* 33, no. 1 (1934): 37; *International Engineer* 66, no. 1 (1934): 12; Richard J. Oestreicher, "The Spirit of '92: Popular Opposition in Homestead's Politics and Culture, 1892–1937," in *Pittsburgh Surveyed: Social Science Reform in the Early Twentieth Century*, ed. Maurine W. Greenwald and Margo Anderson (Pittsburgh, 1996), 200.

5. Eccles, *Beckoning Frontiers*, 165–66, 175; Henry Morgenthau Jr. to Marriner S. Eccles, January 29, 1934, White House Press Release, November 10, 1934, box 2, Eccles to Duncan U. Fletcher, July 2, 1935, box 56, Eccles, "Desirable Changes in the Administration of the Federal Reserve System," box 4, Eccles Papers.

6. *CR*, February 5, 1935, 1501; February 6, 1935, 1514–24; Marriner S. Eccles to Marvin H. McIntyre, February 4, 1935, box 4, Eccles Papers.

7. *News-Week* 4, no. 26 (1934): 4; Marriner S. Eccles to Carter Glass, December 17, 1934, box 56, Eccles Papers; Peter Norbeck to W. L. Baker, March 21, 1933, box 1, Norbeck Papers; *Today* 4, no. 21 (1935): 8; Schlesinger, *Age of Roosevelt*, 3:295–96; Eccles, *Beckoning Frontiers*, 178; Carter Glass to Reed Smoot, Fred Kiesel, Walker Cheeseman, J. H. Devine, Frederick Champ, A. R. Dawson, January 22, 1935, box 304, Glass to N. E. Miller, December 4, 1934, box 317, Glass Papers; Carter Glass to H. Parker Willis, April 3, 1935, box 1, Willis Papers.

8. *Evening Star* (Washington, DC), January 15, 1935, A-2; Franklin D. Roosevelt to Duncan U. Fletcher, March 26, 1935, President's Personal File 1358, Roosevelt Library; Subcommittee of the Senate Committee on Banking and Currency, *Nomination of Marriner S. Eccles to Be a Member of the Federal Reserve Board*, 74th Cong., 1st Sess. (Washington, DC, 1935), 1; *Sun* (Baltimore), April 24, 1935, 2; *CR*, April 24, 1935, 6296; *Washington Post*, February 6, 1935, 1; Subcommittee of the Senate Committee on Banking and Currency, *Banking Act of 1935*, 74th Cong., 1st Sess., (Washington, DC, 1935), 1:83; Carter Glass to E. W. Kemmerer, May 1, 1935, box 317, Glass Papers.

9. *Amalgamated Journal* 34, no. 6 (1932): 24. Despite Roosevelt's initial opposition, he quickly embraced guaranty. See *Wall Street Journal*, February 16, 1934, 13.

10. Eccles, *Beckoning Frontiers*, 197; *Washington Post*, April 23, 1935, 1; Carter Glass to Charles F. Zimmerman, February 16, 1935, box 304, Glass Papers; *Banking* 27, no. 11 (1935): 41; Subcommittee of the Senate Committee on Banking and Currency, *Banking Act of 1935*, 1:71–72. On Warburg's opposition to New Deal financial reform, see Irving S. Michelman, "A Banker in the New Deal: James P. Warburg," *Revue Internationale d'Histoire de la Banque* 8 (1974): 48–59.

11. *Economic Conditions*, March 1935, 47; *Commercial West* 69, no. 24 (1935): 6; S. H. Vance to Wright Patman, May 4, 1935, box 65B, Patman Papers; House

Committee on Banking and Currency, *Banking Act of 1935*, 74th Cong., 1st session (Washington, DC, 1935), 514; Krooss, *Executive Opinion*, 208; R. M. Hanes to Josiah William Bailey, May 17, 1935, box 223, Bailey Papers; *Hartford (CT) Courant*, June 8, 1935, 18; Subcommittee of the Senate Committee on Banking and Currency, *Banking Act of 1935*, 2:522, 516, 901; A. E. Dahl to Peter Norbeck, May 20, 1935, box 13, Norbeck Papers.

12. *New York Times*, May 4, 1935, 19; House Committee on Banking and Currency, *Banking Act of 1935*, 519; Subcommittee of the Senate Committee on Banking and Currency, *Banking Act of 1935*, 2:520; *New York Times*, May 8, 1935, 27; "Resolution adopted at the Twenty-third Annual Meeting," box 223, Bailey Papers; C. George Wolfskill, *The Revolt of the Conservatives: A History of the American Liberty League, 1934–1940* (Boston, 1962), 134, 165.

13. Subcommittee of the Senate Committee on Banking and Currency, *Banking Act of 1935*, 1:76; *Coast Banker* 52, no. 2 (1934): 72; *Review of Reviews and World's Work* 91, no. 2 (1935): 21; *Southern Banker* 63, no. 2 (1934): 14.

14. Stephen R. Ortiz, *Beyond the Bonus March and GI Bill: How Veterans Shaped the New Deal Era* (New York, 2010), 138–40; Alan Brinkley, "Huey Long, the Share Our Wealth Movement, and the Limits of Depression Dissidence," *Louisiana History* 22, no. 2 (1981): 126–27; Brinkley, *Voices of Protest*, 213–14, 225–26; *Cleveland Plain Dealer*, March 1, 1935, 8; "Resolutions of National Monetary Conference," box 18, Thomas Papers; *Washington Post*, January 28, 1935, 2. On the Townsend Plan, see Edwin L. Amenta, *When Movements Matter: The Townsend Plan and the Rise of Social Security* (Princeton, NJ, 2006); Abraham Holtzman, *The Townsend Movement: A Political Study* (New York, 1963).

15. *New York Times*, May 22, 1935, 18; Stuart L. Weiss, "Maury Maverick and the Liberal Bloc," *Journal of American History* 57, no. 4 (1971): 882–83; *New York Times*, March 17, 1935, 33; Richard B. Henderson, *Maury Maverick: A Political Biography* (Austin, TX, 1970), 78; *CR*, March 8, 1935, 3180; March 14, 1935, 3682; January 7, 1935, 137, 165, 177; February 20, 1935, 2358; *Washington Post*, January 8, 1935, 3; *CR*, January 8, 1935, 212.

16. *CR*, January 7, 1935, 178; February 15, 1935, 1999; May 2, 1935, 6801; Junker, *Bank of North Dakota*, 112; Twin Falls Grange to William Borah, March 8, 1935, Canyonside Grange to Borah, March 12, 1935, box 377, Borah Papers; *Kansas Union Farmer* 27, no. 22 (1935): 2.

17. *CR*, March 4, 1935, 2899–900; March 5, 1935, 2961; Subcommittee of the Senate Committee on Banking and Currency, *Banking Act of 1935*, 1:808; Huey Pierce Long, *My First Days in the White House* (Harrisburg, PA, 1935), 34–38; Williams, *Huey Long*, 845–47. On the 100 percent reserve requirement, see Irving Fisher, *100% Money* (New York, 1935). On the origin of this proposal, see William R. Allen, "Irving Fisher, F.D.R., and the Great Depression," *History of Political Economy* 9, no. 4 (1977): 583.

18. *CR*, May 9, 1935, 7270–71; April 19, 1935, 6096; House, *Banking Act of 1935*, 74th Cong., 1st Sess. (1935), H. Rept. 742; *Time* 25, no. 21 (1935): 13–14; Henry

Morgenthau Jr., Diary, May 15, July 3, and May 17, 1935, Henry Morgenthau, Jr., Papers, Franklin D. Roosevelt Presidential Library and Museum, Hyde Park, NY; John Morton Blum, *From the Morgenthau Diaries*, 3 vols. (Boston, 1959), 1:280; Subcommittee of the Senate Committee on Banking and Currency, *Banking Act of 1935*, 2:507; *Chicago Banker* 79, no. 22 (1935): 6.

19. Subcommittee of the Senate Committee on Banking and Currency, *Banking Act of 1935*, 1:76–77; Warburg, "Public-Spirited Bank Policies," 401; *Southern Banker* 63, no. 4 (1934): 24. Lenin stated: "Only the control of the banks, on which the whole of capitalist circulation is pivoted, will allow us to realize . . . control of the whole of economic life, of the production and distribution of the most important products." See N. Lenin, *Preparing for Revolt* (London, 1929), 108–10.

20. *New York Times*, June 16, 1935, E8; Joseph W. Gibson to Carter Glass, May 8, 1935, box 338, Glass Papers.

21. *CR*, April 12, 1935, 5575; January 7, 1935, 178; House Committee on the Post Office and Post Roads, *H.R. 3030*, 74th Cong., 1st Sess. (1935), 4; *Banking* 27, no. 12 (1935): 41; *CR*, May 9, 1935, 7244; February 4, 1935, 1456; *National Cyclopaedia of American Biography*, 54:70.

22. Burns, *American Banking Community*, 159–60; A. P. Giannini to Lawrence Clayton, May 14, 1935, box 20A, Eccles Papers; Bonadio, *A. P. Giannini*, 227–28; A. P. Giannini, "I Favor the Banking Bill," *Today* 4, no. 6 (1935): 8–9.

23. *Minnesota Leader* 6, no. 26 (1935): 4; Paul S. Holbo, "The Farmer-Labor Association: Minnesota's Party *within* a Party," *Minnesota History* 38, no. 7 (1963): 301–9; *Journal of Electrical Workers and Operators* 34, no. 3 (1935): 126; *Farm Holiday News* 2, no. 10 (1935): 3.

24. Charles E. Coughlin, *A Series of Lectures on Social Justice* (Royal Oak, MI, 1935), 152; *Cleveland Plain Dealer*, May 9, 1935, 1; *Cleveland Press*, May 9, 1935, 25; *New York Herald Tribune*, May 23, 1935, 11; *New York Times*, May 23, 1935, 18.

25. *CR*, May 2, 1935, 6891; May 9, 1935, 7256–57; Lawrence Clayton to A. P. Giannini, June 26, 1935, box 20A, Eccles Papers; William Borah to C. F. Yingst, March 16, 1935, Borah to W. R. Bell, March 15, 1935, box 407, Borah Papers.

26. Mark Wayne Nelson, *Jumping the Abyss: Marriner S. Eccles and the New Deal, 1933–1940* (Salt Lake City, UT, 2017), 218; *New York Herald Tribune*, June 4, 1935, 6; Subcommittee of the Senate Committee on Banking and Currency, *Banking Act of 1935*, 2:367; *Washington Post*, June 21, 1935, 21; *New York Times*, June 18, 1935, 17; Isabel Parker to Carter Glass, May 14, 1935, box 338, Glass Papers. On Glass's undemocratic beliefs, see Koeniger, "'Unreconstructed Rebel,'" 9–13, 203–4, 234–35; Allan A. Michie and Frank W. Ryhlick, *Dixie Demagogues* (New York, 1939), 173.

27. Patrick, *Reform of the Federal Reserve*, 264; Morgenthau Diary, June 13, 1935; *CR*, June 27, 1935, 10291; July 1, 1935, 10459.

28. *CR*, July 2, 1935, 10588; July 25, 1935, 11776–77, 11827; Senate, *Banking Act of 1935*, 74th Cong., 1st Sess. (1935), S. Rept. 1007; Chernow, *House of Morgan*, 384.

29. J. Wayne Flynt, *Duncan Upshaw Fletcher: Dixie's Reluctant Progressive* (Tallahassee, FL, 1971), 178; *CR*, July 23, 1935, 11686; July 18, 1935, 11364; July 25, 1935, 11842–43; July 26, 1935, 11906, 11914, 11935; July 29, 1935, 12016; Ronald A. Mulder, "The Progressive Insurgents in the United States Senate, 1935–1936: Was There a Second New Deal?," *Mid-America* 57, no. 2 (1975): 116–17; Frederick Steiwer to A. P. Giannini, July 29, 1935, box 4, Frederick Steiwer Papers, Oregon Historical Society, Portland; *New York Times*, July 27, 1935, 1.

30. *CR*, July 29, 1935, 12016–17; Eccles, *Beckoning Frontiers*, 221; *CR*, August 1, 1935, 12280.

31. Burns, *American Banking Community*, 170–71; Elliot A. Rosen, *Roosevelt, the Great Depression, and the Economics of Recovery* (Charlottesville, VA, 2005), 3; Eccles, *Beckoning Frontiers*, 220–21; *CR*, August 19, 1935, 13709; Patrick, *Reform of the Federal Reserve*, 266–69; House, *Banking Act of 1935*, 74th Cong., 1st Sess. (1935), H. Rept. 1822. The conference substituted a majority vote to change reserve requirements for the Senate's stipulation requiring the support of five of the seven governors.

32. *Evening Star* (Washington, DC), August 23, 1935, 4; *Statutes at Large* 49 (1935): 684–723.

33. *Today* 4, no. 21 (1935): 8; *Wall Street Journal*, August 24, 1935, 3; Eccles, "Desirable Changes."

34. *Southern Banker* 65, no. 5 (1935): 28; *Wall Street Journal*, August 24, 1935, 3; O'Connor Diary, August 20, 1935; *Southern Banker* 65, no. 3 (1935): 17.

35. Greider, *Secrets of the Temple*, 313; Nelson, *Jumping the Abyss*, 232–36; Donald F. Kettl, *Leadership at the Fed* (New Haven, CT, 1986), 53–55; Matias Vernengo, "A Hands-Off Central Banker? Marriner S. Eccles and the Federal Reserve, 1934–51," in *American Power and Policy*, ed. Robert Leeson (New York, 2009); Chandler, *American Monetary Policy*, 243–45; G. Griffith Johnson Jr., *The Treasury and Monetary Policy, 1933–1938* (Cambridge, MA, 1939), 35–38; Romer, "What Ended the Great Depression?"

Chapter Twelve

1. Federal Reserve Bank of Boston, *Fourteenth Annual Meeting* (n.p., 1936), 7; James A. Farley, *Behind the Ballots: The Personal History of a Politician* (New York, 1938), 289; Michael J. Webber, *New Deal Fat Cats: Business, Labor, and Campaign Finance in the 1936 Presidential Election* (New York, 2000), 57–60.

2. *CR*, March 8, 1938, 3008; Senate, S. 3630, 75th Cong., 3rd Sess. (1938); Alexander R. Stoesen, "The Senatorial Career of Claude D. Pepper" (PhD diss., University of North Carolina, 1965), 85–86; Frank S. Tower to Franklin D. Roosevelt, January 25, 1938, box 1, Official File 706, Roosevelt Library; *New York Times*, March 11, 1939, 26. On insufficiency of credit for small businesses, see Howard S. Dye, "Federal Banking Legislation from 1930 to 1938: Its History, Consequences and Related Issues" (PhD diss., Cornell University, 1949), 409–11.

3. William Raspas to Daniel Reed, October 20, 1936, box 14, Daniel Alden Reed Papers, Division of Rare and Manuscript Collections, Cornell University, Ithaca, NY; R. S. Hecht to Marriner S. Eccles, December 14, 1935, box 44, Eccles Papers.

4. Marriner S. Eccles to Herbert E. Gaston, August 3, 1936, box 7, Eccles Papers; William Lemke, "Monetary Reform," August 30, 1937, box 26, Lemke Papers; J. L. Crossley to George Norris, January 15, 1936, box 55, Norris Papers; W. E. Marvin to Jerry Voorhis, July 1, 1937, box 54, Jerry Voorhis Papers, Special Collections, Claremont University Consortium, Claremont, CA.

5. Oregon State Grange, *Sixty-Second Annual Session* (n.p., 1935), 40; idem, *Sixty-Third Annual Session* (n.p., 1936), 175; Subcommittee of the Committee on Agriculture and Forestry, *General Farm Legislation*, 75th Cong., 2nd Sess. (Washington, DC, 1937), 20:4540; Indiana State Federation of Labor, *Fifty-Second Annual Convention* (n.p., 1936), 88.

6. National Grange, *Seventy-Third Annual Session* (Springfield, MA, 1939), 181; Veterans of Foreign Wars, *34th National Encampment* (Washington, DC, 1934), 19; idem, *35th National Encampment* (Washington, DC, 1935), 20; M. L. Gilbert to James E. Murray, May 16, 1939, box 333, James E. Murray Papers, Archives and Special Collections, University of Montana, Missoula; Ortiz, *Beyond the Bonus March*, 176–77. Payment of the bonus raised consumer spending and stimulated employment. See Joshua K. Hausman, "Fiscal Policy and Economic Recovery: The Case of the 1936 Veterans' Bonus," *American Economic Review* 106, no. 4 (2016): 1100–143.

7. *California Banker* 16, no. 11 (1935): 460–61; Federal Reserve Bank of Boston, *Fourteenth Annual Meeting*, 20; Donald Sham to John L. Lewis, November 14, 1936, box 78, Amalgamated Clothing Workers of America Records; American Bankers Association, *The Postal Savings System of the United States* (New York, 1937); National Grange, *Sixty-Ninth Annual Session* (Springfield, MA, 1935), 169; *Labor* 17, no. 15 (1935): 4; *CR*, January 27, 1937, 504; *Wall Street Journal*, March 9, 1937, 6; Lyle H. Boren to C. P. Ellis, April 15, 1937, box 6, Lyle H. Boren Papers, Carl Albert Congressional Research and Studies Center, University of Oklahoma, Norman.

8. Eric Leif Davin, *Crucible of Freedom: Workers' Democracy in the Industrial Heartland, 1914–1960* (Lanham, MD, 2010), 230; *Tow-Sack Tattler*, November 4, 1939, 7; *Progressive* 1, no. 179 (1936): 7; Fred Yeates to A. P. Giannini, July 19, 1938, box 10, Julian Dana Papers, Bancroft Library, University of California, Berkeley.

9. *Daily Oklahoman* (Oklahoma City), March 16, 1934, 2; *Santa Fe New Mexican*, May 6, 1935, 1; Nick A. Komons, *The Cutting Air Crash: A Case Study in Early Federal Aviation Policy* (Washington, DC, 1973); Williams, *Huey Long*, 859–76; *New York Herald Tribune*, February 12, 1936, 14; *Telegraph-Herald* (Dubuque, IA), May 5, 1936, 1; Phelan, *William Green*, 114–18, 152; Taft, *Organized Labor*, 466–70; James O. Morris, *Conflict within the AFL: A Study of Craft Versus Industrial Unionism, 1901–1938* (Ithaca, NY, 1958), 264–66; E. Perrin Schwartz to Andrae Nord-

skog, January 19, 1939, box 16, Nordskog Papers, CSUN; Brinkley, *Voices of Protest*, 265–68. The Union Party made a respectable showing for a third party, receiving almost 2 percent of all ballots cast—892,492 votes—including over 5 percent in Massachusetts, Minnesota, North Dakota, Oregon, and Rhode Island (Diamond, *Congressional Quarterly's Guide*, 290). But these results fell far short of what Coughlin had predicted (Tull, *Father Coughlin*, 141). On the legal and organizational obstacles the party faced, see David O. Powell, "The Union Party of 1936: Organization and Finance," *North Dakota History* 34, no. 2 (1967): 147–56.

10. Howson, "Jacob Sechler Coxey," 403–8; Karl F. M. Sandberg, *Inflation and the Federal Reserve Banks* (n.p., 1942), 24; Paul Bullock, *Jerry Voorhis: The Idealist as Politician* (New York, 1978); Christopher H. Evans, *The Social Gospel in American Religion: A History* (New York, 2017); Peter W. Williams, *Religion, Art, and Money: Episcopalians and American Culture from the Civil War to the Great Depression* (Chapel Hill, NC, 2016), 117–50. On EPIC, see Greg Mitchell, *The Campaign of the Century: Upton Sinclair's Race for Governor of California and the Birth of Media Politics* (New York, 1992); James N. Gregory, "Upton Sinclair's 1934 EPIC Campaign: Anatomy of a Political Movement," *Labor* 12, no. 4 (2015): 51–81.

11. *CR*, April 26, 1937, app. 961; Peter Paul Lucenti to Jerry Voorhis, n.d., box 54, Voorhis Papers.

12. C. B. Deane, ed., *Official Congressional Directory*, 74th Cong., 1st Sess. (Washington, DC, 1935), 65; *Minden (NE) Courier*, August 24, 1950, 1; *CR*, March 19, 1937, 2530.

13. Wright Patman and Charles G. Binderup to steering committee, March 29, 1937, Patman to steering committee, November 17, 1937, box 858B, Patman Papers; Jerry Voorhis, interviewed by John A. Vieg and Enid H. Douglass, Special Collections, Claremont University Consortium, 1971, 28; R. N. Harper to Lyle H. Boren, July 26, 1937, box 20, Boren to Guy L. Berry, November 23, 1937, box 5, Boren Papers; Franklin D. Roosevelt to Marriner S. Eccles, July 9, 1937, box 4, Eccles Papers.

14. Wright Patman to steering committee, November 17, 1937, box 858B, Patman Papers; *Banking* 30, no. 6 (1937): 19; Gene Gum to Elmer Thomas, November 11, 1937, box 30, Thomas Papers; Roosevelt, *Public Papers*, 4:407–8; Marriner S. Eccles to Franklin D. Roosevelt, July 13, 1937, box 4, Eccles Papers.

15. House Committee on Banking and Currency, *Government Ownership of the Federal Reserve Banks*, 75th Cong., 3rd Sess. (Washington, DC, 1938); *CR*, January 24, 1938, 1010; Jerry Voorhis, *Confessions of a Congressman* (Garden City, NY, 1947), 168, 170; Joseph A. Gavagan to Franklin D. Roosevelt, April 16, 1938, box 3, Official File 90, Marvin H. McIntyre to Roosevelt, December 14, 1937, box 3, Official File 230, McIntyre to Roosevelt, February 10, 1938, McIntyre to Roosevelt, January 11, 1938, box 6, Official File 229, Roosevelt Library; James T. Patterson, *Congressional Conservatism and the New Deal: The Growth of the Conservative Coalition in Congress, 1933–1939* (Lexington, KY, 1967), 188–249; D. B.

Hardeman and Donald C. Bacon, *Rayburn: A Biography* (Austin, TX, 1987), 224–26.

16. *Los Angeles Times*, August 27, 1938, 1. On Ham and Eggs, see Chris Ernest Nelson, "The Battle for Ham and Eggs: The 1938–1939 San Diego Campaign for the California Pension Plan," *Journal of San Diego History* 38, no. 4 (1992): 203–25; Tom Zimmerman, "Ham and Eggs, Everybody!," *Southern California Quarterly* 62, no. 1 (1980): 77–96; Jackson K. Putnam, *Old-Age Politics in California* (Stanford, CA, 1970), 89–114.

17. John B. Canterbury, "'Ham and Eggs' in California," *Nation* 147, no. 17 (1938): 408–10; *Life*, September 12, 1938, 18–19; *New York Herald Tribune*, September 1, 1938, 2; *New York Times*, November 5, 1939, 1; *Tow-Sack Tattler*, October 28, 1939, 10; *Los Angeles Times*, September 15, 1938, 1; *Ham and Eggs* 1, no. 1 (1938): 4–5; *Christian Science Monitor*, October 27, 1939, 2. On stamp scrip, see Loren C. Gatch, "The Professor and a Paper Panacea: Irving Fisher and the Stamp Scrip Movement of 1932–1934," *Paper Money* 48, no. 2 (2009): 125–42.

18. *Sacramento (CA) Bee*, May 18, 1939, 1; Robert E. Burke, *Olson's New Deal for California* (Berkeley, 1953), 15–17, 107–12; Culbert L. Olson, *State Papers and Public Addresses* (Sacramento, 1942), 403–5; *San Francisco Examiner*, July 2, 1939, 1; *National Ham and Eggs* 1, no. 42 (1939): 3; idem, 1, no. 43 (1939): 5; idem, 1, no. 44 (1939): 21.

19. *National Ham and Eggs* 1, no. 49 (1939): 18; *Sacramento (CA) Bee*, October 7, 1939, 26; *Ham and Eggs for Californians* 1, no. 1 (1938): 3; *Santa Barbara (CA) News-Press*, October 20, 1939, 16.

20. *National Ham and Eggs* 1, no. 13 (1939): 2; idem, 1, no. 6 (1939): 2; idem, 1, no. 49 (1939): 26; idem, 1, no. 19 (1939): 2; idem, 1, no. 20 (1939): 2.

21. *New York Times*, November 8, 1939, 1; *Christian Science Monitor*, October 27, 1939, 2; *National Ham and Eggs* 1, no. 50 (1939): 20–21; idem, 2, no. 2 (1939): 18.

22. *Covered Wagon*, April 29, 1939, 6; *CR*, March 10, 1939, 2606; House, H.R. 4931, 76th Cong., 1st Sess. (1939); California State Grange, *Sixty-Seventh Annual Session* (n.p., 1939), 198–99; Jerry Voorhis to Andrae Nordskog, February 18, 1941, box 18, Nordskog Papers, CSUN; *CR*, January 30, 1940, 814; January 3, 1941, 14; January 16, 1941, 183; January 6, 1943, 22; January 3, 1945, 21.

23. E. E. Placek to members of Congress, March 27, 1943, box 4, Boren Papers; Robert Sobel, *Inside Wall Street: Continuity and Change in the Financial District* (New York, 1977), 204; Paul M. Sweezy, "The Decline of the Investment Banker," *Antioch Review* 1, no. 1 (1941): 63; Paul Studenski and Herman E. Krooss, *Financial History of the United States* (New York, 1952), 441–42; Greider, *Secrets of the Temple*, 322–24.

24. Minnesota State Federation of Labor, *Sixty-First Convention* (n.p., 1943), 87; Harvey O'Connor, *History of Oil Workers Intl. Union (CIO)* (Denver, 1950), 181; Oil Workers International Union, *Fourteenth National Convention* (n.p., 1943),

209; idem, *Fifteenth National Convention* (n.p., 1944), 107; idem, *Seventeenth National Convention* (n.p., 1946), 369.

25. *National Ham and Eggs* 1, no. 49 (1939): 10; *CR*, May 19, 1944, 4776; April 2, 1945, 3053; July 11, 1947, 8758; June 21, 1949, 8084.

26. California State Grange, *Sixty-Eighth Annual Session* (n.p., 1940), 187; idem, *Seventieth Annual Session* (n.p., 1942), 143–44, 13; Arthur H. Pursell, *Rural Credit Unions in the United States* (Washington, DC, 1958), 2.

27. Minutes of the Farmers Educational & Cooperative Equity Union of America, Wis. Div., 1936, reel 2, Farmers Educational and Co-operative Union of America, Wisconsin Division Records; *Black Worker* 3, no. 3 (1937): 4; Roy F. Bergengren, *CUNA Emerges* (Madison, WI, 1935), 198.

28. *Commercial West* 70, no. 2 (1935): 6; Moody and Fite, *Credit Union Movement*, 359; Elizabeth A. Fones-Wolf, *Selling Free Enterprise: The Business Assault on Labor and Liberalism, 1945–60* (Urbana, IL, 1994), 120. On the postwar growth of credit unions, see Moody and Fite, *Credit Union Movement*, 289–352.

29. Howard M. Wachtel, *The Money Mandarins: The Making of a Supranational Economic Order*, rev. ed. (Armonk, NY, 1990), 46–52; Alfred E. Eckes Jr., *A Search for Solvency: Bretton Woods and the International Monetary System, 1941–1971* (Austin, TX, 1975), 154–61; Eric N. Helleiner, *States and the Reemergence of Global Finance: From Bretton Woods to the 1990s* (Ithaca, NY, 1994), 25–50; Fred L. Block, *The Origins of International Economic Disorder: A Study of United States International Monetary Policy from World War II to the Present* (Berkeley, 1977), 53; Richard N. Gardner, *Sterling-Dollar Diplomacy: Anglo-American Collaboration in the Reconstruction of Multilateral Trade* (Oxford, 1956), 76.

30. *CR*, April 30, 1945, app. 1980; House Committee on Banking and Currency, *Bretton Woods Agreements Act*, 79th Cong., 1st Sess. (Washington, DC, 1945), 597, 679, 780, 1036–37, 1048, 1183; Joseph Gaer, *Bretton Woods Is No Mystery* (New York, 1945), 17; *New York Times*, March 22, 1945, 13; Congress of Industrial Organizations, *5,000,000 Jobs in World Trade: The Promise of Bretton Woods* (Washington, DC, 1944), 11; "Labor-USA," April 7, 1945, box 496, Robert A. Taft, Sr., Papers, Manuscript Division, Library of Congress, Washington, DC.

31. *Washington Post*, March 17, 1945, 5; Rauchway, *Money Makers*, 209–25; Block, *Origins of International Economic Disorder*, 52–55; Eckes, *Search for Solvency*, 174–79; *CR*, June 5, 1945, 5541; June 6, 1945, 5671; Andrae B. Nordskog to Harry S. Truman, May 5, 1945, box 1, Nordskog Papers, MHS. The banking fraternity's opposition to Bretton Woods notably included the American Bankers Association and New York State Bankers Association, but small-town bankers represented by the Independent Bankers Association endorsed the agreement (*New York Times*, March 4, 1945, 26).

32. *CR*, June 6, 1945, 5668; House Committee on Banking and Currency, *Bretton Woods Agreements Act*, 1019; Rauchway, *Money Makers*, 225, 222; Mrs. J. H. Garrison to Elmer Thomas, April 27, 1945, box 58, Thomas Papers; Charles A. Beard, *The Economic Basis of Politics* (New York, 1945), 95.

Chapter Thirteen

1. The epigraph is from Merle Haggard's 1982 song "Are the Good Times Really Over (I Wish a Buck Was Still Silver)."

2. *Chicago Daily Tribune*, May 2, 1944, 4; Mary McSherry Marker, "As We Go Marching On," reel 2, Jacob S. Coxey Papers, Ohio Historical Society, Columbus; *Sunday Star* (Washington, DC), April 30, 1933, A-2.

3. Robert P. Brenner, "The Political Economy of Rank-and-File Rebellion," in *Rebel Rank and File: Labor Militancy and Revolt from Below in the Long 1970s*, ed. Aaron Brenner et al. (London, 2010); Richard M. Abrams, *America Transformed: Sixty Years of Revolutionary Change, 1941–2001* (New York, 2006), 27–42; Lizabeth Cohen, *A Consumers' Republic: The Politics of Mass Consumption in Postwar America* (New York, 2003), 112–29; Gary S. Cross, *An All-Consuming Century: Why Commercialism Won in Modern America* (New York, 2000), 88–109; Nelson N. Lichtenstein, *The Most Dangerous Man in Detroit: Walter Reuther and the Fate of American Labor* (New York, 1995), 276–88; Eichengreen, *Hall of Mirrors*, 318; Robertson, *Comptroller and Bank Supervision*, 7; Fraser, *Every Man a Speculator*, 475–76; Garon, *Beyond Our Means*, 322–23; Paul A. Samuelson, *Economics: An Introductory Analysis*, 6th ed. (New York, 1964), 295.

4. Bankers served as stock villains in movies during the Depression. See, for example, Michael D. Duchemin, *New Deal Cowboy: Gene Autry and Public Diplomacy* (Norman, OK, 2016), 76–80.

5. James G. Patton, address to the International Association of Machinists, September 10, 1964, box 1355C, Patman Papers; Frank S. Levy and Peter Temin, "Institutions and Wages in Post–World War II America," in *Labor in the Era of Globalization*, ed. Clair Brown et al. (New York, 2010); Thomas Piketty and Emmanuel Saez, "Income Inequality in the United States, 1913–1998," *Quarterly Journal of Economics* 118, no. 1 (2003): 1–39; Claudia Goldin and Robert A. Margo, "The Great Compression: The Wage Structure in the United States at Mid-Century," *Quarterly Journal of Economics* 107, no. 1 (1992): 1–34.

6. Abrams, *America Transformed*, 203–4; Alan Brinkley, "1968 and the Unraveling of Liberal America," in *1968: The World Transformed*, ed. Carole Fink et al. (New York, 1998); John Kenneth Galbraith, *American Capitalism: The Concept of Countervailing Power* (Boston, 1952), 151–52; C. Wright Mills with Helen Schneider, *The New Men of Power: America's Labor Leaders* (New York, 1948), 116; Nelson N. Lichtenstein, *Labor's War at Home: The CIO in World War II* (New York, 1982), 233–34; James B. Atleson, *Labor and the Wartime State: Labor Relations and Law during World War II* (Urbana, IL, 1998), 1–2; Harlan Savage to Jerry Voorhis, September 16, 1953, box 54, Voorhis Papers. The CIO opposed tight money policies. See Congress of Industrial Organizations, *Sixteenth Constitutional Convention* (n.p., 1954), 616; idem, *Fifteenth Constitutional Convention* (n.p., 1953), 516. On the Treasury-Federal Reserve Accord of 1951, see Gerald A. Epstein and Juliet B. Schor, "The Federal Reserve-Treasury Accord and the Construction

of the Postwar Monetary Regime in the United States," *Social Concept* 7, no. 1 (1995): 7–48.

7. California State Grange, *Eighty-First Annual Session* (n.p., 1953), 199–200.

8. Washington State Grange, *Seventieth Annual Session* (n.p., 1959), 166–67; F. E. Knowles to Jerry Voorhis, June 18, 1956, box 54, Voorhis Papers; Washington State Grange, *Sixty-Seventh Annual Session* (n.p., 1956), 180–82. In 1962 the Washington State Grange stopped pursuing financial reform. See idem, *Seventy-Third Annual Session* (n.p., 1962), 193. Minnesota State Federation of Labor, *Sixty-Third Convention* (n.p., 1945), 112; idem, *Seventy-Third Convention* (n.p., 1955), 113–14, 127.

9. A. P. Worrell to Andrae Nordskog, February 6, 1964, box 30, Nordskog Papers, CSUN; *Los Angeles Times*, February 13, 1962, 23; *Spokane (WA) Daily Chronicle*, October 17, 1956, 2; *New Yorker* 32, no. 19 (1956): 19.

10. *Washington Post*, January 30, 1963, A2; Joe E. Webb to Wright Patman, September 4, 1964, box 2004-127/111, Henry B. Gonzalez Papers, Center for American History, University of Texas, Austin.

11. Young, *Wright Patman*, 220; Epstein and Schor, "Federal Reserve-Treasury Accord"; William M. McClenahan Jr. and William H. Becker, *Eisenhower and the Cold War Economy* (Baltimore, 2011), 63; Wright Patman, *A Primer on Money* (Washington, DC, 1964), 102–17; House Subcommittee on Domestic Finance, *The Federal Reserve System after Fifty Years*, 88th Cong., 2nd Sess. (Washington, DC, 1964), 1:657.

12. Wright Patman, interviewed by Joe B. Frantz, Lyndon B. Johnson Presidential Library and Museum, 1972, 37–38; *Esquire* 74, no. 3 (1965): 52.

13. AFL-CIO, *Sixth Constitutional Convention* (n.p., 1965), 2:84–86; National Farmers Union, *1965 Policy* (n.p., 1965), 17; Randolph G. Urbanec, "Federal Reserve Discount Rate Policy Actions: 1951–1965" (master's thesis, University of Montana, 1967), 71–75; Robert P. Bremner, *Chairman of the Fed: William McChesney Martin Jr. and the Creation of the Modern American Financial System* (New Haven, CT, 2004), 205–11; Roundup Local 201 Minutes, December 1965, box 15, Montana Farmers Union Records, Montana Historical Society, Helena; Dorothy Ross to Arnold Olsen, January 7, 1966, box 63, Arnold Olsen Papers, Archives and Special Collections, University of Montana, Missoula; Leonard Kenfield to Lee Metcalf, June 16, 1966, Metcalf to Kenfield, July 5, 1966, box 298, Lee Metcalf Papers, Montana Historical Society, Helena.

14. Young, *Wright Patman*, 219; *New York Times*, March 9, 1964, 45; *Saturday Evening Post* 237, no. 9 (1964): 62.

15. Marcia Abramson, *Wallace F. Bennett: Republican Senator from Utah* (Washington, DC, 1972); *Time* 52, no. 24 (1948): 91; *CR*, June 10, 1952, 6893; January 23, 1953, 513; April 1, 1955, 4184; February 26, 1957, 2574; February 3, 1965, 1895; Senate Committee on Post Office and Civil Service, *S. 573*, 83rd Cong., 1st Sess. (1953), 18; J. B. Stenhouse to Wallace F. Bennett, May 15, 1952, Bennett to

George S. Eccles, June 9, 1953, series 2, subseries A, box 623, Wallace F. Bennett Papers, Special Collections, Brigham Young University, Provo, UT.

16. *Sunday Star* (Washington, DC), January 11, 1953, A-3; Arthur E. Summerfield, address to Illinois Chamber of Commerce, October 15, 1958, box 295, White House Central Files, General File, Dwight D. Eisenhower Presidential Library and Museum, Abilene, KS; Arthur E. Summerfield with Charles Hurd, *U.S. Mail: The Story of the United States Postal Service* (New York, 1960), 171; House Subcommittee on Intergovernmental Relations, *Investigation into Federal Agency Competition with Legitimate Industry*, 83rd Cong., 2nd Sess. (1954), 160; *New York Times*, March 1, 1957, 21.

17. Post Office Department, *Annual Report of the Postmaster General, 1966—Financial Supplement* (Washington, DC, 1966), 81; Homer and Sylla, *History of Interest Rates*, 392; United Federation of Postal Clerks, *First Merged Convention* (n.p., 1962), 140; Sham, "Origin and Development," 325; *Postal Bulletin* 78, no. 20031 (1957): 5; Senate Committee on Post Office and Civil Service, *Discontinuance of the Postal Savings System*, 89th Cong., 2nd Sess. (Washington, DC, 1966), 24; *CR*, July 17, 1965, 16351.

18. Senate Committee on Post Office and Civil Service, *Discontinuance of the Postal Savings System*, 29; Carey McWilliams to Lyndon B. Johnson, September 21, 1964, Johnson to McWilliams, October 3, 1964, box PO 3, White House Central File, Lyndon B. Johnson Presidential Library and Museum, Austin, TX.

19. House Subcommittee on Postal Operations, *Dissolution of the Postal Savings System*, 86th Cong., 1st Sess. (Washington, DC, 1965), 13–20; Senate Committee on Post Office and Civil Service, *Discontinuance of the Postal Savings System*, 18–30; *Evening Star* (Washington, DC), March 2, 1965, A-2; Clifford H. Jones to Thomas H. Kuchel, June 23, 1965, Herbert A. Bocka to Kuchel, July 8, 1965, box 514, Thomas H. Kuchel Papers, Bancroft Library, University of California, Berkeley; *Statutes at Large* 80 (1966): 92–93. Abolition of the Postal Savings System left a void that encouraged the subsequent proliferation of fringe banking providers. See Christopher W. Shaw, *Preserving the People's Post Office* (Washington, DC, 2006), 172–84. On fringe banking, see John P. Caskey, *Fringe Banking: Check-Cashing Outlets, Pawnshops, and the Poor* (New York, 1994).

20. *Nation* 202, no. 13 (1966): 350; Brinkley, *End of Reform*, 10; Mary Ann Glendon, *Rights Talk: The Impoverishment of Political Discourse* (New York, 1991), 3–7; Louis R. Hyman, *Debtor Nation: The History of America in Red Ink* (Princeton, NJ, 2011), 173–219.

21. David J. Vogel, *Lobbying the Corporation: Citizen Challenges to Business Authority* (New York, 1978), 35–37; Richard Flacks and Milton L. Mankoff, "Why They Burned the Bank," *Nation* 210, no. 11 (1970): 337–40; *Santa Barbara (CA) News-Press*, February 26, 1970, A-1; *Evening Star* (Washington, DC), September 7, 1971, A-2; Alphonso Pinkney, *The American Way of Violence* (New York, 1972), 194–97; Louis B. Lundborg, "The Lessons of Isla Vista," *Business Lawyer*

26, no. 3 (1971): 943–44. Bank of America offered a sizable reward for information that would help identify and convict the Isla Vista "mob leaders." The chairman of the bank's board of directors labeled the event a "revolutionary gesture
. . . reminiscent of the riots . . . that eventually led to the rise of Adolph Hitler,"
and demanded that the state's governor "make certain with all the means at your
disposal, that citizens and their property are protected." The bank subsequently
rebuilt the branch in a very permanent—"fortresslike"—manner. The despised
new building was called "The Alamo" and subjected to further attacks, including one by a hand grenade. See *Santa Barbara (CA) News-Press*, February 27,
1970, A10–A11; *Los Angeles Times*, February 24, 1980, A1; Crillon C. Payne II, *Deep
Cover: An FBI Agent Infiltrates the Radical Underground* (New York, 1979), 25–26.

22. Eckes, *Search for Solvency*, 238; Block, *Origins of International Economic
Disorder*, 140–63; Robert Kuttner, *The End of Laissez-Faire: National Purpose and
the Global Economy after the Cold War* (New York, 1991), 61; *Time* 85, no. 7 (1965):
81; Gordon L. Weil and Ian Davidson, *The Gold War: The Story of the World's
Monetary Crisis* (New York, 1970), 88.

23. Ernest Mandel, *Decline of the Dollar: A Marxist View of the Monetary Crisis*
(New York, 1972), 88; Joanne Gowa, *Closing the Gold Window: Domestic Politics
and the End of Bretton Woods* (Ithaca, NY, 1983), 163–70; Voorhis, *Confessions of a
Congressman*, 331, 342; Anthony B. Summers with Robbyn Swan, *The Arrogance of
Power: The Secret World of Richard Nixon* (New York, 2000), 46.

24. Jerry Voorhis to Robert L. Faucett, June 4, 1970, box 54, Voorhis Papers;
Helleiner, *States and the Reemergence of Global Finance*, 115–21; Gowa, *Closing the
Gold Window*, 81–86; Block, *Origins of International Economic Disorder*, 198–99;
Barry J. Eichengreen, *Globalizing Capital: A History of the International Monetary
System*, 2nd ed. (Princeton, NJ, 2008), 138–42; Gérard Duménil and Dominique
Lévy, *The Crisis of Neoliberalism* (Cambridge, MA, 2011), 134–37; Wachtel, *Money
Mandarins*, 92.

25. Block, *Origins of International Economic Disorder*, 154; *New York Times*,
March 4, 1973, III-1; George Meany, address at the AFL-CIO Conference on Jobs,
July 12, 1971, Statement by the AFL-CIO Executive Council, February 18, 1971,
box 615B, Patman Papers.

26. Leo Gananian to Wright Patman, February 15, 1972, box 602B, Patman
Papers; *Esquire* 74, no. 3 (1970): 36; Wright Patman, "The Federal Reserve:
A Separate Government," *Vital Speeches of the Day* 34, no. 5 (1967): 138.

27. David Harvey, *The Condition of Postmodernity: An Enquiry into the Origins of Cultural Change* (Cambridge, MA, 1990), 164–65; Noam Chomsky, *Hopes
and Prospects* (Chicago, 2010), 97–99; Joshua B. Freeman, *Working-Class New
York: Life and Labor since World War II* (New York, 2000), 258; Kimberly Phillips-
Fein, *Fear City: New York's Fiscal Crisis and the Rise of Austerity Politics* (New York,
2017). 7–8; Eric A. Lichten, *Class, Power and Austerity: The New York City Fiscal
Crisis* (South Hadley, MA, 1986), 191; *Boston Globe*, October 10, 1975, 39.

28. William F. Haddad et al., *The Banks and the Municipal Crisis: Public*

Responsibility and Private Profit (New York, 1976); David Rockefeller, *Memoirs* (New York, 2002), 393; William K. Tabb, *The Long Default: New York City and the Urban Fiscal Crisis* (New York, 1982), 42–52; John Donald Wilson, *The Chase: The Chase Manhattan Bank, N.A., 1945–1985* (Boston, 1986), 271.

29. Michael Spear, "A Crisis in Urban Liberalism: The New York City Municipal Unions and the 1970s Fiscal Crisis" (PhD diss., City University of New York, 2005), 121–27; *New York Times*, May 21, 1975, 48; *New York Daily News*, June 1, 1975, 3; June 2, 1975, 3; *New York Times*, June 5, 1975, 31; *Newsday*, June 5, 1975, 6; *New York Daily News*, June 5, 1975, 5. Within a few years, the city's labor leaders and bankers had something of a rapprochement. See Jewel Bellush and Bernard Bellush, *Union Power and New York: Victor Gotbaum and District Council 37* (New York, 1984), 412–15.

30. *New York Times*, March 2, 1975, 45; April 5, 1975, 1; April 26, 1975, 11; *Washington Post*, May 12, 1975, D10; *Newsday*, April 26, 1975, 6; *New York Times*, April 25, 1975, 34; *Oakland Tribune*, May 18, 1975, 27; *Chicago Tribune*, May 12, 1975, C8; *Newsday*, June 6, 1975, 17; *Empire State Report* 1, no. 8 (1975): 301–2.

31. *Northwest Labor Press* 99, no. 4 (1998): 2; *Oregonian* (Portland), March 8, 1975, A12; December 31, 1976, A9; *Eugene (OR) Register-Guard*, May 13, 1977, 11A; *Parade*, November 9, 1975, 24.

32. Jerry Voorhis to Edmund G. Brown Sr., February 26, 1973, Brown to Manuel Aragon Jr., November 5, 1973, Voorhis to Brown, April 30, 1975, Samuel Bristol to Voorhis, n.d., box 111, Voorhis Papers; *San Francisco Examiner*, February 27, 1977, 1; *San Francisco Chronicle*, September 20, 1977, 6; *Los Angeles Times*, September 21, 1977, B1; April 26, 1978, B23. Public bank legislation also was discussed seriously in Colorado, the District of Columbia, Florida, and Massachusetts. See Derek N. Shearer, *Public Control of Public Money: Should States and Cities Have Their Own Banks?* (Washington, DC, 1976), 21–24.

33. John L. Eatwell, "The Global Money Trap: Can Clinton Master the Markets?," *American Prospect* 12 (1993): 120; Walter Adams and James W. Brock, *Dangerous Pursuits: Mergers and Acquisitions in the Age of Wall Street* (New York, 1989), 120–23; Bennett Harrison and Barry A. Bluestone, *The Great U-Turn: Corporate Restructuring and the Polarizing of America* (New York, 1988), 53–55.

34. Greider, *Secrets of the Temple*. In 1984 automobile executive Lee A. Iacocca took exception to the Federal Reserve's "curb service for the banking fraternity." "There's a funny orientation at the Federal Reserve Board," he noted. "If a bank goes under for making bad decisions, it gets immediate attention. . . . But when Chrysler and International Harvester, two companies with almost a million jobs at stake, are going under, that's good old free enterprise at work. . . . That's nothing but a double standard and totally unfair" (Iacocca with William Novak, *Iacocca: An Autobiography* [New York, 1984], 242–43). Samuel Bowles, David M. Gordon, and Thomas E. Weiskopf, *After the Waste Land: A Democratic Economics for the Year 2000* (Armonk, NY, 1990), 123–24; William M. Dugger, "The Great Retrenchment: Pecuniary Gains and Industrial Losses," *Journal of Economic Issues* 26, no. 2

(1992): 562–64; Dean Baker, *The United States since 1980* (New York, 2007), 73; *Syracuse (NY) Herald-Journal*, December 22, 1986, A1; Neil E. Harl, *The Farm Debt Crisis of the 1980s* (Ames, IA, 1990), 15; *Syracuse (NY) Herald-Journal*, April 27, 1987, A1.

35. *Gazette* (Cedar Rapids, IA), May 29, 1992, C6; *Washington Post*, November 18, 1990, A18; *Dallas Morning News*, April 6, 1986, 1M–16M; *Seattle Times*, March 4, 1985, A10; *Philadelphia Inquirer*, September 25, 1989, A1; Bennett Harrison and Barry A. Bluestone, *The Deindustrialization of America: Plant Closings, Community Abandonment, and the Dismantling of Basic Industry* (New York, 1982), 61–66.

36. On the impact of deindustrialization on communities, see Laurie Mercier, *Anaconda: Labor, Community, and Culture in Montana's Smelter City* (Urbana, IL, 2001); Judith Schachter Modell, *A Town without Steel: Envisioning Homestead* (Pittsburgh, 1998); William Serrin, *Homestead: The Glory and Tragedy of an American Steel Town* (New York, 1992); Gregory Pappas, *The Magic City: Unemployment in a Working-Class Community* (Ithaca, NY, 1989); David H. Bensman and Roberta Lynch, *Rusted Dreams: Hard Times in a Steel Community* (New York, 1987). Mark Goldman, *City on the Lake: The Challenge of Change in Buffalo, New York* (Buffalo, 1990), 218; *Buffalo News*, May 26, 2008, A1; Brian S. Meyer and David Breslawski, *The World According to Griffin* (Buffalo, 1985), 103; *Buffalo News*, May 5, 1993, A12; *Empire State Report* 7, no. 26 (1981): 330.

37. Robert P. Brenner, *The Boom and the Bubble: The U.S. in the World Economy* (London, 2003), 81–84, 132; Kevin P. Phillips, *Bad Money: Reckless Finance, Failed Politics, and the Global Crisis of American Capitalism* (New York, 2008), 31; Simon H. Johnson and James Y. Kwak, *13 Bankers: The Wall Street Takeover and the Next Financial Meltdown* (New York, 2010), 115–16. On finance's return to economic dominance in the late twentieth century, see L. Randall Wray, "The Rise and Fall of Money Manager Capitalism: A Minskian Approach," *Cambridge Journal of Economics* 33, no. 4 (2009): 807–28. On contemporary subordination of productive economic activity to finance, see Michael Hudson, "From Marx to Goldman Sachs: The Fictions of Fictitious Capital, and the Financialization of Industry," *Critique* 38, no. 3 (2010): 419–44.

38. On the great influence of wealthy individuals and business lobbying groups on policymaking at the close of the twentieth century, see Martin I. Gilens and Benjamin I. Page, "Testing Theories of American Politics: Elites, Interest Groups, and Average Citizens," *Perspectives on Politics* 12, no. 3 (2014): 564–81. On the savings and loan crisis, see William K. Black, *The Best Way to Rob a Bank Is to Own One: How Corporate Executives and Politicians Looted the S&L Industry* (Austin, TX, 2005); Kitty C. Calavita, Henry N. Pontell, and Robert H. Tillman, *Big Money Crime: Fraud and Politics in the Savings and Loan Crisis* (Berkeley, 1997); Martin P. Mayer, *The Greatest-Ever Bank Robbery: The Collapse of the Savings and Loan Industry* (New York, 1990); Stephen P. Pizzo, Mary Fricker, and Paul Muolo, *Inside Job: The Looting of America's Savings and Loans* (New York, 1989). On the 2008

financial crisis, see Alan S. Blinder, *After the Music Stopped: The Financial Crisis, the Response, and the Work Ahead* (New York, 2013); Johnson and Kwak, *13 Bankers*; Joseph E. Stiglitz, *Freefall: America, Free Markets, and the Sinking of the World Economy* (New York, 2010); Dean Baker, *Plunder and Blunder: The Rise and Fall of the Bubble Economy* (Sausalito, CA, 2008). Joseph C. Lewis, "Monster Banks: The Political and Economic Costs of Banking and Financial Consolidation," *Multinational Monitor* 26, nos. 1 & 2 (2005): 31–32; *Statutes at Large* 94 (1980): 132–93; Martin Tolchin and Susan Tolchin, *Buying into America: How Foreign Money Is Changing the Face of Our Nation* (New York, 1988), 129–40.

39. James K. Galbraith, *The Predator State* (New York, 2008), 140–41; Calavita, Pontell, and Tillman, *Big Money Crime*, 88–94; Black, *Best Way to Rob a Bank*, 29–37; Mason, *From Building and Loans to Bail-Outs*, 260; Lester C. Thurow, *Head to Head: The Coming Economic Battle among Japan, Europe, and America* (New York, 1992), 18; Ralph Nader, "Introduction," in *Who Robbed America? A Citizen's Guide to the S&L Scandal*, by Michael Waldman (New York, 1990), xvii.

40. G. Christian Hill, "A Never Ending Story: An Introduction to the S&L Symposium," *Stanford Law and Policy Review* 2 (1990): 24; *Statutes at Large* 108 (1994): 2338–81; Jill Andresky Fraser, *White-Collar Sweatshop: The Deterioration of Work and Its Rewards in Corporate America* (New York, 2001), 161; Steven J. Pilloff, *Bank Merger Activity in the United States, 1994–2003* (Washington, DC, 2004). On the negative consequences of banking consolidation, see Gary A. Dymski, *The Bank Merger Wave: The Economic Causes and Social Consequences of Financial Consolidation* (Armonk, NY, 1999).

41. *Mother Jones* 16, no. 5 (1991): 56–57; Wolfgang H. Reinicke, *Banking, Politics, and Global Finance: American Commercial Banks and Regulatory Change, 1980–1990* (Brookfield, VT, 1995), 96–126; *Washington Post*, May 4, 1990, F1; *New York Times*, October 20, 1993, D2. In 1984 J. P. Morgan & Company had called for amending the Banking Act of 1933 to permit commercial banks to engage in investment banking activities. See J. P. Morgan & Co., *Rethinking Glass-Steagall* (New York, 1984).

42. House Committee on Banking and Financial Services, *H.R. 10 — The Financial Services Modernization Act of 1999*, 106th Cong., 1st Sess. (Washington, DC, 1999), 562; *Business Week*, November 15, 1999, 28; *Mother Jones* 16, no. 5 (1991): 58; *Roll Call* 36, no. 68 (1991): 21; *American Banker* 160, no. 53 (1995): 1; Geoffrey P. Faux, *The Global Class War* (Hoboken, NJ, 2006), 117.

43. Sanford I. Weill and Judah S. Kraushaar, *The Real Deal: My Life in Business and Philanthropy* (New York, 2006), 363–65; *New York*, April 18, 2011, 36–37; Russell Mokhiber, "The Ten Worst Corporations of 1999," *Multinational Monitor* 20, no. 12 (1999): 11; *Statutes at Large* 113 (1999): 1338–481; *CR*, November 4, 1999, 28344; *Christian Science Monitor*, November 1, 1999, 21. Nader and a coalition of consumer groups called for a government ethics investigation of Rubin's "turnstile behavior." The Department of Justice elected not to investigate (*New York Times*, November 18, 1999, C17; *American Banker* 165, no. 248 [2000]: 20).

44. Stiglitz, *Freefall*, 14–15, 162–63; William S. Lerach, "Plundering America: How American Investors Got Taken for Trillions by Corporate Insiders—The Rise of the New Corporate Kleptocracy," *Stanford Journal of Law, Business & Finance* 8, no. 1 (2002): 114–20; Neil D. Fligstein and Adam M. Goldstein, "The Anatomy of the Mortgage Securitization Crisis," *Research in the Sociology of Organizations* 30A (2010): 42–46; Mary Kreiner Ramirez and Steven A. Ramirez, *The Case for the Corporate Death Penalty: Restoring Law and Order on Wall Street* (New York, 2017), 86–89; Robert J. Shiller, *The Subprime Solution: How Today's Global Financial Crisis Happened, and What to Do about It* (Princeton, NJ, 2008), 6–7; Dean Baker, *False Profits: Recovering from the Bubble Economy* (San Francisco, 2010), 1–2; Robert Weissman and James P. Donahue, *Sold Out: How Washington and Wall Street Betrayed America* (Washington, DC, 2009), 39–49.

45. *CR*, September 22, 2008, H8547; Johnson and Kwak, *13 Bankers*, 88–119; Sandra Suarez and Robin Kolodny, "Paving the Road to 'Too Big to Fail': Business Interests and the Politics of Financial Deregulation in the United States," *Politics & Society* 39, no. 1 (2011): 74–102; GAO, *Federal Reserve System: Opportunities Exist to Strengthen Policies and Processes for Managing Emergency Assistance* (Washington, DC, 2011), 131; James Andrew Felkerson, *A Detailed Look at the Fed's Crisis Response by Funding Facility and Recipient* (Annandale-on-Hudson, NY, 2012); *USA Today*, August 10, 2009, 1B; Matthew C. Taibbi, "Wall Street's Bailout Hustle," *Rolling Stone*, March 4, 2010, 48. Despite public anger at the foreclosure crisis, social isolation and ineffective civic organizations yielded a "missing movement." See J. Gregg Robinson, "The White Working-Class and the Foreclosure Crisis: Tracing the Roots of a Failed Movement in Southern California," *Sociological Perspectives* 56, no. 1 (2013): 131–59; Robinson, "The Left and the Foreclosure Crisis: Roots, Resources, and Ideology," *Critical Sociology* 43, no. 2 (2017): 181–98. On the decline of American civic life, see Robert D. Putnam, *Bowling Alone: The Collapse and Revival of American Community* (New York, 2000).

46. *Pittsburgh Post-Gazette*, January 1, 2009, C-1; Barack H. Obama, interviewed by Stephen F. Kroft, *60 Minutes*, CBS, March 22, 2009; *Seattle Times*, March 31, 2009, A3; *Philadelphia Daily News*, December 16, 2008, 10; *Multinational Monitor Editors Blog*, December 12, 2008, http://www.multinational monitor.org/editorsblog/2008/12/12/.

47. Steven Fraser, *The Age of Acquiescence* (New York, 2015), 363–64; Mark Shields, interviewed by James C. Lehrer, *News Hour*, PBS, December 12, 2008.

Epilogue

1. Thomas C. Frank, *Pity the Billionaire: The Hard-Times Swindle and the Unlikely Comeback of the Right* (New York, 2012), 40; Kimberly Phillips-Fein, *Invisible Hands: The Businessmen's Crusade against the New Deal* (New York, 2010); Jason M. Stahl, *Right Moves: The Conservative Think Tank in American Political Culture since 1945* (Chapel Hill, NC, 2016); Nancy MacLean, *Democracy in Chains:*

The Deep History of the Radical Right's Stealth Plan for America (New York, 2017); William Greider, "Rolling Back the 20th Century," *Nation* 276, no. 18 (2003): 11–19; Ronald E. Paul, *End the Fed* (New York, 2009); Paul and Lewis E. Lehrman, *The Case for Gold: A Minority Report of the U.S. Gold Commission* (Washington, DC, 1982); George A. Selgin, *The Theory of Free Banking: Money Supply under Competitive Note Issue* (Washington, DC, 1988); Bettie Ford to Hiram Fong, June 18, 1970, Legislative Series, box 31, Hiram L. Fong Papers, Hawaii Congressional Papers Collection, University of Hawaii, Manoa. Anti-government rhetoric in the United States draws on defenses of slavery. See Robin L. Einhorn, *American Taxation, American Slavery* (Chicago, 2006), 3–8.

2. Jacob S. Hacker, *The Great Risk Shift* (New York, 2006); Elizabeth Warren and Amelia Warren Tyagi, *The Two-Income Trap* (New York, 2003); Tamara Draut, *Strapped: Why America's 20- and 30-Somethings Can't Get Ahead* (New York, 2006); Robert D. Manning, *Credit Card Nation: The Consequences of America's Addiction to Credit* (New York, 2000); Congressional Oversight Panel, *An Overall Assessment of TARP and Financial Stability*, 112th Cong., 1st Sess. (Washington, DC, 2011), 127.

3. *Labor Clarion* 12, no. 35 (1913): 9; *Retail Clerks International Advocate* 36, no. 12 (1930): 32.

4. Roosevelt, *Public Papers*, 2:12. On disembedded economic systems, see Polanyi, *Great Transformation*; R. H. Tawney, *Religion and the Rise of Capitalism: A Historical Study* (New York, 1952). On popular defense of a moral economy, see E. P. Thompson, *Customs in Common* (New York, 1993); George Rudé, *Ideology and Popular Protest* (New York, 1980); Raymond Williams, *The Country and the City* (New York, 1973); Christopher Hill, *The World Turned Upside Down: Radical Ideas during the English Revolution* (New York, 1972); E. J. Hobsbawm and George Rudé, *Captain Swing* (New York, 1968).

5. Michael Gould-Wartofsky, *The Occupiers: The Making of the 99 Percent Movement* (New York, 2015); *St. Louis Post-Dispatch*, September 18, 2016, A12; *New York Daily News*, November 3, 2017, 11; Bernard Sanders, *Our Revolution* (New York, 2016), 296–317; Sanders, address at the Town Hall, Manhattan, January 5, 2016, http://www.presidency.ucsb.edu/ws/index.php?pid=114496; Nigel B. Dodd, *The Social Life of Money* (Princeton, NJ, 2014), 3; Republican National Convention, *Republican Platform, 2016* (n.p., 2016), 3; Democratic Platform Committee, *2016 Democratic Party Platform* (n.p., 2016), 10.

6. *New York Daily News*, March 15, 2012, 46; Bruce Springsteen, *Wrecking Ball*, 2012, compact disc.

INDEX

American Bankers Association (*cont.*)
  banking, 44; on veterans' bonus,
  154; on wage reductions, 127–28
American Farm Bureau Foundation.
  See Farm Bureau
American Federation of Labor: on
  agricultural credit reform, 104;
  and Bretton Woods, 271; on control of credit, 114–15; on credit
  unions, 216; and Goldsborough
  bill, 126; on government banking,
  199; on home lending, 106–7; and
  Jacob S. Coxey Sr., 150; and New
  Deal, 223, 228; on postal savings,
  35, 60, 117, 197; on wage reductions, 128
American Federation of Teachers, 131,
  205–6
American Flint Glass Workers Union,
  110, 129; bank, 214, 369n26
American Legion, 122, 207
American Liberty League, 244
American Society of Equity: on agricultural credit reform, 32, 105–6;
  financial reform program of, 32;
  local in Hendrum, MN, 35, 37; on
  the Panic of 1907, 13–14; on postal
  savings, 69, 71, 106; Wisconsin
  Society of Equity, 85, 170
American Sugar Refining Company,
  321n6
Amherst College, 177
Amlie, Thomas R., 145
Anaconda Copper Mining Company,
  15–17, 124
Ancient Order of Gleaners, 70
Anderson, Benjamin M., Jr., 128
Anderson, Frank B., 19
Andrew, A. Piatt, Jr., 75, 77
Anglophobia, 112, 312n20
anti-monopolism, 5, 29, 40, 49, 83,
  92, 118, 176, 204, 257–58. *See also*
  financial monopoly

anti-Semitism, 10, 85, 112, 163, 262,
  312n20, 355n10
anti-union activity, 114–16, 228, 269
Armour and Company, 216
asset currency, 29, 43, 48–49, 78, 81–
  82, 91, 318n35; opposition to, 30,
  37, 43, 52, 93–95
Associated Farmers of California, 235
automobile industry bailout (2009),
  296–97
Avondale mine disaster (1869), 25,
  317n27
Awalt, F. Gloyd, 167, 171
Ayres, Leonard P., 139

Babson, Roger W., 201
Bailey, Josiah William, 194
Baker, George F., Sr., 40, 48, 76, 85
Ballantine, Arthur A., 171
Baltimore Building Trades Council, 128
bank depositors: blamed for banking
  crisis, 136, 170; and deposit account fees, 110, 132–33; distrust of
  banks, 57–59, 135–41, 167–68; in
  Great Depression, 135–41, 167–68;
  of labor banks, 115; in Panic of
  1907, 17–19, 57. *See also* depositors'
  committees
bankers: as experts, 90–91; public
  image of, 5–6, 23–26, 107, 123–33,
  161, 261, 278, 296; and public relations, 79–80, 208–9; reform agenda
  of, 42–45; and regulation, 51–52,
  196, 293–95
Bankers' Magazine, 34, 53, 56, 66, 87
Bankers' Panic. *See* Panic of 1907
Bankers Trust Company, 209, 244
bank failures, 58, 65; in 1920s, 136; in
  Great Depression, 121, 123, 135–41,
  154, 167–68; in Panic of 1907, 17–18.
  See also Bank of United States;
  Detroit bank crisis (1933); Toledo
  bank crash (1931)